EASTERN EUROPEAN RAILWAYS IN TRANSITION

Modern Economic and Social History Series

General Editor: Derek H. Aldcroft

Titles in this series include:

Eastern European Railways in Transition
Nineteenth to Twenty-first Centuries

Edited by

RALF ROTH
Johann Wolfgang Goethe-Universität, Germany

HENRY JACOLIN
President, International Railway History Association

Routledge
Taylor & Francis Group

LONDON AND NEW YORK

First published 2013 by Ashgate Publishing

2 Park Square, Milton Park, Abingdon, Oxon OX14 4RN

711 Third Avenue, New York, NY 10017, USA

Routledge is an imprint of the Taylor & Francis Group, an informa business

First issued in paperback 2016

British Library Cataloguing in Publication Data
Eastern European railways in transition : nineteenth to twenty-first
    centuries. – (Modern economic and social history)
    1. Railroads – Europe, Eastern – History – 19th century. 2. Railroads Europe,
    Eastern – History – 20th century. 3. Railroads – Europe, Eastern – History – 21st
    century. 4. Railroads – Former communist countries. 5. Cold War – Influence.
    I. Series II. Roth, Ralf.
    385'.0947–dc23

The Library of Congress has cataloged the printed edition as follows:
Eastern European railways in transition : nineteenth to twenty-first centuries / edited by
    Ralf Roth and Henry Jacolin, supported by Marie-Noelle Polino and August
    Veenendaal.
        pages cm. – (Modern economic and social history)
    Includes bibliographical references and index.
    ISBN 978–1–4094–2782–7 (hardcover : alk. paper)
    1. Railroads – Europe, Eastern – History. I. Roth, Ralf. II. Jacolin, Henry.
    HE3008.E27 2013
    385.0947–dc23   2012043451

ISBN 978-1-4094-2782-7 (hbk)
ISBN 978-1-138-24698-0 (pbk)

Contents

PART I: GENERAL SUGGESTIONS AND HISTORICAL OVERVIEWS OF RAILWAYS IN EASTERN EUROPEAN COUNTRIES

PART II: UNDER RUSSIAN PROTECTION

PART III: AFTER THE FALL OF THE IRON CURTAIN: CHANGES – PROBLEMS – MODERNISATION

Contents

List of Figures

List of Tables

Abbreviations

ACNSAS	Arhivele Consiliului pentru Studierea Arhivelor Securitatii (Archives of the National Archives for the Study of Securitate Archives)
ANIC	Arhivele Nationale Istorice Centrale (Central National Historical Archives)
BAM	Baikalo–Amurskaia magistral' (Baikal-Amur Mainline, known formally as the Baikal–Amur Railway from 1980)
BDZ	Balgarski darzhavni zheleznitsi (Bulgarian State Railways)
BKV	Budapesti Közlekedési Zrt. (Budapest Transport Company)
BNB	Böhmische Nordbahn
BPR	Belorussian People's Republic
BRD	Bundesrepublik Deutschland (Federal Republic of Germany)
BSSR	Byelorussian Socialist Soviet Republic
BVG	Berliner Verkehrsbetriebe
CC	Comitetul Central (Central Committee)
ČD	České Dráhy
CEEC	Central and Eastern European Countries
CEH	Conférence Européenne des horaires des trains de voyageurs (European Passenger Train Timetable Conference)
CEM	Conférence Européenne des horaires des trains de marchandises (European Freight Timetable Conference)
CER	Community of European Railways
CFR	Căile Ferate Române (Romanian Railways)
CIM	Convention internationale concernant le transport des marchandises par chemin de fer (Convention Relating to the International Carriage of Goods by Rail)
CIT	Comité international des transports ferroviaires (International Rail Transport Committee)
CIV	Convention internationale concernant le transport des voyageurs par chemin de fer (Convention Relating to the International Carriage of Passengers by Rail)
CIWL	Compagnie internationale des wagons-lits (International Sleeping Cars Company)
CMEA	Council for Mutual Economic Assistance (see also the original Slovak name under RVHP)

COMECON	Совет экономической взаимопомощи (Council for Mutual Economic Assistance; Hungarian: Kölcsönös Gazdasági Segítség Tanácsa)
COTIF	Convention relative aux transports internationaux ferroviaires (Convention on the International Carriage by Rail)
CPSU	Communist Party of the Soviet Union
CR	China Railways
ČSAD	Československá státní automobilová doprava (Czechoslovak State Motorcar Transport)
ČSD	Československé státní dráhy (Czechoslovak State Railways)
CSHAU	Central State Historical Archives of Ukraine in Kiev
ČVUT	České Vysoké Učení Technické
DB AG	Deutsche Bahn AG (German Railway Company)
DB	Deutsche Bundesbahn (State Railway Company of the German Federal Republic)
DR	Deutsche Reichsbahn (State Railway Company of the German Democratic Republic)
DSA	Duna-Száva-Adria Vasúttársaság (Duna-Sava-Adria Railway Company)
ECITO	European Central Inland Transport Organisation
ECMT	European Conference of Ministers of Transport
Ecosoc	Economic and Social Council of the United Nations Organisation
EIM	European Rail Infrastructure Managers
EPPK	Eisenbahn Pilsen-Preisen-Komotau (Pilsen-Preisen-Komotau Railways)
ERA	European Railway Agency of the European Commission and Parliament
ERFA	European Rail Freight Association
ERRI	[European Rescue and Recovery Initiative?]
EU	European Union
EVR	Eesti Vabariigi Raudteede
Ex train	Express train (Czech)
FABLOK	Pierwsza Fabryka Lokomotyw w Polsce
FRG	Federal Republic of Germany
FVA	Fahrzeug Versuchsanstalt (Technical Institute for the Improvement of Carriages)
GCU	General Contract for the Use of Wagons
GDL	Gewerkschaft Deutscher Lokomotivführer (Trade Union for German Locomotive Drivers)
GDR	German Democratic Republic
GySEV	Győr-Sopron-Ebenfurti Vasút (Győr-Sopron-Ebenfurth Railway Company)

HSWP	Hungarian Socialist Workers Party (see also MSZMP)
HUF	Hungarian Forint
HUKO	Hutnícky kombinát Košice (Metallurgical Complex Košice)
IBK	Informationssystem Bahn- und Konzerngeschichte (Information Database for the History of Railways and the Deutsche Bahn AG)
IC train	InterCity train
IRFP	Institut für Regional- und Fernverkehrsplanung (Institute for the Planning of Regional and Far Distance Transport)
IRHA	International Railway History Association
ITF	Integraler Taktfahrplan
KFNB	Kaiser-Ferdinands-Nordbahn (Emperor Ferdinand North Railways)
KFU	Karl-Franzens-Universität Graz (Karl-Franzens University of Graz)
KSČ	Komunistická strana Československa (Communist Party of Czechoslovakia)
LBSSR	Lithuanian-Belorussian Soviet Socialist Republic
LDZ	Latvijas Dzelzceļš
LG	Lietuvos Geležinkeliai
LON	League of Nations
LVD	Latvijas Valsts Dzelzsceli
MÁV	Magyar Államvasutak (Hungarian State Railway)
MÁV-START	Vasúti Személyszállító Zrt. (MÁV-START Railway Passenger Transport Co.)
MDP	Magyar Dolgozók Pártja (Hungarian Workers Party)
MGB	Mährische Grenzbahn
MOL	Magyar Országos Levéltár (National Archives of Hungary)
MPS	Ministerstvo Putei Soobshcheniia – Ministry of Ways of Communication
MSZMP	Magyar Szocialista Munkáspárt (Hungarian Socialist Workers Party, see also HSWP)
NEP	New Economic Policy
NHAB (Grodno)	National Historical Archives of Belarus in Grodno
NHAB	National Historical Archives of Belarus in Minsk
NKVD	Narodnyy komissariat vnutrennikh del (Peoples Commissariat for Internal Affairs)
ÖBB	Österreichische Bundesbahn (Austrian State Railways)
OCTI	Office central des transports internationaux par chemins de fer (Central Office for International Carriage by Rail)
OECD	Organisation for Economic Co-operation and Development
ÖNWB	Österreichische Nordwestbahn (Austrian North-West Railways)

OPW	Obschtchij Park Wagonow / Общий парк вагонов (Common Goods Wagon Park)
ORE	Office for Research and Experiments
Os train	Regional passenger train (Czech)
OSJD or OSZhD	Организация Сотрудничества Железных Дорог or ОСЖД (Organisation for Cooperation between Railways)
OTIF	Organisation intergouvernementale pour les transports internationaux ferroviaires (Organisation for International Carriage by Rail)
PCR	Partidul Comunist Român (Romanian Communist Party)
PKP	Polskie Koleje Państwowe (Polish State Railways)
PLM	Compagnie des chemins de fer de Paris à Lyon et à la Méditerranée (Paris-Lyon-Méditerranée Company)
PMR	Partidul Muncitoresc Roman (Romanian Communist Party)
PPR	Polska Partia Robotnicza (Polish Labour Party)
PV	Passazhieru Vilciens
R train	Speed train (Czech)
RER	Réseau express régional (Regional Express Railways)
RF	Rossiiskaia Federatsiia – Russian Federation
RIC	Regolamento Internazionale delle Carrozze (International Coach Regulations)
RID	Règlement concernant le transport international ferroviaire de marchandises Dangereuses (Agreement on International Rail Transport of Dangerous Goods)
RIV	Regolamento Internazionale Veicoli (International Wagon Regulations)
RSFSR	Rossiiskaia Sovetskaia Federativnaia Sotsialisticheskaia Respublika (Russian Soviet Federal Socialist Republic)
RSHA	Russian State Historical Archives
RVHP	Rada vzájomnej hospodárskej pomoci so sídlom v Moskve
RŽD or RZhD	Российские железные дороги, РЖД; Rossiiskie Zheleznye Dorogi (Russian Railways)
SBB	Schweizer Bundesbahnen (Federal Railways of Switzerland)
SC train	SuperCity train (Czech)
SMGS	Soglashenije o Meshdunarodnom Shelesnodoroshnom Grusowom Soobstschenii (Agreement on International Railway Goods Transport)
SMPS	Soglashenije o Meshdunarodnom Passagierskom Soobstschenii (Agreement on International Passengers Transport by Rail)
SNCF	Société nationale des chemins de fer Français (French State Railways)

SNDVB	Südnord-deutschen Verbindungsbahn (German South-North Connecting Railways)
Sp train	Fast stopping train (Czech)
StEG	Staatseisenbahngesellschaft (State Railway Company)
SŽ	Slovenske Železnice
SZD	Sovetskie Zheleznye Dorogi (Soviet Railways)
TAV	Technikbasierte Abfertigungsverfahren (Technical Oriented Service Processing)
TEE	Trans-Europe Express
TEN	Trans-European Network
TEN-T	Trans-European Transportation Network
TEŽ	Tatranské elektrické železnice (Tatra Electric Railway)
TGV	Train à grande vitesse (French Highspeed Railways)
THRSC	Taiwan High Speed Rail Corporation
TINA	Transport Infrastructure Needs Assessment
TRA	Taiwan Railways Administration
TSFSR	Transcaucasian Soviet Federative Socialist Republic
UECC	Union Européenne des Chambres de Commerce et d'Industrie (Union of European Chambers of Commerce)
UIC	Union Internationale des Chemins de Fer (International Union of Railways)
UIP	Union internationale des wagons privés (International Union of Private Wagons)
UkrSSR	Ukraine Soviet Socialist Republic
USSR	Union of Socialist Soviet Republics
ÚV KSČ	Ústřední výbor Komunistické strany Československa (Central Committee of Communist Party of the Czechoslovakia)
VEB	Volkseigener Betrieb (company owned by the state)
VILG	Valstbine Imone Lietuvos Geležinkeliai
ŽSR	Železnice Slovenskej Republiky (Railway of the Slovak Republic)
ZSSK Cargo	Železničná Spoločnosť Cargo Slovakia, a. s. (later abbreviated as ZSCS
ZSSK	Železničná spoločnosť, a. s., later Železničná Spoločnosť Slovensko, a. s.

Notes on Contributors

Viktor Borza holds a transport engineering degree from Budapest University of Technology and Economy, an MBA degree from Budapest Corvinus University and pursues PhD studies in transport science at Budapest University. He contributed essential work to the first pilot project of the Integraler Taktfahrplan (ITF) involving three Budapest suburban lines (70, 71, 100) and was engaged in planning the hubs of the ITF-OST-system, a regular timetable scheme covering eastern Hungary.

Zsuzsa Frisnyák is a senior research fellow at the Institute of History of Hungarian Academy of Sciences. Recent publications include 'A hazai vasúti közlekedés jellemzöi és válsága 1949–1953 között (Features and Crisis of Railway Transportation 1949–1953)', in István Mezei (ed.), *Vasúthistória* Évkönyv (Budapest 1999), 263–301, and *A magyarországi közlekedés krónikája 1750–2000* (Chronicle of Transport in Hungary 1750–2000) (ed.) Ferenc Glatz (Budapest 2001), and 'Az ÁVH és a vasúti kémelhárítók, 1953 (The State Defence Authority and the Counter-espionage of the Railway in 1953)', in István Mezei (ed.), *Vasúthistória* Évkönyv (Budapest 2003), 253–69.

Anthony Heywood is Senior Lecturer in Modern European History at the University of Aberdeen, Scotland. His many publications on the history of the Russian and Soviet railways include *Engineer of Revolutionary Russia: Iu. V. Lomonosov (1876–1952) and the Railways* (Farnham 2010); *Modernising Lenin's Russia: Economic Reconstruction, Foreign Trade and the Railways* (Cambridge 1999), and (with I.D.C. Button) *Soviet Locomotive Types: The Union Legacy* (Malmö 1995). He is currently preparing a history of the Russian railways in the First World War.

Peter F.N. Hörz teaches Cultural Anthropology at the Rheinische Friedrich-Wilhelms-Universität, Bonn. He studied cultural science, ethnology and paedagogic at Eberhard Karls Universität, Tübingen and at Vienna University. He gained his PhD 2001 at Vienna University with a dissertation about Jewish culture in the Austro-Hungarian border region. Hörz is author and co-author of numerous publications on Jewish culture, the history of German anthropology (*Volkskunde)*, and aspects of the German inner unification and difference. With Marcus Richter he shares the interest in the anthropology of labour and economy and in the East German transformation process. Together with Marcus Richter he is recently working on a research project on the cultural history of the former cigar industry of Schöneck/Vogtland in Saxony.

Henry Jacolin is a retired French diplomat who served in Africa (Ethiopia), Asia (Indonesia), Oceania (Fiji) and Europe (Cyprus, Vienna and the Balkans: Bulgaria, Greece, Yugoslavia and Bosnia-Hercegovina). He studied Russian, Rumanian and Serbo-Croatian at the École *des langues orientales,* Geography at the Sorbonne and Political Sciences at the *Institut d'*études *politiques de Paris.* He published *Les transports ferroviaires dans l'Europe orientale et danubienne,* Cahiers de l'Institut de science économique appliquée (Paris 1965), and articles on the railways of Balkan states in railway and geographical reviews. He is president of the International Railway History Association.

Ivan Jakubec is Professor of Economic and Social History at the Institute of Economic and Social History (Faculty of Arts, Charles University Prague). In 1992/1993, 1995, and 2002 he was scholar of the Alexander von Humboldt foundation in Berlin. Scientific research fields are transport history and the role of economic elites. In 2006 he published *Schlupflöcher im 'Eisernen Vorhang'. Tschechoslowakisch-deutsche Verkehrspolitik im Kalten Krieg. Die Eisenbahn und Elbeschiffahrt 1945–1989* (Loopholes in the 'Iron Curtain'. Czech-German Transport Policy in the era of the Cold War. Railway and Navigation on River Elbe, 1945–1989) (Stuttgart 2006).

Vit Janoš is a transport scientist at the Technical University in Prague of which he holds a degree in engineering (1999) and a PhD (2002). He is a counsellor to the Czech Ministry of Transport in the area of commissioning long-distance transport services. He pursued studies at the Technical University of Dresden in 2001 and was an emploeyee at the Bayerische Eisenbahngesellschaft (Bavarian Railway Company) in Munich and at the regional board of SBB in Luzern in 2002.

Andrej Kishtymov is an Associated Professor at the Institute of Parliamentary and Enterprise Development in Minsk. He got his PhD in History at the Institute of History at the National Academy of Science of Belarus where he was engaged from 1979 to 2005. His main fields of research are geopolitics, history, ethnic identity, religious history, history of science and technology, socio-economic history, history of entrepreneurship in Belarus and the problems of historiography. He is author of numerous publications on these topics and published in scientific journals in Belarus, Germany, United States, Poland, Czechoslovakia, Russia, Ukraine, Lithuania, Estonia and Kyrgyzstan. He is one of the authors of the *Handbuch der Geschichte Weissrusslands* (Handbook of the History of Belorussia) (Göttingen 2001) and of the fourth volume of the *History of Belarus* in six volumes entitled *Belarus in the Russian Empire: From the End of the Eighteenth to the Beginning of the Twentieth Centuries* (Minsk 2005).

Milan Klubal studied engineering at the Railway University in Prague and got the grade of a diploma engineer in 1959. After a professional career in railway service he worked at the Railway Directorate in Bratislava and became Director of the Transport Department of the Slovak Republic. After his retirement in 1996 he gave lectures in logistic and railway history at the University of Transport and Communication of Zilina and the University of Logistics in Přerov. He together with Jiří Kubáček and other colleagues wrote *Dejiny železníc na území Slovenska* (History of Railway Transport in Slovakia) (Bratislava 1999). He is vice president of *Zväz slovenských vedeckotechnických spoločností* (The Association of Slovak Scienticific and Technological Societies) (ZSVTS).

Martin Kvizda is a senior Lecturer at the Department of Economics, Masaryk University, Brno, Czech Republic. Recent publications include 'The State and Railways: A Historical Comparison of Economic Policy in Relation to Railways', in Edward Shinnick (ed.), *Issues in Economic Performance: Business, Regional and Transport Issues* (Berlin 2009), 115–137, and 'Managing the Czech Joint-Stock Companies – Failure of Economic Transformation', *Zagreb International Review of Economics and Business*, 9, 2006, 89–110.

Rainer Mertens is Head of Collections and Exhibitions at the DB Museum in Nuremberg, Germany. He studied history, political science and economics at the University of Erlangen and obtained a doctorate at Bayreuth. He published numerous essays on railway history and was responsible for the renewing of the permanent exhibitions and collections in the Deutsche Bahn Museum in Nuremberg.

Jan Musekamp, PhD, is a Lecturer at the Department of Eastern European History at European University Viadrina in Frankfurt (Oder) in Germany. He is working on the history of forced migrations, entangled German–Russian–Polish–Czech history and cultural history of communication. Recent publications include *Zwischen Stettin und Szczecin. Metamorphosen einer Stadt von 1945 bis 2005* (Wiesbaden 2010) and 'Szczecin's Identity after 1989: A Local Turn', in J. Czaplicka, N. Gelazis and B. Ruble (eds), *Cities after the Fall of Communism: Reshaping Cultural Landscapes and European Identity* (Baltimore and Washington 2009), 305–34.

István Neumann has been active on behalf of Hungarian non-Governmental Organisations in the area of branch railways and regional transport since 2006. The networker with a German–Swiss–Austrian background moved to northeastern Hungary next to Slovakia in 1994.

Tomáš Nigrin is a Senior Lecturer at the Institute for International Studies at the Faculty of Social Sciences, Charles University in Prague. His publications focus on West Berlin, the time of the Second Berlin Crisis and on the reflection of history in schoolbooks. One of his latest articles together with Zdeněk Beneš is 'Ideologie und Leben. Das Bild des Sozialismus in tschechischen, slowakischen, polnischen und deutschen Geschichtsschulbüchern', in Volker Zimmermann, Peter Haslinger and Tomáš Nigrin (eds), *Loyalitäten im Staatssozialismus. DDR, Tschechoslowakei, Polen* (Freiburg 2010), 347–68.

Imre Perger, born 1953 in Csorna in Hungary, got his professional training as an economist. He was director of the MÁV and is now consultant of MÁV-START (Railway Passenger Transport Company) which he has co-founded. His specialities are railway passenger tariffs, tariff policy, railway passenger transport operation and transport alliances. He published several books on railway transportation such as *Vasúti Nagylexikon* (Railway Encyclopaedia), 2 vols (Budapest 2005) which was edited by Magyar Államvasutak Rt., and several issues of *Magyar Vasúti Almanach* (Hungarian Railway Almanack) which were edited by MÁV Zrt. Vezérigazgatóság.

Marcin Przegiętka is a PhD student at the Faculty of History at the Nicolaus Copernicus University in Torun in Poland and is interested in history of transport in nineteenth and twentieth centuries in connection with political history. Currently he is writing his doctoral dissertation about 'Transport and policy: Railways, roads and river navigation in German–Polish relationships during the interwar period, 1918–1939'.

Marcus Richter, MA, is a freelance cultural anthropologist. He studied European Ethnology, Political Science and Sociology at the University of Bamberg, Germany. He wrote his master thesis about 'Precarious Consumption', a research on everyday consumption with limited resources. He published among other articles together with Peter F.N. Hörz, 'Preserved as Technical Monuments, Run as Tourist Attractions: Narrow-Gauge Railways in the German Democratic Republic', in *The Journal of Transport History*, 32(2), 2011, 192–213, and also together with Peter F. N. Hörz, 'Old Know-how for New Challenges: East Germans and Collective Creativity? Anthropological Case Studies', in G. Fischer and F. Vassen (eds), *Collective Creativity: Collaborative Work in the Sciences, Literature and the Arts* (Amsterdam and New York 2010), 59–69.

Ralf Roth is Professor of History at the *Historische Seminar, Johann Wolfgang Goethe-Universität* in Frankfurt am Main, Germany. His numerous articles published in German, American, British, Ukrainian, and Spanish journals are focused on the social and cultural history of cities and communication networks. After his research on the development of urban elites he completed a project about the impact of the railways on German society from 1800 to 1914. Together with Günter Dinhobl he published *Across the Borders: Financing the World's Railways in the Nineteenth and Twentieth Centuries* (Aldershot 2008); with Karl Schlögel he edited *Neue Wege in ein neues Europa. Geschichte und Verkehr im 20.*

Jahrhundert (New Roads to a New Europe: History and Transport in the Twentieth Century) (Frankfurt am Main 2009); and *Städte im europäischen Raum. Verkehr, Kommunikation und Urbanität im 19. und 20. Jahrhundert* (Cities in the European Space: Transport, Communication and Urbanism in the Nineteenth and Twentieth Centuries) (Stuttgart 2009). Together with Colin Divall he is editor and author of *From Rail to Road and Back Again? A Century of Transport Competition and Interdependency* (Aldershot forthcoming).

Adelina Oana Ştefan is PhD student at the University of Pittsburgh working on a thesis about 'Mass tourism and the making of consumer culture in socialist Romania, 1960s–1980s'. She is also a research associate at the Centre for Administrative, Cultural and Economic Studies in Bucharest. Her latest publications are *Călătorii si Frontiere Ieri si Azi: Întâlniri, Despărtiri, Regăsiri* (Travels and Frontiers, Yesterday and Today: Meetings, Separations, Reunions) (Bucharest 2009) and 'The socialist state and workers' leisure in Communist Romania of the 1950s', *Interstitio: East European Review of Historical Anthropology*, 1, issue June, 2007, 119–130.

Kevin Sutton is Associate (*agrégé*) and a PhD candidate in geography at the University of Savoy, in the laboratory EDYTEM, Chambéry. Recent publications include 'Railway "Space", Traverser les Alpes par l'affiche', in Zembri Varlet (ed.), *Mobilités contemporaines* (Ellipse 2009), 191–203, and 'Les nouvelles traversées alpines: la "cité-Europe" à l'épreuve de l'acceptabilité alpine', *Belgeo*, 1–2, 2010, 79–88.

Augustus J. Veenendaal, Jr. PhD, was trained as a historian and worked, until his recent retirement, for the Institute of Netherlands History at The Hague. He has written a number of books and articles on Dutch and American railway history and in 2000 he was commissioned by Netherlands Railways to write a comprehensive history of railways in the Netherlands, published under the title *Spoorwegen in Nederland van 1834 tot nu* (Amsterdam 2004, second edition Amsterdam 2008).

Paul Véron currently holds responsibilities as Director of Communications, and in parallel as Director for the coordination of the UIC's Middle Eastern Region. He was a graduate of the University of Bordeaux III with a Master's degree in German and a diploma in Russian. He also studied at the *Institut des hautes études internationales* (IHEI) (Institute of High International Studies) at the University of Paris II, as well as graduating in political science from the *Institut d'études politiques* (IEP) (Paris Institute of Political Studies – international relations section). He has held responsibilities at France's Ministry of Defence (in charge of international media relations for SIRPA – the Department of Information and Public Relations of the Armed Forces), then within the political publications branch of a media information group (Société générale de Presse SGP) before joining the International Union of Railways (UIC), the professional association comprising 200 railway companies around the world.

Ihor Zhaloba is Professor of History at the Diplomatic Academy of Ukraine where he teaches the history of international relations. His publications include *Infrastructural Policy of the Austrian Government in the Northern East of the Monarchy in the late 18th Century to the 1860s* (Chernivtsi 2004). He is currently writing *Communicative Factor in the International Relations of Nineteenth Century.*

Modern Economic and Social History Series
General Editor's Preface

Economic and social history has been a flourishing subject of scholarly study during recent decades. Not only has the volume of literature increased enormously but the range of interest in time, space and subject matter has broadened considerably so that today there are many sub-branches of the subject which have developed considerable status in their own right.

One of the aims of this series is to encourage the publication of scholarly monographs on any aspect of modern economic and social history. The geographical coverage is worldwide and contributions on the non-British themes will be especially welcome. While emphasis will be placed on works embodying original research, it is also intended that the series should provide the opportunity to publish studies of a more general thematic nature which offer a reappraisal or critical analysis of major issues of debate.

Derek H. Aldcroft
University of Leicester

Preface

In September 2009 the International Railway History Association (IRHA), which is dedicated to the history and heritage of transport by rail and its networks, organised its third International conference on railway history in Bratislava, the capital of Slovakia. The topic of the conference entitled 'Railways in Transition – Eastern Europe Railways, their Past, Present and Future in the 20th and 21st Centuries' sparked a lot of interest in the scientific community. The papers for the conference and the discussions that took place there raised questions and started discussions that are of importance for our understanding of the history of the railway as well as for economic history in general. The theme stressed an important aspect of Europe that has been growing together for 60 years and since 20 years together with many countries in the Eastern parts. We personally believe that the construction of railway systems is something that cannot be considered separately for each country. The great shifts in the European history after World War One and after World War Two formed a world very different from the time up to World War One and after the end of the Cold War from 1990 onwards. We envisaged again: railways are transnational communication systems that form continental and even intercontinental networks.

All papers presented at the Bratislava conference have been extensively rewritten and enlarged for inclusion in this book. Some other papers have been acquired especially for this anthology. We thank our authors who come from Belarus, the Czech Republic, France, Germany, Hungary, the Netherlands, Poland, Romania, Slovakia, Ukraine and the United Kingdom for having answered our questions and for the fruitful dialogues about their work and our suggestions. The present book broadens our view of the past and deepens our understanding of how the modern world came to be what it is today. It gathers information from numerous countries of the Eastern European world, covering regions from the Baltic States in the north to Serbia, Slovenia and Romania in the south, from Germany in the west to Poland, the Czech Republic, Slovakia and the Ukraine in the east. We believe that some breakthroughs in comparative social, political and railway history may result from what is still a first step in a very promising field.

We wish to thank Derek Aldcroft, general editor of Ashgate's Modern Economic and Social History series, the Ashgate publishers and Thomas Gray for their patient help. We also wish to extend our gratitude to those who made possible the conference in Bratislava in September 2009. We want to mention especially the Slovak Railways Železnice Slovenskej Republiky (ŽSR) (Slovak railways, infrastructure), Železničná Spoločnosť Slovensko (ZSSK) (passenger company); Železničná Spoločnosť Cargo Slovakia (ZSSK Cargo) (freight company). The publication was also supported by the Union internationale des chemins de fer (UIC). This book would not have reached its level of quality without the engaged, competent and critical proofreading of our supporters Marie-Noëlle Polinoe and Augustus J. Veenendaal. There had been an intense exchange of emails and telephone calls between Paris, 't Harde in the Netherlands and Sinntal in Germany.

We collect in this anthology a lot of authors from non-English speaking countries who expressed their ideas in a foreign language. We therefore thank Nathan Horowitz for his professional editing of all English texts.

Henry Jacolin and Ralf Roth
Paris, France and Sinntal, Germany, April 2013

Introduction

Eastern European Railways in Transition

Ralf Roth

Some General Lines of Railway Development in Eastern Europe

Our goal is not to clarify all problems of European transport or railway history in 400 pages, but to provide an opening to the world of railways in Eastern European countries and their history. The intention of the book is therefore, to get a clearer insight in three central topics. At first we ask for the main lines of historical development of railways in Eastern European countries since the beginnings in the mid nineteenth century. Secondly we raise the question of the political, geopolitical and economic context in Eastern Europe in the period between 1945 and 1989. Thirdly our interest is to learn more about the impact of the transition starting in 1989 on the railway systems as a whole and the national railway companies in particular. From this focus the question derived about the efforts that have been undertaken for technological and administrative modernisation and about the consequences of the radical transformation as for example the drastic increase in competition from other modes of transport. Last but not least we look at the role that West European plans and visions played for a Trans-European Railway Network (TEN) including the east of Europe. According to these questions we separated the chapters in three sections. First we start with papers on 'General Suggestions and on Historical Overviews of Railways in Eastern European Countries'.

Looking back to the time before Europe was shattered by two world wars we find not a homogeneous but an undivided European space which was structured by railways for more than 60 years. We can recognise conspicuous particularities which distinguish the Eastern parts of the network from the Western ones. First, they were characterised by vaster and less densely populated territories. This was one of the main causes of the less dense network. Second, this network had been constructed with a delay of two or three decades compared with the Western parts of Europe. Third, Eastern Europe and its railway networks belonged to the so-called 'periphery' of Europe which formed a ring surrounding the centre with states as France, Great Britain, Belgium, the Netherlands and Germany. This ring includes besides Eastern Europe also parts of southern and northern Europe. Eastern Europe is the region between Russia's Asian territories and Greece (which is considered to be a southern European country belonging to the

Mediterranean world).[1] The railways there were created and developed under the rule of four multi-ethnic empires: the German, Habsburg, Ottoman and the Tsarist Russian empire.[2] All four stood for authoritarian rule and at least two of them, the Tsarist and Ottoman empires, belonged to the so-called 'catch up' societies, i.e. they tried to minimise the economic gap between them and the nations and empires of the Western world. The other ones also included in their territories vast areas that were longing for modernisation. We could mention the German east, including Polish territories or Habsburg Galicia, even Hungary or provinces as Bohemia, Slovakia or the newly conquered countries of the Balkans.[3] They achieved this goal with less success.[4]

Railways in Eastern Europe can be described also as a network between two important lines of the world's railway system: the Trans-Siberian Railway and the Orient Railway (later extended by the Baghdad Railway) which both connect Europe with Asia's Far and Middle East. This network developed the wide spaces of Middle and Eastern Europe and formed the structure of settlement along the lines. There, villages, cities and industrial sites grew up whereas other places which did not succeed in becoming connected to the tracks were retarded in their development.[5]

But this network formed no homogeneous entity and was by far not dominated by economic reasons. We find in every region of the space certain particularities. To start with, Russia did not develop a ground-covering network with many railway junctions, but a structure with only a few centres because of the vast distances

---

[1]   On the term 'periphery' refer to the theory of Immanuel Wallerstein. In his view the world system is characterised by fundamental differences in social development, accumulation of political power and capital. Contrary to affirmative theories of modernisation, Wallerstein does not conceive of these differences as mere residues or irregularities that can and will be overcome as the system evolves. In his opinion a lasting division of the world in 'core' and 'periphery' is an inherent feature of the world system. See Immanuel Wallerstein, *World-Systems Analysis: An Introduction* (London 2004).

[2]   On the role of empires see Timothy H. Parsons, *The Rule of Empires: Those Who Built Them, Those Who Endured Them, and Why They Always Fall* (Oxford 2010), and Jane Burbank and Frederick Cooper, *Empires in World History: Power and the Politics of Difference* (Princeton and Oxford 2010).

[3]   See the discussion about this topic in the issue of *Zeitschrift für Weltgeschichte*, 12, 2, autumn 2012, especially the articles of Andrea Komlosy, Manuela Boatca, Hans-Heinrich Nolte and Dariusz Adamczyk.

[4]   See the papers of the Fifth International Conference on Railway History: 'The Great Longing for Railways' – How the Periphery Became Connected with the Centres of Industrialisation' organised by the International Railway History Association and the Centre for Urban History of East Central Europe in Lviv (Ukraine) on 3–5 November 2011.

[5]   Thomas Bremer, Osteuropäische Eisenbahngeschichten, *OST-WEST. Europäische Perspektiven. Zeitschrift für Mittel- und Osteuropa* (online publication, last accessed 15 September 2009).

and because of the tradition of central government.[6] Russia's first railway line with a length of 27 kilometres was built between the metropolis St Petersburg and Zarskoje Selo, the country seat of the Tsarist family – as in Prussia (Berlin-Potsdam) and France (Paris-Versailles, exactly one year after the first line from Paris to Saint Germain en Laye).[7] After this prestige project further lines were constructed not for economic but chiefly for strategic reasons – for example the line from Warsaw to Skérnewizy (poln. Skierniewice) in the border regions of Tsarist Russia, later extended to St Petersburg. However, in 1851 followed the first long-distance line from St Petersburg to Moscow – currently rebuilt as a high-speed rail connection. In the 1850s railway development stagnated but flourished again after the defeat in the Crimean War. The construction of the 4,300 kilometres-long line from Moscow to Sewastopol – also for strategic reasons – was made possible by French capital organised by the *Crédit mobilier* of the brothers Pereire. This was the beginning of Russia's rapidly increasing state debt which had skyrocketed to several billion British pounds by 1913.[8]

However, the network had grown from 27,000 to 76,250 kilometres in 1910. This was at that time the biggest but by far not the most dense railway network in Europe. One of the particularities of the Russian railway network was that the main lines had been built for administrative and military reasons. Moscow always formed the centre of the Russian network. In a star structure most lines were directed to the capital. In this way it became possible to govern the whole of Russia with its vast distances and to create a central administration in the capital. The railways served as a kind of backbone of the empire. It made the Tsarist rule more efficient and stabilised the territories occupied in the southern and Eastern regions during the eighteenth and nineteenth centuries. It structured and developed the economic resources for the purpose of the central government.[9] Characteristic for this kind of network were long-distance lines.

---

[6] Bremer, Osteuropäische Eisenbahngeschichten. See also Walter Sperling, *Der Aufbruch der Provinz. Die Eisenbahn und die Neuordnung der Räume im Zarenreich* (Frankfurt am Main 2011).

[7] The Russian line was planned and built by the Austrian railway pioneer Franz Anton von Gerstner from 1834 to 1837. The opening event took place seven years after the Liverpool–Manchester Railway and two years after the first continental lines in Belgium and Germany.

[8] Although the state paid nearly 90 per cent of the Russian railway the government controlled not more than 10 per cent around the turn of the century. See Ralf Roman Rossberg, *Geschichte der Eisenbahn.*, 2nd edn (Frankfurt am Main 1984), 102–3. See also Ralf Roth, 'Eisenbahn', in Dan Diner and Markus Kirchhoff, (eds), *Europäische Traditionen – Enzyklopädie jüdischer Geschichte und Kultur*, 5 vols (Stuttgart and Weimar 2011), vol. 2, 195–201.

[9] Frithjof Benjamin Schenk, 'Mapping the Empire: Die Neuvermessung des Russländischen Reiches im Eisenbahnzeitalter', paper presented at Osteuropa kartiert – Mapping Eastern Europe. Conference organised by Christophe von Werdt (Osteuropa-Bibliothek, Bern), Mira Jovanovíc, and Jörn Happel in Bern from 25 to 27 September 2008.

Obviously, these elements worked together when the biggest railway project of Europe was undertaken at the end of the nineteenth century – the so-called Trans-Siberian Railway.[10] This railway made possible the continuation of the imperialistic expansion of the empire and served as an infrastructure for Russia's imperialistic interests in Far East Asia – to compete there with other European countries and Japan. The expansion programme of Russia at the beginning of the twentieth century was focused on territories in China. With the Trans-Siberian Railway the empire had direct railway access to China's northwest and northeast. At this time railways were considered to be of supreme geo-strategic importance. The colonial powers of Europe saw railway lines as surrounded by spheres of imperialistic interests. This was why Russia established a 'railway colony' in Manchuria. The struggle for China failed and ended up in a serious conflict with another imperialistic power – Japan. The Russo-Japanese War of 1904 resulted in a severe defeat that in turn led directly to the turmoil of Russia's first Revolution of 1905. This was the beginning of Russia's decline, the loss of territories during and at the end of World War One, and the establishment of independent states as a consequence of the Brest-Litowsk and Trianon treaties of 1918 and 1920. With this loss of territories the Russian railway network declined from 76,000 to 72,000 kilometres. The retreat of the collapsed empire opened the way for an independent development of railways in the Baltic States, Poland and the Ukraine.

After the collapse of the Tsarist state, the October Revolution, the Civil War and the establishment of the Bolshevik government the Soviet Union continued the tradition of Tsarist Russia and developed its eastern territories in Asia by the expansion of the railway network there. To mention only a few, the Turksib, or the most Nordic railway line of the world to the mines of Norilsk, or the famous Baikal–Amur main line. All in all the length of the network doubled in these decades and reached 143,000 kilometres in 1983.[11]

The situation in Russia is not comparable with the railways of other Eastern European countries. In southeast Europe most of the railway lines were relics of the Habsburg and Ottoman Empires.[12] As in Russia there existed a transcontinental railway for colonial reasons, the so-called Orient Railway which crossed Austria and Hungary as well as Romania, Bulgaria or on a second track Serbia and the

---

[10] On the history of the Trans-Siberian Railway see A.I. Dimitrijew-Mamonow and A.F. Zdiarski, *Wegweiser auf der großen Sibirischen Eisenbahn* (St Petersburg 1901), and S.V. Sabler and I.V. Sosnovskii, *Sibirskaia zhelenaia doroga v ee proshlom i nastoiaschem* (The Siberian railway in its history and today) (St. Petersburg 1903). For its role for settlement see Ivan Nevzgodine, 'The Impact of the Trans-Siberian Railway on Architecture and Urban Planning of Siberian Cities', in Ralf Roth and Marie-Noëlle Polino, (eds), *The City and the Railway in Europe* (Aldershot 2003), 79–104.

[11] This was the biggest railway network of the world after the gigantic deconstruction of the American railways. See Arfon Rees, *Stalinism and Soviet Rail Transport, 1928–1941* (Basingstoke and New York 1995), and Rossberg, *Geschichte der Eisenbahn*, 104–9.

[12] Bremer, *Osteuropäische Eisenbahngeschichten*.

European territories of the Ottoman Empire.[13] The key figure behind the railway investment in the Ottoman part of this line was not a single state as in Russia but Baron Maurice de Hirsch, who established the Société impériale des chemins de fer de Turquie d'Europe in 1870 and a bit later the Société générale pour l'exploitation des chemins de fer Orientaux based in Paris.[14] The construction work was taken over by the Compagnie générale pour l'exploitation des chemins de fer de Turquie d'Europe which was set up 10 days later by Hirsch with Austrian and French capital. The main financial sponsors of this company were the French Société générale de Paris, the Anglo-Austrian Bank of Vienna, and the Banque Bischofsheim de Hirsch of Brussels.[15] Baron de Hirsch sold all the finished lines to the Deutsche Bank in 1890 which handed them over to the Zurich Bank for Oriental Railways which had been established by German, Austrian and Swiss banks.[16] The other parts of the line were built by the Habsburg empire, Serbia and Bulgaria, and either by the state or by private investors, and in many cases by foreign companies.[17] The first through train between Vienna and Istanbul ran on 12 August 1888. Afterwards the scramble for concessions in the Asian parts of the Ottoman empire began including the plans for the construction of a line as far as Baghdad, by investors from Great Britain, France and Germany and from other European states.[18]

One can see the Orient Railway as the starting point of Germany's imperial interest in the Near and Middle East but many other European countries were engaged in this railway project. However, as the railway imperialism of Russia failed in the Far East, so did the European in the Near East and all ended up in World War One and the breakdown of all four empires that had dominated the Eastern European space. Between the losers of the war – Germany, Austria, the Soviet Union and the modern Turkey – and themselves, the winners established a *cordon sanitaire* of independent states. We have not enough room in these short remarks to present all of the new states and their particular railway history.

---

[13]   For information on the Balkan railways in the Ottoman Empire see in general B.C. Gounaris, *Steam over Macedonia, 1870–1912. Socio-Economic Change and the Railway Factor* (Boulder, CO 1993). See also A. Nurdoğan, 'Dersaadet-Selanik İltisak Demiryolu', Marmara University MA thesis, 1999, and S.H. Beaver, 'Railways in the Balkan peninsula', *The Geographic Journal*, 5, 1941, 273–95.

[14]   On Baron Maurice de Hirsch see K. Grunwald, *Türkenhirsch: A Study of Baron Maurice de Hirsch, Entrepreneur and Philanthropist* (Jerusalem 1966).

[15]   Gounaris, *Steam over Macedonia*, 42–3.

[16]   Y.N. Karkar, *Railway Development in the Ottoman Empire, 1856–1914* (New York 1972), 68.

[17]   Rossberg, *Geschichte der Eisenbahn*, 99.

[18]   Bülent Bilmez, 'European Investments in the Ottoman Railways, 1850–1914', in Ralf Roth and Günter Dinhobl, (eds), *Across the Borders – Financing the World's Railways in the Nineteenth and Twentieth Centuries* (Aldershot 2008), 183–206. See also Manfred Pohl, *Von Stambul nach Bagdad. Die Geschichte einer berühmten Eisenbahn* (Munich and Zurich 1999).

One can imagine the complexity in this fragmented world when looking at the particularities of the multi-ethnic kingdom of Yugoslavia and the role played by Serbia in this kingdom, as well as in the People's Republic established after World War Two. Henry Jacolin has analysed this in his contributions 'Serbia's Access to the Sea, 1830–2006' and 'Yugoslavia: The Sub-Savian Magistral'. Step by step the author uncovers a 180-year-long story how the intention of Serbia to increase its potential by open access to the advantages of sea transport affected railway construction in the region. The state formed in its modern beginning a landlock between the Ottoman and Habsburg empires since its liberation in 1830. Already in 1856 first plans for a railway line to the coast were formulated but these plans could not be realised before 1985. The long struggle for this line without success demonstrates very well that the realisation of strategic suggestions depends on many factors and a constellation of powers that would allow it. Serbia depended on the strategic interests of no fewer than four powers, directly on the Habsburg and Ottoman empires, but also on the interests of Italy and Russia. Not by accident the Habsburg–Serbia conflict was the burning fuse that brought the antagonisms between the empires in Eastern Europe to explosion. But the outcome of World War One did not end up in a solution of Serbia's infrastructural problems. Jacolin summarises:

> The Yugoslavians, who were disappointed as they did not gain control of Trieste and Fiume, which were indispensable for Yugoslavia, felt the burden of Italian imperialism and realised that, although the Austro-Hungarian Empire had disappeared, their outlet in the north Adriatic was at the mercy of an expanding power, extremely focused on its interests. (52)

The story continued even after World War Two and even after the breakdown of socialism in Eastern Europe and the fall of the Iron Curtain, which the author explains in his second contribution for this anthology. There, the author describes and discusses the importance of one single line in former Yugoslavia which was planned in the 1970s to connect the less homogeneous republics of the socialist federation. Therefore he drew an impressive sketch of the geographical as well as political circumstances of this project – which had particular importance for the countries of former Yugoslavia as for through going transport from Eastern Europe to the Balkans and vice versa.

However, with the collapse of Yugoslavia after 1990 and its 'bloody' transformation into a series of new states, the railways were split into separate companies of Serbia, Slovenia, Croatia, Bosnia and Herzegovina, Montenegro and Macedonia, all in all a network originating in the Habsburg, Hungarian and Ottoman railway lines with a length of 11,000 kilometres, including the isolated railway of Albania.[19]

---

[19]   Rossberg, *Geschichte der Eisenbahn*, 99.

As in the former territories of Yugoslavia, the state railway construction in Bulgaria and Romania started with a delay of three decades. One can see the Orient Railway as a backbone of the developing network in these countries. Together the two countries constructed a railway network of 15,000 kilometres. The particularity of the Romanian network was that it was not only influenced by the Habsburg and Ottoman empires, but also by Germany, i.e. Prussia. The first Romanian line was built by the German railway 'king' Henry Bethel Strousberg. Between 1869 and 1873 he constructed four railway lines in Romania, all four starting in Bucharest and from there leading to Roman, Bîrlad, Galaţi and Piteşti. He planned an infrastructural backbone that would have been able to support Romania's rapid evolution into a modern state.[20] The plan failed. The Franco-Prussian War of 1870–71 caused his railway and industrial empire to crumble and the first project that went bankrupt was his railway system in Romania. This caused a shock wave that even had its repercussions in Germany because the default of Strousberg marked the beginning of a new debate on the nationalisation of Germany's railways. At first Reichskanzler Bismarck failed with several initiatives but in 1879 he achieved the nationalisation of the Prussian Railways (not those of the German empire). The other German states followed him. This is why one can say that the origins of Germany's state railways can be found in Romania. However, after the breakdown of Strousberg the Romanian state took over the railways and formed the Căile Ferate Române (CFR).[21]

Next to Romania lies the Ukraine and in the neighbourhood of both we have to consider Hungary, part of the double monarchy of the Habsburg empire. Whereas we have from Romania and Ukraine one chapter of each, we have several contributions on the railway history of Hungary. A general overview is presented by Imre Perger 'The History of Railway Passenger Transportation in Hungary – From the Monarchy to the Twenty-First Century'.[22] Although the Kingdom of Hungary was one constituent of the double monarchy and therefore was closely tied to the Habsburg empire, we have to face the fact that in Hungary the railways developed independently from Austria. Hungary possessed an independent railway organisation. The beginnings are in the 1840s, therefore a decade earlier then in many other Eastern European countries and they were initiated by Austria. But already in 1867 both networks became separated and the Magyar Államvasutak (MÁV) was founded in 1868. The company still exists today under the same

---

[20] For the railway projects in Hungary and Romania see Bethel Henry Strousberg, *Dr. Strousberg und sein Wirken. Von ihm selbst geschildert* (Berlin 1876), 331–47, Joachim Borchart, *Der europäische Eisenbahnkönig Bethel Henry Strousberg* (Munich 1991), 115–25, and Ralf Roth, 'Difficulties of International Railway Investments in Germany: The Example of the Railway King Henry Bethel Strousberg, 1855–1875', in Roth and Dinhobl, *Across the Borders*, 33–47.

[21] Rossberg, *Geschichte der Eisenbahn*, 99.

[22] We also get informed about Hungary and its railways in the chapters by Zsuzsa Frisnyák and of Viktor Borza, Vít Janoš and István Neumann.

name, even when its structure and the territory of its service have changed several times.[23] But further development was similar to a long and winding road and was characterised by rapidly shifting borders and wars and its integration into the hemisphere of the Soviet Union after World War Two. The permanent shift of borders in the aftermath of World Wars One and Two and the consequences this had on the railway system, its structure and economic, political and public use is not a particularity of Hungary but a widespread element of the unstable conditions of railways in Eastern Europe. Because of this it is a central theme of argumentation and runs through more than half a dozen chapters of this anthology. Perger describes also the consequence of the opening of the Iron Curtain and the shift from a centrally planned economy to a market system of the Western World, inclusive EU membership and renewal of the transport market, as for example the planning of inter-modality in urban regions, the competition with motorcars and the renewal of infrastructure and rolling stock despite lack of investment capital. He draws an optimistic conclusion:

> The history of the Hungarian railway shows that the future of the railway can only be ensured in the framework of European integration. A place has to be found for the existing network, and there is a pressing need for renewal of the infrastructure and rolling stock. Services must be improved and the results will surely come. At all times during the history of this railway system, inaction and the dismantling of infrastructure have brought only negative effects. (71)

For the development of railways in the Czech Republic and Slovakia – especially in the period of socialism and people's democracies – we have the contributions of Martin Kvizda, Ivan Jakubec and Milan Klubal, who shed light on the history of railways in both countries, which inherited the Habsburg and Hungarian railway lines in their newly formed territories. Contrary to the Czech Republic, Slovakia and Hungary, the railways of Poland (Polskie Koleje Państwowe – PKP) were formed out of parts of the Russian, Austrian and German railways. The network had a length of 16,000 kilometres and was not very dense with the exception of the industrial regions in the west.[24] The Polish Republic added further lines to the network and that is what Marcin Przegiętka is writing about in his contribution '1918, 1945 and 1989: Three Turning Points in the History of Polish Railways in the Twentieth Century'. The chapter looks back to the origin of the Polish railway system in the times when the Polish state did not exist. The empires of Prussia (then Germany), Russia and Habsburg supported railway networks of different density. The most densely developed in the German part, the less densely in the Russian one. As a consequence the newly erected state after World War One possessed a railway system with different track gauges. As in Hungary, Romania and the Ukraine the

---

[23]   http://de.wikipedia.org/wiki/Magyar_%C3%81llamvasutak#cite_note-M. C3.80V_Cargo-2 (last accessed 2 May 2010).

[24]   Bremer, *Osteuropäische Eisenbahngeschichten.*

next decades brought shifting borders and great destructions. Germany occupied the country, lost again the war and Poland was shifted westwards, lost territories in the east to the Soviet Union and gained new territories in the west from Germany. Together with the state the railway system had to be restructured again. A new chapter was opened and its importance summarised Przegiętka as follows:

> During the Cold War, the railways in Poland were strategically important. They were used to transport Soviet forces, because the People's Republic of Poland (*Polska Rzeczpospolita Ludowa*), like other countries in Eastern Europe, was a signatory to the Warsaw Pact, the defence treaty signed in 1951. The Red Army stayed in Poland and the German Democratic Republic until the beginning of 1990s. (111)

Until 1980 2,200 kilometres of new railways were built, among them the line from Kattowitz (Katowice) to Warsaw (Warszawa) and further on to Danzig (Gdansk) as a new main line. In the 1980s the Polish state railways ran a network of 24,305 kilometres length.[25]

The railways of Estonia, Latvia, Lithuania and Belorussia were all a part of the Tsarist empire and then of the Soviet Baltic Railroad during the Soviet era. The lines are not designed according to the present national borders and the trains are still mostly the same which were 'inherited' from the Baltic Railroad of the Sovetskie Zheleznye Dorogi (SZD) at the time when the Baltic States regained their independence. Some of them have a long tradition, such as the Lithuanian railway which goes back to 1857. They became independent state railways in 1992. The history of railways in this northeastern part of Europe is not very well researched. But with the contributions of Augustus Veenendaal and Andrej Kishtymov we found two excellent authors who filled that gap in this volume. In 'The Baltic States – Railways under Many Masters' Augustus Veenendaal stated:

> Today they are independent nations and members of the European Union, but the three Baltic countries, Estonia (Estland, Eesti), Latvia (Lettland, Latvija) and Lithuania (Litauen, Lietuva), suffered much political turmoil and went through many changes in borders and overlords in previous centuries. (3)

From 1721 up to the 1990s they were part of Russia and the Soviet Union. All three countries belonged to the more developed parts of the empire including some important ports. The first line was constructed in 1869 and was of importance for the growing grain export of Russia to Western Europe. The capacity of this line was never enough and there was a permanent need to attract foreign investment capital and know-how from Germany. The twentieth century changed between independence and Soviet control and therefore several changes of the gauge

---

[25] Bremer, *Osteuropäische Eisenbahngeschichten*, and Rossberg, *Geschichte der Eisenbahn*, 99.

of the network. After World War Two the main freight shifted from corn to oil and with it the railways there experienced the competition with other transport modes – such as pipelines.

The neighbouring country, respectively province of the former Tsarist empire has been explored by Andrej Kishtymov in his chapter 'The Construction and Modernisation of Railways in Belorussia/Belarus in the Late Nineteenth and Twentieth Centuries'. His conviction is:

> Railways have contributed greatly to the development of the economy and society
> of Belorussia since the middle of the nineteenth century. Like a locomotive,
> literally and figuratively, they pulled the Belorussian economy upwards. (19)

On the background of this thesis he delivered a chronology of the development of the railway system in Belorussia and modern Belarus. We find very early proposals for railway construction – not very much later than in Western Europe, but differing from them in a strong emphasis on military aspects. However, the proposals were rejected and there was no serious engagement before the 1850s. First successful railway construction was a part of the strategic line from St Petersburg to Warsaw. Landlords in agrarian regions tried to initiate additional lines in the 1860s. But instead of an increase in investments it ended up in a 10-year break in the 1870s. Only in the 1880s a strong engagement of the state including nationalisation in the 1890s, had more success and resulted in initiatives for a long series of construction projects.

Last but not least, Germany has to be mentioned. Of course it is not a part of Eastern Europe but in the past it had a great and powerful influence on its Eastern neighbours, a position that shifted to the Soviet Union after 1945. It was no accident that the so-called Prussian Eastern Railway was built with enormous support from the state. Moreover a most important debate sprang up about the principal purpose of railway construction – economic reasons or administrative and military ones. This debate was initiated by the question of financing and caused indirectly the revolution of 1848 when liberals (among them railway entrepreneurs David Hansemann and Ludolf Camphausen) at the Vereinigte Landtag in Berlin rejected the states' wish of financial contributions to the Eastern Railway from Berlin all the way to Königsberg.[26] Jan Musekamp tells us more about the further history of 'The Royal Prussian Eastern Railway (Ostbahn) and its significance for East–West Transportation' and of its strategic importance. So far he directs our attention to one of Europe's traffic axis to the East between Berlin and Warsaw and on to Moscow. The line reflects the turbulent history of Germany's influence in this part of the continent in the twentieth century and in the course of the renewal of Poland as a sovereign state. Not only in the case of the Prussian Eastern Railway, but in many railway projects in central, northeast, east and southeast Europe, German

---

[26]   See Ralf Roth, *Das Jahrhundert der Eisenbahn. Die Herrschaft über Raum und Zeit 1800 – 1914* (Ostfildern 2005), 80–88.

investors played an important role in the development of railways. The Orient Railway and the activities of Deutsche Bank in the Balkans and Ottoman empire have already been mentioned. The railway 'king' Henry B. Strousberg and his activities in Russia, Hungary and Romania have also to be added.

However, historical overviews from the Eastern border regions of Germany up to the northern parts of the Balkans, all of this formed the first section of the book.

Breaks and Disruptions in the Twentieth Century

The second part of the book includes contributions with focus on the time of the Cold War entitled 'Under Russian Protection'. But before we jump to this section of the book, we have to focus our attention on a further general phenomenon that characterises the railways in Eastern Europe. When we summarise the particularities of railway history in Eastern Europe we find not only the dominance of multi-ethnic empires, not only economic latecomers and shattered and geographical instable societies that influenced the development of the railways there, but also many striking examples of non-economic factors that have driven the railway system forward. One example is the construction of lines for strategic and military reasons only. Our author Martin Kvizda analyses this in his chapter 'Czech Military Railways – History and a Comparative Analysis of the Czech Railway Network's Efficiency'. As said, the growth of the economy was not the only reason for the construction of railways. Especially in Eastern Europe we find administrative and military-strategic reasons. Kvizda discusses this matter in the example of the Czech Railways – one of the densest networks in this region of Europe. He is of the opinion that the recent view of a rational railway considering only economic aspects would fail and asks the question:

> Who was so enthusiastic about building a railway in hilly terrain just to connect a few sleepy villages? A wealth of material in railway history helps us arrive at answers. Generally speaking, railway networks were created in three ways: First, the state planned lines and then built tracks of its own, and with its own money; second, the state gave orders and licenses to private companies to build tracks according to the state's plans; and third, the state gave privileges to private companies to plan, build and run railways without any restrictions on route planning. In continental Europe, starting in the middle of the nineteenth century the state usually combined all these approaches to network creation, but the first prevailed. (76)

A lot of authors in the volume come directly or indirectly to similar results and deliver impressive cases which might open a flourishing debate about this point. We have to face that this is probably a main characteristic that distinguishes the Eastern European railway system very clearly from that of Western Europe.

However, the system of the four dominant empires Russian, Germany, Habsburg and Ottoman lost its stability in the beginning of the twentieth century. With the defeat of Germany in World War One and the collapse of its imperialistic strategies, it lost territories to the new states of Poland and Czechoslovakia and with it important railway lines. Many more changes were caused by the breakdown of the Habsburg empire for Southeastern Europe, and that of the Ottoman empire for the Balkans. After the decline of three of these former empires, only Russia survived in the form of the Soviet Union. The Soviet Union had a tremendous impact on the Eastern European railway system in the following decades of the new century. Initially this was obviously only the case in Ukraine, but after World War Two the Soviet hegemony reached out to all countries of this part of Europe. This meant that most of these railway systems became part of the planned economy carried through by the Soviet Union at the beginning of the Cold War.

The divided Europe of the Cold War period was marked by severed traffic routes, dead end railway stations along the new frontiers, limitations of the right to move and travel, a general slowdown, and bureaucratic obstacles. The people in the Soviet sphere were separated from the networks in middle and Western Europe. It became difficult to travel from west to east and in many cases even impossible to make journeys vice versa from east to west. Moreover, for the Eastern European countries this meant regulation by the state, less dynamic, bureaucratic structures and limited resources, but on the other hand less competition from other means of transport such as motor cars and air transport, because railways ranked more highly in the economic order and in the systems of transport infrastructure as compared to the Western countries which supported competition by motorisation.[27]

A series of contributions underline this thesis. Ivan Jakubec analyses in his chapter 'Transport under Socialism: The Case of the Czechoslovak State Railways 1948–1989' as well 'the political level', i.e. the Soviet political model and the orientation of foreign policy on Moscow and the 'economic level' what he defined as:

> the Soviet-style planned economy, the Eastern economic bloc, the dependence
> on the import of raw materials from the Soviet Union, and the creation of the
> material and technological basis of Communism. (115)

Railways continued as a state enterprise, and thus formed a stabilising element in the political, economic, military-strategic, and even in social and cultural fields. The Czech railways, the Československé státní dráhy (ČSD) were fully integrated in the transformation of Czechoslovak society and economy on the model of the Soviet command economy.

After being informed about the railways of the Czech Republic, Milan Klubal continued in his chapter 'The Modernisation of Railways in Slovakia After 1945' with an overview of the modernisation of railways in Slovakia in this period. But

---

[27]   Christoph Maria Merki, *Verkehrsgeschichte und Mobilität* (Stuttgart 2008), 52ff.

he includes also an overview from the beginning onwards. As the Czech Republic, Slovakia experienced a transformation from a region inside the Habsburg empire to a part of the first Czechoslovakian Republic, then to an independent state that depended on the will of Germany and then again it became a part of the ČSSR under Soviet hegemony. One of the conspicuous facts was the increase in freight transport because of the requirements of the central economic planning in COMECON which led to the construction of new lines. Although the ČSD successfully realised some modernisations of the railway system as electrification and some automatic safety infrastructure, Jakubec, just as Klubal, shows the lack of investment resources for necessary innovations. This had radical consequences which Jakubec summarised as follows:

> This situation led to plans that were difficult or impossible to fulfil, neither from Czechoslovakia nor from the Council for Mutual Economic Assistance, COMECON. (125)

Zsuzsa Frisnyák focused her chapter 'The Centrally Planned Economy and Railways in Hungary' nearly parallel to Jakubec and Klubal on the Czech Republic and Slovakia also on the period of central economic planning after World War Two. Command economy in Hungary started astonishingly two years before the one party state was erected. She writes:

> The most important features of the Soviet model of transportation were the following: total state control over transport vehicles, party oversight, the merging of control and implementation, central command, the economy of shortage, and Stakhanovite labour competitions. (144)

As in the ČSSR Republic Slovakia and the Czech Republic forced industrialisation on the model of the Soviet Union led to an increase in freight transport. But very similar to the conclusion of Jakubec, the close personal union between the board of the MÁV and the Ministry of Transportation increased the political influence in railway administration and led to 'wishful thinking'. The whole transport organisation lost its way to reality up to a first collapse of railways transport in 1952. For Frisnyák the history of socialist Hungary is a failed 'experiment in modernisation' (154).

Ihor Zhaloba presents us a further chapter on this topic entitled 'The Railways of the Ukrainian Soviet Socialist Republic: 1920–1990'. In Ukraine the Soviet rule lasted seven decades – a quarter of a century longer than in Hungary, Czech Republic or Slovakia. Nevertheless the railway network itself came from many masters, i.e. territories that had belonged to Romania, Poland and Czechoslovakia or before to the Habsburg empire and not only to Russia and the Tsarist empire. There had been a long period of transition with shifting borders in the decade between 1920 and 1941. This made Ukrainian history compatible with that of Lithuania, Estonia, Latvia or Belorussia. Not only shifting borders, but also the destruction of two World Wars and Civil Wars impacted the development with decades of intense construction that were followed by periods of destruction and decline and 'graveyards of broken engines and wagons' at locomotive depots and railway stations – with losses of billions of roubles. Zhaloba also mentions drastic methods to keep the machine running – including death penalties for railway directors. After a long period of reconstruction after World War Two the railway system fell into stagnation in the 1970s and 1980s a consequence of a failed command economy. The author summarises:

> This led to numerous accidents with casualties and material losses. The goals of the plans were not reached. In the 1970s, the railway industry met the USSR national economy demands only by 88 per cent and in the 1980s by 94 per cent. The population's demands were met only by 80 to 92 per cent (...) The majority of accidents, collisions, train crashes, derailments, and other violations of road safety regulations took place because of the low level of operational and technological discipline. (171)

Whereas Jakubec, Klubal, Frisnyák (also Perger and Przegiętka) and Zhaloba describe more general aspects of the development of railways in the time of the Cold War and Soviet hegemony over Eastern Europe, Adelina Oana Ştefan concentrates more on the quality of the service for customers in this time. Her chapter 'Passengers' Railway Identity in Socialist Romania during the 1950s and 1960s' therefore made use of methods of oral history and focuses our attention to railways as 'means of showing the regime's strength and empathy towards the ordinary people's style of living' (187).

Especially in the post-Stalinist era when the social glue of the system changed from terror to consumerism and therefore, consumption and service became more important for railways. But most Romanian railways authorities concentrated on freight transport as Jakubec, Klubal, Frisnyák and Zhaloba have stressed for their countries. But even this was the case in Romania too they tried to use passenger transport for agitation. This is the aspect Ştefan starts with. After she has pointed out 'the official policies of the Communist regime regarding railways, paying attention to legislation, official directives and practices', she analysed 'the way passengers remember the experience of the everyday use of railways'. Her aim is:

> to investigate the role of passenger transportation within the railway system, the passengers' uses of railway lines, the conditions provided by various types of trains, and last but not least the cultural and social impact of railways on passengers. (189)

Thanks to her investigation we get insight in everyday arrangements of the people there with the system. Ştefan concluded:

At the same time their testimonies show that a compromise was set up with the communist regime, which in exchange for poor services, offered citizens the freedom to officially deceive the system by smuggling and creating an underground economy. This helps explain the incapacity of the communist regime to fulfil its promises of prosperity and good life, and part of the syndrome that eroded them in the end. (201)

With Tomáš Nigrin's chapter 'Cold War Crisis on the Railway: Construction of the Berlin Wall' we include an informative chapter on the absurdity of the Cold War and on the example of the railway system in Berlin. Because of increasing differences between the former allies, the common administration of the former German capital failed. But as relics of the war alliance they preserved the administration of all railways in and around Berlin by the Deutsche Reichsbahn, while the rest of the railway system was divided according to the occupation zones. This led to the absurd situation of an undivided railway organisation in a divided city. Whereas the Iron Curtain became closer and closer in Berlin the 'East' drove literally speaking to the 'West' and West Berliners were employees of an East German company. Moreover it was planned by the government of the former German Democratic Republic (GDR) to use the railways passing through West Berlin as a kind of showcase for the superiority of their system, while the West developed the rest of the city as showcase for their superiority. Lack of resources of the GDR let their ambitious plans fail. The S-Bahn system declined and the Western parts were sold to the magistrate of West Berlin in the 1980s. This was more than a sign at the wall for the later breakdown of all Eastern European economies in 1989.[28]

Reunification of the European Hemisphere

One can imagine that more than the planned economy system itself, the isolation from the West caused a certain delay in the technological development and that was at the end what caused the breakdown in the late 1980s. However, since 1990 Europe's two halves, torn apart by the Cold War, are beginning to come together again. The political changes were accompanied by tremendous economic and social changes, including changes in the transport industry. Europe has made an effort to reconnect severed railway lines and to repair and reopen decommissioned and blocked East–West connections. Of course there are a lot of problems with this transition accompanied by shrinking railway networks, reduction of employment and serious problems in financing the railway infrastructure. But there are signs for a better future which back up the optimistic view that the railway could survive when the new management will face the problems. There is not necessarily an end to the existence of railways. It is obvious that a modern and reunited Europe

---

[28] One can read more about the details in Burghard Ciesla, *Als der Osten durch den Westen fuhr. Die Geschichte der Deutschen Reichsbahn in Westberlin* (Cologne et al. 2006).

cannot exist without a unified and modernised transportation system in which the railway mode has an important part to play. High-speed connections between the regions should link them closer together. But in between we have a transition period of unknown length – not only for the East, but also for the south, where the modernisation efforts began in the 1980s, 30 years ago. For the Eastern parts of Europe the transition meanwhile has lasted 20 years, and these 20 years had our particular interest in this volume.

The situation after 1990 will be addressed by chapters of the third section: 'After the Fall of the Iron Curtain: Changes – Problems – Modernisation'. The chapters shed light on the understanding of this fact and they improved our knowledge of what has been done afterwards, after 1990 – the great transition from a planned economy to a free market system as in Western Europe. One of the most important contributions is Anthony Heywood's 'Back to the Future? Russia's Railway Transport and the Collapse of the Soviet Union in Historical Perspective'. He convincingly explains how the railways of the Soviet Union expanded up to the end of the USSR. Astonishingly enough, there was no sign of stagnation there contrary to the economy in general. But at the end of the Soviet Union railways suddenly declined and were partitioned into 15 separate national railway organisations in 1991. Heywood aims to situate this upheaval in a long-term history and compared it with the collapse of the transport system in the Civil War between 1917 and 1920 and with the second transport crisis in the time of German invasion from 1941 to 1943. After a short description of the development of the network from the beginning on he draws the conclusion that:

> the crisis of the 1990s (…) involved a collapse of turnover that proportionately was worse than the Second-World-War experience but was not nearly as bad as the crisis during the Civil War. (238)

However, the collapse forced the system to reform. Obviously there were some changes, as Heywood writes:

> Some of the key Soviet transport policies like centrally planned inter-modal coordination have disappeared, and some momentous reforms have been instigated. But there are also significant continuities in mindset and policy that are deeply rooted in the culture and traditions of the Russian railways. Faced with an uncertain future, the Russian railways have not simply rejected their past, but have sought to meld large parts of it with the new national priorities associated with running a mixed state-private economy. (252)

And this is what happened in other countries of the former socialist East too. The most dynamic experienced the sovietised part of Germany whose railways, the Deutsche Reichsbahn of the former GDR, became unified with the railways of the former Federal Republic of Germany (FRG), the Deutsche Bundesbahn. That is what Ralf Roth's chapter 'The Unification of East and West German Railways into the Deutsche Bahn' is about. He writes in his chapter about the separation of a national railway system – one of the most dense in Europe – into two parts as a consequence of World War Two and the policy of the allies and the outbreak of the Cold War. Then he analyses the long list of problems which appears when both systems were merged again after the reunification of both German states in 1990. The cure was harsh:

> In 15 years, the *Deutsche Bahn AG* invested in new, modern technology, and it modernised tracks and railway stations, trains and locomotives. The number of employees declined from nearly 500,000 to 230,000; they run service on a shrinking network. But at the same time, new strategic lines have been constructed for high speed travel. The *Deutsche Bahn* has transported an increasing number of passengers and an increasing amount of goods. And important international activities have led to a diversification of the staff, with ten% located outside Germany. (266)

In addition to Roth's chapter about the change of German railways after 1945 and 1990 Peter F.N. Hörz and Marcus Richter give with 'Seen from the Driving Cab: The Consequences of German Railway's Privatisation since the Reunion of Deutsche Bundesbahn and Reichsbahn from the Engine Drivers' Perspective' insight in the consequences of the reform of German railways by analysing the everyday working lot of Deutsche Bahn employees – especially the locomotive drivers. As Ştefan did in the case of Romania, they made use of oral-history methods and interviewed engine drivers; they deliver us insight from the driving cab about changes in working conditions. For them:

> the market-oriented reform of the *Deutsche Bahn* carried out since the reunion of the two German railways in 1994 means more than a loss of income and habitual social benefits. For engine drivers, it means a sudden farewell to high technical qualification standards, long training periods and vast decision-making competence and authority. Today, they feel they have become mere operational assistants, carrying out instructions which they can barely influence. (280)

The fall of the Iron Curtain brought back one key player on the field of international cooperation of railways and increased its possibilities to influence the modernisation of railways in Eastern European countries. Paul Véron describes this in his excellent contribution 'Railway Integration in Europe: UIC – a Key Player of East–West Railway Integration'. He presents an overview of the development of the World Union of Railways, its historic origins and its role during the Cold War. But the main focus lies on the subject of railway integration between East and West in the decades that followed after. He stated:

> From the moment the borders began to open, UIC examined the impact of this new geopolitical and economic environment on the pan-European rail sector through

a specially created body, the UIC East-West Task Force (it rapidly published a White Paper on the perspectives that the new political situation opened for the European rail sector). UIC immediately initiated closer cooperation with railways of all countries concerned (and with the Community of European Railways (CER), representing the railways of the European Union) in order to accelerate railway harmonisation at European level. The UIC East-West Task Force focused on the harmonisation of legislative, regulatory, technical and administrative measures between East and West. (225–6)

He demonstrates how the current European railway integration is carried out at four levels that he summarises in the following way: (1) Political decision-making process in EU institutions, (2) professional representation towards political and economic institutions, (3) professional/technical cooperation mainly at UIC with focuses on interoperability, development of a seamless, non-discriminatory rail transport system, and (4) last but not least the business level, with a trend towards European alliances, joint ventures, private–public partnerships and new forms of joint business.

How the development of strategic European transport axis influenced local and regional policies shows Kevin Sutton in his chapter 'The Reopening of Murska Sobota–Zalalövő Railway: A Paradox of the European Reunification in Central Europe?' He shifts our attention from north Central Europe and Germany again to the southeast and Alpine region between Hungary and Slovenia and analyses how fragile European transport axes could be and how speedy new routes can open competition to older lines which had worked for decades. Or older ones – how in his case of the Murska Sobota–Zalalövő Railway experience a renaissance after they were blocked for nearly one hundred years. Nothing shows the effect of a European-wide network clearer than this case.

Another aspect is delivered by our three authors Viktor Borza, Vít Janoš and István Neumann in their chapter "More is Less': Regular Interval Timetable in Central Eastern Europe'. They discuss the effects of a new schedule system and present the experiences of Western European railways with the so-called Interval Timetable and its advantages for Eastern European railways on the experiences of the Hungarian MÁV:

An ITF-based system favours an expedient concept of infrastructure development priorities as it points out which possible developments are not a priority. It favours efficient management of human resources, which still makes up for 45 per cent of MÁV's cost structure. Due to ITF's transparent, periodic nature, planning efforts can be reduced to a fraction of previous levels. (307)

Like a mosaic, all these aspects of modernisation presented together in the chapters of the book formed a panorama of the ongoing process of railways in transition. Many details afford of course more and intensified research, but based on the modernisation of railways in Eastern Europe there existed extrapolations of the progress in mobility, and not only a few estimated that the time-space correlation of Europe will shrink further – also in its Eastern part.[29] This means that more and more centres will be connected by a more dynamic railway network. This and of course innovations in all other transport modes should lead to a more homogeneous development in economic wealth, social harmony and political freedom and stability. That is the long-term vision of a united Europe.

However, this is not the end of the book. At the end of the third section we attach two chapters that introduce two institutions where railway heritage is professional preserved. This provides an additional access to history. Not only the historical description and interpretation but also the heritage is important for the understanding of railway history in our time. Zsuzsa Frisnyák informs us in 'Railway Heritage Protection Policy in Hungary' about the history of the Museum of Science, Technology and Transport in Budapest. Beside all impressive achievements that could be reached in the last decades, she identifies a long list which things in heritage protection could be improved:

> The history of the Hungarian railway heritage protection is not an unbroken chain of successes. Today's institutional structure with its multiple players is relatively stable, but there is still a lack of methodical and predictable development in the area of vehicle restoration. That era of the Hungarian railway heritage protection has not yet arrived. Because the state's contributions are unpredictable, and the railway companies are encumbered with debts, planning is impossible even for the short term. (320)

Rainer Mertens did the something similar in his chapter 'The Heritage of the Deutsche Reichsbahn and its Presentation in the Deutsche Bahn Museum in Nuremberg'. Contrary to the Museum in Budapest, the Museum in Nuremberg is not a state but a private institute financed by the Deutsche Bahn. He resumes some remarkable changes in the last decade:

> Since its renovation, the Nuremberg Railway Museum has changed from a technology-oriented museum of the West German *Bundesbahn* and pre-war railways to a culture-oriented museum of the pan-German Deutsche Bahn and its predecessors. The history of the *Deutsche Reichsbahn* in East Germany is one of the central topics of the new *DB Museum*. The exhibition 'On separate

---

[29] See Klaus Spiekermann and Michael Wegener, 'Trans-European networks and unequal accessibility in Europe', *European Journal of Regional Development (EUREG)*, 4, 1996, 35–42. Their outlines are based on a research project for the Network of European Communications and Transport Activities Research. There they developed time maps in dependency of the high-speed railway network. On the Trans-European Transportation Network (TEN-T) see Michèle Merger, 'The Great European Infrastructure Projects and their Outcome', in Ralf Roth and Karl Schlögel, (eds), *Neue Wege in ein neues Europa. Geschichte und Verkehr im 20. Jahrhundert* (Frankfurt am Main 2009), 414–27.

tracks' in the main museum in Nuremberg contains one of the largest and most important presentations of GDR history in Germany. (332)

We hope that this volume will contribute to our understanding of the ongoing process of the transformation of Eastern and Southeastern Europe.

Bibliography

Beaver, S.H., 'Railways in the Balkan peninsula', *The Geographic Journal*, 5, 1941, 273–95.

Bilmez, B., 'European Investments in the Ottoman Railways, 1850–1914', in Ralf Roth and Günter Dinhobl (eds), *Across the Borders – Financing the World's Railways in the Nineteenth and Twentieth Centuries* (Aldershot 2008), 183–206.

Borchart, J., *Der europäische Eisenbahnkönig Bethel Henry Strousberg* (Munich 1991).

Bremer, Th., Osteuropäische Eisenbahngeschichten, *OST-WEST. Europäische Perspektiven. Zeitschrift für Mittel- und Osteuropa* (online publication, last accessed 15 September 2009).

Burbank, Jane and Cooper, Frederick, *Empires in World History: Power and the Politics of Difference* (Princeton and Oxford 2010).

Ciesla, Burghard, *Als der osten durch den Westen fuhr. Die Geschichte der Deutschen Reichsbahn in Westberlin* (Cologne et al. 2006).

Dimitrijew-Mamonow, A.I. and Zdiarski, A.F., *Wegweiser auf der großen Sibirischen Eisenbahn* (St Petersburg 1901).

Gounaris, B.C., *Steam over Macedonia, 1870–1912: Socio-Economic Change and the Railway Factor* (Boulder, CO 1993).

Grunwald, K., *Türkenhirsch: A Study of Baron Maurice de Hirsch, Entrepreneur and Philanthropist* (Jerusalem 1966).

Karkar, Y.N., *Railway Development in the Ottoman Empire, 1856–1914* (New York 1972).

Merger, Michèle, 'The Great European Infrastructure Projects and their Outcome', in Ralf Roth and Karl Schlögel (eds), *Neue Wege in ein neues Europa. Geschichte und Verkehr im 20. Jahrhundert* (Frankfurt am Main 2009), 414–27.

Merki, Chr. M., *Verkehrsgeschichte und Mobilität* (Stuttgart 2008).

Nevzgodine, Ivan, ,The Impact of the Trans-Siberian Railway on Architecture and Urban Planning of Siberian Cities', in Ralf Roth and Marie-Noëlle Polino (eds), *The City and the Railway in Europe* (Aldershot 2003), 79–104.

Nurdoğan, A., 'Dersaadet-Selanik İltisak Demiryolu', Marmara University MA thesis, 1999.

Parsons, Timothy H., *The Rule of Empires: Those Who Built Them, Those Who Endured Them, and Why They Always Fall* (Oxford 2010).

Pohl, Manfred, *Von Stambul nach Bagdad. Die Geschichte einer berühmten Eisenbahn* (Munich and Zurich 1999).

Pinheiro, M. (ed.), *Railway Modernization: An Historical Perspective, 19th and 20th Centuries* (Lisbon 2009).

Rees, Arfon, *Stalinism and Soviet Rail Transport, 1928–1941* (Basingstoke and New York 1995).

Rossberg, R.R., *Geschichte der Eisenbahn*, 2nd edn (Frankfurt am Main 1984).

Roth, R., 'Difficulties of International Railway Investments in Germany: The Example of the Railway King Henry Bethel Strousberg, 1855–1875', in R. Roth and Günter Dinhobl (eds), *Across the Borders – Financing the World's Railways in the Nineteenth and Twentieth Centuries* (Aldershot 2008), 33–47.

Roth, R., 'Eisenbahn', in Dan Diner and Markus Kirchhoff (eds), *Europäische Traditionen – Enzyklopädie jüdischer Geschichte und Kultur*, 5 vols (Stuttgart and Weimar 2011), vol. 2, 195–201.

Roth, R., *Das Jahrhundert der Eisenbahn. Die Herrschaft über Raum und Zeit 1800–1914* (Ostfildern 2005).

Roth, R. and Dinhobl, G. (eds), *Across the Borders: Financing the World's Railways in the Nineteenth and Twentieth Centuries* (Aldershot 2008).

Sabler, S.V. and Sosnovskii, I.V., *Sibirskaia zheleznaia doroga v ee proshlom i nastoiaschem* (The Siberian railway in its history and today) (St Petersburg 1903).

Schenk, F.B., 'Mapping the Empire: Die Neuvermessung des Russländischen Reiches im Eisenbahnzeitalter', paper presented at Osteuropa kartiert – Mapping Eastern Europe. Conference organised by Christophe von Werdt (Osteuropa-Bibliothek, Bern), Mira Jovanovíc and Jörn Happel in Bern from 25 to 27 September 2008.

Sperling, Walter, *Der Aufbruch der Provinz. Die Eisenbahn und die Neuordnung der Räume im Zarenreich* (Frankfurt am Main 2011).

Spiekermann, Klaus and Wegener, Michael, 'Trans-European Networks and Unequal Accessibility in Europe', *European Journal of Regional Development (EUREG)*, 4, 1996, 35–42

Strousberg, B.H., *Dr. Strousberg und sein Wirken. Von ihm selbst geschildert* (Berlin 1876), 331–47.

Wallerstein, Immanuel, *World-Systems Analysis: An Introduction* (London 2004).

PART I
General Suggestions and Historical Overviews of Railways in Eastern European Countries

Chapter 1

The Baltic States – Railways under Many Masters

Augustus J. Veenendaal, Jr.

Introduction

Today they are independent nations and members of the European Union, but the three Baltic countries, Estonia (Estland, Eesti), Latvia (Lettland, Latvija) and Lithuania (Litauen, Lietuva), suffered much political turmoil and went through many changes in borders and overlords in previous centuries. In the Middle Ages, the Teutonic Knights pushed in from the West and, beginning in the sixteenth century, the Swedish kings established themselves as overlords of Estonia, and of Livland and the Duchy of Kurland, in what is now Latvia. At the 1721 Peace of Nystadt, Sweden lost most of its Baltic possessions, and Czarist Russia became the new master, while Litauen was, at least officially, part of the Polish-Lithuanian Commonwealth. With the partitions of Poland in the later eighteenth century, Polish Litauen became Russian as well, with the exception of Klaipeda, then known as Memel, which was part of East Prussia.[1] The Vienna Congress of 1815 mostly confirmed the existing borders. Estland, Livland, Kurland and Kowno (the northern part of Litauen) remained Russian; the southern part of Litauen was officially Polish, but under Russian domination, as Poland did not exist as a separate nation before 1918. Memel was still part of Prussia, and then, after 1871, part of the German Empire. Reval and Riga, with their generally ice-free harbours, were important commercial ports for the export of Russian grain, and Libau, while also being an important mercantile port, became the home base for a large part of the Russian Imperial Navy.

Generally, the Baltic provinces of Russia were more developed than the vast plains to the east and south, with a number of ancient but still thriving cities, and somewhat more industrialised than the still predominantly agricultural rest of Russia. Shipping and trade with Western Europe from the Baltic ports went back to the sixteenth century, and Western influence was always much more important there than it was in landlocked Russia. Even Peter the Great did not change this, although his new capital of St Petersburg did attract a number of foreigners who introduced

---

[1] For the survey of the developments before 1918, the generally acknowledged contemporary German versions of place names are used; after 1918, the locally recognised versions. In Table 1.1 a list of places is given in both German and national languages.

modern methods in trade and industry. The modern textile industry, in the form of a huge cotton mill, was brought by Englishmen to Kränholm near Narva in 1857, employing British capital and know how. This factory town was nicknamed 'a piece of England on Russian soil'.[2] Industrialisation on a large scale came to Russia only late, certainly not before 1875, and, according to modern scholars, only in the last decade of the nineteenth century. Heavy industry, based on the coal and iron deposits of the Donetz area, began to be developed late in the nineteenth century, necessitating railway construction on a large scale, including to the Baltic ports to export the industrial products. The many wars in which the Russian empire was involved also played an important role in the construction of railways.[3]

Table 1.1   Names of places mentioned in the text in German and national languages

Dorpat	Tartu (Estonia)
Dünaburg	Daugavpils (Latvia, Dwinsk in Russian)
Eydtkuhnen	Chernyshevskoye (Russia)
Königsberg	Kaliningrad (Russia)
Kovno	Kaunas (Lithuania)
Kreuzburg	Krustpils (Latvia)
Libau	Liepaja (Latvia)
Memel	Klaipeda (Lithuania)
Mitau	Jelgava (Latvia)
Narwa	Narva (Estonia)
Pernau	Pärnu (Estonia)
Pillau	Baltisk (Russia)
Reval	Tallinn (Estonia)
Tauroggen	Taurage (Lithuania)
Tilsit	Sovetsk (Russia)
Walk	Valga (Estonia), Valka (Latvia)
Wilna	Vilnius (Lithuania)
Windau	Ventspils (Latvia)
Wirballen	Virbalis (Lithuania)

---

[2] W.O. Henderson, *The Industrial Revolution on the Continent: Germany, France, Russia, 1800–1914* (London 1961), 212.

[3] Ibid., 28, 33.

At the same time, the grain of the vast Russian plains was exported to a hungry Western Europe. However, transportation was the greatest problem everywhere in Russia, with bad or non-existent roads, and rivers that froze over every winter. Railways were sorely needed to boost the industrial and agricultural growth. The first most important outlet for Russian grain was Odessa, with – before 1853 – more than half of total exports over the Black Sea. Only 0.3 per cent went through Riga.[4] At that time there were no railways to any Baltic port, and although Odessa too lacked a railway, distances there for ox-drawn carts were shorter, and the rivers were more navigable. After the railway reached the Baltic, Riga, Reval and Windau became the chief ports for the export of Russian grain. But despite the presence of railways, even as late as 1894, more than 1.5 million tons of grain reached the Baltic ports by road, not by rail.[5]

The growth of heavy industry and railways was helped in no small way by the influx of foreign capital, foreign managers and staff, and foreign methods, as solicited by the Russian minister Count Sergej Witte late in the nineteenth century. Many of the Russian railways were financed from Western Europe. They were considered eminently safe vehicles for investment, as most were guaranteed by the Russian government.[6] Initially, domestic labour was poorly educated and generally uninterested in any development. Serfdom was only abolished in 1861, although there were men from this class who became entrepreneurs. Foreign labour was prominent, especially among foremen and the higher echelons of managers. For instance, the Russo-Baltic Company in Riga, a maker of railway rolling stock which opened in 1869, depended heavily on German entrepreneurs and foremen.[7] The large Lugansk locomotive factory was founded in 1896 by Gustav Hartmann, a close friend of Witte, a son-in-law of Alfred Krupp of Essen, and connected to Richard Hartmann's *Sächsische Maschinenfabrik* in Chemnitz. Similarly, the Russian Locomotive and Construction Company of Kharkov, founded in 1895, was initiated by a Frenchman, Philippe Bouhey.[8]

---

[4]   *Russian Rail Transport 1836–1917* (St Petersburg State Transportation University Faculty 1999), 45.

[5]   Henderson, *The Industrial Revolution*, 226.

[6]   See for the importance of foreign capital in Russia in general, see Herbert Feis, *Europe, the World's Banker 1870–1914* (New Haven 1930), 210–34.

[7]   The Russo-Baltic rolling stock company was founded back in 1869 by the German firm of Van der Zypen and Charlier of Cologne. By 1900, production had reached the 50,000 mark. Herman G. Hesselink and Norbert Tempel, *Eisenbahnen im Baltikum* (Münster 1996). See also John P. McKay, *Pioneers for Profit: Foreign Entrepreneurship and Russian Industrialization 1885–1913* (Chicago 1970), 252. *Russian Rail Transport*, 171.

[8]   McKay, *Pioneers for Profit*, 48, 217.

Railways in the Russian Baltic Provinces

In the still largely undeveloped economy, communications were primitive. Bad roads, impassable in winter and dusty in summer, hampered movement. A regular service of stagecoaches between St Petersburg and Moscow was first initiated in 1820. The coaches took four to five days for the whole route. A similar service between St Petersburg and Riga by way of Pskov was started only in 1841.[9] Before that it could take days to travel over the few hundred miles between the two cities. River traffic was always popular, but in winter the rivers froze over and became useless. Boatmen used to winter *en route* and continue their journey in the next spring.

Figure 1.1   Railways in the Russian Baltic provinces, 1914
Source: Map drawn by Dick van der Spek, Emmen, the Netherlands.

---

9   *Russian Rail Transport*, 2.

The first railway in Russia was the short line from St Petersburg to Tsarskoye Selo, a summer palace of Czar Nicholas I. The line, some 14 miles long, was designed by Franz Anton von Gerstner, a leading Austrian engineer, and opened late in 1837. Steam locomotives came from England and Belgium initially; only in 1856 was the first Russian one built. The gauge chosen by von Gerstner was six feet, not for strategic reasons but for technical ones.[10] In 1899 the line was taken over by the recently formed Moscow, Windau & Rybinsk Railway, and in 1903 the gauge changed to the then-standard Russian gauge of five feet.

The second railway in Russia was the Nicholas Railway between Petersburg and Moscow. Its first section opened in 1847. Engineered by the American George Washington Whistler and his sons, this line was to set the example for the Russian network that was to come.[11] Whistler chose a gauge of five feet, because it would be cheaper than the six feet of the Tsarskoye Selo line. There is no proof that military strategic reasons were involved in the choice of the five-foot gauge. Whistler argued that the six-foot gauge would be too expensive for the whole network, but did value the greater stability and capacity of the wide gauge. As he needed to placate the proponents of the six-foot gauge, he came up with five-foot gauge as a compromise. Apparently he did not foresee that the Russian network might one day be connected with Western Europe.[12] Most of the capital needed for the construction – 121 million rubles in all – of the Nicholas Railway was provided by Dutch and German investors. No less than 70 million rubles came from Amsterdam and Berlin in the form of five loans at 4.5 per cent interest.[13] The Netherlands would remain a large investor in Russian railways, although some contemporaries compared this to David financing Goliath. British and French interests later took over the leading role, but the Dutch capital market remained an important source for Russian railways and governments.

The first line to a Baltic port was from Dünaburg to Riga (135 miles), opened in 1861. The Riga Board of Trade was behind this successful scheme. Dünaburg (in Latvia; known as Dwinsk starting in 1893 and Daugavpils since 1917) was already

---

[10]   *Russian Rail Transport*, 18. In the early years of railway construction there was no consensus among engineers as to the ideal gauge. Apart from the Stephensonian gauge of 4 feet 8.5 inches (1435 mm), now standard in most countries, engineers used gauges from 4 feet 10 inches to 7 feet.

[11]   About George Washington Whistler (1800–1849), one of the foremost American railway engineers, see *Encyclopedia of North American Railroads* (Bloomington, IN 2007), 1105. Whistler died of cholera in St Petersburg when the St Petersburg–Moscow line was almost finished.

[12]   A.D. de Pater and F.M. Page, *The Railway Locomotives of Russia*, vol. 1 (Sutton Coldfield 1987), 107; *Russian Rail Transport*, 37. About the choice of gauge see Douglas J. Puffert, *Tracks across Continents, Paths through History* (Chicago and London 2009), 178–81.

[13]   D.C.M. Platt, *Foreign Finance in Continental Europe and the United States 1815–1870* (London 1984), 46, 68.

on the St Petersburg–Pskov–Wilna line that went on to Warsaw, so connections with Western Europe were ensured. The main reason behind this scheme, though, was the link with the Russian heartland. The government guaranteed that loans would be repaid at 4.5 per cent interest, making this an excellent investment for foreign capitalists.[14] An English consortium obtained the concession for a Dünaburg–Vitebsk line, again on very favourable conditions for the shareholders, including a five per cent interest guarantee.[15] A competitor for the grain export was the Moscow, Windau & Rybinsk Railway. This opened in stages between 1899 and 1904, and gave Windau and Riga a fairly straight, 1,523-mile-long connection with the Russian agricultural regions.[16] In 1899 a guaranteed loan was floated for this company, with bonds of £500 at 4 per cent; the text of the bond was in Russian, English and German, a clear sign of the interest of foreign capitalists.

An earlier line from Riga to Mitau, begun by Russian entrepreneurs in 1859 without any government guarantee, was finished only in 1868. More important was the Baltic Railway Company's St Petersburg–Tallinn line, which opened in 1870.[17] In 1893, that line was combined with the Pskov–Riga Railway of 1889 to form a new Baltic & Pskov–Riga Railway, which, in 1906, became part of the state-controlled North-Western Railway.[18] Another line important for the grain export was the Libau-Romny Railway. The first section from Libau was opened in 1871, followed two years later by the section through Wilna to Romny, making it an ideal outlet to Western Europe for the grain from Kiev province.[19] Originally a private company, the line was taken over by the government in 1901.

As will be seen on the map (Figure 1.1 above), most of the main lines ran east to west, reflecting the original purpose of the construction. In Estonia and Latvia there was a regional line that connected Riga with Dorpat and further north, and another line, originally constructed on narrow gauge, connecting Tallinn and Pernau with the Moscow, Windau & Rybinsk Railway. Foreign travellers – in first class of course – were generally satisfied with rail travel in Russia. The trains

---

[14]   *Russian Rail Transport*, 52, 56. In 1868 the Orel-Smolensk-Vitebsk line is still shown as under construction, while the Vitebsk-Dünaburg section is open for traffic, in H. König, *Geschäfts- und Reisekarte von Europa* (Berlin 1868).

[15]   J.N. Westwood, *Geschichte der Russischen Eisenbahnen* (Zürich 1966), 41. The line from Vitebsk was later extended in a southeasterly direction to Orel.

[16]   *Russian Rail Transport*, 133.

[17]   Another clear indication of the influence of foreign capitalists on Russian railway construction is provided by the first issue of shares by this Baltische Eisenbahn Gesellschaft in 1868. The text is in Russian, German and English, while the amount is given as 125 gold rubles, 136 German thalers, or 500 French francs.

[18]   Pater and Page, *Russian Locomotives*, 20–23.

[19]   Pater and Page, *Russian Locomotives*, 63–7; *Russian Rail Transport*, 65.

were slow but on time, the distances enormous, and the station buffets clean and well provided with food and drinks.[20]

Before the outbreak of World War One, the Russian Baltic provinces were fairly well provided with railways. Connections with the big cities such as St Petersburg, Moscow, Minsk and others were ensured, and from Western Europe, trains from Berlin on the Preussische Ostbahn went all the way to Eydtkuhnen/Wirballen, where the change of gauge took place.[21] From there a traveller took the train to Wilna, and then on to St Petersburg. Beginning in 1890 the Russian government's policy had been to bring the railways under control of the State, uniting them in larger organisations. The Baltic–Pskov–Riga and the St Petersburg-Warsaw became a part of the new North-Western Railway, with a total length of about 2500 kilometres for the new company. One of the few remaining private corporations was the Moscow, Windau & Rybinsk Railway.[22]

In 1870 the Czarist government permitted the construction of narrow gauge railways as feeders for the main lines. Over the years fairly extensive systems were built in Estonia and Lithuania on 750 millimetres gauge, chiefly to transport agricultural products. Some were later converted to the standard Russian gauge; the rest continued to serve only regional purposes.[23]

World War One and Independence

The First World War brought great changes. The Russian mobilisation proceeded with many problems, and civilian traffic came to a virtual standstill. The Russian offensive in East Prussia came to a quick end when the German armies defeated the Russians in several bloody battles. In 1915 the German offensive began, ending in 1917 in an almost complete occupation of the Baltic provinces.[24] During their retreat the Russian armies destroyed the railway infrastructure wherever they could, and took the rolling stock with them. The Germans reacted by bringing in

---

[20]   A German engineer who travelled a lot in Russia in the 1870s wrote about his experiences in Russian trains: 'Das Reisen mit Dampf ist in keinem Land so bequem gemacht wie hier. Langsam freilich geht's und die Entfernungen sind riesig. Aber die Zeit wird pünktlich eingehalten, und so weisz man wenigstens, was man zu erwarten hat.' Max Eyth, *Im Strom unserer Zeit. Aus Briefen eines Ingenieurs*, 3 vols (Heidelberg 1905), here vol. 2, 180.

[21]   See the contribution of Jan Musekamp in this volume.

[22]   Westwood, *Geschichte der Russische Eisenbahnen*, 70–73, 137–8.

[23]   Hesselink-Tempel, *Eisenbahnen im Baltikum*, 15–17.

[24]   On the role of the railways in the Baltic provinces between 1914 and 1919, see Andreas Knipping, *Eisenbahnen im Ersten Weltkrieg* (Freiburg 2004). On Russia's economic situation in 1914 see Peter Gatrell, 'Poor Russia, Poor Show: Mobilising a Backward Economy for War, 1914–1917,' in Stephen Broadberry and Mark Harrison (eds), *The Economics of World War I* (Cambridge 2005), 235–75.

their own locomotives and rolling stock, but could use these only after converting the broad gauge tracks to European standard gauge. Toward the end of the hostilities, the standard gauge tracks covered all of Lithuania and reached north in Latvia as far as Riga. The German armies also constructed an extensive network of narrow gauge feeder tracks.[25]

German armies occupied Estonia in 1917, but with the general collapse of Germany in 1918, the Estonian republic was proclaimed. Attempts to take over and keep the country in the Russian sphere of influence were prevented by strong local opposition against the poorly organised Bolsheviks. With the Peace of Tartu of February 1920, Estonia was recognised by the Soviets as 'forever' independent. In Latvia, the story was much the same and the republic was proclaimed in November 1918. With the help of German volunteers, the Bolsheviks were expelled, and the Treaty of Riga of August 1920 ended hostilities and recognised Latvian independence. Lithuania followed as an independent republic in 1920. Reconstruction in the three young republics could then begin.[26]

Early in 1919 the Germans completed their retreat from their last outpost, Lithuania (though Lithuania would only acquire Klaipeda / Memel in 1923), and the Baltic railways transferred to the new owners. These were Estonian State Railways or in their original name Eesti Vabariigi Raudteede (EVR), Latvian State Railways or Latvijas Valsts Dzelzsceļi (LVD), and Lithuanian State Railways original named Lietuvos Geležinkeliai (LG), and the new companies were in a sorry shape. The railways in all three new states had suffered heavily, and reconstruction took a long time. Lithuania kept the Western European standard gauge, while Latvia changed back to Russian broad gauge, apart from a single line in the south. Because of the political problems between Lithuania and Poland, which had occupied the large area around Wilna/Vilnius, of all three new companies the LG had the most severe problems in reorganising its services.

Estonia had suffered the least from the war, but maintenance used up a lot of scarce capital. New lines were planned but only a few were actually finished. Important was the electric suburban service in Tallinn, opened in 1924 with 1200 volt DC and gradually extended. New stations were built, and new bridges constructed, obviating many slow orders. Some 400 kilometres of new narrow gauge feeder lines were built. Rolling stock was generally in bad shape, and the ex-Russian steam locomotives were ancient and poorly maintained, resulting in slow speeds and many breakdowns. Little by little, improvements were made, train speeds rose and frequencies improved. Night trains between Tallinn and Riga began running in 1921, with sleeping cars provided by the Compagnie internationale des wagons-lits.

---

[25]   On the military network of narrow gauge lines in Poland and the Baltic area, see Rüdiger Fach and Günter Krall, *Heeresfeldbahnen der Kaiserzeit* (Nordhorn 2002), 165–82.

[26]   There are few publications about the railways in Estonia: V. Gussarova, O. Karma and G. Lukin, *Sada Aastat Eesti Raudteed* (Tallinn 1970); and Jüri Loog, *125 Aastat Raudteid Eestis* (Tallinn 1997), the latter with an English summary. On Latvian railways in the interbellum, see *Latvijas Dzelzsceļi 1918–1938* (Riga 1938).

An international line between Tallinn and Prague by way of Riga and Warsaw began in 1923, with a connection in the Polish capital to Berlin. Passengers had to change trains at Zemgale in south-eastern Latvia, where the broad gauge ended and the standard gauge in Wilna Territory, then occupied by Poland, began.[27] After the end of the war, the Polish government forbade the passage of goods traffic over its territory between Germany and the Soviet Union, and a route from Königsberg was developed, with a change of gauge in Daugavpils/Dünaburg. Later on the Polish government relented and a more southern route was opened.[28]

In Latvia the situation was much the same at war's end, although the damage from the war was greater. Large numbers of Latvians had fled to Russia during the war, and the contents of workshops and factories had been taken away by the retreating Russian army. Railway workshops in Riga and Daugavpils needed to be reequipped with modern tools; the Dutch government donated some 700,000 guilders for this purpose.[29] The LVD soon re-converted the lines that had been narrowed by the Germans into broad gauge, although one standard gauge line was retained between Riga and Jelgava so that the international traffic could go as far as Paris and Ostend without change of gauge. The important connection between the Latvian port of Liepaja and Jelgava and Riga caused a political problem. Part of the line ran through Lithuanian territory, and the two governments involved could not agree about free transit. So a new line was constructed between Liepaja and Jelgava, more to the north, wholly on Latvian soil. It opened in 1929. British capital played an important role in this new construction.

For practical reasons, after the end of the war Lithuania retained the European standard gauge, as used by the German occupation forces. The Polish occupation of Vilnius Territory meant not only the loss of the capital, but also of many railway trains. Kaunas became the new capital and the headquarters of the LG. Landlocked Lithuania had no access to a port on the Baltic, and laid claim to Liepaja in Latvia. Under international pressure, the Lithuanian government backed out, but in 1923 occupied the German territory of Memel, with its harbour of Memel, now Klaipeda. Henceforth it could compete with the two other new states for traffic between Western Europe and the Soviet Union. For many years after 1920, railway traffic remained unimpressive, but after a new line connected Klaipeda to the East in 1932, a slow growth set in.

For all three Baltic countries, the often-changing transportation policies of the Soviet Union were highly important. Moscow tried to direct as much goods traffic as possible through Leningrad and the Black Sea ports instead of the Baltic ports. As a result, goods traffic between the Baltic ports and the Russian heartland, once of supreme importance, declined during the 1930s. At the same time, passenger

---

[27]   On the railway situation in the Wilna Territory, which was officially part of Lithuania but occupied by Poland, during the interbellum, see Hesselink-Tempel, *Eisenbahnen im Baltikum*, 51–2.

[28]   Hesselink-Tempel, *Eisenbahnen im Baltikum*, 53.

[29]   Ibid., 39.

train service was severely hurt by competition from buses that could offer more comfort, higher speed and lower fares. New steam locomotives generally of modern construction, went into service in all three countries, but motor traction, which became so popular in Western Europe in the 1920s and 1930s, was used only on a small scale. Estonia started in 1927 with some four-wheeled railcars and the other two countries followed suit, but on a limited scale. On the narrow gauge in Latvia some modern articulated units were introduced in the late 1930s, but in general, steam traction continued to reign supreme everywhere.[30] Electric traction existed only on a short suburban line to Tallinn starting in 1924.

World War Two and under Russian Domination Again

In the Treaty of Non-Aggression between Germany and the Soviet Union of 23 August 1939, Estonia and Latvia, although still nominally independent, were designated as being in the sphere of interest of Soviet Russia. A second secret protocol agreed to in September 1939 reassigned the majority of Lithuania to the USSR, and Estonia and the USSR concluded a pact of 'mutual assistance', which in reality meant complete loss of independence and total Russification. Latvia was forced to sign a similar pact with Moscow in October 1939, and Soviet forces occupied all three countries in 1940. With this move, the Soviets acquired some 7,000 kilometres of railway line: 2,840 in five-foot gauge, 2,000 in standard gauge, and 2,100 in narrow gauge.[31] Soon after the takeover, the Soviets widened the standard gauge of some strategic lines in Lithuania to the Russian gauge. The German offensive that started in June 1941 shattered this relatively quiet period.

In its first year, the German offensive was very successful, and by the end of August, 1941, the German armies occupied practically the entire territory of the three Baltic countries. They were incorporated into a new 'Ostmark' under German supervision. To supply the front better, the Germans almost immediately began narrowing the wide gauge lines in the newly acquired territories. By the end of 1941, most of the strategic lines had been narrowed, and a large number of bridges destroyed by the retreating Russians, had been rebuilt. A fairly 'normal' railway service was maintained for some years, naturally first of all in the interests of the German authorities and armies, but also for the local population.

The Soviet counterattack began in the summer of 1944, and by the end of that year, most of the former 'Ostmark' had been reoccupied by the Soviets.

Under the new Soviet occupation, the three countries were incorporated into the Soviet Union as separate Soviet republics. The railway infrastructure had been severely damaged by the war, and it took time before everything was rebuilt. One of the first things that had to be done was to widen all the standard gauge lines, this time including those in Lithuania, although the last standard gauge there

---

[30]   Ibid., 100–107.

[31]   Ibid., 110.

disappeared only in 1951.[32] The narrow gauge tracks in the three republics were either abandoned or – especially in Estonia as late as the 1960s – widened to the Russian gauge. Under the influence of the strong centralization tendencies of the Soviet government, the railways in the three republics were organised in a single unit until 1956, divided into three separate units in 1957, but reunited in 1963 and subsequently known – in the West – as the Baltic Railway.[33] Goods traffic always had priority over passenger trains, and new infrastructure was almost always intended for freight. Passenger trains tended to be slow, as everywhere in the Soviet Union in those years.[34] As the Baltic ports again became of supreme importance for the export of Russian oil and other goods, many of the harbour installations, including marshalling yards and engine terminals, were reconstructed or enlarged. The lines around Tallinn were reconstructed; some of the old narrow gauge lines there were rebuilt to the Russian standard gauge and the rest abandoned. In the 1960s and 1970s, the lines around the junctions of Riga were extended and partially electrified with 3,000 volts DC.[35] As is to be expected, passenger traffic was mainly oriented towards Russia, and much less so toward Western Europe. In 1975 the Kaunas–Vilnius line in Lithuania was electrified with 25,000 volts AC, as part of a planned connection between Kaliningrad and Minsk in Byelorussia. After the renewed independence of Lithuania, this electrification was not extended. Diesel electric locomotives and multiple units were introduced on a large scale in the 1970s, and the faithful but outmoded steam locomotive finally laid to rest.[36]

A new connection with the West was opened in 1986 in the form of a ferry service between the Lithuanian port of Klaipeda and Mukran on the German island of Rügen; because of the insecure political situation in Poland, the governments of the Soviet Union and the German Democratic Republic (GDR) had decided to open a connection that avoided Polish territory and rails. The ferry carried broad gauge goods wagons, and some of them could be fitted with standard gauge bogies to enable them to be carried on the main lines of the GDR. Other freight was transferred to standard gauge wagons in Mukran. The revolutions in the old Soviet bloc after 1989 made this service largely superfluous, but in recent years traffic has been growing again.[37]

Renewed Independence

With the new developments in the Soviet Union that began with Soviet President Mikhail Gorbachev's *perestroika*, the three Baltic countries were quick to declare

---

[32]   Ibid., 120.

[33]   Westwood, *Russsische Eisenbahnen*, 249, 303–4.

[34]   Ibid., 259.

[35]   Hesselink-Tempel, *Eisenbahnen im Baltikum*, 121.

[36]   Westwood, *Russische Eisenbahnen*, 269.

[37]   Hesselink-Tempel, *Eisenbahnen im Baltikum*, 123.

their independence once again. In 1991 they were officially recognised as independent states by the former Soviet government, without becoming members of the newly founded and Moscow-oriented Commonwealth of Independent States. However, the presence of strong Russian minorities in all countries, especially Estonia, to this day continues to create problems that disturb the peace and retard economic development. The three countries also left the ruble zone, which meant a complete reorientation to Western Europe in economic aspects, resulting initially in a somewhat chaotic situation, which they only slowly overcame. After being included in the centrally directed economic policies of Soviet Russia for more than 50 years, it was only natural that this reorientation took time. The entry of the three countries into the European Union in 2004 strengthened their new political and economic position.

After 1991, the railway systems had to be extricated from the former Soviet Railway Administration, the rolling stock divided, and the staff redeployed. Former through trains now ended at the new frontiers, established traffic flows suddenly stopped, and new directions had to be found. The new relationship between Russia and its former Baltic provinces took a lot of time to stabilise. All this meant a sharp downturn in the number of passengers and the volume of freight in the three countries.

In Estonia the railways, 1024 kilometres long and broad gauge, are run mostly run for goods traffic by the national railway company Eesti Raudtee (ER). Since 2001, the ER has had an important foreign influence in both technical and managerial spheres, including a large number of second hand American diesel locomotives. Around Tallinn, the electric suburban services are operated by Elektriraudtee. Passenger service on the non-electrified network declined substantially when the state subsidy to Edelaraudtee, the operator, was ended in 2001. International trains to Moscow and St Petersburg still run, but bus companies provide a lot of competition.[38] Political tensions between Estonia and Russia in 2007 caused a closure of the border stations between the two countries for some months.

The ER, partly privatised in 2001, was taken back into government hands in 2007, and in 2009 the company was restructured into a holding company, AS Eesti Raudtee, with two subsidiaries, AS EVR Infra for the infrastructure and AS EVR Cargo for the goods traffic. Goods traffic has declined severely over the years, as the Russian government directs more and more of its oil exports to its own ports. The ER's passenger traffic has also been declining. To boost rail traffic in the Baltic countries, the European Union has initiated a programme called Rail Baltica, which envisages the modernisation of the Warsaw–Bialystok–Kaunas–Riga–Valga–Tartu–Tallinn corridor, with new signalling and higher speeds. Lines radiating from Tallinn will also be modernised and made suitable for higher speeds up to 120 kilometres per hour.

---

[38]   For the particulars of the railways in the three countries for the years since 2004, I have used the series of guides by Richard Latten, *Spoorwegen 2005* (Alkmaar 2004) through *Spoorwegen 2010* (Alkmaar 2009).

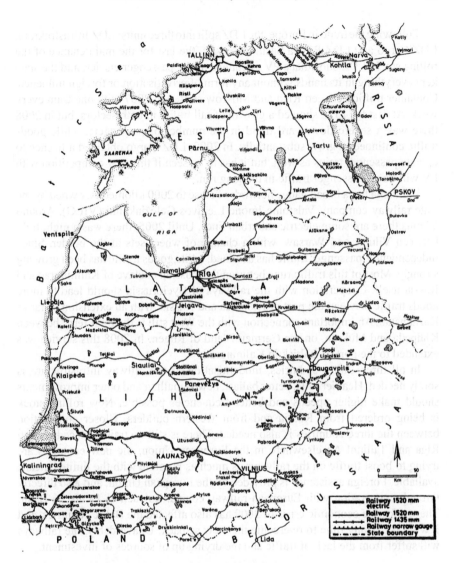

Figure 1.2   Railways in the Baltic States, 2000
Source: Map drawn by Dick van der Spek, Emmen, the Netherlands.

In Latvia, the railway network measures some 2,373 kilometres, also with the Russian gauge, with electric suburban lines around Riga. The *Latvijas Dzelzceļš* (LDZ) is the state organisation, and runs only goods trains, while the passenger services are provided by a subsidiary, Passazhieru Vilciens (PV). International trains to Moscow, St Petersburg, Minsk and Vilnius are run by a private company, L-Expressis. Here too, bus companies generally offer better service, higher speeds and cheaper rates.

Following the trend in Europe, the LDZ split into three units: LDZ Infrastruktura, LDZ Cargo and LDZ Ritosa Sastava Serviss, the last for the maintenance of the rolling stock. LDZ subsidiary PV continued as the passenger carrier, and the state kept everything in its hands without any form of privatisation or foreign influence. Container traffic between Riga and Moscow started in 2007 with one train every week. At first the LDZ showed a growth of rail traffic in both sectors, but in 2008 there was a severe downward trend in the number of passengers, while goods traffic continued to grow substantially. In 2009, LDZ Cargo obtained a licence to operate passenger trains as well, but it has to be seen if this new competition with PV will boost passenger traffic in the long run.

Lithuania has a broad gauge network of close to 2000 kilometres, owned by the state railway company Valstbine Imone Lietuvos Geležinkeliai (VILG). Around Vilnius there are some electric suburban lines. Until 2005, there was a night train between Vilnius and Warsaw, with a change of wheel sets at the border. Since independence, passenger traffic has declined, while goods traffic has been growing strongly. Most of this traffic runs between the Russian enclave of Kaliningrad and Russia itself. Cooperation with the railways of Byelorussia should lead to more goods traffic between the port of Klaipeda and Russia, with an extension as far as Kazakhstan. An important connection with the West still is the train ferry between Klaipeda and Mukran, on the German island of Rügen. In 2008 this service was extended to the port of Baltisk in Kaliningrad.

In all three Baltic countries, modernisation of the railway infrastructure is sorely needed. Heavier rails, better ballast, new signalling and other improvements should make higher speeds and better frequencies possible. New rolling stock is being ordered from Russia and from Western builders. Closer cooperation between the three countries is also needed. There is still no train service between Riga and Tallinn! As elsewhere in the European Union, the new countries are trying to boost traffic on the railways as much as possible with the limited means available. Foreign assistance is provided by the European Union, and also directly through cooperation with European railway companies such as Deutsche Bahn. The worldwide economic crisis of 2009 has also affected the Baltic countries, and it will take a long time to overcome this new setback. Unavoidably, the railways will suffer from the lack of traffic and the drying up of sources of investment.

Bibliography

Eyth, Max, *Im Strom unserer Zeit. Aus Briefen eines Ingenieurs*, 3 vols (Heidelberg 1903–1905).

Fach, Rüdiger and Krall, Günter, *Heeresfeldbahnen der Kaiserzeit* (Nordhorn 2002).

Feis, Herbert, *Europe, the World's Banker 1870–1914: An Account of European Foreign Investment and the Connection of World Finance with Diplomacy before the War* (New Haven 1930).

Gatrell, Peter, 'Poor Russia, Poor Show: Mobilising a Backward Economy for War, 1914–1917', in Stephen Broadberry and Mark Harrison (eds), *The Economics of World War I* (Cambridge 2005), 235–75.

Gussarova, V., Karma, O. and Lukin, G., *Sada Aastat Eesti Raudteed* (Tallinn 1970).

Henderson, W.O., *The Industrial Revolution on the Continent: Germany, France, Russia, 1800–1914* (London 1961).

Henderson, W.O., *The Industrialization of Europe 1780–1914* (London 1970).

Hesselink, Herman G. and Tempel, Norbert, *Eisenbahnen im Baltikum* (Münster 1996).

Knipping, Andreas, *Eisenbahnen im Ersten Weltkrieg* (Freiburg 2004).

König, Th., *Geschäfts- und Reise-Karte von Europa, mit Angabe aller Eisenbahnen, Dampfschiffslinien und Haupt Poststrassen* (Berlin 1868).

Latten, Richard, *Spoorwegen 2005* (Alkmaar 2004).

Latten, Richard, *Spoorwegen 2010* (Alkmaar 2009).

Latvijas Dzelzceļi 1918–1938 (Riga 1938).

Loog, Jüri, *125 Aastat Raudteid Eestis* (Tallinn 1997), with an English summary.

McKay, John P., *Pioneers for Profit: Foreign Entrepreneurship and Russian Industrialization 1885–1913* (Chicago and London 1970).

Middleton, William D., Smerk, George M. and Diehl, Roberta L. (eds), *Encyclopedia of North American Railroads* (Bloomington 2007).

Pater, A.D. de and Page, F.M., *Russian Locomotives*, vol. 1: *1836 to 1904* (Sutton Coldfield 1987).

Platt, D.C.M., *Foreign Finance in Continental Europe and the United States, 1815–1870: Quantities, Origins, Functions and Distribution* (London 1984).

Puffert, Douglas J., *Tracks across Continents, Paths through History: The Economic Dynamics of Standardization in Railway Gauge* (Chicago and London 2009).

Russian Rail Transport 1836–1917 (St Petersburg State Transportation University Faculty 1999).

Westwood, J.N., *Geschichte der Russischen Eisenbahnen* (Zürich 1966).

Chapter 2

The Construction and Modernisation of Railways in Belorussia/Belarus in the Late Nineteenth and Twentieth Centuries

Andrej Kishtymov

Railways have contributed greatly to the development of the economy and society of Belorussia since the middle of the nineteenth century. Like a locomotive, literally and figuratively, they pulled the Belorussian economy upwards. It was railways that mainly determined Belorussian economic integration into Russian and then European markets. The dynamics of social change and social mobility increased significantly due to railways. With the beginning of railway construction, Belorussia and its European neighbouring countries obviously entered a new age, the age of industrial society. This article deals with the timeline of Belorussian railway history, focusing on the following issues:

- construction of new railway lines
- improvement of existing railway tracks and railway operation
- proposals for new railway lines and their design.

Belorussia is a landlocked country in Eastern Europe, bordered clockwise by Russia to the northeast, Ukraine to the south, Poland to the west, and Lithuania and Latvia to the northwest. Its capital is Minsk; other major cities include Brest, Grodno (Hrodna), Gomel (Homiel), Mogilev (Mahilyow) and Vitebsk (Viciebsk).[1] Its strongest economic sectors are agriculture and manufacturing. We can distinguish at least five different periods in the late nineteenth and twentieth centuries. In early modern times, the lands of modern-day Belarus belonged to several countries, including the Principality of Polotsk, the Grand Duchy of Lithuania, the Russian empire, and the Polish-Lithuanian Commonwealth. In the eighteenth century, the territories of modern-day Belarus were acquired by the Russian empire under the

---

[1]   United Nations Organisation, (ed.), *UN Statistics Division. Standard Country and Area Codes Classifications (M49)*. http://unstats.un.org/unsd/methods/m49 /m49regin. htm#europe (last accessed 3 March 2011).

reign of Catherine II, and held until their occupation by the German empire during World War One.[2]

The Beginnings up to World War One

When people think of a railway transportation system, they generally think of an engine and rolling stock. But the most important thing in a railway transportation system is actually a railway line. The principle of moving along a railway line underlies the whole railway sector. Railways had already been used in the second half of the eighteenth century: freight and passenger cars were drawn by horses before the introduction of steam traction. From the 1840s to the 1860s the railway of Starinka metallurgical and machine works, which belonged to retired Lieutenant Alexander von Benckendorff, operated in the surroundings of the village of Starinka. The region was called Cherikov *uyezd* (now Slavgorod district). The railway line should be considered the predecessor of the main Belorussian railway lines. Horse railway tracks with a total length of about six versts (6.4 kilometres) connected different shops and a landing stage on the River Sozh.[3]

Certainly, we can speak about the real onset of the railway era only with the emergence of public railways. Back in 1835, an Austrian subject named Franz Anton von Gerstner had a private audience with Emperor Nicholas I. Von Gerstner wanted to obtain a concession for the construction of the Tsarskoye Selo railway line. He tried to assure the Tsar of the brilliant future of railways by adducing the following argument:

> If St. Petersburg, Moscow and Grodno or Warsaw had been connected by a railway line, it would have been possible to subdue the Polish uprising in four weeks.[4]

The argument had its effect, as the uprising of 1830 and 1831 was still a recent memory, and there had been also upheavals in the Belorussian province that hindered the transportation of troops to quell the uprising in Poland. That is why the Belorussian issue was discussed too in the context of railway construction. Then, retired Lieutenant Anton Golievsky proposed a different project. He offered to construct railway lines from St Petersburg to Odessa and from Moscow to Warsaw in a period of nine years. According to Golievsky's plan, the authorities of the 15

---

[2]   Susanne Michele Birgerson, *After the Breakup of a Multi-Ethnic Empire* (Westport, CT 2002), 101.

[3]   Andrej L. Kishtymov, *Ural i sudby chernoi metallurgii Belarusi v XIX v. // Razvitie metallurgicheskogo proizvodstva na Urale. Sbornik dokladov i soobshchenii istoriko-ekonomicheskoi sektsii Mezhdunarodnogo kongressa, posvyashchennogo 300-letiyu metallurgii Urala i Rossii* (Ekaterinburg 2001), 72.

[4]   A.M. Solovyeva, *Zheleznodorozhnyi transport Rossii vo vtoroi polovine XIX v.* (Moscow 1975), 39.

provinces which the railway lines would pass through would be required to provide manpower to do the job. This meant one man with an axe and a spade for every 500 peasants. In addition, local landowners would supply the workers with food, and the financial costs would be imposed on the whole population. According to his calculations, every group of 500 peasants would be assessed with a surtax of 72 roubles. The project looked semi-fantastic even for the Russian empire, and was rejected by the Central Administration of Communications and Public Buildings.[5]

Then in the years 1838 and 1839, five memoranda to 'his Majesty' were submitted by the former governor of Novgorod, Nicholas Muravyov, in which he justified the construction of an extensive railway network centred on Moscow:

> Please see, wrote Muravyov to the tsar, that the Moscow state iron road will beget roads similar to itself: to Palangen, Kovno, Warsaw, Kalisz and up to Odessa and Kazan available to meet the needs of the increased population.[6]

It is obvious that western railway routes would have passed through Belorussian provinces, but all these memorandas were left without substantial answer.

In early 1852, the Administration of Railways of the Tsarist Government developed the first state plan of the future railway network of the Russian empire under the guidance of engineer Pavel Melnikov. The Ministry of War also submitted preliminary reports to a Special Committee for Railways Construction. According to the military authorities, the St Petersburg to Pskov and Warsaw line was among the main railway lines to be constructed in the first order. The line from Riga to Vitebsk was given the second priority.[7] However, out of all proposed lines, Nicholas I approved only the construction of the 1,288-kilometre line from St Petersburg to Warsaw. This took quite a long time to build, from 1852 till 1862, initially at public expense and then at the expense of a private joint-stock company.

In December 1862, after the Lentvaris to Warsaw section was put into operation, Grodno became the first Belorussian town reached by railway civilisation. In 1861, before railway tracks had reached Grodno, the Prussian Society of the Königsberg–Lyki Railway, through the former governor of the Kingdom of Poland Mikhail Gorchakov made an offer to the Russian government to extend its own tracks 'across the Augustów province to the town of Grodno or any other place in Russia' and to Pinsk in the future. This issue was carefully discussed at the meetings of the Railways Committee until, finally, it was favourably resolved on 10 November 1867. But there were some preconditions: the new railway line should conform to the organisational and technical standards of Russian railways; the railway construction from the Prussian border to Bialystok – the imperial authorities preferred this direction – should not outpace the construction of the

5   Anonymous, 'Pervye zheleznye dorogi v Rossii,' *Krasnyi arhiv*, 3, 1936, 88–9.

6   Ibid., 122.

7   L.G. Beskrovnyi, *Russkaya armiya i flot v XIX veke. Voenno-ekonomicheskii protentsial Rossii* (Moscow 1973), 401.

railway line from Bialystok to Brest. The last requirement was caused by fear that the Prussian company would not continue the construction after the connection of the first line with the existing railway line from St Petersburg to Warsaw. The Russian–Prussian Convention on Railway Freight Transportation had already been signed by this time (1866). The variant offered by the Railways Committee did not suit the Prussian side, and it withdrew its offer.[8]

The first local initiatives were founded in the early 1860s and sparked a public debate on the economic effects of railway policy. At the very beginning of railway construction, a group of major Belorussian and Ukrainian landowners, among whom were Prince Edwin Drutsky-Lubetsky, Princes Vladislav and Roman Sangushko, Prince Peter Wittgenstein, who was also aide-de-camp and belonged with this title to the retinue of the emperor, Count Ivan Tyshkevich, Count August Zamoyski, Counts Stephen and Konstantin Pototsky, and landowner Casimir Skirmunt, petitioned for the construction of a railway line from Bialystok across Pruzhany to Pinsk and further to Volhynia. Alexander II gave his permission on 28 June 1862. The engineering survey started. The Lithuanian Railways joint-stock company was created to finance the project. It was planned to start the construction in the autumn of 1863, to open the Bialystok to Pinsk line in two years and, upon successful completion of the project, to extend the line to Volhynia from the spring of 1866.[9] The expenses for the Bialystok to Pinsk line construction were estimated at 7.91 million roubles.[10] In the 'Explanatory note on the petition of the founders of the Lithuanian Railways joint-stock company', every detail was taken into account.[11] For example, there was an extensive discussion of how the railway traffic would influence the lives of bison in the Belovezhskaya Pushcha Forest.

The project had also ardent opponents, and, as often happens in history, politics frustrated the economic project.[12] In 1863 and 1864 the insurrection against Czarist rule that spread out to Polish, Lithuanian and Belorussian regions buried this interesting and promising railway project. Having considered the issue of the Bialystok to Pinsk railway line construction, the Western Committee, created for strengthening the administrative supervision in the insurgent provinces, came to the conclusion that its construction:

> does not meet the intended purpose and will only lead to the connection of
> the Western Provinces with the Kingdom of Poland, which contradicts the

---

[8]   The Russian State Historical Archives (RSHA), F.1272. L.1. F.20.5–6, 33–6 bs.

[9]   The Central State Historical Archives of Ukraine in Kiev (CSHAU), F.442. L.39. F.763, 2–3, 19 bs.-20,23; The National Historical Archives of Belarus (NHAB), F.295. L.1. F.1458, 1–2 bs.

[10]   CSHAU, F.442. L.39. F.763.17bs, 19 bs.-20.

[11]   Ibid., 55–60.

[12]   See Anonymous, *Pamyatnaya knizhka Minskoi gubernii na 1864 god* (Minsk 1864), 12–44.

intentions of the Government to connect the Western Provinces with the centre of the empire but not with the Kingdom of Poland by the railway.[13]

This decision by the Committee received the imperial approval on 29 May 1863. However, in 1867, the original initiative was resurrected by a person undoubtedly devoted to the Russian throne, one of the largest Belorussian-Lithuanian landowners, Prince Peter Wittgenstein. He was one of the founding shareholders of the Lithuanian Railways, and he now individually petitioned for a concession for the construction of a 314-kilometre railway line from Bialystok through Pinsk to Dombrovitsy at the confluence of the rivers Horyn and Sluch.[14] This railway was intended to replace 'the inconvenient and difficult way along the Dnepr-Bug and the Oginski Canal systems' and become a part of the 853-kilometre track from Volhynia to Libau, an important port on the Baltic Sea, after the completion of the projected railway from Kovno to Libau. The plan was to spend 21.8 million roubles for the construction of the 'Pinsk Way', 74,000 roubles per mile.

After these first lines had been built, there followed a series of additional connecting lines (see Table 2.1). On 26 May 1867, the Minister of Communications, Pavel Melnikov, pointed out to the Tsar that if Bialystok were linked with the Prussian Königsberg–Lyki Railway, this short way of 519 kilometres would be preferred to the other that went 866 kilometres to Libau for transportation of goods from Volhynia. He also reminded the Tsar of the decision of the Western Committee of 29 May 1863. As a result, Wittgenstein's petition for the concession was rejected.[15]

The operating railway from St Petersburg to Warsaw had been created by Petersburg military strategists, who soon underlined its important role in the suppression of the January Uprising. The Minister of War, Dmitry Milyutin, said:

> If the St. Petersburg-Warsaw railway line had not been built, the uprising would not have been so easily suppressed, and the rebels would have played the game of a country at war, and hostile to us, the Western European states – calculating our disability of a mobilisation right on time – would have supported them with arms.[16]

A new project, 'The Network of the Main Railway Lines of European Russia', with a total length of 4,802 kilometres, was discussed by the Committee of Ministers in

---

[13]   RSHA, F. 1272. L.1.F.26, 79 bs.-80.

[14]   Vladimir Mihailovich Verkhovsky mistakenly indicated the line from Bialystok to Minsk. See V. Verkhovsky, *Kratkii istoricheskii ocherk nachala i rasprostraneniya zheleznyh dorog v Rossii po 1897 g. vklyuchitelno* (St Petersburg 1898), 312.

[15]   RSHA, F. 1272. L. 1. F. 26, 74–5, 77 bs, 83 bs, 148.

[16]   Dmitry Milyutin quoted at Anonymous, *Nasha zheleznodorozhnaya politika po dokumentam arhiva Komiteta ministrov*, vol. 1 (St Petersburg 1902), 173.

January 1863. Among other lines, it provided for the construction of the Western railway line from Orel to Smolensk, Vitebsk, Dinaburg and further to Libau.[17]

Immediately after the Petersburg–Warsaw Railway was put into operation in August 1862, an engineering survey started for the section between Bialystok and Minsk.[18] However, Vitebsk became the second Belorussian provincial town after Grodno that the railway line passed through. The railway from Riga to Orlov was constructed through it. Three private railways operated along this route from the 1860s up to 1893: the Riga–Dvina Railway, the Dvina–Vitebsk Railway and the Orlov–Vitebsk Railway, each with its own administration. The Dvina–Vitebsk Railway, founded in 1863, was the only line in the Russian empire that was wholly owned by a foreign company. Its headquarters were in London and the management acted in accordance with British laws.[19]

Brest was the third regional centre of Belorussia that the railway reached. The construction of the 220-kilometre line took from 1867 to 1870.[20] At the end of 1868, the Tsar approved a new plan of railway construction 'of primary importance'. Private companies were granted 15 concessions for this purpose for a total of 3,634 kilometres of railway tracks, including the construction of the line from Smolensk to Brest (674 kilometres), the line from Brest to Berdichev (579 kilometres), and the line from Brest to Grajewo (217 kilometres).[21]

The military authorities also continued to put forward railway plans. In 1868, on behalf of the Minister of War, Dmitry Milyutin, General Nicholas Obruchev prepared a special Memorandum on Railways Required for Military Communications for the Committee of Ministers. The highest priority lines were the ones that would run from Smolensk to Brest (through Minsk and Mogilev), the Volhynia Railway (from Kiev to Zhitomir, Rovno, Brest with the Rovno to Brody branch line), the Polessye Lateral Railway (from Kiev to Chernigov and Mogilev up to the intersection with the Smolensk–Brest Railway) and the line from Brest or Kobrin to Grodno. Though Alexander II marked this memorandum as 'very sensible', the Committee of Ministers rejected the project on 11 February 1869, pointing to the fact that the lines from Smolensk to Brest and from Kiev to Brest had already been approved for construction.[22] Between 1871 and 1874, many lines were opened, and Minsk became the first Belorussian junction station.

---

[17]   Solovyeva, *Zheleznodorozhnyi transport Rossii*, 90.

[18]   *Promyshlennost* of August 1862, 200.

[19]   A. Golovachev, *Istoriya zheleznodorozhnogo dela v Rossii* (St Petersburg 1881), 73; Anonymous, *Nasha zheleznodorozhnaya politika po dokumentam arhiva Komiteta ministrov*, vol. 3 (St Petersburg 1902), 111; K.A. Oppenheim, *Rossiya v dorozhnom otnoshenii. Opyt kratkogo istoriko-kriticheskogo obozreniya dannyh, otnosyashchihsya do razvitiya putyeǐ soobshcheniya v Rossii i parallelno v drugih vazhnyeǐshih stranah* (Moscow 1920), 67.

[20]   Oppenheim, *Rossiya v dorozhnom otnoshenii*, 67.

[21]   Solovyeva, *Zheleznodorozhnyǐ transport Rossii*, 108.

[22]   Beskrovnyi, *Russkaya armiya i flot*, 406–407.

This was important, if not decisive, for its future economic, political and cultural development (see Table 2.1).[23] Brest also became an important railway hub, when lines stretching out to Kiev and to the Grajewo station at the border with Prussia were opened on 27 July 1873. The joint-stock company of the Brest–Grajewo Railway had been founded back in 1860.[24]

Then there was a 10-year pause in railway construction in Belorussia. However, the second railway line of the section from Smolensk to Brest was put into operation in 1879, and new projects were still being proposed.[25] On 16 April 1873, the Minister of Communications provided the concession for the construction of new railway lines to the Railways Committee. Among them were lines from Bryansk to Brest (1,339 kilometres) and from Vitebsk to Gomel.[26] In summer 1874 several surveying teams prepared different sections of these two lines for construction.[27] Though neither project was implemented at that time, the railway from Bryansk to Brest with branch lines to Grodno, Rovno and Kovel became the predecessor of the future Polessye Railway. The railway from Vitebsk to Zhlobin was an extension of the Vitebsk to Gomel line.

Starting in the early 1880s, the Tsarist policy drastically changed in respect of private railway construction. Now, the state began a large-scale railway nationalisation project. Between 1891 and 1896, the main railway lines of the Belorussian provinces were taken into state ownership: the Libau–Romny Railway was nationalised on 1 May 1891, the St Petersburg–Warsaw Railway on 1 January 1894, the Dvina–Vitebsk and the Orlov–Vitebsk Railways in 1894, the South-Eastern Railways with the branch line from Kovel to Brest and Grajewo in 1895, and the Moscow–Brest Railway in 1896.

Since then, the railways in the territory of Belorussia have been constructed by the state. One of the most impressive examples of that became the construction of railways in the Polessye region. At a secret meeting of the General Staff of the army in 1873, it was essentially decided to construct an extensive network of military railway lines in the Polessye region; a year later, the Minister of Communications, Count Alexey Bobrinsky, with the concurrence of the Minister of War, proposed the project of a strategic line from Brest to Bryansk with branches to Grodno, Rovno

---

[23]   On the completion of the Moscow–Brest Railway see Anonymous, *Putevoditel po Aleksandrovskoi zheleznoi doroge* (Moscow 1912), 6. We should note that during the construction of the railway section from Naujoji Vilnia to Minsk, the initially planned route from Oshmany to Boruny and Gorodok was changed to Smorgon–Molodechno. RSHA, F. 1272. L.1.F.40, 5,26,40.

[24]   See Oppenheim, *Rossiya v dorozhnom otnoshenii*, 67, and Ministerstvo putyei soobshcheniya, *Statisticheskii sbornik Ministerstva putyei soobshcheniya. Zheleznye dorogi v 1907*, vol. 102 (St Petersburg 1910), 70.

[25]   *Putevoditel po Aleksandrovskoi zheleznoi doroge*, 6.

[26]   RSHA, F. 1272. L.1.F.44, 1–3,10–10bs; *Belorussiya v epohu kapitalizma*, vol. 2 (Minsk 1990), 103–106.

[27]   NHAB, F.295. L.1. F.2441, 1,2,3.

and Kovel.[28] In March 1875, the next Minister of Communications, Adjutant General Konstantin Possiet, suggested limiting this construction, in view of the considerable financial expenses. Specifically, he proposed putting into operation only the line from Gomel to Bryansk, and doubling the tracks along the Orel–Vitebsk and the Moscow–Brest railways.[29] In the same year, the Committee of Ministers dismissed as 'premature' a petition in which Lieutenant General Ivan Chekmaryov requested a concession for the construction of a railway from Vilnia to Rovno with branch lines to Grodno and Kovel.[30] Ivan Chekmarey, a landowner of the Volhynian Governorate, did not conceal his interest in the construction of the new railway, which he, as Prince Wittgenstein had previously, called the 'Pinsk' one.[31]

In 1882, Konstantin Possiet again initiated a public debate on the necessity of new railways in Polessye.[32] In September 1883, the Polessye Railway, previously under the control of the Ministry of War, was transferred to the administration of the Ministry of Communications. On 14 February 1883, the railway network plan of the Polessye region was finally approved by Alexander III, and its implementation began on 12 May. Within three years, an impressive network was opened by the Minister of Communications and set into operation (see Table 2.1).[33] It differed from other Belorussian railways of the nineteenth century by its comparatively small maintenance costs per mile: they amounted to only 35,100 roubles per year, in comparison with 83,300 roubles of the Libau–Romny Railway, 122,600 roubles of the Moscow–Brest Railway, 136,000 roubles of the Riga–Orlov Railway by the end of 1900.[34] The beneficial effect of the Polessye railways on the regional

---

[28]   Anonymous, *Nasha zheleznodorozhnaya politika po dokumentam arhiva Komiteta ministrov*, vol. 3, 209.

[29]   Verkhovsky, *Kratkii istoricheskii ocherk nachala i rasprostraneniya zheleznyh dorog*, 311.

[30]   Ibid., 312.

[31]   I. Chekmarev, *Zapiska o gosudarstvennom i ekonomicheskom znachenii Pinskoi zheleznoi dorogi, predpolozhennoi voiti v set stroyushchihsya zheleznyh dorog, pod nazvaniem: Vilno-Rovenskaya s vetvyami na Grodno i Kovel, s soedineniem onoi s Bryansko-Brestskoi zheleznoi dorogoi* (St Petersburg 1875), 29, in which it was proposed to name it the 'Vilnia–Rovno Railway', build branch lines to Grodno and Kovel, and include it in the railway network that connected with the Bryansk–Brest railway.

[32]   Anonymous, *Nasha zheleznodorozhnaya politika po dokumentam arhiva Komiteta ministrov*, vol 3, 192.

[33]   Anonymous, *Nasha zheleznodorozhnaya politika po dokumentam arhiva Komiteta ministrov*, vol 3, 221. On the Zhabinka to Pinsk line see Anonymous, *Otchet Zhabinko-Pinskoi zheleznoi dorogi za vremya s 1-go sentyabrya 1883 po 1-ye yanvarya 1884 goda* (St Petersburg 1910), 1. On the construction costs see A. Radtsig, *Vliyanie zheleznyh dorog na selskoe hozyaistvo, promyshlennost i torgovlyu* (St Petersburg 1896), 77. On the line from Lunitets to Pinsk see ibid., 209. On the line from Luninets to Gomel and on the Baranovichi to Bialystok line see ibid., 211–2.

[34]   Solovyeva, *Zheleznodorozhnyi transport Rossii*, 301.

economy very soon became evident.[35] At the same time, the importance of Brest increased with the construction of a new line to Kholm that was built in 1887.[36]

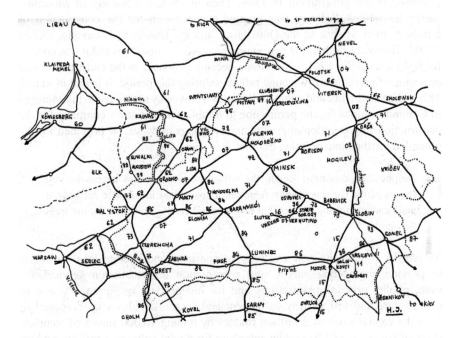

Figure 2.1   Railways in Belorussia, 1861–1915
Source: Created by Henry Jacolin.

At the end of the century, construction work started again, this time to complete some gaps in the network between Grodno to Suwalki and Olita (now Alytus). Starting in 1899, a big semi-circular railway line was put into operation, running from Grodno to Suwalki, Olita and Orany, and connected to the St Petersburg–Warsaw Railway at both ends. Although the state dominated the field of railway construction there had survived some private companies, but their importance

---

[35]   Andrej L. Kishtymov, *Ekonomicheskii potentsial Polesya v nachale XX veka // Zagarodze-3: Materyaly navukova-krayaznauchai kanferentsyi 'Palesse u XX stagoddzi', 1–4 iunya 2000 g.* (Belastok-Minsk 2001), 115.

[36]   The Minister of War Peter Vannovskiy proposed to construct this railway and the idea was approved by Alexander III on 17 March 1884. See Verkhovsky, *Kratkii istoricheskii ocherk nachala i rasprostraneniya zheleznyh dorog*, 316, and Anonymous, *Nasha zheleznodorozhnaya politika po dokumentam arhiva Komiteta ministrov*, vol. 1, 210–12. Later, on 14 December 1892, it was decided to double the track along the Brest to Kholm line. Verkhovsky, Verkhovsky, *Kratkii istoricheskii ocherk nachala i rasprostraneniya zheleznyh dorog*, 380.

steadily declined. The construction of the St Petersburg–Vitebsk Railway, which later became a part of a main line from St Petersburg to Kiev and Odessa, was discussed in the government in 1896. Then in 1898, the Society of Moscow–Ventspils–Rybinsk Railway was granted a concession for the construction of a railway from Vitebsk to the Dno station and the Dno to St Petersburg line in 1900.[37] The total length of the new main line was 370 kilometres and it was opened for regular traffic in 1904.[38] Belorussia became a pioneer in the construction and operation of private narrow-gauge railways during this period. It began in March 1890, when councillor and engineer Boleslav Yalovetsky petitioned to the Ministry of Communications for the permission to establish a joint-stock company for the construction and operation of private narrow-gauge railways. He provided a well-grounded justification, pointing out that:

> Despite their enormous length, the railways and waterways within the vast spaces of the Russian empire represent a sparse and incomplete network of main communication arteries, but they were relatively convenient for the areas they cross.[39]

Yalovetsky wanted the new company to construct and operate local railways; to provide engineering survey and construction documentation services for state, public, private organisations and for independent entrepreneurs; and to manufacture and sell railway equipment and supplies. Yalovetsky proposed to form the capital stock of 3 million roubles by issuing 10,000 shares of common stock of par value of 100 roubles per share for a total value of 1 million roubles and bonds for a total value of 2 million roubles. Dividends were supposed to be not less than between 15 and 30 roubles per 100-rouble share.

Yalovetsky's petition and the draft charter of the new joint-stock company were carefully examined by the Ministry of Communications, endorsed by the Ministry of Finance and then submitted to the Committee of Ministers on 15 November 1891. The final approval of the charter was made by Emperor Alexander III on 26 March 1892.

The first part of the projection was the construction of a railway line from the Sventsiany station of the St Petersburg–Warsaw Railway to Glubokoe, a large Belorussian centre. In February 1894, at the instance of the joint-stock company, the Governor General of Vilnia, Grodno and Kovno and the Minister of Interior petitioned the emperor for permission for this construction and received

---

[37]   P.P. Migulin, *Nasha novyeĭshaya zheleznodorozhnaya politika i zheleznodorozhnye zaimy (1893–1902)* (Kharkov 1903), 77 and 79.

[38]   I. Tikhotsky, *Kratkii ocherk razvitiya nashyeĭ zheleznodorozhnoĭ seti za desyatiletie 1904–1913 gg.* (St Petersburg 1914), 27.

[39]   B. Yalovetsky, *Obyasnitelnaya zapiska po povodu uchrezhdaemogo inzhenerom B.A. Yalovetskim Pervogo Obshchestva podezdnyh zheleznyh putei v Rossii* (St Petersburg 1892), 1.

it on 27 June 1894. The company was granted a concession for 85 years but the government could use the right of full repurchase in 18 years. The concessionaires received some benefits, including the right of alienation of the state lands for the construction, but were obliged to deliver mail for free and to carry freight and troops at a low price.[40] Within three years the new lines were built, with a gauge of 75 centimetres.[41] After the Sventsiany–Berezvech Railway construction, some other narrow-gauge railways were built and successfully exploited by the Yalovetsky's company, the First Joint-Stock Company of Russian Local Railways in the Baltics and Ukraine. In 1913, it owned 1,226 kilometres of railway tracks, almost half the total length of Russian narrow-gauge railways. It was the largest railway company of its kind in the Russian empire, far ahead of the Moscow Joint-Stock Company of Local Railways, its closest competitor, which owned 321 kilometres of narrow-gauge railway tracks.[42] After the completion of the narrow-gauge railway from Novo–Sventsiany to Ponevezh, the total length of the Sventsiany local railway increased to 272 kilometres. It operated very effectively. According to the freight traffic statistics for 1913, its total freight turnover amounted to 137,000 tons, including 13,000 tons of grain, 3,000 tons of rock and common salt, 1,000 tons of oil and kerosene, 6,000 tons of coal and 27,000 tons of timber and a long list of different goods of no less than 87,000 tons.[43] There were some more narrow-gauge railway lines built or projected.[44] The emergence of numerous proposals for local railway construction was peculiar to that time. Landowners of the Slutsky district headed by Edward Voynilovich supported the project of a railway line from the Gorodeya station to Slutsk. Moreover, they agreed to the cession of their lands, which the future railway was going to use. Their petition to the administration of the Moscow–Brest Railway was also supported by the Minsk governor.[45]

The state project of a railway line from Grodno to Volkovysk and Kobrin was presented in 1898. Having learned about it, the citizens of Pruzhany requested that the railway be routed through their town. This project was not carried out, but after

---

[40]   Verkhovsky, *Kratkii istoricheskii ocherk nachala i rasprostraneniya zheleznyh dorog*, 547–8.

[41]   Train speeds reached 27 to 32 kilometres per hour. The second-class passenger coaches were equipped with soft spring high-back seats. Moreover, sleeping compartments were arranged there. See ibid.

[42]   Anonymous, *Rossiya 1913 god. Statistiko-dokumentalnyi spravochnik* (St Petersburg 1995), 112.

[43]   Anonymous, *Zheleznodorozhnyi transport v 1913 g. (Statisticheskie svedeniya)* (Moscow 1925), 112, 116, 117, 120, and 127.

[44]   On projected branches from Lyntupy to Svir or Lyntupy to Shemetovo, Izha and Molodechno see Anonymous, *Fabriki i zavody, kazennye lesnye dachi, lesa chastnyh vladeltsev i vydayushchiesya selskie hozyaistva v 50-ti verstnom raione. Vilenskaya guberniya* (Vilnia 1900), 91. And on Brest-Litovsk lines see Beskrovny, *Russkaya armiya i flot v XIX veke*, 419.

[45]   NHAB, F.295. L.1. F.3716, 1–2 bs, 3, 4.

the imperial decree for the construction of the Bologoye to Sedlets railway line had been issued, the District Marshal of Nobility and the municipal government of Pruzhany asked the Grodno governor to intercede and get this railway routed through the district centre of Pruzhany. The Ministry of Communications rejected the request, as the railway route to Sedlets through Volkovysk could not be changed.[46]

Just before the First World War, a petition requesting the construction of a railway line from Ruzhany to the Ozernitsa station of the Polessye Railway was submitted to the Kiev Area Committee for Railway Freight Regulation. On 18 June 1914, the Committee approved the idea but proposed to route the railway line to Volkovysk through Noviy Dvor and Porozovo instead of Ozernitsy. It also asked the Polessye Railway Administration to conduct the preliminary survey.[47] There were also a number of local proposals which failed to be accepted and implemented, as they did not pass through all the stages of approval. However, some initiatives for the construction of relatively short local railway lines were successfully implemented (see Table 2.1).[48]

We find some bigger projects after 1900 – for example, the line from Pinsk to Kovel and Vladimir–Volhyniasky, and the one from from Polotsk to Sedlets which was routed through Vileyka, Molodechno, Lida, Mosty, Volkovysk, Svisloch and

---

[46]   The National Historical Archives of Belarus in Grodno (NHAB in Grodno), F.13, L.1, F. 177, 1–2, 5. The question of railway routing to the district town was also brought up twice by landowners and entrepreneurs of Igumen District. In 1902, it was offered to build the 94-kilometre local railway from Borisov through Igumen to Maryina Gorka at the expense of a joint-stock company. Ten years later, in 1911, two variants of the railway construction were discussed: to route the railway either from Igumen to Minsk through Smilovichi or from Igumen to the Pukhovichi station (26 kilometres). Andrej L. Kishtymov, *Yelskie: opyt selskih hozyaev (19 - nachalo 20 v.)*, in Aleksei Paznajkov, (ed.), *Dzelya blizkih i pryshlastsi: Materyaly mizhnarodnai navukova-praktychnai kanferentsyi 'Universitety Yelskih' (da 165-goddzya z dnya naradzhennya A. Yelskaga* (Minsk 1999), 112–4.

[47]   NHAB in Grodno, F.13, L.1, F.1257,5.

[48]   On the Osipovichy to Starye Dorogi branch line, see Anonymous, *Materialy dlya obsledovaniya zheleznyh dorog. Libavo-Romenskaya zheleznaya doroga* (St Petersburg 1911), III. On the Moscow-Brest Railway, see Anonymous, *Putevoditel po Aleksandrovskoi zheleznoi doroge*, 234. On the Polessye Railway see Anonymous, *Ocherk razvitiya Dobrushskoi pischebumazhnoi fabriki knyazya Paskevicha. 1882–1896* (St Petersburg 1896), 61. On the discussion of a 75-kilometre line from Orsha to Mogilev, see RSHA, F. 268. L. 1. F. 223, 11–12, 13–16. On the project to connect St Petersberg with Kiev through Mogilev, see RSHA, F. 1272. L. 1. F. 44, 1, 10 bs. Even the detailed project of the 1,093-kilometre railway from Kiev to St Petersburg through Chernobyl, Zhlobin, Rogachev, Mogilev, Shklov, Orsha, Vitebsk and Velikie Luki of the early 1890s failed to be realised. Its construction costs were calculated at 55.5 million roubles. See K. Zavadsky, *O postroike Kievo-Peterburgskoi zheleznoi dorogi* (Kiev 1892), 5–6. Mogilev became the last of Belorussian provincial towns that got the railway. On the Vitebsk to Zhlobin line see Anonymous, *Otchet po postroike Vitebsk – Zhlobinskoi zheleznoi dorogi. 1899–1902* (St Petersburg 1904), 35.

had a branch line from Mosty to Grodno. The latter project was financed by a French loan (see Table 2.1).[49] Local initiatives also continued to propose projects on the construction of new railway lines. Again the region around Mogilev was very active, and in 1909 the management board of the First Joint-Stock Company of Russian Local Railways applied to the Ministry of Finance for the permission to construct and operate the Donetsk–Baltic broad-gauge railway, with a total length of 1,066 kilometres.[50]

---

[49] On the line from from Pinsk to Kovel and Vladimir–Volhyniasky, see Oppenheim, *Rossiya v dorozhnom otnoshenii*, 105, and V. Feldt, *Zheleznodorozhnye voiska i ih nyeotlozhnye nuzhdy* (St Petersburg 1910), 14–15. On the line from Polotsk to Sedlets see B. Ananjich, *Rossiya i mezhdunarodnyi kapital 1897–1914. Ocherki istorii finansovyh otnoshenii* (Leningrad 1970), 63. The construction of the latter line was supervised by Vladimir Timofeev-Ryasovsky (1856–1913). His son, Nikolay Timofeev-Ryasovsky, remembered about his father: 'He only constructed railways and never dealt with their operation. He constructed about 15,000 versts (16,000 kilometres) of railway tracks in the former Russian empire and was a prominent railway engineer, who created a kind of practical engineering school'. N. Timofeev-Ryasovsky, 'Istorii Timofyeeva-Ryasovskogo, rasskazannye im samim', *Chelovek* 6, 1992, 134–61, here 137. His engineering talent and organisational skills Vladimir Timofeev-Ryasovsky brilliantly displayed on Belarusian land. He managed to save more than 12 million roubles, i.e. more than 15 per cent of the initially estimated project costs of nearly 81 million roubles. There was no precedent for this, as outrageous embezzlement was typical within railway construction projects in the Russian empire. See Anonymous, *Otchet po postroike Polotsk-Sedletskoi zheleznoi dorogi, 1902–1907* (St Petersburg 1910), 12 and 27.

[50] Engineering surveys were carried out during September and November of 1909 for the construction of railways from Bryansk to Mogilev (293 kilometres), from Roslavl to Mogilev (169 kilometres), and from Mogilev to Minsk and Mosty (451 kilometres). This project was called the Belarusian Railway. See F. Tiesenhausen, *Proekt sooruzheniya zheleznodorozhnyh linii Bryansk-Mogilev, Roslavl-Mogilev, Mogilev-Minsk i Minsk-Grodno, po izyskaniyam, proizvedennym v 1909 g.*, 2 vols. (St Petersburg 1910), vol. 1, 2. It was supposed to establish the direct railway communication between 35 old Belarusian towns including Hotimsk, Klimovichi, Cherikov, Chausy, Berezino, Igumen, Korelichi, Mstislavl, Novogrudok, and Dyatlovo. Representatives of towns and some locations which the new railway was to pass through, held meetings in Mogilev on 17 July and in Novogrudok on 8 September 1909. Special public committees were set up to facilitate its construction. See ibid., vol. 2, 1, 8 and 9. On the first joint-stock company of Russian local railways, see anonymous, *Dopolnitelnaya poyasnitelnaya zapiska Pravleniya Pervogo Obshchestva podezdnyh putyei v Rossii k proektu Donetsko-Baltiiskoi zheleznoi dorogi s umenshennym zadaniem.1910* (St Petersburg 1910), 1, and 4. It was to go from the Lgov station – the North Donetsk Railway terminal – to the provincial town of Mogilev and further to Postavy, partly along the line of the existing Sventsiany narrow-gauge line to Riga through the town of Bauska. Moreover, another railway line to Libau through the Ponevezh station was planned. The construction was expected to cost 65.5 million roubles.

Table 2.1   Opening of lines in Tsarist Russia on the territory of later Belarus from 1867 up to World War One

Line	Year	Length in km	Cost in roubles
Dwinsk to Polotsk	1866	161.0	n. a.
Polotsk to Vitebsk	1866	100.0	n. a.
Vitebsk, Smolensk to Roslavl	1867		n. a.
Warsaw to Terespol	1867	213.0	n. a.
Vitebsk to Orel	1868	521.0	n. a.
Brest to Terespol	1870	7.5	n. a.
Smolensk to Orsha, Borisov, Minsk and Brest	1871	674.0	n. a.
Naujoji Vilnia to Minsk	1872	185.0	n. a.
Minsk to Bobruisk	1873	152.0	n. a.
Minsk to Gomel	1873	150.0	n. a.
Libau-Romny Railway			
Brest via Bialystok to Grajewo	1873	212.0	n. a.
Brest via Berdichev to Kiev	1873	1051.0	n. a.
Zhabinka to Pinsk	1882	143.0	4,370,275
Gomel to Bryansk	1887	273.0	45,293*
Vilnia to Luninets with a branch line from Lunitets to Pinsk	1884	377.0	n. a.
Luninets to Rovno	1885	194.0	42,288*
Luninets to Gomel	1886	303.0	36,141*
Baranovichi to Bialystok	1886	204.0	46,678*
Brest to the Kholm station	1887	114.0	41,710*
Dobrush to Polessye Railway	1889	7.0	n. a.
Sventsiany to Postavy	1895	70.0	n. a.
Osipovichy to Starye Dorogi	1896	42.0	n. a.
Sventsiany to Glubokoe	1897	57.0	n. a.
Grodno to Suwalki and Olita	1899	197.0	n. a.
Vitebsk to Zhlobin	1902	280.0	17,960,000
Vitebsk to St Petersburg	1904	370.0	n. a.
Starye Dorogi to Verhutino	1906	19.0	n. a.
Verhutino to Urechye	1907	11.0	n. a.
Polotsk to Sedlets	1907	630.0	69,000,000

Khlustino to Vydritsa	?	6.0	n. a.
Vasilevichi to Hoiniki	1911	47.0	n. a.
Verejtsy to Grodzyanka	1911	36.0	n. a.
Zhlobin to Shepetovka	1915	?	n. a.
Urechye to Slutsk	1916	?	n. a.
Glubokoe to Krulevschizna	1916	?	n. a.
Narva to Pskov and Polotsk	1916	453.0	n. a.
Unecha to Kommunary	1918	77.0	n. a.

Note: * average costs for building 1 verst (1.067 kilometres) of the railway line.
Source: Compiled by the author.

But beside local initiatives, the military department of Imperial Russia remained one of the main 'project owners' that initiated the construction of new railway lines. In 1900, it insisted on the construction of the 555-kilometre East Polessye Railway in the near future, which was to pass from Zhlobin through Mozyr, Ovruch, Novograd and Volhyniask to the Shepetovka station and further to Proskurov. The construction costs amounted to 23 million roubles and were included in the extraordinary expenses of the Ministry of Communications. But the Russo-Japanese War frustrated these plans.[51] Later, it was assumed that the railway from Zhlobin to Kiev through Chernihiv would be built by railway troops from Chernihiv. The project and cost sheets had been prepared for the Ministry of Communications by 1910.[52] It was also proposed to build a railway from Baranovichi to Rechytsa.[53] It was still essential to shorten the route in the south-north direction. Eventually, a railway engineer from St Petersburg named Ivan Bernatovich established the Surveying Office of the Zhlobin–Staro–Konstantinov–Polonnoe–Zhmerinka line. Design work for the future railway line was carried out from 1909 to 1910 and financed by major banks such as the St Petersburg International Commercial Bank, the Russian-Chinese Bank and the Northern Bank. The Council of Ministers approved the construction of this line on 16 March 1910. It was also found as 'meriting attention and highly desirable' by the staff of Kiev Military District. On 6 June 1910, the St Petersburg International Commercial Bank gave Bernatovich a loan of 5,000 roubles 'for the completion of the project'.[54] The future 434-kilometre railway would shorten the route from St Petersburg to Kiev by 160 kilometres and from St Petersburg to Odessa by 213

---

[51] G.A. Lashkarev, *K voprosu o sooruzhenii zheleznodorozhnoi magistrali Zhlobin-Mozyr-Ovruch-Starokonstantinov-Kamenets-Podolsk* (St Petersburg 1910), 12 and 27.

[52] See Feldt, *Zheleznodorozhnye voiska*, 57 and 63, and V. Feldt, *Proekt Kievskoi voennoi zheleznoi dorogi* (St Petersburg 1911), 14.

[53] Lashkarev, *K voprosu o sooruzhenii*, 14.

[54] CSHAU, F.882. L.2. F.32, 2–3, 9.

kilometres. The project was widely discussed by the public. The Minsk Provincial Committee for District Affairs decided:

> to support petitions composed by cities, districts, agricultural societies and industrial groups which requested that the railway construction be completed within the shortest possible period of time.[55]

Newspapers of that time referred to the project as a part of the future Slav Railway which:

> will become an essential element of the direct route to the South Slavic lands connecting Kamenets-Podolsk with Mamalyga near the Romanian border, with the Kamenets-Podolsk to Romania section as the last part of the Slav Railway linking St Petersburg and the Balkan Peninsula through Romania in the shortest way while bypassing Austria.[56]

Just before the First World War, at the request of the French General Staff, the doubling of railway tracks along the Bryansk to Gomel, Luninets and Zhabinka line and quadrupling of railway tracks along the Zhabinka to Brest line was initiated. In 1913, it was decided to double-track the railway lines from Minsk to Naujoji Vilnia, from Mosty to Grodno, from Vilnia to Luninets, from Baranovichi to Volkovysk, from Minsk to Gomel. At the same time, priority was given to the construction of a new railway from Ryazan to Warsaw through Tula, Sukhinichi, Mogilev, Bobruisk, Baranovichi and Bielsk. The second priority was to construct railway lines from Baranovichi to Kovel or from Pinsk to Kovel and from Lida to Orany.[57]

Before the First World War, Russia, with French help, developed the railway system in its western regions and increased its improvements for mobilisation. Because of this, the German General staff demanded a gigantic increase in armament in December 1912. The arms race and tensions in international affairs increased again.[58] Certainly, the construction of railways in Belorussia was only part of the national state rail policy. In this western region of the Russian empire, the railway was given a special military-strategic importance. That is why it was carefully designed and constructed.

In a relatively short period of time the core network of the Belorussian Railways grew to a complex structure. For the region itself, the importance of the railway was not so much military or political, but economic. Railways contributed to the

---

[55]   *Torgovo-promyshlennaya gazeta*, of 20 October 1910.

[56]   *Kievlyanin* of 7 March 1911, and CSHAU, F.882. L.2. F.32, 4 bs., 8.

[57]   K. Ushakov, *Podgotovka voennyh soobshchenii Rossii k mirovoi voine* (Moscow and Leningrad 1928), 29, 50, 51, 187 and 189.

[58]   See Helmut Altrichter and Walther L. Bernecker, *Geschichte Europas im 20. Jahrhundert* (Stuttgart 2004), 25–7.

development of the economy and promoted trade and urbanisation.[59] Thanks to them, Belorussia gained importance as a transit region.

However, with the beginning of the First World War, the railway network of the Russian empire was divided into two districts: the western district, which was under the control of the Military Field Office, and the eastern one, which was still managed by the civil Department of Railways. The boundary between the districts passed to the west of the conventional line from St Petersburg to Bologoye, Smolensk, Bakhmac, Kharkov and further to the south. Thus, Belorussian railway facilities came under military control.[60] This led to an intensification of railway construction. Lines became double tracked, and for strategic reasons gaps were closed (see Table 2.1).[61] It was also decided to build the railway line from Minsk via Rakov and Ivenets to Lida but its construction was interrupted by the German offensive and a new front line, which was established in the autumn of 1915.[62] The railway network of Belorussian provinces was intensively exploited during the First World War, increasing its value. It was in Belorussia during First World War that the Supreme Command of the Russian army settled: first at the major junction, Baranovichi, and then from August 1915 onwards, in Mogilev. Now some lines were built that had been planned before the war. Nevertheless gaps in traffic service remained because of a lack of rolling stock which led ultimately to paralysis of railway traffic.

Railways in the Time of the Byelorussian Socialist Soviet Republic

The first time Belorussia declared its independence happened on 25 March 1918 during the negotiations of the Treaty of Brest-Litovsk. The Belorussian People's Republic (BPR) was created while under German occupation and it was one of the first attempts to 'Westernise' Belorussia. But immediately after the formation

---

[59]   See Andrej L. Kishtymov *Zheleznodorozhnoe stroitelstvo kak faktor urbanizatsii Belarusi // Garady Belarusi u kantekstse palityki , ekanomiki , kultury* (Grodna 2007), 96–100.

[60]   Anonymous, *Kratkii ocherk deyatelnosti russkih zheleznyh dorog vo vtoruyu otechestvennuyu voinu*, 2 vols (Petrograd 1916), vol. 2, 7, 36 and 42.

[61]   Russian researchers deny this obvious fact for some reason: 'During the First World War, the construction of new railways had practically ceased in Russia. Only the Murmansk railway line was provisionally built, along with a number of short branch lines required for military purposes. The line from Vologda to Arkhangelsk was converted to the standard gauge.' G. Kumanev, *Na sluzhbe fronta i tyla* (Moscow 1976), 26. On the line from Zhlobin to Kalinkovichi, Ovruch, Korosten and Shepetovka and from Urechye to Slutsk and from Glubokoe to Krulevschizna see Ushakov, *Podgotovka voennyh soobshchenii Rossii*, 60. Railway construction continued even during the Civil War. See A. Yakobi, *Zheleznye dorogi SSSR v tsifrah. Statisticheskii sbornik* (Moscow 1935), 11.

[62]   Oppenheim, *Rossiya v dorozhnom otnoshenii*, 104.

of the BPR, the Polish–Soviet War started, and Belorussia was torn between resurgent Poland and Soviet Russia. Belorussia was divided into two parts and the part of Belorussia under Russian rule became a constituent of the Russian Soviet Federative Socialist Republic (RSFSR) in 1919. Soon that part was merged into the Lithuanian-Belorussian Soviet Socialist Republic (LBSSR). Belorussian lands then were partitioned between Poland and the Soviet Union after the Polish–Soviet War ended in 1921. On 28 December 1922, a conference of plenipotentiary delegations from the RSFSR, the Transcaucasian Soviet Federative Socialist Republic (TSFSR), the Ukrainian Soviet Socialist Republic (UkrSSR) and the Byelorussian Socialist Soviet Republic (BSSR) approved the Treaty of the Creation of the Union of Soviet Socialist Republics (USSR). This is why the Byelorussian SSR became a founding member of the Union of Soviet Socialist Republics. At the same time, Western Belorussia remained part of Poland.[63] A set of agricultural reforms, culminating in the Belorussian phase of Soviet collectivisation, began in the 1920s. A process of rapid industrialisation was undertaken during the 1930s, following the model of Soviet five-year plans.

At the same time, quite extensive railway construction was undertaken on both sides of the border in the 1920s and 1930s. One railway line after another was put into operation in Belorussia (see Table 2.2).[64] But because of lack of resources after the long war period some projects could not be realised, for example the line from Lepel through Vitebsk to Sychevka, which was proposed by the government of the BSSR in the mid 1920s. Also some double-track lines again became single-tracked, for example the ones from the Bogdanovo station to the national boundary and from Mikashevichy to Zhabinka.[65] As the standard-gauge network was expanding, several narrow-gauge railways were also opened.[66] Near Belgres, narrow-gauge railways supported the development of peat deposits and logging operations. Two other narrow-gauge lines were laid down to the east of Smolevichi and Zhodino stations, and one operated on the route from Minsk to Borovliany.[67]

---

[63]   Ibid., 105–106, Julian Towster, *Political Power in the U.S.S.R., 1917–1947: The Theory and Structure of Government in the Soviet State* (Oxford 1948), 106, and Grigory Ioffe, *Understanding Belarus and How Western Foreign Policy Misses the Mark* (Toronto 2008), 57. See also David Marples, *Belarus: A Denationalized Nation* (New York 1999), 5.

[64]   On openings between 1923 and 1930, see Yakobi, *Zheleznye dorogi SSSR v tsifrah*, 11–12. On the lines from Pruzhany to Oranchitsy and from Voropaevo to Druya opened in 1932, see T. Khachaturov, *Zheleznye dorogi zapadnyh oblastyei Belorussii i Ukrainy* (Moscow 1940), 12 and 18. On the opening of the branch line from Porechye to Druskeniki, see Migulin, *Nasha novyeĭshaya zheleznodorozhnaya politika*, 189.

[65]   According to the project, about 160 kilometres of the railway line should have crossed the territory of Belarus. See Anonymous, *Belorusskaya Sovetskaya Sotsialisticheskaya Respublika* (Minsk 1927), 366.

[66]   See examples in Khachaturov, *Zheleznye dorogi zapadnyh oblastyei*, 19 and 23.

[67]   V. Zhuchkevich, *Dorogi i vodnye puti Belorussii* (Minsk 1977), 102–103.

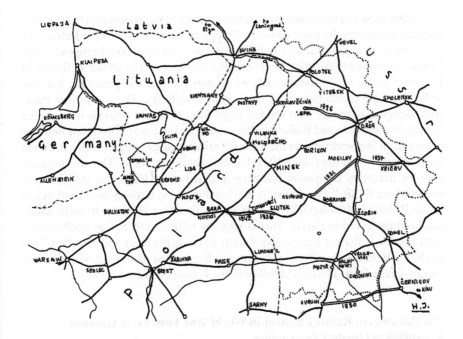

Figure 2.2   Railways in the Byelorussian Socialist Soviet Republic, 1922–1945
Source: Created by Henry Jacolin.

Table 2.2   Opening of lines in the interwar period of Socialist Belorussia since
1919 up to 1939

Line	Year	Length
Polotsk to Idritsa	1923	
Kommunary to Orsha	1923	176.0
Orsha to Lepel	1926	131.0
Chernigov to Novobelitsa	1930	105.0
Bobruisk to Ratmirovichi	1930	
Chernigov to Ovruch	1930	178.0
Roslavl to Mogilev	1931	189.0
Osipovichy to Mogilev	1931	132.0
Ratmirovichi to Starushki	1932	134.0
Pruzhany to Oranchitsy and Voropaevo to Druya	1932	89.0
Porechye to Druskeniki	1932	18.0
Slutsk to Timkovichi	1936	35.0

Source: Compiled by the author.

Beside these improvements, the greatest change in the system derived from the decision to convert the track gauge to European standard in Western Belorussia. The railway heritage of the new Polish government included both European gauge (former German and Austrian lines) and Russian gauge. The choice in favour of European gauge was made not only to support national independence, but also to facilitate the connections with the European railways. This meant that trains with express passengers who wanted to go from Minsk to Warsaw were routed through Baranovichi and Bialystok. Passengers had to transfer from one network to another at the border due to the different railway gauge. Bogies with a different width of axles were used since 1938, but only for freight trains. This was possible after the necessary equipment had been installed at the Negoreloe station at the border of the BSSR.[68] Freight traffic and handling went through from Zhitkovichi in the BSSR to Mikashevichy in Poland. On the other side, the Russian gauge had been preserved in Latvia. That is why the railway traffic went unobstructed from Bigosovo, the last Belorussian station, to Indra, the first Latvian station.[69] All in all, the Belorussian railway network was fragmented into broad, standard and narrow-gauge lines. The compatibility of the system decreased.

The Belorussian Railway System in World War Two: From Greatest Expansion to Greatest Destruction

The final unification of the modern-day Belorussian lands took place in 1939, when lands that were part of the Second Polish Republic were united with the Byelorussian Soviet Socialist Republic as a result of the Soviet invasion of Poland.[70] In 1939, Nazi Germany and the Soviet Union invaded and occupied Poland, marking the beginning of World War Two. Much of northeastern Poland, which had been part of the country since the Peace of Riga two decades earlier, was annexed to the Byelorussian Soviet Socialist Republic; this area is now known as West Belorussia. The Soviet-controlled Belorussian People's Council officially took control of the territories that had a predominantly ethnic Belorussian population on 28 October 1939, in Bialystok.

In the autumn of 1939, the unity of the Belorussian railway network was restored. And moreover, during a short period of time before the Soviet–German War (1941–45), this network had the highest length and density rates for the whole history of the Belorussian railway system. Since then the length of our main lines

---

[68]   Ibid., 77.

[69]   Anonymous, *Vneshnetorgovyi transport* (Moscow and Leningrad 1938), 267.

[70]   See Rawi Abdelal, *National purpose in the world economy: post-Soviet states in comparative perspective* (Ithaca, NY 2001), and Клоков В. Я. Великий освободительный поход Красной Армии. (Освобождение Западной Украины и Западной Белоруссии).- Воронеж 1940.

significantly decreased and caused a greater reduction of the capacity of the railway network than wartime destruction.

Nazi Germany invaded the Soviet Union in 1941. The Brest Fortress, which had been annexed in 1939, received one of the fiercest of the war's opening blows. BSSR was the hardest-hit Soviet republic in the war and remained in Nazi hands until 1944. The territory and its nation were devastated in World War Two, during which Belorussia lost about a third of its population and more than half of its economic resources.[71] Germany destroyed 209 out of 290 cities in the republic, 85 per cent of the republic's industry, and more than 1 million buildings. As historian Helen Fodor has written:

> Casualties were estimated to be between two and 3 million, while the Jewish population of Belorussia was devastated during the Holocaust and never recovered. The population of Belorussia did not regain its pre-war level until 1971.[72]

In the years between 1941 and 1944, the Belorussian railways were severely damaged. Following the logic of war, the opposing sides had the same intention to cause as much damage as possible to the railway system. For example, 83 per cent of the railway tracks along the section from Polotsk to Idritsa were undermined.[73] But after this, the railways were restored, because they were necessary for the transport of troops and supplies. Moreover, a railway line between Timkovichami and Baranovichi was completed in 1942, during the years of German occupation, and is still in operation today. This section connected Baranovichi with Slutsk, Osipovichy and Mogilev. Although its construction had started before the war, it was the whistle of a German troop train that was heard first along the railway line.[74]

While the Soviet Army was moving to the West, railway lines were restored. On 9 July 1944, the Soviet railway workers brought a train to Minsk again. By the end of 1945, the traffic had been restored in all sections of modern Belorussian railway lines.[75] The peculiarity of the years between 1939 and 1950 was that the Russian broad gauge was used simultaneously with West European standard gauge within the integrated railway system. However, some main lines were converted thrice from one kind of gauge to another, and the final conversion of Belorussian railway lines to the Russian Soviet standard took place during the first post-war five-year plan.

---

[71]   Albert Axell, *Russia's Heroes, 1941–45* (New York 2002), 247.

[72]   Helen Fodor, 'Belarus – Stalin and Russification', in Helen Fedor, (ed.), *Belarus: A Country Study* (Washington 1995), see under: http://countrystudies.us/belarus/ (last access 3.3.2011).

[73]   Kumanev, *Na sluzhbe fronta i tyla*, 301.

[74]   Ibid., 50.

[75]   Boris Zivica, Valentin Sozinov, *Entsyklapedyya gistoryi Belarusi*, vol. 1 (Minsk 1993), 421.

The existence of two main gauge standards is one of the most complicated and controversial problems of the railways. During the Second World War, after the Belorussian operation had been finished, railway workers converted only main routes in each direction to the Russian gauge, leaving other railway lines with the European standard gauge. That was done to facilitate further attacks of the Soviet Army. This combination allowed the maximum success. Broad-gauge track was laid all the way to the capital of Germany. On 6 May 1945, the first direct train from the Soviet Union arrived at the Berlin East railway station.[76]

Railways of the Byelorussian SSR after World War Two

The republic was redeveloped in the post-war years. In 1945 the Byelorussian SSR became a founding member of the United Nations, along with the Soviet Union and the Ukrainian SSR. Intense post-war reconstruction was initiated promptly. During this time, the Byelorussian SSR became a major centre of manufacturing in the west of the USSR, increasing jobs and bringing an influx of ethnic Russians into the republic. Josef Stalin implemented a policy of Sovietisation to isolate the Byelorussian SSR from Western influences. This policy involved sending Russians from various parts of the Soviet Union and placing them in key positions in the Byelorussian SSR government.

After 1945, six district centres – Braslav, Rossony, Novogrudok, Luban, Pruzhany and Lelchitsy – were deprived of railway communication; the towns of Ivanovo (the Yanov-Polessky station) and Gantsevichy ceased to be railway junctions. In Eastern Polessye, tracks were removed in the Ratmirovichi to Starushki railway line; this was part of Stalin's first five-year plan. In the early 1960s, the operation of the narrow-gauge railway line from Lyntupy to Kobylnik was stopped. That line was the last part of what had once been almost 500 kilometres of Belorussian narrow-gauge railway.

The construction of new railways was started as well. In February 1946, the construction of the 20-kilometre branch line from Luzhesno to Ruba began. Thus, the railways were one of the first Belorussian economy branches to overcome the consequences of the war. The reasons for the quite sharp decrease in the length of the Belorussian railways have not been of economic origin: the Soviet and post-Soviet planned economy deliberately ignored and is still ignoring economics, preferring strong-willed political decisions to economic ones.

In the post-war period, as a result of geopolitical changes in Central and Eastern Europe, the Belorussian railway construction lost the incentives that had provided its development before. The military lost interest in the railways and turned its focus to highways, for example the one from Moscow to Brest and the one from Minsk to Lida and Grodno. Road transportation became increasingly popular. Furthermore, for the transportation of oil and gas from the East to the West, the

---

[76] Ibid., 347.

Soviet Government preferred to develop pipeline systems. The Soviet economy had no more need for a number of railway corridors from Belorussia to Europe. Sections from Grodno to Suwalki, from Baranovichi to Bialystok, from Volkovysk to Sedltes, from Brest to Bialystok, and from Brest to Kholm and Lublin were among the ones whose use was discontinued. Certainly, no one raised the question of further railway line construction between Oranchitsy to Bielsk through Belavezha, which had been started in the years 1940 and 1941. Railways were not constructed any more, but dismantled. By the end of 1959, the Belorussian railways working mileage was 5,358 kilometres, 385 kilometres less than before the war.[77] Although the mileage again increased to 5,500 kilometres by the year 2000, the loss of almost 200 kilometres of railway length, notably in the most important directions, has not yet been acknowledged by modern Belorussian politicians and economists.[78]

In 1963, the first section of the electrified railway line from Minsk to Olekhnovichi (48 kilometres) was put into operation. Electrification was intermittently carried out until 1989 and it has not been finished yet. There is also not much construction of new railway lines. New railway construction has been limited to laying down branch lines to large energy and chemical enterprises.[79]

Belarusian Railways after the Breakdown of the Soviet Union

The parliament of the republic declared the sovereignty of Belarus on 27 July 1990, and during the collapse of the Soviet Union, Belarus declared independence on 25 August 1991. Despite many critiques, Soviet-era policies, such as state ownership of the economy, have been continued.[80] In 2000, Belarus and Russia signed a treaty for greater cooperation, with some hints of forming a Union State.

Currently, the operational length of the Belarusian Railway is 5,511 kilometres, including 3,884 kilometres of double-track sections, and 898 kilometres of

---

[77]   L. Lych, *Adnaulenne i razvitche chygunachnaga transpartu Belaruskai SSR* (Minsk 1976), 82.

[78]   Anonymous, *The Belarusian railways* (Minsk 2000), 5.

[79]   For example one could mention Novopolotsk (1959, 12 kilometres), Beloozersk (1959, 18 kilometres), Soligorsk (1960, 55 kilometres), Novolukoml (1965, 21 kilometres). Moreover, the speed of this construction a hundred years ago would have been considered just ridiculous, as it took the whole year to construct the 45 kilometres branch line of the first order from Slutsk to the construction site of the potassium plant. The line was opened on 2 July 1959. But it took more than a year to include this section into the official schedule. See Anonymous, *Zheleznodorozhnaya magistral Belorussii. K stoletiyu so dnya vvedeniya v stroi* (Minsk 1971), 127. In contrast, the Smolensk to Brest railway line (674 kilometres) was completed in less than a year and a half (from 2 May 1870 till 24 September 1871), with the first work trains running along the whole distance; i.e. an average of 1.3 kilometres were put into operation daily.

[80]   United Nations Office in Belarus, (ed.), 'About Belarus – Population 2003' see: http://un.by/en/aboutbelarus/population/ (last accessed 3.3.2011).

electrified lines. The Belarusian Railway is a member of the Railway Transport Council of the Commonwealth of Independent States, the Organisation of Railways Cooperation, the International Union of Railways, the Coordinating Council on Transsiberian Transportation and several others. Belarusian territory is crisscrossed by two pan-European transport corridors defined by the International Classification No. 2 (East–West) and at No. 9 (North–South) with a branch line 9b. Permissible speed of freight trains is 80 to 90 kilometres per hour and for passenger trains up to 140 kilometres per hour.

Today, Belarusian Railways is the leader of the national system of transportation. It currently carries more than 85 per cent of the freight of all kinds of public transport and about 50 per cent of passenger traffic. In 2010, the Belarusian Railways transported almost 140 million tons of cargo including 90 million tons on international routes. The most important railway junctions are in Minsk, Brest, Gomel, Orsha, Baranovichi, Mogilev, Vitebsk and Polotsk. The administration of the Belarusian Railways is divided into six departments: Minsk, Baranovichi, Brest, Gomel, Mogilev, Vitebsk. All in all they organise 373 large and small stations, including 21 railway junctions, and 17 locomotive repair shops and 12 depots. If the state programme of development of rail transport in Belarus from 2011 to 2015 will be successful, 387 more kilometres of railway lines are supposed to be electrified.

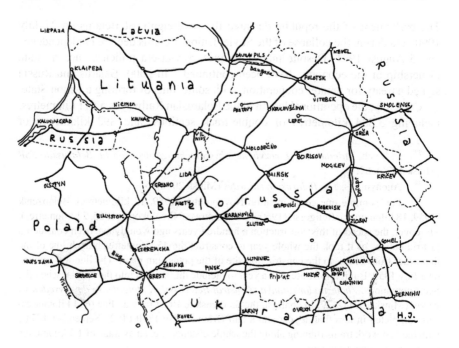

Figure 2.3   Railways in the Byelorussian SSR after World War Two
Source: Created by Henry Jacolin.

Conclusion

On the basis of the foregoing, we can divide Belorussian railway construction history into the following periods: the middle of the nineteenth century up to 1881, 1882 to 1914, 1915 to 1939, and 1939 to the present.

We started with the first railway projects. Railway lines were constructed mainly by private joint-stock companies with the participation of foreign capital, but according to the state plans and under the government control. The railway network connected all Belorussian provincial towns except Mogilev. Also we find the first cases of locally capitalised railway initiatives. Then, starting in 1881, the railways were constructed mainly by the state. The local railway lines were built to serve regional commercial interests; more projects for the construction of such lines were put forward by local entrepreneurs. Unlike the majority of other railways, the Polessye Railway, the Polotsk to Sedlets railway line, and the Belorussian railway projects primarily served the national market and were not segments of big transit routes passing through Belorussia.

The next step was the war and interwar period, from 1915 to 1939. The Belorussian railway network was divided by the front line, and later by national boundaries. Military and economic necessity led to quite intensive railway construction. The construction of narrow-gauge railway lines was recommenced in Western Belorussia. New railway lines passed through Orsha in Eastern Belorussia. Mogilev and Krichev became railway junctions.

The periods after 1939 were characterised by extreme political interruptions, foreign rule, military suffering, a planned economy in the COMECON system, and the more recent search for an independent way. After the restoration of the Belorussian railway system, which had been destroyed during the war, the construction of new railway lines was practically stopped, except for some railway branch lines specially laid down to new industrial and energy enterprises. The length of the railway network has been decreasing. Belorussia has lost five out of seven broad-gauge railway corridors leading to the West and one leading to the East. The operation of narrow-gauge railways has been terminated. From 1963 to 1989, some railway lines were electrified; however, this work has not been finished yet. In 2010, the operational length of the Belarusian Railways amounted to 5,511 kilometres. Belarusian Railways are an important part of Asia–Europe rail transit lines.

Bibliography

Abdelal, Rawi, *National Purpose in the World Economy: Post-Soviet States in Comparative Perspective* (Ithaca, NY 2001).

Altrichter, Helmut and Bernecker, Walther L., *Geschichte Europas im 20. Jahrhundert* (Stuttgart 2004).

Ananjich, B., *Rossiya i mezhdunarodnyi kapital 1897–1914. Ocherki istorii finansovyh otnoshenii* (Leningrad 1970).

Anonymous, 'Pervye zheleznye dorogi v Rossii', *Krasnyi arhiv*, 3, 1936, 88–9.

Anonymous, *Belorusskaya Sovetskaya Sotsialisticheskaya Respublika* (Minsk 1927).

Anonymous, *Dopolnitelnaya poyasnitelnaya zapiska Pravleniya Pervogo Obshchestva pod,ezdnyh putyei v Rossii k proektu Donetsko-Baltiiskoi zheleznoi dorogi s umenshennym zadaniem.1910* (St. Petersburg 1910).

Anonymous, *Fabriki i zavody, kazennye lesnye dachi, lesa chastnyh vladeltsev i vydayushchiesya selskie hozyaistva v 50-ti verstnom raione. Vilenskaya guberniya* (Vilnia 1900).

Anonymous, *Kratkii ocherk deyatelnosti russkih zheleznyh dorog vo vtoruyu otechestvennuyu voinu*, 2 vols (Petrograd 1916).

Anonymous, *Materialy dlya obsledovaniya zheleznyh dorog. Libavo-Romenskaya zheleznaya doroga* (St. Petersburg 1911).

Anonymous, *Nasha zheleznodorozhnaya politika po dokumentam arhiva Komiteta ministrov*, vol. 1 (St. Petersburg 1902).

Anonymous, *Nasha zheleznodorozhnaya politika po dokumentam arhiva Komiteta ministrov*, vol. 3 (St. Petersburg 1902).

Anonymous, *Ocherk razvitiya Dobrushskoi pischebumazhnoi fabriki knyazya Paskevicha. 1882–1896* (St. Petersburg 1896).

Anonymous, *Otchet po postroike Polotsk-Sedletskoi zheleznoi dorogi, 1902–1907* (St. Petersburg 1910).

Anonymous, *Otchet po postroike Vitebsk – Zhlobinskoi zheleznoi dorogi. 1899–1902* (St. Petersburg 1904).

Anonymous, *Otchet Zhabinko-Pinskoĭ zheleznoĭ dorogi za vremya s 1-go sentyabrya 1883 po 1-ye yanvarya 1884 goda* (St. Petersburg 1910).

Anonymous, *Pamyatnaya knizhka Minskoi gubernii na 1864 god* (Minsk 1864).

Anonymous, *Putevoditel po Aleksandrovskoi zheleznoi doroge* (Moscow 1912).

Anonymous, *Rossiya 1913 god. Statistiko-dokumentalnyi spravochnik* (St. Petersburg 1995).

Anonymous, *The Belarusian Railways* (Minsk 2000).

Anonymous, *Vneshnetorgovyi Transport* (Moscow and Leningrad 1938).

Anonymous, *Zheleznodorozhnaya magistral Belorussii. K stoletiyu so dnya vvedeniya v stroi* (Minsk 1971).

Anonymous, *Zheleznodorozhnyi transport v 1913 g. (Statisticheskie svedeniya)* (Moscow 1925).

Axell, Albert, *Russia's Heroes, 1941–45* (New York 2002).

Beskrovnyi, L.G., *Russkaya armiya i flot v XIX veke. Voenno-ekonomicheskii protentsial Rossii* (Moscow 1973).

Birgerson, Susanne Michele, *After the Breakup of a Multi-Ethnic Empire* (Westport CT 2002).

Chekmarev, I., *Zapiska o gosudarstvennom i ekonomicheskom znachenii Pinskoi zheleznoi dorogi, predpolozhennoi voiti v set stroyushchihsya zheleznyh dorog, pod nazvaniem: Vilno-Rovenskaya s vetvyami na Grodno i Kovel, s soedineniem onoi s Bryansko-Brestskoi zheleznoi dorogoi* (St. Petersburg 1875).

Fedor, Helen, 'Belarus – Stalin and Russification', in Helen Fedor (ed.), *Belarus: A Country Study* (Washington 1995) (see under: http://countrystudies.us/belarus/ (last accessed 3 March 2011).

Feldt, V., *Proekt Kievskoi voennoi zheleznoi dorogi* (St. Petersburg 1911).

Feldt, V., *Zheleznodorozhnye voiska i ih nyeotlozhnye nuzhdy* (St. Petersburg 1910).

Golovachev, A., *Istoriya zheleznodorozhnogo dela v Rossii* (St. Petersburg 1881).

Grigory Ioffe, *Understanding Belarus and How Western Foreign Policy Misses the Mark* (Toronto 2008).

Ioffe, Grigory, *Understanding Belarus and How Western Foreign Policy Misses the Mark* (Toronto 2008)

Khachaturov, T., *Zheleznye dorogi zapadnyh oblastyei Belorussii i Ukrainy* (Moscow 1940).

Kishtymov, Andrej L., *Polesya v nachale XX veka // Zagarodze-3: Materyaly navukova-krayaznauchai kanferentsyi 'Palesse u XX stagoddzi', 1–4 iunya 2000 g.* (Belastok-Minsk 2001).

Kishtymov, Andrej L., 'Yelskie: opyt selskih hozyaev (19 - nachalo 20 v.)', in Aleksei Paznajkov (ed.), *Dzelya blizkih i pryshlastsi: Materyaly mizhnarodnai navukova-praktychnai kanferentsyi "Universitety Yelskih" (da 165-goddzya z dnya naradzhennya A.Yelskaga* (Minsk 1999), 112–4.

Kishtymov, Andrej L., *Zheleznodorozhnoe stroitelstvo kak faktor urbanizatsii Belarusi // Garady Belarusi u kantekstse palityki, ekanomiki, kultury* (Grodna 2007).

Kishtymov, Andrej L., *Ural i sudby chernoi metallurgii Belarusi v XIX v. // Razvitie metallurgicheskogo proizvodstva na Urale. Sbornik dokladov i soobshchenii istoriko-ekonomicheskoi sektsii Mezhdunarodnogo kongressa, posvyashchennogo 300-letiyu metallurgii Urala i Rossii* (Ekaterinburg 2001).

Kumanev, G., *Na sluzhbe fronta i tyla* (Moscow 1976).

Клоков В. Я. Великий освободительный поход Красной Армии. (Освобождение Западной Украины и Западной Белоруссии).-Воронеж 1940.

Lashkarev, G.A., *K voprosu o sooruzhenii zheleznodorozhnoi magistrali Zhlobin-Mozyr-Ovruch-Starokonstantinov-Kamenets-Podolsk* (St. Petersburg 1910).

Lych, L., *Adnaulenne i razvitche chygunachnaga transpartu Belaruskai SSR* (Minsk 1976).

Marples, David, *Belarus: A Denationalized Nation* (New York 1999).

Migulin, P.P., *Nasha novyeĭshaya zheleznodorozhnaya politika i zheleznodorozhnye zaimy (1893–1902)* (Kharkov 1903).

Ministerstvo putyei soobshcheniya, *Statisticheskii sbornik Ministerstva putyei soobshcheniya. Zheleznye dorogi v 1907*, vol. 102 (St. Petersburg 1910).

Oppenheim, K.A., *Rossiya v dorozhnom otnoshenii. Opyt kratkogo istoriko-kriticheskogo obozreniya dannyh, otnosyashchihsya do razvitiya putyeĭ soobshcheniya v Rossii i parallelno v drugih vazhnyeĭshih stranah* (Moscow 1920).

Radtsig, A., *Vliyanie zheleznyh dorog na selskoe hozyaistvo, promyshlennost i torgovlyu* (St. Petersburg 1896).

Solovyeva, A.M., *Zheleznodorozhnyi transport Rossii vo vtoroi polovine XIX v.* (Moscow 1975).

Tiesenhausen, F., *Proekt sooruzheniya zheleznodorozhnyh linii Bryansk-Mogilev, Roslavl-Mogilev, Mogilev-Minsk i Minsk-Grodno, po izyskaniyam, proizvedennym v 1909 g.*, 2 vols (St. Petersburg 1910).

Tikhotsky, I., *Kratkii ocherk razvitiya nashyeĭ zheleznodorozhnoĭ seti za desyatiletie 1904–1913 gg.* (St. Petersburg 1914).

Timofeev-Ryasovsky, N., 'Istorii Timofyeeva-Ryasovskogo, rasskazannye im samim', *Chelovek* 6, 1992, 134–61.

Towster, Julian, *Political Power in the U.S.S.R., 1917–1947: The Theory and Structure of Government in the Soviet State* (Oxford 1948).

Ushakov, K., *Podgotovka voennyh soobshchenii Rossii k mirovoi voine* (Moscow and Leningrad 1928).

Verkhovsky, V., *Kratkii istoricheskii ocherk nachala i rasprostraneniya zheleznyh dorog v Rossii po 1897 g. vklyuchitelno* (St. Petersburg 1898).

Yakobi, A., *Zheleznye dorogi SSSR v tsifrah. Statisticheskii sbornik* (Moscow 1935).

Yalovetsky, B., *Ob,yasnitelnaya zapiska po povodu uchrezhdaemogo inzhenerom B.A.Yalovetskim Pervogo Obshchestva pod,ezdnyh zheleznyh putei v Rossii* (St. Petersburg 1892).

Zavadsky, K., *O postroike Kievo-Peterburgskoi zheleznoi dorogi* (Kiev 1892).

Zhuchkevich, V., *Dorogi i vodnye puti Belorussii* (Minsk 1977).

Zivica, Boris and Sozinov, Valentin, *Entsyklapedyya gistoryi Belarusi*, vol. 1 (Minsk 1993).

Chapter 3

Serbia's Access to the Sea, 1830–2006

Henry Jacolin

Having access to the Adriatic Sea was long a dream of Serbia. Landlocked between Austria-Hungary and the Ottoman empire, Serbia sought to escape from the dominance of its two powerful neighbours starting at its liberation in 1830, even though Serbia nominally remained a vassal of the Sublime Porte.

The Council to Improve Trade in Serbia reported to the Serbian Parliament on 20 February 1856 that access to the sea 'shall only be possible when Serbia has good transport infrastructure; in other words, when it builds railways, first running to the Adriatic Sea, which is only 45 hours away from our border, then to Constantinople or to the Black Sea'.[1] At the 18 February 1856 meeting, this same Council requested 'that our government do everything in its power so that a railway system does not bypass Serbia, and in particular that the Skadar railway line runs through Bosnia to Belgrade, as this railway line is essential to our fatherland'.[2]

For almost three-quarters of the century, railway construction projects in the Balkans aroused the passions of diplomatic chanceries, businessmen and financial circles to such an extent that these projects nearly provoked wars. Although many projects were planned over the years, only a handful were completed. And none would fulfil the dream that haunted Serbia.

The Impossible Dream: 1833–1918

Before 1918, there were five main reasons why Serbia was unable to fulfil its dream of access to the Adriatic Sea.

1. Turkish and Austro-Hungarian Hostility towards Serbia

Austria-Hungary and Turkey might have agreed to a proposed railway line running through Serbia between Vienna–Budapest and Constantinople–Salonica, had the empires been granted full control of the entire route. However, both of them were concerned about rising Serb nationalism, which sought to unite and liberate all the southern Slavs. Serbia expressed its desire to undertake the construction and

---

[1] Jezdimir Nikolić, *Istorija železnica Srbije, Vojvodine, Crne Gore i Kosova* (Beograd 1980), 20.

[2] Ibid., 21.

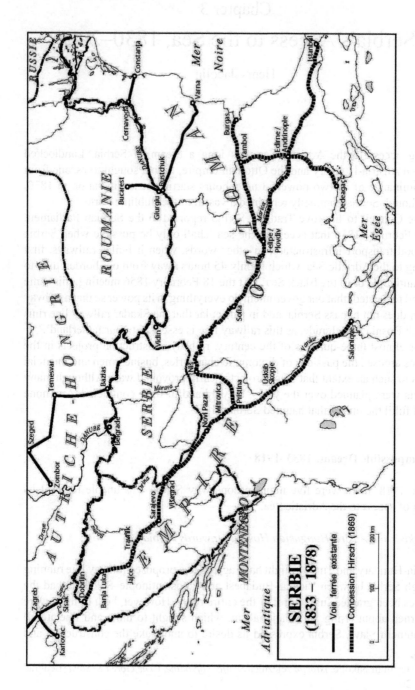

Figure 3.1   Map of Serbia, 1833–1878.

Source: Drawn by the author with the support of Jean-Pierre Pirat.

control the railway link running through its territory. Austria-Hungary and Turkey both tried to isolate Serbia. Turkey threatened to circumvent Serbia's territory by linking its railway network to the Austro-Hungarian line, either to the east, through Romania (Vidin), or to the west, through Novi Pazar Sandžak and Bosnia (with a connection in Sisak, near Zagreb, in the furthest outpost of Bosnia). The solution finally opted for in 1869 – the concession was granted to Baron Hirsch – would give Turkey a threefold advantage: the largest portion of the railway line would be in Turkey, and it would bypass Serbia while providing a means of keeping Serbia's border under close control. However, construction of the planned railway stopped in 1874, and it only got as far as Mitrovica, Kosovo. At the other end, a short railway link connecting Dobrljin (at the Croatian border) to Banja Luka remained isolated.

2. The Construction of the Vienna–Constantinople Line through Serbia

In 1878, the Great Powers were in a hurry to connect Central Europe to Constantinople. In the Treaty of Berlin they stipulated the construction of a railway line running through Serbia, Bulgaria and Eastern Rumelia, compelling each interested country to build the portion of the railway line that ran through its territory.

Serbia found this decision satisfactory, as it could finally start building a railway network connecting it to Europe. However, this project also presented a major drawback for the country: it tied up Serbia's financial resources for a decade, and thus diverted its attention away from access to the Adriatic Sea. What's more, in accordance with the Treaty of Berlin, Austria-Hungary's control of Bosnia cut Serbia off from one of its potential accesses to the Adriatic.

3. Austria-Hungary and Russia's Rivalry for Control over the Balkans

The two-headed Austro-Hungarian empire had a threefold ambition in the Balkans. Its first ambition was geographic: to control the Slavs, 'who were the main population in the region that could provide Austria-Hungary with access to the sea. Austria-Hungary also sought to control Bosnia-Herzegovina, the Adriatic provinces, and the surrounding areas of Trieste and Fiume.'[3] This explains why the Austro-Hungarian empire wanted to annex Bosnia-Herzegovina, which is sandwiched between Dalmatia and Croatia. Its second ambition was commercial: to open up a new market for its industry. Thirdly, Austria-Hungary wanted to stem the tide of Serbian and Albanian nationalism. The Berlin Congress granted Austria-Hungary control over the Novi Pazar Sandžak region, which presented the advantage of splitting Serbia off from Montenegro.

Russia backed Slavic liberation in the peninsula against Austro-Hungarian and Turkish domination. In this way it sought to wreak its revenge on Vienna for

---

[3] Isaiah Bowman, *Le monde nouveau* (Paris 1928), 410.

drawing the plan for the first trans-Balkan railway line, which kept Russia out of the Balkans. Since the late nineteenth century, Russia had offered to Serbia that it would build a railway line that would connect the Danube to the Adriatic Sea. Some of the goals of this project included 'uniting the diverse peoples of the Balkans (...) and by bringing them to the Mediterranean Sea via the Adriatic, they would thereby be liberated from Austro-Hungarian domination'.[4]

4. The Competing Trans-Balkan Railway Projects

To gain a direct link with the Ottoman empire while circumventing Serbia, Austria-Hungary developed two plans. The first was to run a railway line along the Adriatic shoreline and was to connect Split to Salonica via Metković, the Bay of Kotor, Bar (in Montenegro) and, in Turkish territory, Scutari, Durazzo and Monastir, where it would meet up with the existing railway line leading to Salonica. This project was mainly based on the narrow gauge Bosnian-Herzegovinian railway network. It would be extremely long, and would run through very mountainous regions. However, this project could not compete with the standard-gauge line from Belgrade via Niš to Constantinople and Salonica.

This is why Austria-Hungary then promoted the project called the Sandžak Railway. This project was intended to link Bosnia-Herzegovina to Mitrovica, the terminus of the line that had been built by the Oriental Railways Company through Novi Pazar Sandžak. Although this railway plan was far from ideal (it was to be started on the narrow gauge Bosnian-Herzegovinian network, and would be difficult to build), it would have indeed 'split Serbia from Montenegro' and prevented Serbia from having a sea exit.[5]

In contrast, the Russo-Serb Danube-Adriatic railway project started from a bridge that was to be built on the Danube between Serbia and Romania. To the east, it was connected to the Russian railways via the Romanian network at Reni, near Galați. To the west, the Adriatic line was to be built from scratch.

The planned route in Serbia went through Niš to the Merdare Pass, which demarcated Serbia's border and provided access to the Kosovo Plain in Turkish territory. This project stirred disputes between Serbia and Romania about the location of the bridge and between Serbia and Montenegro about the seaward route. Montenegro wanted this railway line to run through its territory up to the Bar (Antivari) port, while Serbia wanted it to run exclusively through Turkish territory. The purpose of Serbia's plan was to avoid Novi Pazar Sandžak, where the Treaty of Berlin had given some rights to Austria-Hungary, as well as the Antivari port, where Austria-Hungary exercised a right as a public health authority.

---

[4] Jean Larmeroux, *La politique extérieure de l'Autriche Hongrie, 1875–1914*, 2 vols (Paris 1918), vol. 2, 402.

[5] Albert Sauzède, 'Les voies ferrées transbalkaniques', *Questions diplomatiques et coloniales*, issue 404, of 16 décember 1913, 713.

Figure 3.2   Map of Serbia, 1878–1913

Source: Drawn by the author with the support of Jean-Pierre Pirat.

The proposed route from the Merdare Pass crossed the Skopje-Mitrovica line at Ferizović/Uroševac and from there reached the port of Saint Jean de Medua.

The Danube-Adriatic project suffered a number of setbacks due to the opposition from Austria-Hungary; the intermittent support of Russia, which hesitated to anger Vienna; Turkey's wavering attitude; and Serbia's lack of money.

In 1908, Austria-Hungary attempted to force a decision. In February, it sent a request to the Sublime Porte for the construction of the Sandžak railway line, to which the Porte responded positively. This news provoked 'a real emotion throughout Europe'.[6] Serbia saw itself as surrounded, while Montenegro saw its hopes for a railway line dashed. Soon thereafter, on 19 March, Serbia submitted a similar request for the construction of the Danube-Adriatic line, which was backed by Russia, France and Italy.

Austria-Hungary then used every diplomatic endeavour to block the Russo-Serb project, for example encouraging Bulgaria to propose a more southern Sofia-Skopje-Adriatic route.

Austria-Hungary sought to punish Serbia, which audaciously wanted to open up its own access to the Adriatic Sea and which had managed to defeat the embargo that Vienna had imposed on Belgrade in 1906 in the so-called 'Pig War'. The Young Turk Revolution which broke out in 1908, gave Austria an opportunity to 'place new chains on Serbia in order to shackle it in every direction'.[7]

On 5 October 1908 in Tărnovo, King Ferdinand proclaimed Bulgaria's independence. On 6 October, Austria-Hungary announced the annexation of Bosnia-Herzegovina, which put Serbia's plans to gain access to the Adriatic Sea on hold for a while. French engineers carried out some studies on the Danube-Adriatic route, which provoked hostility of Albanian populations – probably stoked by Austrian agents. Since Austria-Hungary returned the Novi Pazar Sandžak to Turkey in exchange for annexing Bosnia-Herzegovina, the Sandžak project was shelved as well.

5. The Creation of Albania

The Treaty of Bucharest, which put an end to the Balkan Wars in August 1913, extended Serbia's territory to the south as it annexed part of Macedonia. But Greece prevented Serbia's access to the Aegean Sea, since the new border was drawn 77 kilometres from Salonica. This, however, did not stop Serbia from sending increasing traffic volumes to Salonica, which became Serbia's main sea exit. Decided under pressure exerted by Vienna, the creation of Albania thwarted Serbia's access to the Adriatic. In 1913, Serbia was still landlocked.

---

[6]   Larmeroux, *La politique extérieure de l'Autriche-Hongrie*, vol. 2, 60.

[7]   René Pinon, *L'Europe et la jeune Turquie. Les aspects nouveaux de la question d'Orient* (Paris 1913), 213.

Figure 3.3   Map of Serbia, 1913–1918

Source: Drawn by the author with the support of Jean-Pierre Pirat.

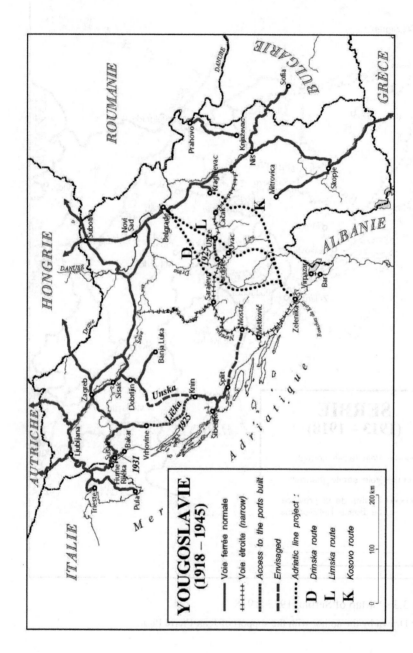

Figure 3.4   Map of Yugoslavia, 1918–1945

Source: Drawn by the author with the support of Jean-Pierre Pirat.

A Possible but Unfulfilled Dream: 1918–1945

With the 1918 creation of the Kingdom of the Serbians, Croatians and Slovenians, which had a long coastline and numerous harbours, did Serbia still need to have its own access to the Adriatic? If we examine this question more closely, we find that the harbour network that the kingdom inherited did not come close to meeting the needs of the new state for the following reasons:

1. Fiume/Rijeka, the only harbour served by a standard-gauge railway line, was not under Yugoslavian control after the 1919 surprise attack by Gabriele d'Annunzio, who set up this city-port as an independent state.
2. Split and Šibenik were connected by a standard-gauge railway line, which served only the nearby surrounding areas, as it did not go further than Knin.
3. Metković (Neretva Delta), Gruž (Dubrovnik) and the Bay of Kotor (Zelenika) were linked by the Bosnian-Herzegovinian narrow gauge railway network, and were practically cut off from the rest of Yugoslavia.
4. Bar (Montenegro) was only linked to Lake Scutari by a narrow gauge forestry line.

'The Yugoslavians, who were disappointed as they did not gain control of Trieste and Fiume, which were indispensable for Yugoslavia, felt the burden of Italian imperialism and realised that, although the Austro-Hungarian empire had disappeared, their outlet in the north Adriatic was at the mercy of an expanding power, extremely focused on its interests.'[8] Henceforth, it became clear that Yugoslavia needed its own ports so as not to rely on those of foreign powers. This explains why from the inception of Yugoslavia, a notion prevailed that Belgrade must be connected directly to the Adriatic. Serbia had always strived to fulfil this dream, but previously through foreign territories. Now, for the first time, the dream was within reach as it could be achieved within national territory.

However, a number of obstacles stood in the way of Serbia realising this dream before World War Two. The first was that the Adriatic line project sparked a debate that continued until 1941. A series of conferences, bringing together the society of engineers and architects of Yugoslavia, representatives from the Railway Authority and from the relevant Ministries, were held to discuss the railway projects in the new state. However, no clear agenda emerged from these conferences, as each region, and sometimes each district within the same region, each port, and each corporation backed its own project, and did not take into account the interests of the country as a whole. To get back to the connection between Belgrade and the Adriatic, 'there were as many proposals as there were

---

[8] Dragomir Arnaoutovitch, *Histoire des chemins de fer yougoslaves 1825–1937* (Paris 1937), 333.

intervening parties'.[9] In short, this debate opposed the Adriatic line supporters and opponents.

The Serbian Government succeeded in getting American business concerns to finance this project – (Railway and Port Construction Co. of Yugoslavia and the bank Blair and Co. Inc.) to finance this project. A 100-million-dollar loan was concluded in 1922 under terms unfavourable to Yugoslavia. Although the Skupština, the Serbian Parliament, approved this financial arrangement, opposition to the Adriatic line came from the Conference of Engineers, requesting that the loan be put first towards completing construction of the railway lines started prior to the war.

Then a dispute arose among Serbs regarding the route of the Adriatic line. For some Serbs, it was essential that Belgrade have direct sea access by rail. The supporters of the Adriatic line proposed to link the narrow gauge network of western Serbia to Bosnia-Herzegovina by building a short link between Užice and Vardište (57.4 kilometres), which would give Belgrade access to the sea via the Neretva River. The plan's opponents, who were in the majority, opposed it because its route largely ran through Bosnia-Herzegovina, and because its capacity was too low, as it was made up of narrow gauge railway lines. The counter-proposal was a line between Belgrade and the Bay of Kotor that would cover the longest possible distance through Serbia. However, within this proposal there were three variants as to where to lay the track: through the Drina Valley, through central Serbia (Lim Valley) and through Kosovo.

The Croats opposed the Adriatic line in any form, because its construction would have taken years. They put forward two other priorities: building a port near Rijeka on Yugoslavian territory close to the Zagreb–Rijeka railway line, and completing the line between Zagreb and the Split and Šibenik ports, the extremities of which had already been built. The Austrians and the Hungarians had delayed construction of this line for decades: the Austrians, because they wanted to keep the Croat nation divided, and the Hungarians, because they did not want the Split and Šibenik ports to compete with that of Fiume. For the Croats, this project was as significant as the Adriatic line was for the Serbs.

More pressing and realistic projects supplanted the Adriatic line, like rebuilding and adjusting the network that Yugoslavia had inherited. In the early enthusiasm resulting from the creation of Yugoslavia, an unrealistic railway plan had been adopted in 1920, which involved 1,400 kilometres of rehabilitation and 3,000 kilometres of new constructions. This plan soon faced harsh realities. First, the new state had to repair the extensive damage that the war had caused. Then it had to increase the capacity of a network almost exclusively made up of single tracks with a great number of narrow gauge lines. Lastly, it had to join unconnected and isolated pieces of the network inherited from Austria, Hungary and Turkey.

The urgency of finding a substitute for the Rijeka-Fiume line came after. Given Italy's occupation of Fiume, and that no solution to the dispute with Italy was in

---

[9]   Zvonimir Jelinović, *Borba za jadranske pruge i njeni ekonomski ciljevi* (Zagreb 1957), 240.

sight, the Croats proposed the construction of a short line to the port of Bakar. In the nineteenth century, Bakar had been the main port on the Kvarner Bay, the development of which was superseded by that of Rijeka. In 1920, the Yugoslavian Ministry of Transport cited financial and technical difficulties (a rack track line was then planned to run through the coastal mountain) delaying this project, which had the backing of the 1920 Conference of Engineers. In 1927, the government finally decided to build this line. But by the time this project was commissioned in 1931, the Rijeka issue had been settled. The Treaty of Rome, signed in January 1924, stipulated that Fiume was to be annexed by Italy; however, the Sušak suburbs, on the eastern shore of the Fiumara River, were left to Yugoslavia. In addition, Yugoslavia was allowed to use facilities in the Italian port of Fiume while it developed its own facilities in Sušak, which partially settled the sea access issue. 'When the Bakar railway line was needed most, as Jelinović writes, it was not built because Belgrade did not understand its importance; when the construction was finally decided on, the fate of Rijeka had already been settled.'[10]

The urgency of unlocking Split and Šibenik was the third pressing problem. As soon as the Croats gained control over the region, and even before proclaiming the Kingdom of the Serbs, Croats and Slovenes on 1 December 1918, the National Council of Zagreb had granted to a private company the concession of the missing link of the Lička line (*Lička Pruga*), between Vrhovine and Knin. But in February 1919, the Ministry of Transport halted the work and sent the project's engineers to Sarajevo to build the narrow gauge Užice–Vardište line, which was intended to create a link between Belgrade and the Neretva sea exit.

After that, things start to get muddled. Only one-fourth of the amount required to complete the Lička project was allocated in the 1920–21 budget. Other routes were proposed, such as the Una Valley line, which would divert traffic from Split and Šibenik towards Serbia, and the Mostar–Imotski–Split line which were mainly intended to benefit Belgrade. Despite these delaying tactics, the Lička line (155.6 kilometres long) was finally commissioned on 25 July 1925, five months after the Belgrade–Neretva line. 'Due to lack of resources, and because there was a misunderstanding about the urgency of building this line, its construction took seven years', even though more than half of its construction had been completed by 1918.[11]

Another obstacle was the fact that the Belgrade-Adriatic line was too long and too expensive, and would not be profitable enough:

1. Too long: regardless of the route, this project involved constructing a line approximately 500 kilometres long because there were practically no railway lines in the region; therefore, it was an all or nothing proposition.
2. Too expensive: the cost of this link would have postponed constructing shorter, albeit critical lines (for example, the Lička line), and would have

---

[10]   Ibid., 81.

[11]   Ibid., 131.

tied up Yugoslavia's financial resources for years to come. At any rate, the Blair loan would not have covered the cost of this project.

3. Not profitable enough: according to studies, the forecasted traffic volumes would have been too low to make the line profitable. In addition, it was improbable that goods produced in southern Serbia and Macedonia could have been diverted from Salonica to the Bay of Kotor (Boka Kotorska). Lastly, the military port would have had to be converted into a commercial one, and, given the limited size of Boka Kotorska, this would have been a difficult undertaking.

As there were no ports in the south of Yugoslavia, and due to the distance between Niš or Skopje from Rijeka or Split, the Salonica harbour was more and more used by Yugoslavia. In accordance with a convention concluded in 1923 with Greece, Yugoslavia obtained a free zone in the harbour of Salonica. Consequently, from 1918 to 1945, not a single kilometre of the Adriatic line was built.

The Dream Fulfilled: 1945–1991

At the end of World War Two, Yugoslavia annexed the port of Rijeka, then completed the access from Belgrade to Split and Šibenik with the Unska line, which ran from Bihać to Knin, and was put into service in 1948. At that point, constructing a special line between Belgrade and the Adriatic did not appear to be as necessary as it had between the world wars. However, as early as 1948, planners decided to study two routes: the Drinska route (Drina valley): Belgrade–Obrenovac–Šabac–Zvornik–Bajna Bašta–Uvac–Priboj–Bijelo Polje–Kolašin–Titograd–Bar, and the Limska route (Lim valley): Belgrade–Valjevo–Kosjević–Požega–Užice–Priboj–Bijelo Polje–Kolašin–Titograd–Bar. In 1951, the Federal Economic Council decided to build a line along the Limska route, which was 105 kilometres shorter than the Drinska route. There were three reasons for undertaking this massive project, which were political, geographical and economic in nature.

The political reason was based on the rationale of the federal system set up in 1945. Each republic reckoned it was within its rights to have its own steel plant or refinery. For the Republic of Serbia, this right would be extended to having access to the sea, and it would have been politically tricky for the other republics to argue against Serbia's dream. Furthermore, having sea access was in line with Yugoslavia's objective of reducing disparities between the rich and poor regions of the country: southern Serbia, Kosovo, Sandžak and Montenegro were among the poor regions, and were almost completely devoid of railway lines. The planned line would cover 49 per cent of Yugoslavia and would serve approximately 10 million inhabitants.

The geographical reason was based on the concept that each harbour should have its own hinterland (gravitation zone) in order to optimise traffic flows and prevent too many goods from travelling across all of Yugoslavia to reach Rijeka.

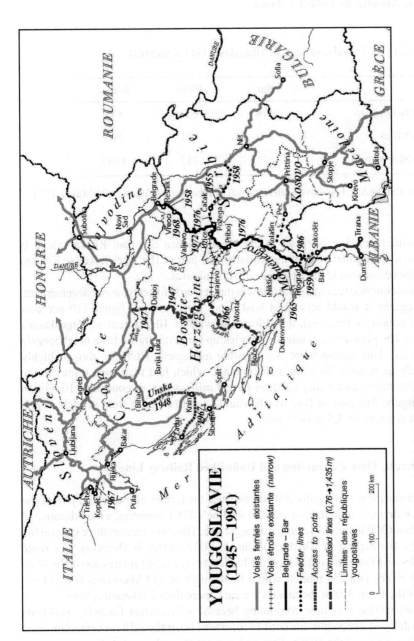

Figure 3.5   Map of Yugoslavia, 1945–1991

Source: Drawn by the author with the support of Jean-Pierre Pirat.

The Belgrade-Bar line significantly reduced distances between eastern Yugoslavia and the Adriatic, as Table 3.1 shows.

Table 3.1   Travel distances in Yugoslavia (in kilometres)

	Bar	Ploče	Rijeka
From Belgrade to	476	629	643
From Niš to	560	621	865
From Skopje to	673	733	1,085

Source: Red Vožnje Jugoslovenskih železnica (Timetables of Yugoslav Railways), 1974.

Furthermore, Bar is closer to the Mediterranean Sea than Rijeka, which is located at the northern end of the Adriatic. The port of Bar, once linked to Kosovo and Macedonia, could have competed with Salonica.

The economic reason for the line was that it would foster resource development. The regions it would serve had lead, zinc, bauxite, coal, lignite (10 per cent of the country's reserves), agriculture, as well as 10 per cent of Yugoslavia's forests. The planners also intended to pick up some rail traffic from neighbouring countries. This arrangement was feasible as regards Hungary, though highly unlikely as regards Bulgaria and Romania, which had their own routes to the sea. The anticipated traffic volumes were 5 million tons of goods and 10 million passengers. The port of Bar, which would need to be built from scratch, would have a capacity of 4.5 million tons.

A Difficult, Time-Consuming and Unfinished Railway Line

This project was technically difficult because the terrain of the central part of the line is extremely mountainous. Out of the line's 476 kilometres, a total distance of only about 300 kilometres runs in a straight line. The route crosses three geographic saddles, the highest of which, Kolašin, is 1,032 metres in elevation. The route includes 14 kilometres of bridges (the highest bridge is 201 metres above the Mala Rijeka river), and 254 tunnels with a total length of 114 kilometres (i.e., 24 per cent of the line); five of the tunnels are each more than 5 kilometres long.

Construction was time-consuming because of recurrent financing problems which delayed its commission until 1976; otherwise, it should have been completed at the beginning of the 1970s. This project went through several stages.

In 1952 construction began at the two extremities of the line. In the north, from Resnik to Valjevo, work was started to replace the narrow gauge network of western Serbia; in the south, between Bar and Titograd, a tunnel at sea level was to replace the Bar–Virpazar narrow gauge line. In 1954 and 1955, drilling was also started on the longest tunnels.

In 1955 the Federal Economic Council decided to stop all work because of lack of funds. However, work continued on two sections, Resnik–Vreoci (38 kilometres), which started service in 1958, and Titograd-Bar, which came in to service in 1959, after completion of the 6,171-metre Sozina tunnel, which runs under the Sutomore coastal mountain.

In 1966, in an effort to complete construction, the Federal Parliament passed a law stating that the Federation would cover 85 per cent of the construction cost; the remaining 15 per cent would be assumed by the Republics of Serbia and Montenegro, which were interested in this project. Nevertheless, it was only after the World Bank extended a \$50 million loan that work on this project could resume. There was some progress with the commissioning of the Vreoci–Valjevo line in 1968 (40.2 kilometres), as well as the Valjevo–Titovo Užice in 1972 (88.1 kilometres). Out of a total of 476.1 kilometres, 232.8 kilometres had been constructed; therefore, 243.3 kilometres, or 51 per cent of the project, remained to be built to complete the line.

In 1971, new financing problems arose. 'As the federation's investment was set and not subject to review, the republics had to bear the rising costs of the bill.'[12] In Serbia, the problem was solved by putting in a call to the banks and by floating a public loan. However, Montenegro was unable to cover the difference, while half the line was on its territory (117 kilometres out of 241 kilometres). Not only was Montenegro only one tenth as populous as Serbia, its per capita income was only 60 per cent of that of the Yugoslav average. Montenegro considered that it should not bear the burden of this investment, which had a national character. As finally Montenegro ended up contributing 60 per cent instead of 15 per cent, it thereafter threw in the towel. However, in 1974 a compromise was reached. The other republics agreed to open a 700 million dinar credit facility for Montenegro, which was financed by the National Bank of Yugoslavia (300 million dinar), the republics (300 million), and Serbia (100 million). 'The Belgrade–Bar railway line was therefore saved.'[13]

The final 243.3-kilometre stretch of line was put into service on 21 May 1976. Of it, 117.9 kilometres are in Montenegro, 109 kilometres are in Serbia and 16.4 kilometres are in Bosnia-Herzegovina.

Apart from the line itself, the broader project remained incomplete because only one of the planned feeder lines was built. It is 32.5 kilometres long and was put into service in 1976. It connects Požega to Čačak, linking Belgrade–Bar to the Belgrade–Niš and Belgrade–Kosovo main lines. One of the terms of the World Bank's 1971 loan was that this link had to be built. The World Bank was of the

---

[12]   Jacques Marville (alias Henry Jacolin), 'Où en sont les travaux de la ligne Belgrade-Bar', *La vie du rail*, issue 1411, of 7 October 1973, 42–3.

[13]   Ibid., 42–3.

view that without the traffic from eastern Serbia, Kosovo and Macedonia, the traffic on the Belgrade–Bar line would be insufficient to turn a profit. In addition, the narrow line connecting Titovo Užice to Sarajevo was suppressed in 1978. Yet surprisingly, another feeder line, connecting Montenegro to Albania, was built in 1986, which added 1 million tons of traffic to the Belgrade-Bar.

However, the feeder line that was intended to link Kolašin (Montenegro) to Peć (Kosovo), which provided the shortest route between Bar and Skopje, and which was a sound alternative to the Salonica line, was not built. The connections to neighbouring states, which were supposed to divert some traffic to Bar, were not improved.

Ten years after completion, only 50 per cent of the 7 million-ton capacity of the Belgrade–Bar line was utilised.[14] Belgrade–Bar is not an ordinary railway line because it offers several considerable advantages. It connects some of Yugoslavia's very isolated areas, opens up a new sea access closer to Yugoslavia's southern regions, and offers a credible alternative to the northern ports. Paul Delacroix hit the nail on the head when he wrote: 'Belgrade–Bar is mainly a collective act of faith in railways.'[15] We might ask, what would have happened if this line had not been built? This indeed was a question the Serbs were asking themselves when Yugoslavia collapsed in 1991.

The Vanishing Dream? The Years between 1991 and 2006

The Belgrade–Bar line suddenly became vital to Serbia when Yugoslavia collapsed. It was Serbia's sole sea exit, because Bakar became Slovenian; Rijeka, Split and Šibenik, Croatian; and Ploče at the service of Bosnia-Herzegovina. This is one of the reasons why when faced with an international boycott, Serbia tried until the last minute to maintain the illusion of a Yugoslav Federation, even if at the time this federation consisted only of Serbia and Montenegro.

Did this dream vanish when Montenegro became independent in 2006? As it stands now, Serbia no longer has its own access to the Adriatic. Yet, in a way, the Belgrade–Bar line did help foster an interdependent relationship between Serbia and Montenegro. It serves Montenegro's domestic rail traffic but would be unprofitable without Serbia's traffic. In addition, the port of Bar was built for a higher traffic capacity than for handling Montenegro's goods exclusively.

To conclude, the dream has not completely died, because Serbia and Montenegro now share in it.

---

[14] Anonymous, 'La première décennie de la ligne Belgrade-Bar', *Revue générale des chemins de fer*, June 1986.

[15] Paul Delacroix, 'Le défi de Belgrade-Bar', *La vie du rail*, issue 1554, of 1 August 1976, 8–14.

Bibliography

Anonymous, 'La première décennie de la ligne Belgrade-Bar', *Revue générale des chemins de fer*, of June 1986.

Arnaoutovitch, Dragomir, *Histoire des chemins de fer yougoslaves 1825–1937* (Paris 1937).

Bowman, Isaiah, *Le monde nouveau* (Paris 1928).

Delacroix, Paul, 'Le défi de Belgrade-Bar', *La vie du rail*, issue 1554, of 1 August 1976, 8–14.

Jelinović, Zvonimir, *Borba za jadranske pruge i njeni ekonomski ciljevi* (Zagreb 1957).

Larmeroux, Jean, *La politique extérieure de l'Autriche Hongrie, 1875–1914*, 2 vols (Paris 1918).

Marville, Jacques (alias Henry Jacolin), 'Belgrade – Bar: premier train en 1976', *La vie du rail*, issue 1458, of 15 September 1974, 42–3

Marville, Jacques (alias Henry Jacolin), 'Où en sont les travaux de la ligne Belgrade-Bar', *La vie du rail*, issue 1411, of 7 October 1973, 42–3

Nikolić, Jezdimir, *Istorija železnica Srbije, Vojvodine, Crne Gore i Kosova* (Belgrade 1980).

Pinon, René, *L'Europe et la jeune Turquie. Les aspects nouveaux de la question d'Orient* (Paris 1913).

Sauzède, Albert, 'Les voies ferrées transbalkaniques', *Questions diplomatiques et coloniales*, issue 404, of 16 December 1913, 713.

Chapter 4
The History of Railway Passenger Transportation in Hungary – From the Monarchy to the Twenty-First Century

Imre Perger

The first railway line in Hungary was operated with steam locomotives, and it was opened between Pest and Vác on 15 July 1846. This occasion is regarded as the birthday of the Hungarian railways. Sándor Petőfi (1823–49), a famous Hungarian Romantic poet, travelled on the first train and wrote a poem predicting that rails would connect cities and villages of Hungary like the blood vessels in the human body.

At this time, Hungary included not only the wide plain on both banks of the Danube and Tisza rivers, which was mainly inhabited by Hungarians, but many other territories, the majority of whose population was of Slavic origin: Slovakia (Slovaks), Sub Carpathian Ruthenia (Ukrainians), Banat (mixed), Bačka (mixed), Transylvania (primarily Romanians, but with many Hungarians), Croatia-Slavonia (Croats) and Fiume (Italians). Up to 1867, the railway policies were decided by the government of the Austro-Hungarian empire in Vienna. And up to that time, 2,282 kilometres were built.

After the Compromise (*Ausgleich/Kiegyezés*) that was agreed upon between Austria and Hungary in 1867, the Hungarians obtained autonomy for the territories situated to the east of the Leitha River. This area, known as Trans-Leithania, comprised 325,411 square kilometres. From then on, the parliament and the government of Pest determined the railway policies of the Hungarian part of the Double Monarchy. One of their first decisions was the creation of the Hungarian State Railways on 30 June 1868.

The network of the state railways was extended by building new lines and by nationalising unprofitable private railway companies. As Under-Secretary of State and later as Minister of Transport (1883–92), Gábor Baross brought 62 per cent of the railway lines into public ownership and helped to restore the financial equilibrium of the country. The whole network was now united. However, fares for passengers in Hungary were the second highest in Europe, surpassed only by Turkey. Moreover, passenger trains were few, and ran with a seat occupancy of only 20 per cent.

In order to solve these problems, Baross created a totally new tariff system. The zone tariff system, based on dumping prices, was introduced on 1 August

1889 and remained in operation with some minor changes until 1912. Baross famously said, 'I want an honourable woman from Brasov [a town 703 kilometres away from Budapest, today in Romania] to come to Budapest to buy a hat.'[1] The peculiarity of this system was that Budapest and the River Danube were meant to be a point of intersection, so passengers wishing to travel from the eastern part of the country to Vienna had to pay twice as much as to Budapest. This placed the Hungarian capital in a much more competitive position than the Austrian one. The system also resulted in lower prices for passenger trips and goods transport, which in turn resulted in a rapid increase of both, bringing higher overall profits. As a consequence of the zone tariff system, the number of passengers increased from 9.056 million in 1889 to 28.624 million in 1912, an increase of 215 per cent, with revenues increasing by 40 per cent to 19,685 million kronen.[2] The number of journeys below 25 kilometres grew from 1.2 million to 12 million, and journeys of more than 225 kilometres from 163,000 to 657,000. As a consequence of this, the operation of the railways became profitable by 1908. In 1900 the total length of the Hungarian railway network was 17,281 kilometres, with 2,917 engines, 5,730 passenger carriages and 72,513 freight wagons in operation. With 64.4 million passengers, 2.3 billion passenger kilometres, 42.6 million freight tons, 5.3 billion ton kilometres and working expenses of 149.3 million kronen, the MÁV managed to produce an income of 375.3 million kronen and a profit of 126 million. At that time 89,479 men and women were working for the railway.[3] The essence of the introduction of the zone tariff system was the drastic reduction of passenger fares. The new system divided the stations into well-defined zones: the lowest one was five kilometres, the longest one 225 kilometres. The biggest price reduction was provided for railway journeys of less than 25 kilometres and for those of over 225 kilometres (the so-called infinity distance). This meant that travelling to Budapest from Kolozsvár (Cluj-Napoca), a journey of 400 kilometres, cost as much as from Brasso (Brasov), 731 kilometres.

So that Vienna would not reap the benefits from the price reductions in case of long-distance travels through Budapest, the calculation of distances was revised. With this measure, Baross assured the central position of Budapest in respect to trade and tourism, and soon the benefits of the new pricing policy became visible. Domestic trade and tourism to Budapest began to pick up. Many people travelled to Budapest from great distances to go shopping, for work and for pleasure. The increased traffic had a positive effect on industry, necessitating the purchase of new rolling stock and locomotives.

---

[1] Magyar Államvasutak Rt. (ed.), *Vasúti Nagylexikon*, 2 vols (Budapest 2005), vol. 1, 89.

[2] Magyar Államvasutak Rt., *Vasúti Nagylexikon*, vol. 1, 90.

[3] Figures are taken from MÁV Zrt. Vezérigazgatóság (ed.), *A magyar vasút krónikája a XIX. Században* (Budapest 2009), 379, 381, 386 and 388.

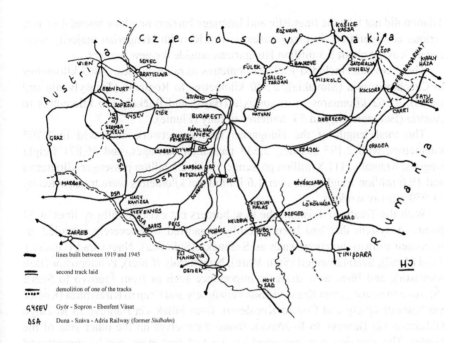

Figure 4.1 Railway network of Hungary, 1919–1938

Source: Map created by Henry Jacolin.

By the beginning of World War One, the Hungarian railways had become the leading driver of the economy. At the end of the war, the length of the Hungarian railway network stood at 22,869 kilometres. At that time, 5,504 engines, 10,668 passenger cars and 119,360 freight wagons were in operation. A total of 263 million passengers, 12.031 billion passenger kilometres, 74.5 million freight tons and 9.9 billion ton kilometres were serviced by a workforce of 167,163 men and women.[4]

Under the 1920 Treaty of Trianon, the former Kingdom of Hungary (Hungary and Croatia-Slavonia) lost more than two-thirds of the 325,411 square kilometres of its territory; the country – without Croatia-Slavonia – decreased from 282,870 square kilometres to about 92,963 square kilometres. The country also lost more than half of its population, from 20,886,487 (without Croatia-Slavonia 18,264,533) in 1910 to 7,615,117 in 1920.

In 1910, the ethnic Hungarian population living in the Kingdom of Hungary had accounted for approximately 48.1 per cent of the whole population (not including Croatia-Slavonia even 54.6 per cent). Although the majority of people living in the newly lost territories were not ethnic Hungarians, the Treaty of

---

4 Figures are taken from MÁV Zrt. Vezérigazgatóság (ed.), *A magyar vasút krónikája a XX. Században* (Budapest 2005), 390–94.

Trianon did not take the linguistic and language barriers or ethnic boundaries into serious consideration. In many cases, territories with Hungarian majority were ceded, leaving about 3.3 million Hungarians outside the new borders.

These cessions included 13,920 kilometres of railway lines: 3,803 kilometres to Czechoslovakia (Slovakia), 5,540 kilometres to Romania (Transylvania and Banat), 4,262 kilometres to Yugoslavia (Banat and Bačka), 310 kilometres to Austria (Burgenland), and 5 kilometres to Italy (Fiume).

The total length of the Hungarian railway network decreased to 8,705 kilometres, with 2,195 engines, 3,533 passenger carriages, and 36,871 freight wagons. Annually, 111.8 million passengers with 2.5 billion passenger kilometres and 19.6 million freight tons over 1.6 billion ton kilometres were transported by 71,950 railway workers.[5]

With the Treaty of Trianon, the new borders cut existing railway lines at 51 points. A system that had been carefully organised was severely curtailed, as important railway junctions such as Szabadka (Subotica), Nagyvárad (Oradea), Arad (Arad), Szatmárnémeti (Satu Mare), Nagykároly (Carei), Pélmonostor (Beli Monastir), and lines with strategic importance such as from Štúrovo to Szenc (Štúrovo to Senec), from Kassa via Sátoraljaújhely and Csap to Királyháza (Košice via Sátoraljaújhely and Čop to Korolevo), from Fülek via Bánréve to Rozsnyó (Fiľakovo via Bánréve to Rožňava), found themselves on the other side of the border. The situation was worsened by the fact that many newly unemployed railway workers migrated to Hungary from the other side of the new frontiers. The peace treaty also prescribed the demolition of one of the tracks on the line from Békéscsaba via Lőkösháza, Soroksár and Kiskunlacháza to Kelebia and on the line from Hatvan to Salgótarján as well.

The damage of World War One and the consequences of the Treaty of Trianon resulted in recession and decline. Due to the scarcity of resources, only a moderate development of the railway network was built. As a replacement for a lost connection, a new line of 11 kilometres was built between Kocsord and Fehérgyarmat. The construction of a new line between Dunaföldvár and Solt (11 kilometres) created a new crossing over the River Danube. In Budapest, branch lines and side tracks were built, and new connections were constructed all over the country. There were also line and curve corrections on the main lines, such as from Budapest to Hegyeshalom, Budapest to Hatvan, and Budapest to Lake Balaton. A second track was built between Kápolnásnyék and Szabadbattyán via Székesfehérvár (33.6 kilometres), between Szajol and Debrecen (101.9 kilometres), and between Sárbogárd and Rétszilas (9.1 kilometres). Railway stations were rebuilt, 203 kilometres of narrow-gauge lines were constructed, and the line from Budapest to Hegyeshalom was electrified.[6]

---

[5] Figures are taken from MÁV Zrt. Vezérigazgatóság, *A magyar vasút krónikája a XX. Században*, 390–94.

[6] Figures were taken from MÁV Rt. (ed.), *Magyar vasúttörténet*, 7 vols (Budapest 1996), vol. 5, 121.

One way to escape the economic crisis was seen by the nationalisation of the remaining private railways. Between 1926 and 1931 no fewer than 58 lines, with a total length of 4,052 kilometres, were transferred to public ownership. On 1 July 1932, the Duna-Száva-Adria Railway Company (DSA), the former *Südbahn*, with a length of 560.7 kilometres, was taken into public ownership. Magyar Államvasutak (MÁV) became the only major railway operator in Hungary, and the impact of the remaining independent railway companies, such as Győr-Sopron-Ebenfurti Vasút (GySEV), was negligible. There were several reasons for the nationalisation, including the quest for efficiency and the hope of resulting financial savings. It was decided to rationalise the whole network and all business procedures. As a side note, today Hungary is preparing to privatise parts of the nationalised railways using the same argumentation.

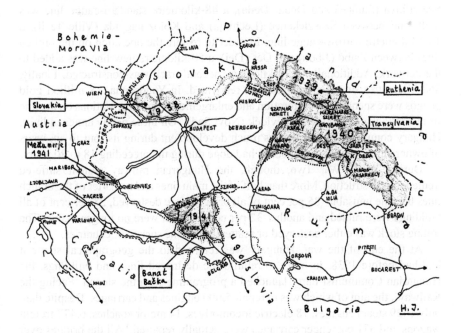

Figure 4.2   The railway network of Hungary, 1938–1945
Source: Map created by Henry Jacolin.

As mentioned above, in the interwar period the developments focused on existing multiple-track lines, and most main lines got a second track. Based on inventions by Kálmán Kandó, an electrification process was started on the single-phase 16,000 volts 50 Hz system, and Kandó's newly designed MÁV Class V40 locomotive was put into operation. Despite the economic crisis, new MÁV Class 424 general purpose steam locomotives were purchased between 1924 and 1958.

For service on branch lines, in order to attract more passengers, four- and six-wheeled gasoline (and later diesel) railcars were purchased, beginning in 1928.

In accordance with two successive Vienna arbitrations during the Nazi regime, in November 1938 Hungary recovered the southern part of Slovakia (1,069 kilometres of railway lines), in March–April 1939 Ruthenia (440 kilometres), in 1940 part of Transylvania (2,204 kilometres), and in 1941 Bačka, Banat and Međumurje (1,114 kilometres).

During the Second World War, an intensive development of the railways took place between 1938 and 1943 in the regions temporarily recovered by Hungary. In all, 418 million gold pengős were invested: in Czechoslovakia, 48 million gold pengős were used for the construction of a 16.9-kilometre-long new line between Taracköz (Teresva) and Aknaszlatina (Slatina), and 352 million were invested in the renovation of 695 kilometres of superstructure in Romania. Moreover, between Szeretfalva (Sărăţel) and Déda (Deda), a 48-kilometre standard-gauge line was built, and between Szászlekence (Lechinţa) and Kolozsnagyida (Viile Tecii), a 16.2-kilometre narrow-gauge line. In order to restore the operation on the broken lines between Zsibó (Jibou) and Dés (Dej), a 50-kilometre new line was added to the network. Additionally, a 76-kilometre second track was constructed. Finally, 468 kilometres of superstructure was renovated. In Yugoslavia, 18 million gold pengős were spent on the restoration and enlargement of railway stations on the line from Szabadka (Subotica) to Újvidék (Novi Sad).[7] On these newly annexed lines, Hungary completed three times as much development during its four to six years of ownership as the successor states had done during the preceding 18 to 20 years.

During World War Two, though, the Hungarian railway system suffered tremendous destruction. More than half of the main lines and a quarter of the branch lines became unusable: 85 per cent of all bridges were destroyed, 28 per cent of all buildings were ruined and another 32 per cent of them were no longer usable. The rolling stock was either destroyed or scattered over the successor countries.

At the end of the war, Hungary was returned to the geographical shape it had had before 1938. In order to rebuild the destroyed lines and buildings, the Hungarian Communist Party launched a programme with the slogan 'Facing the Railway', the aim of which was to repair 5,000 engines and carriages. Despite that, only 1429 steam engines, 18 electric locomotives, 14 motor coaches, 6,477 freight wagons and 571 passenger carriages were actually repaired.[8] All the bridges over the biggest rivers had been destroyed, and it took 10 years to rebuild them. There was a moderate improvement in new building after the repair of war damage: connecting lines and the construction of 178 kilometres of new tracks and a new 282-kilometre second track. Traffic between Hungary and the Soviet Union increased enormously, which made it necessary to improve the border station

[7]   Figures are taken from MÁV Rt., *Magyar vasúttörténet*, vol. 5, 137–47.

[8]   Figures were taken from István-Szabó András Heinczinger, *Vasút és közpolitika – Magyarország politikai* évkönyve *2008-ról*, (ed.) by DKMKA (Budapest 2009), 931.

of Záhony. Furthermore, all the private railway companies that still remained in private hands except the GySEV were nationalised.

Due to the development of road transport, the renewal of the railway became more and more important. A general plan for this was the 'Concept for Transport', a scheme launched in 1968: passenger traffic on secondary lines was either to be ended or centralised in order to economise and to improve the level of service of passenger and freight transport. The concept was intended to enable the technical renewal of railways in the 1970s.

Between 1959 and 1980, railway lines with a total length of 1,888 kilometres (712 kilometres narrow-gauge and 1,176 kilometres standard-gauge) were closed down and the track dismantled. In those years passenger and freight traffic were significant and the railway made full use of its capacity. That is why every autumn severe restrictions in freight transport had to be imposed, and freight over short distances had to be transferred to the roads. Passenger rates of MÁV had shown a remarkable stability, remaining unchanged between 1951 and 1980. In that last year the tariff rates were increased according to the value of the forint, and the number of zones was decreased, but the general tariff level remained unchanged. In 2010, passenger rates were 70 times higher than in 1980.

The collapse of the Communist regime in 1990 – in parallel with the development of the road network – dealt the railways a heavy blow. Factories were closed down and many people became unemployed. Fewer people purchased monthly passes and there was a decline in the number of commuter journeys at the weekend. The number of the passengers with reduced fares steadily went up. The number of families with cars increased significantly, and the quality of the cars themselves improved greatly. The amount of freight traffic plummeted, and because so little cash was entering the system, investment in infrastructure was postponed or even cancelled.

Foreign consulting companies uncovered a debt of 1,000 billion forint at the Hungarian railways. This amount went up to 5,000 billion forint by 2005. The average age of passenger carriages had been 17 years in 1980 and had grown to 30 years by 2008. Between 1964 and 1983, 3,090 new carriages had been purchased, between 1983 and 2009 only 428. The successive governments and politicians have not yet found the means to combat the decline of railway traffic. Due to the high-pressure lobbying from road and motor interests, governments have consistently paid more attention to the construction of the motorway system. At the same time the railway infrastructure and the network of minor roads have been neglected. Due to the decrease in freight transport, the cross-financing possibilities of the railway have declined drastically. Road transport, especially heavy trucks, have benefited from this situation. And while passenger rail traffic was scaled back, bus companies were able to continuously enlarge their services with more modern coaches.

The railway lost its positive image. The name MÁV acquired a negative connotation. The only positive development in the first decade of the twenty-first century was the opening of the Hungarian Railway Museum, currently operated by MÁV-Nostalgia Ltd. The foundation stone was laid on 22 November 1999 on the site of the former Budapest North Depot of the Hungarian State Railways. The main activity of MÁV-Nostalgia Ltd. is the running of nostalgic railway trips in restored vintage trains. It owns approximately 50 different types of vehicles, all of historic interest, including some that are well known throughout Europe. They are available for hire both for domestic use and international travel.

The Hungarian government was looking for new methods for the reconstruction of the Hungarian railways and engaged private consulting firms such as Knight Wendling, Mercer, Halcrow Fox, Boston Consulting and IFUA-Horvath. All advocated nearly identical measures: reducing costs, improving the main lines, rationalising the network, outsourcing the branch lines, ensuring more state support, increasing passenger tariffs, reducing the number of discounts and outsourcing non-core activities. As a consequence of the implementation of some of these actions the new MÁV Co. was split into several legally independent companies between 2000 and 2008. The aim was to provide the most efficient operational framework for all members of the group. In 2006 the former freight division was the first to be set up as an independent unit under the name MÁV CARGO Plc. Two years later this company was privatised. As of 2010, it belongs to Rail Cargo Austria and operates under the name of Rail Cargo Hungaria. The second unit, MÁV-START Railway Passenger Transport Co., was created on 1 July 2007 out of MÁV's Passenger Transport Division as a separate company with more than 7,000 employees.

On 1 January 2008, MÁV Co.'s traction operations became a separate company, MÁV-TRAKCIÓ Railway Traction Company Ltd. The new company took over the employees of the original parent company who had worked in the traction sector, a total of around 5,100 people. MÁV-GÉPÉSZET Railway Vehicle Maintenance and Repairs Co. started its operations on 1 January 2008, too. The basic activities of this new company are the maintenance, repair and modernisation of railway rolling stock. The new unit has just over 5,000 employees. The mentioned above companies together with several small and medium-sized undertakings and the remaining MÁV Co. (Infrastructure, Finance, Property, Investment and Portfolio) form the so-called MÁV Group.

Due to the lack of adequate financial resources of its own, Hungary has tried to modernise its railway network and service level with the help of EU structural funds. The aims are higher speeds, electrification and the modernisation of the signalling system. The modernisation of passenger transport in Hungary has generated huge political and economic disputes. According to one opinion, there should be a more generous timetable based on regular interval, improvement of services, cooperation with other forms of public transportation and more competitive tariffs. At the other end are those who emphasise a reduction of costs, i.e. rationalisation, a general reduction of services and an increase in ticket prices.

Some specialists have been in favour of modernisation of the existing railway lines, providing a new and modern mission for the railway. They urged the creation of a level playing field for road and railway transport by the externalising railway costs and making up for the cancelled or postponed investments. They see the future of the railway passenger transport in the creation of the regular interval timetable system by ensuring more and better connections and a higher level of service. They also support the creation of alliances with other systems of light and heavy rail. To improve the condition of the track on branch lines, they advocated the use of discarded materials from the rebuilt main lines.[9]

However, the majority of the economists and foreign consultants urged the cutting back of the rail network, and a reduction of service by the closure of unprofitable lines. They judged the losses of the railway to be caused chiefly by the operation of branch lines, ignoring the fact that the losses were generated primarily in the traffic on the main lines and on European transit routes. These people's arguments were successful and their recommendations were adopted. But in effect the results show that the closing down of branch lines with low passenger traffic had virtually no positive impact on the overall costs of the railway system.

It must be regarded as a positive development that the Budapest Transport Association, which targets the suburban area of Budapest and is similar to transport systems already in place for many years in Western European regions and urban areas, was created by the Budapesti Közlekedési Zrt. (BKV Zrt.), Volánbusz Zrt. and MÁV Co. on 1 September 2005. The Association's goal is to provide viable solutions for public transport and a reduction of the well-known unfavourable effects of motorisation. Now holders of a combined pass called the Budapest Pass are entitled to board all commuter trains and buses within Budapest. The harmonisation of the tariffs and the timetables are still a problem that remains to be solved. But the Budapest Transport Association is commercially viable. According to transport experts the annual financial situation of the city needs the revenue of the Budapest Transport Association which is as high as the cost of building two kilometres of motorway.

Out in the countryside, the fundamentals of a transport association have not yet been worked out. In the field of public service, bus and railway transport are still competing and the intermodal points and the harmonisation of timetables are still lacking. The connection of small villages efficiently and economically to the transport network also needs to be solved. In recent years the advocates of rationalisation and reduction of services have had the upper hand: passenger fares were increased to the level of that of bus fares in 2007, and in the same year on 19, and in 2009 on 27 railway lines the passenger services were ended, on a total of 1,302 kilometres altogether. However, the expected savings failed to appear, and this policy led to the loss of many passengers and much revenue.[10]

There are burning questions on the future of the Hungarian railways that have not been properly addressed for years: how extensive should the network be? What should be the future of branch lines? The improvement of the main lines is clearly in the interest of the national economy, but the future of branch lines

---

[9]   See the contribution of Borza, Janos and Neumann, 'More is Less', in this volume.
[10]   MÁV Zrt. Vezérigazgatóság (ed.), *Magyar Vasúti Almanach* 2009 (Budapest 2009), 320.

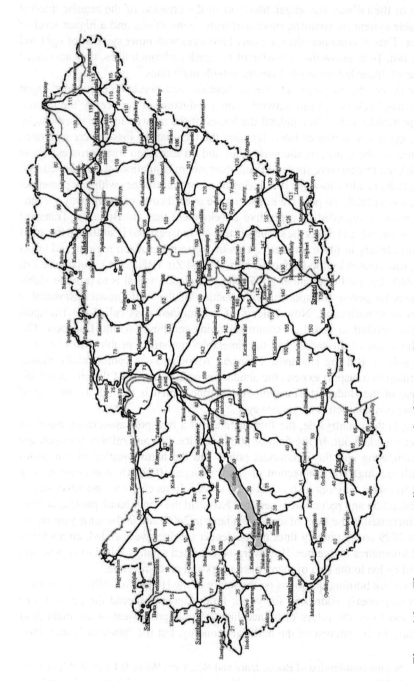

Figure 4.3   The passenger railway network of Hungary, 2010

Source: MÁV-START Co. (http://www.mav-start.hu/res/magyarorszag_vasuti_terkepe_2010–10–01.pdf, last accessed on 22 August 2012).

is more debatable. Options include modernisation, conservation, abolishing the passenger traffic temporarily or permanently, complete closure and re-activation. They could be operated as part of the united railway network, or as part of a regional network in cooperation with other modes of transportation. However, the required resources for all of these solutions are missing.

With the enlargement of the European Union in 2004 and the accession of Hungary and its neighbours in 2007, a new situation was created and a new question arose: what should be done with the many severed international railway connections in a united Europe? From Hungary there are now trains running every hour via Hegyeshalom and Sopron to Austria, and by way of Lőkösháza every two hours to Romania. However, at the other border points, to Serbia, Slovenia, Croatia, Slovakia and the Ukraine, an average of only two to five trains daily were running. At four of the eight border stations between Slovakia and Hungary, there is now no passenger traffic at all. With a little investment, direct railway connections could be re-established with Slovakia on the Nógrádszakál–Bušince, Ipolytarnóc–Lučenec, Tornanádaska–Košice, and Hont–Šahy lines. The same could be done with Romania between Battonya–Pecica and Körösnagyharsány–Oradea, and with Slovenia between Rédics–Lendava.

Hungary still has one of the most dense railway networks in Europe, although it is neglected and the resources for investment are lacking. Due to the severe competition from the road, fewer and fewer people choose the railway. There are two possible solutions: either the railway should be modernised and developed, or it should be closed down. The decision should be taken rationally without emotion and personal feelings. At the moment no one knows the total costs of road and rail transport. The current calculations are based on artificial cost and revenue structures. All costs in connection with rail transport have to be paid by the railway company, whereas the costs of road transport are partly paid by the community.

The history of the Hungarian railway shows that the future of the railway can only be ensured in the framework of European integration. A place has to be found for the existing network, and there is a pressing need for renewal of the infrastructure and rolling stock. Services must be improved and the results will surely come. At all times during the history of this railway system, inaction and the dismantling of infrastructure have brought only negative effects.

Conclusion

At the birth of the Hungarian railway network, the railway was able to develop without any competitors. The radial railway system with its centre at Budapest helped that city to become a major metropolitan and industrial centre. As the lines connecting the major towns 200 kilometres or more from Budapest were transferred to other countries, the importance of branch lines decreased, and the resources for their modernisation were not available. Furthermore, road development became a priority of the government. Today, railways in bad technical shape provide inadequate service. In the political debates of the first decade of the twenty-first century, the Hungarian railways – quite in contrast to those elsewhere in Europe – were seen as a losing proposition, especially the branch lines. While the Hungarian population may have remained emotionally railway-friendly, the slow trains, long journey times, high rates, poor service and infrastructure, the inadequate timetable and the unreliable traffic have led people to prefer other modes of transport.

The political decision-makers and economists should take the external costs of all modes of transport into consideration. They should create a transparent and clear situation by giving preference to public transport over individual transport. In order to maintain the service level of the Hungarian railways, 200 kilometres of the railway network should be modernised every year, 200 kilometres completely rebuilt, 70 new passenger carriages purchased, 70 passenger carriages modernised, 30 new engines purchased and another 30 modernised. In the twentieth century, these requirements were rarely fulfilled. The railway company lacked resources and the state did not provide them. These are the chief reasons for all the railway's problems, past and present. However, there is a good example in the history of the Hungarian railway: let us return to the ideas of Gábor Baross! This should be the thing to do now.

Bibliography

Heinczinger, István-Szabó András, *Vasút és közpolitika – Magyarország politikai évkönyve 2008-ról*, (ed.) DKMKA (Budapest 2009).

Kovács, László (ed.), *Geschichte der Ungarischen Eisenbahnen 1846–2000* (Budapest 2000).

MÁV Zrt. Vezérigazgatóság (ed.), *A magyar vasút krónikája a XIX. Században* (Budapest 2009).

MÁV Zrt. Vezérigazgatóság (ed.), *A magyar vasút krónikája a XX. Században* (Budapest 2005).

MÁV Rt. (ed.), *Magyar vasúttörténet*, 7 vols (Budapest 1996).

MÁV Zrt. Vezérigazgatóság (ed.), *Magyar Vasúti Almanach 2009* (Budapest 2009).

Magyar Államvasutak Rt. (ed.), *Vasúti Nagylexikon*, 2 vols (Budapest 2005).

Chapter 5
Czech Military Railways – History and a Comparative Analysis of the Czech Railway Network's Efficiency

Martin Kvizda

Introduction

At the present time, railway transport in the European Union is going through a renaissance, at least at the level of plans and goals of transport policy.[1] An indispensable core component of these reforms is the liberalisation and privatisation of transport services, which are believed to bring competitiveness to the railway industry. These principles are the basis of proposals, conceptions and strategies for reform of the railway industry's institutional structure in EU member countries, including the Czech Republic. The general instrument of the reform is the separation of operations from the administration and ownership of the infrastructure, the network of tracks with its necessary technological facilities. This separation is known as unbundling.[2] Competition is often viewed as an instrument per se: the ability of competition to promote efficiency of services is generally presupposed.[3] So unbundling is based on a competition for the market of train-operating companies as the general condition. These companies compete within a framework that is or should be formed by the railway network, separated from operations, and usually regulated and owned by the state.

---

[1] The text was prepared within the 'Competitiveness and Competition in Railway Transport – Opportunities and Limits of Economic Policy' project, supported by grant GAČR 402/08/1438.

[2] For more details, see European Commission, *White Paper – European Transport Policy for 2010: Time to Decide* (Brussels 2001), D. Seidenglanz, 'Vývoj železniční dopravy v Evropě a její pozice v evropské dopravní politice', *Národohospodářský obzor – Review of Economic Perspectives*, 4, 2005, 92–104 and J. Barrot, 'Rozvíjení železničního trhu', *Doprava – ekonomicko technická revue*, 6, 2005, 3–4.

[3] See A. Estache and G. de Rus, 'The Regulation of Transport Infrastructure and Services: A Conceptual Overview', in A. Estache and G. de Rus (eds), *Privatization and Regulation of Transport Infrastructure* (Washington, D.C. 2000), 5–50.

Unbundling, and the reforms based on it, is connected to several problems.[4] One of these is the fact that the railway network, created in the second half of the nineteenth century, may not cover the economically relevant destinations and directions relevant to our own time.[5] It is generally believed that these railway networks were formed on the basis of economic necessities, providing transport services and ensuring profits by supplying the demand in the regions they served. But this belief is not true for every railway line. At present when train-operating companies are about to compete for the market that was created by the railway network established 170 years ago, they ask the fundamental question: does the network offer something worth competing for? Economic efficiency in the railway industry does not depend on operational costs alone, but of course also on the costs of the network as well. Previous studies suggest that the efficiency of railway operations is connected with the shape of a railway network by means of economies of scale, economies of density, and network economies.[6] Many studies report that the density of transport is the major factor in turning a profit from railway operations, while other factors – economies of scale, network economies – are closely connected with, or simply based on, the density of transport.[7] That means that the network, its technical standards and shape, is a limiting factor for the railway industry's efficiency and competitiveness.

The issue at hand is not the technical condition of the infrastructure (even if the infrastructure is generally heavily underfunded, as it is in Eastern Europe); the issue, rather, is the network itself – its compactness, its shape, the points or places it connects, its capacity, whether the lines duplicate other ones, et cetera – and whether the network is suitable for the companies' business plans, and for potential customers who may want to consume its services. The bigger the gap between the network's limits and the companies' and customers' demands, the higher the level

---

[4]   See J.D. Bitzan, 'Railroad Costs and Competition: The Implications of Introducing Competition to Railroad Networks', *Journal of Transport Economics and Policy*, 37, 2003, 201–25, R. Pittman, 'Structural separation to create competition? The case of freight railways', *Review of Network Economics*, 3, 2005, 181–96 and M. Asmild, T. Holvad, J.L. Hougaard and D. Kronborg, 'Railway reforms: Do they influence operating efficiency?', *Transportation*, 36, 2009, 617–38.

[5]   M. Kvizda, 'Ekonomické dějiny železniční sítě České republiky – mýty, omyly a iluze v hospodářské politice a path dependence železných drah', Masaryk University, PhD, 2006, 66–73.

[6]   See the review by C. Nash, M. Wardman, K.J. Button and P. Nijkamp (eds), *Railways* (Cheltenham 2002), xiii–xxiii.

[7]   D.W. Caves, L.R. Christensen and J.A. Swanson, 'Productivity in U.S. railroads, 1951–1974', *Bell Journal of Economics*, 1, 1980, 166–81, C. Winston, 'Conceptual developments in the economics of transportation: An interpretative survey', *Journal of Economic Literature*, 23, 1985, 57–94, M.L. Katz and C. Shapiro, 'Network externalities, competition, and compatibility', *The American Economic Review*, 3, 1985, 424–40, and P. Cantos, 'A subadditivity test for the cost function of the principal European railways', *Transport Reviews*, 20, 2000, 275–90.

of the network's operational inefficiency. In regard to transport policy, the level of this inefficiency correlates to the sum paid out from public budgets to rebuild and improve railway infrastructure. Some current studies analyse network suitability using large-scale demand models, and others identify problems relating to the models used.[8] My aim here is not to criticise the models, but rather to analyse the historical reasons for the inefficiency of some lines, and to explain differences among the potential effectiveness of some parts of the railway networks. The case of the Czech railway network is presented.

The principal method used here is to apply the principle of path dependence to railway transport, just like this principle is used in the works of Paul A. David, W. Brian Arthur, Douglas J. Puffert and Zdeněk Tomeš.[9] The concept of path dependence of economic processes emerged in economics literature in the 1980s and 1990s.[10] Later the term appeared more frequently in popularised texts, its use becoming sufficiently widespread to lead Brian Arthur to define the concept in terms of a 'lock-in by historical events'. All economic processes to a certain degree are influenced by their own history; they can depend on their own previous development. This concept can explain present market failures which otherwise cannot be accounted for by the economic theory.

The hypothesis to be examined requires a look at the empirical evidence of path dependency in the Czech railway network: some lines of the Czech network were originally established for other than economic reasons, and at present, these non-economic reasons are influencing the performance of the lines. The aim of the commentary is to identify the former so-called military lines – those lines constructed in a different geopolitical situation and clearly for military purposes – and raise the question of their importance and potential effectiveness today. The

---

[8] See also L. Kane and R. del Mistro, 'Changes in transport planning policy: Changes in transport planning methodology?', *Transportation*, 30, 2003, 113–31, B. Flzvbjerg, M.K.S. Holm and S.L. Buhl, 'Inaccuracy in traffic forecasts', *Transportation Review*, 1, 2006, 1–24, A. Talvitie, 'Model, process, technique, and the good thing', *Transportation*, 35, 2008, 375–93, and P. Timms, 'Transport models, philosophy and language', *Transportation*, 35, 2008, 395–410.

[9] See P.A. David, 'Path Dependence and Predictability in Dynamic Systems with Local Network Externalities: A Paradigm for Historical Economics', in D. Foray and C. Freeman (eds), *Technology and the Wealth of Nations: The Dynamics of Constructed Advantage* (London 1993), 208–25, W.B. Arthur, *Increasing Returns and Path Dependence in the Economy* (Ann Arbor 1994), D.J. Puffert, 'Path dependence in spatial networks: The standardization of railway track gauge', *Explorations in Economic History*, 39, 2002, 282–314, and Z. Tomeš, 'Applying the life-cycle theory: The rise and fall of railways', *The Journal of Transport History*, 1, 2008, 120–24, and S.J. Liebowitz and S.E. Margolis, 'Dependence, lock-in and history', *Journal of Law, Economics, and Organization*, 11, 1995, 205–26.

[10] A good review is provided by Stanley J. Liebowitz and Stephen E. Margolis, Path Dependence, Lock-in and History, http://www.utdallas.edu/~liebowit/paths.html (last accessed 18 August 2012).

problem is relevant because the Czech Republic, as mentioned above, is currently engaged in carrying out reforms to improve the efficiency and competitiveness of railway transport. Once these lines are identified, the transport density on them is compared with the transport density on the rest of the network. It appears these lines have a considerably lower transport density, making parts of the network less efficient and competitive. The study offers an alternative view of railway transport's performance, aiming to stimulate the current debate on economic policy and regulation of the railway industry.

Principles of Railway Building

Analysing various railway networks today, quite interesting questions arise. Why were some lines constructed at all? Were the operations efficient at the time of the network origin? Were profitable operations on them ever possible? Who was so enthusiastic about building a railway in hilly terrain just to connect a few sleepy villages? A wealth of material in railway history helps us arrive at answers. Generally speaking, railway networks were created in three ways: first, the state planned lines and then built tracks of its own, and with its own money; second, the state gave orders and licences to private companies to build tracks according to the state's plans; and third, the state gave privileges to private companies to plan, build and run railways without any restrictions on route planning. In continental Europe, starting in the middle of the nineteenth century the state usually combined all these approaches to network creation, but the first prevailed.

From the beginning of the railway industry, private railway companies aimed at their own business goals, trying to compete and win within the transport market and increase their worth. However, in the railway transport market, the competition, profit and efficiency were not always common. The history of railways around the world shows that the profitability of services was very different – even among similar but different lines in the same country in the same time. The reason for this was that only parts of railway lines were built by private companies to make a profit; these contrast with lines built by the state or by private companies by order of the state to support political goals, among which were strategic military plans. The building of railways ordered by the state resulted in a mixed railway network: part of it was highly profitable, the other part less profitable or even losing money. Governments contracted railway companies to build some lines with little economic functionality but great strategic importance.[11]

Nineteenth-century Austria is a good example of a country building military railways. The military lines that appeared within the Austrian network doubled existing older lines and served strategic border regions. Most of these went across hilly areas and operated at high costs, creating little if any profit. The

---

[11]   See E.A. Pratt, *The Rise of Rail-Power in War and Conquest, 1833–1914* (London 1915), 1–13, or J. Westwood, *Railways at War* (London 1980), 88–93.

important fact for the Czech territory was that Austria bordered three German states: friendly Bavaria in the southwest, friendly Saxony in the northwest and hostile Prussia in the north.

The general problem of a military railway's performance can be shown through the example of the Czech Republic. The territory of the present Czech Republic went through several major changes; it had belonged to the Austrian empire for centuries when the first Czechoslovak Republic was constituted in 1918; in 1993, the Czech Republic was created by splitting up the former Czechoslovakia. The Czech railways are among the oldest on the continent: 95 per cent of the railways were built from 1828 to 1914 under the Austrian empire. The density of the Czech network is one of the highest in the world, and the current Czech Republic's railway heritage contains a significant percentage of former Austrian military lines.

Military Lines

Private railways were built in Austria at the very beginning of the railway age – between 1828 and 1841 – without any state subsidy. The state licensed the railways without any restrictions or requests for route planning; the first lines were clearly built with regard to economic criteria, connecting the most important cities that were the hubs of the economy. The first railway was built between České Budějovice[12] and Linz in 1828, crossing the Danube–Elbe watershed. In 1839 the next railway, the Kaiser-Ferdinands-Nordbahn (KFNB), connected Vienna with Brno. This railway became one of the biggest private enterprises on the continent; finished in 1855, the line connected Vienna with Bochnia via Ostrava and Kraków.

At the beginning of the 1840s, the state completely changed its policy towards the railways: the empire's authorities decided to build the railway network themselves, with the empire's own money. The first state trunk line was opened in 1841 and connected Praha with Vienna via Olomouc. The next line was opened in 1849, and shortened the journey between the same end points by going through Brno. The last state line was opened in 1850, connecting Praha with Dresden via Podmokly, and connecting Vienna, the capital of Austria, with Dresden, the capital of Saxony. For the Czech network, these lines constituted a real transport backbone of the east-west economy, intersecting and connecting the major north–south line from Vienna to Kraków.

In 1850, an important and consequential affair occurred. The Punctation of Olmütz was a treaty between Prussia and Austria, according to which Prussia gave up its claim for leadership of the German Confederation (*Deutscher Bund*), which at that time was dominated by Austria. Nevertheless, Prussia had a powerful and well-trained army, and was inclined to start a war against Austria. The Austrian military authorities decided to prepare for a war, and moved troops and requisite

---

[12]   To avoid misunderstanding see Table 5.4 – both the Czech and German names of local sites are documented there.

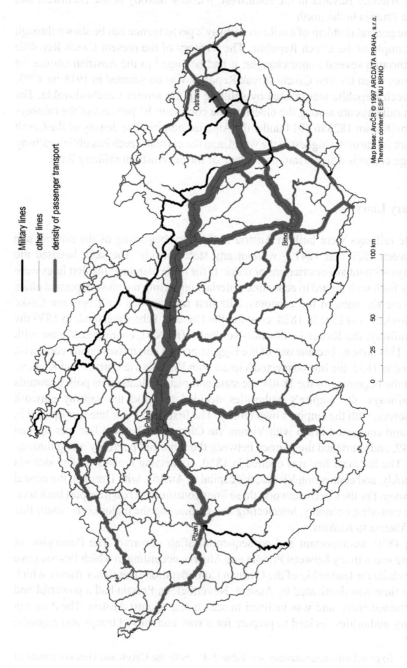

Figure 5.1   Density of passenger transport on the Czech railway network and military lines, 2002 (passengers/kilometres – relatively)

Source: Created by the author on data taken from Czech Railways, NATURAL2000 database (Praha 2000).

Military lines
other lines
density of passenger transport

Praha
Plzeň
Brno
Ostrava

0   25   50   100 km

support by train towards the borders to deter the enemy. Austria was able to move 75,000 men and 8,000 horses some 230 kilometres to the northern border with Prussia in 26 days. It was not just the speed of the deployment that was important: it was also that the troops were in much better condition after riding the trains than they would have been if they had gone on foot. The Austrian strategy worked, and Prussia saw that Austria would be victorious if it came to war.

The leaders in the Austrian military recognised that the railway was an important military tool. In 1851, the Austrian army organised another great manoeuvre, moving 14,500 men, 2,000 horses, 48 cannons and 464 wagons from Kraków to Uherské Hradiště, a distance of 280 kilometres, in two days.[13] Moving troops on railways now became a fundamental of military strategy. Nevertheless, at the same time, the state stopped funding the construction of railways due to financial difficulties.

The next stage of building private railways began in 1855, but thereafter the state would influence the routing of private lines according to political and strategic concerns. For example, an order was enacted requiring that a railway passing an imperial military stronghold had to make a stop there. The first railway built under this rule was opened in 1859: the line of Süd-norddeutschen Verbindungsbahn (SNDVB) connecting Pardubice and Liberec. The line had to go from Pardubice to the north to reach the strategic stronghold of Josefov, and only after calling there was it allowed continuing westward to Liberec.[14] The line did not traverse the shortest connection, and had higher construction and operating costs. In return, the state supported the railway company with a guarantee of a minimal gain from invested capital (5 per cent), a direct subsidy and purchase of railway shares.

Even if in 1850 the Austrian military leaders recognised the importance of railways for transport of troops and supplies during wartime in connection with the Punctation of Olmütz, the importance of railways increased even further after Austria lost a war against Prussia in 1866.[15] Prussia strongly boosted the military usage of railways during the 1850s and 1860s; in 1864, during the war against Denmark, the Prussian army moved 15,500 men and 4,600 horses 280 kilometres from Minden to Hamburg on 42 trains in six days. This transfer showed that congestion during loading and unloading was the biggest problem, and the Prussians learnt from it. They established specialised railway troops and rail repair units so that Prussia was able to more effectively use their railways in the 1866 war against Austria and open a 300-kilometre-long front. In three weeks, they deployed 200,000 men and 55,000 horses.[16] The success

---

[13]   See Pratt, *The Rise of Rail-Power*, 9, and Westwood, *Railways at War* (London 1980), 9.

[14]   P. Schreier, *Zrození železnic v Čechách, na Moravě a ve Slezsku* (Praha 2004).

[15]   Westwood, *Railways at War*, 55, and J. Hons, M. Hlavačka, Z. Maruna and K. Zeithammer, *Čtení o Severní dráze Ferdinandově* (Praha 1990), 120.

[16]   Westwood, *Railways at War*, 56–8.

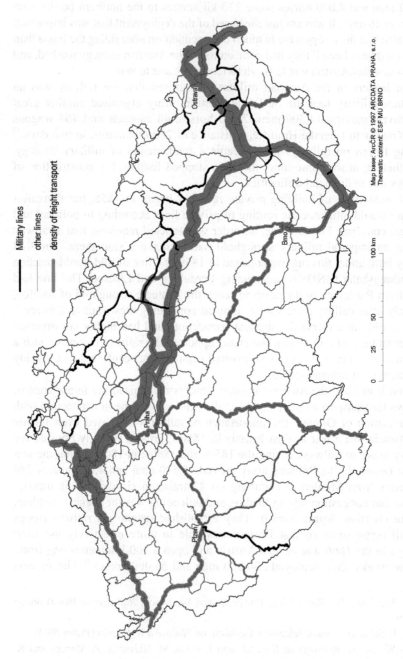

Figure 5.2   Density of freight transport on the Czech railway network and military lines, 2002 (tons/kilometres – relatively)

Source: Created by the author on data taken from Czech Railways, NATURAL2000 database (Praha 2000).

Military lines
other lines
density of feight transport

Praha
Plzeň
Brno
Ostrava

Map base: ArcČR © 1997 ARCDATA PRAHA, s.r.o.
Thematic content: ESF MU BRNO

0   25   50   100 km

of the invasion was based in part on a sufficiently well-routed Prussian railway network in the border regions. Such expert strategic planning was missing in the Austrian railways of that time.

The lost war ended the complacency, and the absence of foresight was recognised by the state. Austria soon contracted railway companies to build several lines that bolstered Austria's defences – in particular, two lines that ran to the strategic Lichtenau Pass. The construction of these lines had a straightforward reason: in the name of the so-called 'Prague Peace', Prussia required Austria to build a new connecting railway across their mutual border, enabling transportation of Prussian goods to southern ports and vice versa. On the other hand, the Austrian military saw that it was in its own self-interest to build a railway towards Prussian border – in case it became necessary to transport troops. The first line to Lichtenau Pass was built by the private company Mährische Grenzbahn (MGB) and opened in 1873. The line goes from Šternberk, via Šumperk and Bludov to Lichkov, a total distance of 95 kilometres. Though the state did not compel the building of this line directly, the construction was heavily affected and supported by the state.

The other line built towards the Lichtenau Pass was constructed by Österreichische Nordwestbahn (ÖNWB), a company that had operated very successful and profitable lines since 1871. When in 1874 the company asked for a licence to build an extension of its line from Nymburk via Litoměřice to Děčín, the state compelled the ÖNWB to build another line connecting Hradec Králové via Letohrad with Lichkov, coupled with a line connected to Ústí nad Orlicí on the trunk railway line.[17] These lines (a total distance of 97 kilometres), together with the MGB line, not only created an important strategic railway along the northern border, but also duplicated and backed up the trunk line from Olomouc to Praha. Rather than developing other additional lines towards Prussia that might be used for invasion, Austria instead built several lines to reinforce the vital connection to its allies, the kingdoms of Bavaria and Saxony. In 1870 the company Eisenbahn Pilsen-Preisen-Komotau (EPPK) asked for a licence to build a new line from Plzeň towards the north Bohemian coal mines close to Chomutov. In granting the licence, the state compelled the EPPK to build, on its own expense, another line from Plzeň via Klatovy to Železná Ruda on the Bavarian frontier, a total distance of 97 kilometres. Even though neither the EPPK nor any other company wanted to build a line like that, because only low transport density was anticipated for it, the Plzeň and Železná Ruda line was completed in 1877.[18] In 1872–73 the same rationale led the state to compel the company Böhmische Nordbahn (BNB) to build two very short lines in the border region of Czech-Saxon; earlier, in 1870, they had already compelled the private company Staatseisenbahngesellschaft (StEG) to build a short but strategic line between Znojmo and Hrušovany and Jevišovka, a distance of 26 kilometres. All

---

[17] See S. Hendrych, *Stopou dějin železnic v Podorlicku* (Hradec Králové 1987).

[18] See Schreier, *Zrození železnic v Čechách* (Praha 2004), 140.

of these railways went across hilly areas with little economic importance, and involved high operating costs.

One of the longest duplicate strategic lines built for military reasons doubled one section of the old line from Vienna to Kraków. The licence for the KFNB Vienna and Kraków line expired in 1886, leading the company to ask for a renewal. The state took advantage of the occasion and required the KFNB to build a new strategic railway at its own expense. The new line duplicated the old KFNB line along the section which went close to the Prussian border, from Kojetín via Hulín and Valašské Meziříčí to Český Těšín, a total distance of 102 kilometres. To accomplish this, the KFNB had to build five other local lines to intensify the transport network in this strategic border region – Suchdol nad Odrou and Budišov nad Budišovkou, Suchdol nad Odrou and Fulnek, Studénka and Bílovec, Hostašovice and Nový Jičín, Opava and Svobodné Heřmanice – and another line in the southern region to connect to Hungary via Rohatec, a total distance of 98 kilometres.[19] The KFNB was not eager to build such branch lines because operational losses were expected.[20] In this way the state used private capital to build fallback railway lines.

Comparison and Conclusion

The list of all the military lines in the territory of present the Czech Republic is shown in Table 5.1. These lines were built between 1859 and 1892; their total distance is 717 kilometres. We can easily see a disparity when measuring the density of transport on the Czech railway network (the relative volume of transport flow on particular lines as ratios of tons/kilometre or passengers/ kilometre is shown at Figure 5.1 and 5.2; the exact transport data are displayed in Tables 5.2 and 5.3 below). Given the railway reform currently underway, it is important to take into account the historical circumstances of the origins of particular lines. This may support the hard work of predicting the effect of privatisation and liberalisation on the service's efficiency. Even when the generally positive influence of competition is obvious, its effects work differently in each instance within the network. A background analysis of the lines' origin can help to understand these differences and predict potential changes in demand for transport services.

---

[19]   See J. Hons, *Šťastnou cestu* (Praha 1961), 74, and Hons, Hlavačka, Maruna and Zeithammer, *Čtení o Severní dráze Ferdinandově* (Praha 1990), 120–22.

[20]   Hons, Hlavačka, Maruna and Zeithammer, *Čtení o Severní dráze Ferdinandově* (Praha 1990), 159.

Table 5.1   Military railways in the Czech Republic

Line	Railway company	Year of opening	Distance km
Pardubice–Liberec	SNDVB	1859	161
Hrušovany nad Jevišovkou–Znojmo	StEG	1870	26
Česká Lípa–Benešov	BNB	1872	20
Rumburk–Mikulášovice	BNB	1873	21
Šternberk–Lichkov	MGB	1873	95
Ústí nad Orlicí–Lichkov	ÖNWB	1874	35
Hradec Králové–Letohrad	ÖNWB	1874	62
Plzeň–Klatovy–Železná Ruda	EPPK	1877	97
Frýdek-Místek–Český Těšín	KFNB	1888	27
Bystřice pod Hostýnem–Frýdlant nad Ostravicí	KFNB	1888	66
Kojetín–Kroměříž	KFNB	1888	9
Hostašovice–Nový Jičín	KFNB	1889	10
Rohatec–Skalica	KFNB	1889	7
Suchdol nad Odrou – Budišov nad Budišovkou	KFNB	1891	39
Suchdol nad Odrou–Fulnek	KFNB	1891	10
Studénka–Bílovec	KFNB	1891	7
Opava–Svobodné Heřmanice	KFNB	1892	25
Total			**717**

Note: M. Hlavačka, *Dějiny dopravy v českých zemích v období průmyslové revoluce* (Praha 1990), 103, Z. Hudec et al. (eds), Atlas drah *České* republiky 2004–2005 (Praha 2004), I. Jakubec and Z. Jindra (eds), *Dějiny hospodářství českých zemí od počátku industrializace do konce habsburské monarchie* (Praha 2006), 254, S. Pavlíček, *Naše lokálky. Místní dráhy v Čechách, na Moravě a ve Slezsku* (Praha 2002), 144, P. Schreier, *Zrození železnic v Čechách, na Moravě a ve Slezsku* (Praha 2004), 236.

Table 5.2   Density of passenger transport in 2002

Military lines	passengers/ kilometres (pkm)	Distance km	pkm/km
Pardubice–Liberec	83,682	161	520
Hrušovany n. J.–Znojmo	13,318	26	512
Česká Lípa–Benešov n. P.	12,079	20	604
Rumburk–Mikulášovice	3,992	21	190
Šternberk–Lichkov	45,216	95	476
Ústí n. O.–Lichkov	10,363	35	296
Hradec Králové–Letohrad	57,709	62	930
Plzeň–Železná Ruda	36,693	97	378
Frýdek-Místek–Český Těšín	24,189	27	895
Bystřice p. H.–Frýdlant n. O.	43,476	66	657
Kojetín–Kroměříž	13,689	9	1,521
Hostašovice–Nový Jičín	752	10	75
Rohatec–Skalica	5,017	7	717
Suchdol n. O.–Budišov n. B.	3,389	39	87
Suchdol n. O.–Fulnek	253	10	25
Studénka–Bílovec	660	7	94
Opava–Svobodné Heřmanice	5,932	25	237
Main trunk lines			
Praha–Přerov	1,301,084	320	4,065
Přerov–Bohumín	314,235	106	2,964
Brno–Česká Třebová	214,315	93	2,304
Praha–Děčín	420,757	139	3,027
Praha–Plzeň	356,428	130	2,741

Source: ČD Telematika a.s.

Inefficient and/or duplicate lines appeared within the Czech network. The major problem of these lines, their operational inefficiency, derives from the fact that the original motivation for being planned and built was essentially strategic and not economic. Comparing the density of transport on the Czech railway network, we can see the differences among the lines. There is low transport density on all of the identified military railways. This finding corresponds to the initial hypothesis: if a given line was built for non-economic strategic reasons, the line at present has low transport density. One closing *caveat*: I have presupposed that the deficiency of particular lines was affected by circumstances of their origin, but I have not claimed that the historical method is without obvious limitations in solving the problems of the railway networks. Discussion of these limitations is beyond the scope of this study, but the issues raised here warrant further investigation. The railway problem is a complex one; in analysing networks, we should take into account their path dependence. Overall, the conclusions presented here may have quite important implications for development of transport policy.

Table 5.3   Density of freight transport in 2002 (tons/kilometres – millions tkm, kilometres – km)

Military lines	tons/ kilometres (tkm)	Distance km	tkm/km
Pardubice–Liberec	53.30	161	0.33
Hrušovany n. J.–Znojmo	16.10	26	0.62
Česká Lípa–Benešov n. P.	6.71	20	0.34
Rumburk–Mikulášovice	0.21	21	0.01
Šternberk–Lichkov	10.40	95	0.11
Ústí n. O.–Lichkov	49.90	35	1.42
Hradec Králové–Letohrad	89.90	62	1.45
Plzeň–Klatovy–Železná Ruda	5.59	97	0.06
Frýdek-Místek–Český Těšín	0.65	27	0.02
Bystřice p. H.–Frýdlant n. O.	7.91	66	0.12
Kojetín–Kroměříž	0.62	9	0.07
Hostašovice–Nový Jičín	0.01	10	0.00

continued

Table 5.3　*concluded*

Military lines	tons/ kilometres (tkm)	Distance km	tkm/km
Rohatec–Skalica	0.00	7	0.00
Suchdol n. O.–Budišov n. B.	1.45	39	0.04
Suchdol n. O.–Fulnek	0.04	10	0.00
Studénka–Bílovec	0.01	7	0.00
Opava–Svobodné Heřmanice	1.12	25	0.04
Main trunk lines			
Břeclav–Přerov	872.90	101	8.64
Přerov–Bohumín	1,649.00	106	15.56
Přerov–Nymburk	3,219.00	279	11.53
Nymburk–Děčín	2,265.00	141	16.06
Praha–Plzeň	325.80	130	2.50

Source: ČD Telematika a.s.

Table 5.4　　Czech and German names of local sites

Czech names (in present time)	German names (in present time)	Czech names (in time of opening of a line)	German names (in time of opening of a line)
Benešov nad Ploučnicí	Bensen	Lichkov	Lichtenau
Bílovec	Wagstadt	Litoměřice	Leitmeritz
Bludov	Blauda	Mikulášovice	Nixdorf
Bochnia	Salzberg	Nový Jičín	Neutitschein
Brno	Brünn	Nymburk	Nimburg
Budišov nad Budišovkou	Bautsch	Olomouc	Olmütz
Bystřice pod Hostýnem	Bistritz / Hostein	Opava	Tropau

Chomutov	Komotau	Ostrava	Ostrau
České Budějovice	Budweis	Pardubice	Pardubitz
Český Těšín	Teschen	Plzeň	Pilsen
Děčín	Tetschen	Podmokly	Bodenbach
Frýdek-Místek	Friedek	Praha	Prag
Frýdlant nad Ostravicí	Friedland	Rohatec	Rohatetz
Fulnek	Fulneck	Rumburk	Rumburg
Hostašovice	Hostaschowitz	Skalica	Szakolca
Hradec Králové	Königgrätz	Studénka	Stauding
Hrušovany nad Jevišovkou	Grusbach	Suchdol nad Odrou	Zauchtel
Hulín	Hullein	Svobodné	Frei Heřmanice Hermersdorf
Josefov	Josefstadt	Šternberk	Sternberg
Klatovy	Klattau	Šumperk	Mährische Schönberg
Kojetín	Kojetein	Uherské Hradiště	Hradisch
Kraków	Krakau	Ústí nad Orlicí	Wilden schwert
Kroměříž	Kremsier	Valašské Meziříčí	Wallachisch Meseritsch
Letohrad	Geiersberg	Znojmo	Znaim
Liberec	Reichenberg	Železná Ruda	Eisenstein

Source: Created by the author.

Bibliography

Asmild, M., Holvad, T., Hougaard, J.L. and Kronborg, D., 'Railway reforms: Do they influence operating efficiency?', *Transportation*, 36, 2009, 617–38.

Arthur, W.B., *Increasing Returns and Path Dependence in the Economy* (Ann Arbor 1994).

Barrot, J., 'Rozvíjení železničního trhu', *Doprava – ekonomicko technická revue*, 6, 2005, 3–4.

Bitzan, J.D., 'Railroad costs and competition. The implications of introducing competition to railroad networks', *Journal of Transport Economics and Policy*, 37, 2003, 201–25.

Cantos, P., 'A subadditivity test for the cost function of the principal European railways', *Transport Reviews*, 20, 2000, 275–90.

Caves, D.W., Christensen, L.R. and Swanson, J.A., 'Productivity in U.S. Railroads, 1951–1974', *Bell Journal of Economics*, 1, 1980, 166–81.

Czech Railways, *NATURAL2000 database* (Praha 2000).

David, P.A., 'Path Dependence and Predictability in Dynamic Systems with Local Network Externalities: A Paradigm for Historical Economics', in D. Foray and C. Freeman (eds), *Technology and the Wealth of Nations: The Dynamics of Constructed Advantage* (London 1993), 208–25.

Estache, A. and Rus, G. de, 'The Regulation of Transport Infrastructure and Services: A Conceptual Overview', in A. Estache and G. de Rus (eds), *Privatization and Regulation of Transport Infrastructure* (Washington, D.C. 2000), 5–50.

European Commission, *White Paper – European Transport Policy for 2010: Time to Decide* (Brussels 2001).

Flyvbjerg, B., Holm, M.K.S. and Buhl, S.L., 'Inaccuracy in Traffic Forecasts', *Transportation Review*, 1, 2006, 1–24.

Hendrych, S., *Stopou dějin železnic v Podorlicku* (Hradec Králové 1987).

Hlavačka, M., *Dějiny dopravy v českých zemích v období průmyslové revoluce* (Praha 1990).

Hons, J., *Šťastnou cestu* (Praha 1961).

Hons, J., Hlavačka, M., Maruna, Z. and Zeithammer, K., *Čtení o Severní dráze Ferdinandově* (Praha 1990).

Hudec, Z. et al. (eds), *Atlas drah České republiky 2004–2005* (Praha 2004).

Jakubec, I. and Jindra, Z. (eds), *Dějiny hospodářství českých zemí od počátku industrializace do konce habsburské monarchie* (Praha 2006).

Kane, L. and Mistro, R. del, 'Changes in transport planning policy: Changes in transport planning methodology?', *Transportation*, 30, 2003, 113–31.

Katz, M.L. and Shapiro, C., 'Network externalities, competition and compatibility', *The American Economic Review*, 3, 1985, 424–40.

Kvizda, M., 'Ekonomické dějiny železniční sítě České republiky – mýty, omyly a iluze v hospodářské politice a path dependence železných drah', Masaryk University, PhD 2006.

Liebowitz, S.J. and Margolis, S.E., 'Dependence, lock-in and history', *Journal of Law, Economics, and Organization*, 11, 1995, 205–26.

Nash, C., Wardman, M., Button, K.J. and Nijkamp, P. (eds), *Railways* (Cheltenham 2002).

Pavlíček, S., *Naše lokálky. Místní dráhy v Čechách, na Moravě a ve Slezsku* (Praha 2002).

Pittman, R., 'Structural separation to create competition? The case of freight railways', *Review of Network Economics*, 3, 2005, 181–96.

Pratt, E.A., *The Rise of Rail-Power in War and Conquest, 1833–1914* (London 1915).

Puffert, D.J., 'Path dependence in spatial networks: The standardization of railway track gauge', *Explorations in Economic History*, 39, 2002, 282–314.

Schreier, P., *Zrození železnic v Čechách, na Moravě a ve Slezsku* (Praha 2004).

Seidenglanz, D., 'Vývoj železniční dopravy v Evropě a její pozice v evropské dopravní politice', *Národohospodářský obzor – Review of Economic Perspectives*, 4, 2005, 92–104.

Talvitie, A., 'Model, process, technique and the good thing', *Transportation*, 35, 2008, 375–93.

Timms, P., 'Transport models, philosophy and language', *Transportation*, 35, 2008, 395–410.

Tomeš, Z., 'Applying the life-cycle theory: The rise and fall of railways', *The Journal of Transport History*, 1, 2008, 120–24.

Westwood, J., *Railways at War* (London 1980).

Winston, C., 'Conceptual developments in the economics of transportation: An interpretative survey', *Journal of Economic Literature*, 23, 1985, 57–94.

Chapter 6

The Royal Prussian Eastern Railway (Ostbahn) and its Importance for East–West Transportation

Jan Musekamp

As Jürgen Osterhammel has recently shown, the long nineteenth century was a time of radical change in all spheres of society.[1] Numerous innovations ushered in an irrevocable acceleration of globalisation. The revolution in transport and communication was of vital importance. It started with improved mail services and the construction of a modern road network, included the steamship and the telegraph, and would eventually cumulate in the development of a European railway system.[2] At first, the railway revolutionised transport in Great Britain and the United States, but continental Europe was not far behind. In the fifteen years that followed the construction of the first railway in a German state in 1835, a whole network was being built, including numerous connections to the neighbouring states. East of the Stettin (Szczecin)–Berlin–Breslau (Wrocław) line, though, railway construction lagged. Mainly due to a lack of private funds, the Prussian East and the Russian empire could be duly considered underdeveloped in terms of railway infrastructure.[3] Once they were established, railways often led to an unprecedented jump in a region's development and markedly influenced the relations between metropolitan centres and peripheral regions. Roland Cvetkovki has shown that this was the case in Russia.[4] The Royal Prussian Eastern Railway (Ostbahn), connecting Prussia's capital of Berlin with Eastern Prussia's capital of Königsberg (Kaliningrad), was the line that would revolutionise Prussia's East.[5]

---

[1] J. Osterhammel, *Die Verwandlung der Welt. Eine Geschichte des 19. Jahrhunderts* (Munich 2009).

[2] W. Kaschuba, *Die Überwindung der Distanz. Zeit und Raum in der europäischen Moderne* (Frankfurt am Main 2004), 78.

[3] I use the German geographic names of the nineteenth century, giving today's Polish/ Russian equivalent in brackets upon first mention. For developments after 1945, the current place names are given.

[4] R. Cvetkovski, *Modernisierung durch Beschleunigung. Raum und Mobilität im Zarenreich* (Frankfurt am Main 2006).

[5] Scientific literature on the Ostbahn is scarce: K. Born, *Die Entwicklung der Königlich Preußischen Ostbahn* (Berlin 1911); A. Piątkowski, *Kolej wschodnia w latach*

In 2007, German and Polish towns along the historic Royal Prussian Eastern Berlin-Königsberg Railway celebrated the 150th anniversary of its existence. The celebrations increased public interest (if only for a short time) in a run-down line that had been the most important route of Prussia's east–west transportation network some 100 years ago. What were the origins of the almost-forgotten former major transport axis? At the time, as in most states, railway construction in Prussia was a private business, and led to the development of a privately owned network, especially in the western half of the monarchy.[6] As the Rhineland was already industrialised and densely populated, investment in transportation was a lucrative business. As far as Prussia's eastern provinces were concerned, it had been possible to build only two major lines in the 1840s. Starting in 1843, the Berlin–Stettin Railway linked the capital to its natural harbour of Stettin – a line that would be extended to Posen (*Poznań*) five years later. In the same year, Silesia's capital, Breslau, was connected to Berlin when the Niederschlesisch-Märkische Eisenbahn was completed. Still, Eastern Prussia's capital of Königsberg, the monarchy's coronation city, could only be reached via a week-long stagecoach journey. As nearly no important cities were situated directly on a possible line between Berlin and Königsberg, the railway line's financing was problematic: private capital was not interested in the risky investment. On the other hand, more and more government authorities were convinced of the necessity to create a network of railway lines in all directions to ensure economic development and the ability to defend the state militarily. As early as the 1830s, visionary railway pioneers like the economist Friedrich List dreamt of railways connecting all European economies, thus preventing wars.[7] This optimistic dream of a peaceful world through railways did not come true. Nonetheless, the railway was one of the important carriers of globalisation, contributing to a dramatic rise in worldwide commerce (tenfold between 1850 and 1913).[8] The rising mobility of ever larger population groups was followed by an international exchange of ideas, technical and cultural innovation, workforce and tourists.[9] As awareness of these developments increased, in 1842 a memorandum concerning the Ostbahn claimed that it would be necessary to expand it to the Russian border to cope with the rising needs of east–west transportation. With military and economic interests merging, a solution to the financing problem needed to be found. Part of this was seen in the

---

1842–1880. Z dziejów transportu kolejowego na Pomorzu Wschodnim (Olsztyn 1996); recently, M. Przegiętka of Nicolas Copernicus University at Toruń is working on inter-war railway traffic between Eastern Pussia and the rest of Germany; please refer to his contribution in this volume.

[6]   R. Roth, *Das Jahrhundert der Eisenbahn. Die Herrschaft über Raum und Zeit 1800–1914* (Ostfildern 2005), 61–4.

[7]   L. Gall, 'Eisenbahn in Deutschland. Von den Anfängen bis zum Ersten Weltkrieg', in M. Pohl and L. Gall (eds), *Die Eisenbahn in Deutschland. Von den Anfängen bis zur Gegenwart* (Munich 1999), 13–70.

[8]   Osterhammel, *Die Verwandlung der Welt*, 1018, 1033.

[9]   Kaschuba, *Die Überwindung der Distanz*, 102.

state-owned railway fund, which allowed subsidising of private railway construction. In fact, only with its help was it possible in 1846 to start some essential works on the Vistula and Nogat rivers south of Danzig (Gdańsk), where a huge region had to be dyked. At Dirschau (Tczew) and Marienburg (Malbork), sophisticated bridges were planned, whose construction proved to be costly both with regard to time and money invested. The bridge at Dirschau is a good example of Europe-wide exchange of knowledge in the nineteenth century: planning this bridge, the architect Carl Lenze went on a voyage to Great Britain, where he studied the construction of the famous Britannia Bridge.[10]

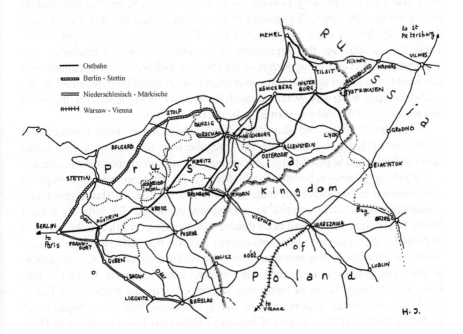

Figure 6.1   Railway map of the Ostbahn showing its development between 1842 and 1918

Source: Map created by Henry Jacolin.

King Friedrich Wilhelm IV himself decided to support the Eastern Railway as a state-owned enterprise, financed by public bonds. But when Friedrich tried to obtain the mandatory approval of his plan, the Prussian Estates (*Vereinigter Landtag*) rejected it. Most members of this quasi-parliament were supporters of the Eastern Railways, but just before the Revolution of 1848 they connected their

---

[10]   W. Ramm, 'Der Bau und das bewegte Schicksal der Dirschauer Brücke', in W. Ramm and C. Groh (eds), *Zeugin der Geschichte: die alte Weichselbrücke in Dirschau. Świadek przeszłości: Dawny most przez Wisłę w Tczewie* (Kaiserslautern 2004), 61–77.

approval with the King's granting of new political rights – a deal angrily rejected by the ruler, who ordered the complete cessation of construction work on the line.[11] It was only in 1849, after the granting of a constitution, that the newly elected Prussian parliament agreed upon the public bonds. From then on, construction work proceeded quickly.

After the completion of the bridges at Dirschau and Marienburg, which then qualified as major feats of engineering, the first train running from Berlin reached East Prussia's capital of Königsberg in 1857.[12] From then on, travellers and goods could be transported by train from Paris to East Prussia and vice versa. In 1858, more than 1 million passengers made use of the Ostbahn. The number rose tenfold during the next 30 years. The amount of goods transported developed even more dynamically from a mere 216,000 tons in 1857 to 16.5 million tons in 1884.[13] These figures illustrate the importance of the line for Prussia's economy – an importance that even the supporters of the Ostbahn had been sceptical about, as it had been thought that agricultural goods from Prussia could be transported by the well-developed waterway system at much lower costs. In the long term, the speed and reliability of the railway proved to be decisive factors.

After the Prussian and Russian railway networks had been connected at Eydtkuhnen (Chernyshevskoye) in 1861, regular train services were established between Berlin and St Petersburg. Concerning the transport of goods, the merchants of Insterburg (Chernyakhovsk) fought fiercely for this connection to improve their position in the important trade with the nearby Russian Baltic provinces. Simultaneously, Danzig wanted to re-establish economic ties with its natural Polish hinterland: the city had been Poland's Baltic Sea port prior to the partition of Poland at the end of the eighteenth century and was now suffering from the new borders and mediocre transportation conditions on the river Vistula. Consequently, in 1862 connections were created with Warsaw and Vienna via Thorn (Toruń). However, Danzig's hopes of being able to compete with the harbours of Trieste and Hamburg proved, with time, to be overly ambitious. With the completion of the Schneidemühl (Piła) – Konitz (Chojnice) – Dirschau (Tczew) shortcut in 1873, travelling between Berlin and Königsberg became even quicker, diminishing the importance of the line that ran through Bromberg (Bydgoszcz). After the completion of yet another bypass in the same year connecting Thorn (Toruń) via Osterode (Ostróda) and Allenstein (Olsztyn) with Insterburg (Chernyakhovsk), the latter gained major importance for the traffic of passengers to the southern part of East Prussia as well as for the traffic of goods to the Russian empire.[14]

---

[11]   Roth, *Das Jahrhundert der Eisenbahn*, 86–8.

[12]   Until 1867, train services followed the Berlin–Frankfurt (Oder) –Küstrin (Kostrzyn) –Schneidemühl (Piła) –Bromberg (Bydgoszcz) –Dirschau (Tczew) – Königsberg (Kaliningrad) route. In 1867 a shortcut was created between Berlin and Küstrin.

[13]   Born, *Die Entwicklung der Königlich Preußischen* Ostbahn, 135.

[14]   Ibid., 122.

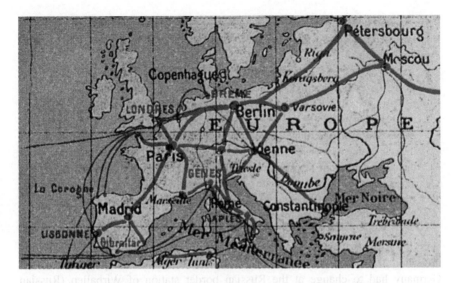

Figure 6.2   The International Sleeping Car Company network, 1904

Source: Collection of Albert Mühl and Jürgen Klein, in A. Mühl and J. Klein, Reisen in Luxuszügen. Die Internationale Schlafwagen-Gesellschaft. Die großen Expresszüge und Hotels. Geschichte und Plakate (Freiburg im Breisgau 2006), 157 (ill. 127).

Between 1896 and 1914, the famous Nord Express linked the French capital to the Russian one in 48 hours. In Paris, passengers had connecting trains to the French Riviera, London, Spain and Portugal. In Russia, travellers could easily change for the Trans-Siberian Railway, thus being able to continue their voyage to the Pacific and China. A Belgian businessman, Georges Nagelmaeckers, established a network of luxury railway connections between major European metropolises.[15] His Compagnie internationale des wagons-lits (International Sleeping Car Company) offered the most comfortable way to travel of the time – comparable to today's airlines. Most high-level private, economic and political contacts between Germany and France on the one side and the Russian empire on the other side were linked to the Nord Express. The Russian and Polish nobles made use of the line to reach the spas on the Mediterranean coast.[16] German nobles visited relatives in Russia or Great Britain. International companies from

---

[15]   Concerning the history of the International Sleeping Car Company and the Nord Express, please refer to A. Mühl and J. Klein, Reisen in Luxuszügen. Die Internationale Schlafwagen-Gesellschaft. Die großen Expresszüge und Hotels. Geschichte und Plakate (Freiburg im Breisgau 2006), 11–31, 112–16; on the Nordexpress: R. Commault, 'Le Nord-Express', La vie du rail, 1777, 1981, 9–14/ 1779, 1981, 46–9/ 1781, 1981, 41–5.

[16]   E. Razvozjaeva, 'L'Histoire du tourisme russe en France 1885–1914', Bulletin de l'Institut Pierre Renouvin, 25, 2007, 5–7.

Paris opened new offices in Berlin, Königsberg, St Petersburg and Moscow. The Russian writer Vladimir Nabokov describes his family's journeys with the Nord Express as follows:

> In the far end of my mind I can unravel, I think, at least five such journeys to Paris, with the Riviera or Biarritz as their ultimate destination. In 1909, the year I now single out, our party consisted of eleven people and one *Dachshund*. Wearing gloves and a travel cap, my father sat reading a book in the compartment he shared with our tutor. My brother and I were separated from them by a washroom. My mother and her maid Natasha occupied a compartment adjacent to ours. Next came my two small sisters, their English governess, Miss Livingston, and a Russian nurse. The odd one of our party, my father's valet, Osip (...) had a stranger for companion.[17]

With the Russian gauge ending at the German border at Eydtkuhnen, passengers travelling from Russia had to change trains there, whereas passengers from Germany had to change at the Russian border station of Wirballen (Russian *Verzhbolovo*, Lithuanian *Virbalis*). The German and Russian border stations became showcases of the two empires. Huge palace-like buildings and logistical facilities were created, serving not only passengers but also (and especially) the rising number of goods trains. All goods coming and going had to be unloaded and reloaded here. Not only official trade flourished at the time, but also smuggling – with significant parallels to the situation at today's Schengen borders. As a result, the border at Wirballen became a *topos* in Russian literature. The border town was the symbolic westernmost point of Russia and the symbolic easternmost point of Europe. Here, the civilised West seemed to clash with the uncivilised East.[18]

World War One and the Russian Revolution put an end to unlimited trans-European transport of people and goods. With Germany's new frontiers, the Ostbahn had to pass through Polish territory. One of the main aspirations of Poland's movement for independence had been access to the Baltic Sea. With the Treaty of Versailles, this request was fulfilled. As a result, Germany lost its direct land connection to its province of East Prussia. Poland's land bridge to the Baltic Sea, the so-called Polish Corridor, became a major issue in both Polish and German politics and led to territorial claims, especially on the German side. As the Weimar Republic did not accept its own Eastern borders, and Poland imposed high tariffs on transit, the number of services between the two Prussian metropolises of Berlin and Königsberg was significantly reduced, as was traffic to and from the Soviet Union. As a result, regular state-subsidised ferry connections between Germany's Baltic Sea harbours and Königsberg were established, the so-called *Seedienst Ostpreußen*. Germany and Poland settled the most important questions

---

[17]   V. Nabokov, *Speak, Memory: An Autobiography Revisited* (London 1999), 107–8.

[18]   Refer to Erenburg's poem of 1913: I.G. Erenburg, 'Rossii', in I.G. Erenburg, *Sobranie sochinenij*, vol. 1 (Moskva 1990), 28.

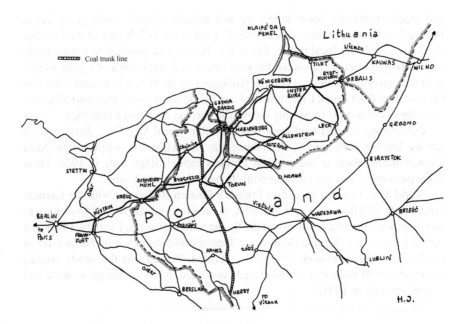

Figure 6.3   Railway map of the Ostbahn showing its development between 1920 and 1939

Source: Map created by Henry Jacolin.

of the transit problem in long and difficult talks that started in 1920 and led to an agreement in 1921. As a result of this agreement, railway services on the Ostbahn regained importance after July 1922. Both sides agreed on direct train services between Germany and East Prussia using sealed trains to avoid border and tariff controls on Polish territory. This was a great inconvenience for passenger traffic on the line.[19] Nevertheless, in the last years before the Second World War, eight fast passenger trains connected Berlin and Königsberg. Fifteen regular goods trains and up to nine occasional ones were established; as a result, the Ostbahn contributed substantially to Germany's preparation for the invasion of Poland.[20] At the time, Eastern Prussia underwent the construction of numerous new barracks

---

[19]   On Polish–German transit in the interwar period, please refer to M. Przegiętka, 'Der Transitverkehr durch Polen nach Ostpreußen in der Zwischenkriegszeit. Anlass für eine verstärkte Zusammenarbeit oder Ursache für den Zweiten Weltkrieg?', in Institut für angewandte Geschichte (ed.), *Die Ostbahn im Spiegel der Zeit. Eine Reise von Berlin nach Königsberg* (Frankfurt (Oder) 2010), 22–3, at http://www.kuwi.euv-frankfurt-o.de/de/lehrstuhl/kg/osteuropa/ forschungs-projekte/Projekt_Ostbahn/Ostbahn/Die_Ostbahn_im_Spiegel_der_Zeit_pdf.pdf (last accessed 22 December 2010).

[20]   Concerning the traffic on the line, please refer to the railway guides of the time.

and roads, sparking a boom in the region's underdeveloped economy. As far as Poland is concerned, it did not extensively exploit the Polish part of the line, but used it primarily for local traffic. The reborn Polish state invested in a completely new railway line that connected the coal mines and steelworks of Upper Silesia with the emerging harbour at Gdynia (Gdingen) on the Baltic Sea coast. This was the so-called Coal Trunk Line. It served as a major north–south transportation axis for Poland's economy, bypassing the nearby harbour of Gdańsk (Danzig).

Concerning international train services after World War One, direct regular service linking Paris and St Petersburg was not reinstated, while a new Nord Express linked Paris to independent Latvia's capital, Riga, only in 1926. From Riga, passengers had convenient connections to the Soviet Union.

World War Two put an end to Prussia's Eastern Railways. With the German border only 80 kilometres east of Berlin, the majority of the former Ostbahn was now in possession of the Polish and the Soviet State Railways. Until the 1970s, the border between the German Democratic Republic and Poland could not be crossed easily. For military reasons, the border between Poland and the newly created Soviet region of Kaliningrad was closed even more tightly to foreign visitors, and opened up only in 1991.

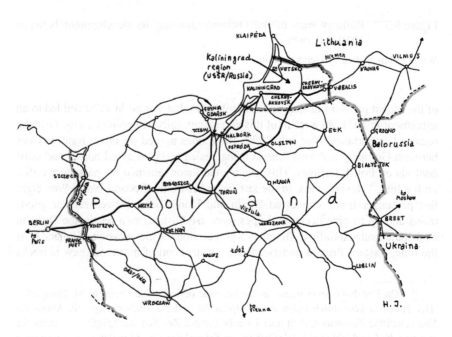

Figure 6.4   Railway map of the Ostbahn showing its development after 1945
            until today

Source: Map created by Henry Jacolin.

When passenger train services between Germany and the Soviet Union were renewed in the 1960s, it was no longer the historic route between Berlin, Königsberg and St Petersburg (Leningrad) that was in use. Beginning at the end of World War Two, a new east–west route was established from Berlin to Moscow through Warsaw and Brest. This then served as the main traffic artery between Eastern and Western Europe. The Ostbahn became one of the symbols of Germany's loss of its Eastern territories. The line served Soviet troops as important means of transport between garrisons in Berlin, Kostrzyn (Küstrin) and Kaliningrad. The Polish section of the former Ostbahn linked the new border town of Kostrzyn to the cities of Bydgoszcz (Bromberg), Gdańsk (Danzig) and Warsaw. The short German section served local transportation only. The Russian section between Kaliningrad and the Russian mainland was the only remaining part of any great importance, with the former connection of Imperial Germany with Imperial Russia still being Kaliningrad's most important link to Moscow and St Petersburg today.

When Kaliningrad was opened up to foreign visitors and trade in the beginning of the 1990s, railway service with Germany was renewed at a very low level. Until 2009, there was one daily through carriage running between Berlin and Kaliningrad on a regular basis. In 1939, the distance was covered in six and a half hours, while the average travelling time in 2009 was sixteen and a half hours. As a consequence, the Ostbahn is a good example of the stretching of space caused by new borders and severed railway lines – and illustrates the opposite of how Wolfgang Schivelbusch characterised early railway development, as an 'elimination of space and time'.[21]

What about the future of this historically important railway? Another important East–West axis – the Berlin–Warsaw Express, linking the German and Polish capitals – has undergone modernisation in the last years. It now crosses the 563 kilometres in less than six hours. This distance is comparable to the Berlin–Kaliningrad line (592 kilometres), though the latter is in a considerably worse condition. Parts of its Polish section between Kostrzyn and Bydgoszcz have undergone reconstruction; the line is due to be fully modernised in the near future. The German section is currently being modernised, as is the Russian section between Kaliningrad and the Russian-Lithuanian border. The latter has to serve the privileged transit of goods and passengers between the Kaliningrad exclave and the Russian mainland. Currently there are no signs on the horizon of a complete reconstruction or restoration befitting of the Ostbahn's former importance. As the line as a whole is running through three different countries (with the Schengen border dividing Russia from Poland), and, further, belongs to three different railway companies undergoing partial privatisation and regionalisation, reconstruction plans have to cope with significant obstacles. As the Berlin–Küstrin–Kostrzyn–Bydgoszcz trans-border connection is not part of the planned Trans-European Network (TEN), it will be modernised to serve trains running at 120 kilometres

---

[21] W. Schivelbusch, *Geschichte der Eisenbahnreise. Zur Industrialisierung von Raum und Zeit im 19. Jahrhundert* (Frankfurt am Main 1989), 35.

per hour maximum. This is far slower than the trains that ran on it prior to World War Two. As a consequence, no high-speed long-distance trains will serve the line, only regional trains. Its future importance depends on the good will of regional officials ordering public transport services.

But there are signs of hope. To promote rail service on the line, an Ostbahn European Interest Group has been founded. It acts as a German-Polish pressure group in local, regional, national and European politics, bundling the interests of towns and institutions between Berlin and Krzyż (Kreuz) – half the distance from Berlin to Kaliningrad. As the western Polish voivodship (province) of Lubuskie is once again part of the German capital's migrational hinterland, public interest in trans-border transportation is rising. For the anniversary celebrations in 2007, the big cities like Berlin, Bydgoszcz, Toruń and Kaliningrad did not organise conferences and expositions, but the small towns and even villages on both sides of the German-Polish border did. People in the region seem aware of their cultural heritage and of the prospects of revitalised direct connections to Berlin. At the moment, a couple of railway stations on both the German and the Polish sides are being modernised and adapted to commuter needs. With modernisation going on and EU programmes giving the green light, common technology is being installed on both sides of the border. Unfortunately, it seems that this positive development is limited to no more than half of the former line. The connection between Kaliningrad and Berlin as a whole is unlikely to be improved in the near future.

Bibliography

Born, K., *Die Entwicklung der Königlich Preußischen Ostbahn* (Berlin 1911).

Commault, R., 'Le Nord-Express', *La vie du rail*, 1777, 1981, 9–14/ 1779, 1981, 46–9/ 1781, 1981, 41–5.

Cvetkovski, R., *Modernisierung durch Beschleunigung. Raum und Mobilität im Zarenreich* (Frankfurt am Main 2006).

Erenburg, I.G., 'Rossii', in I.G. Erenburg, *Sobranie sochinenij*, vol. 1 (Moskva 1990).

Gall, L., 'Eisenbahn in Deutschland. Von den Anfängen bis zum Ersten Weltkrieg', in M. Pohl and L. Gall (eds), *Die Eisenbahn in Deutschland. Von den Anfängen bis zur Gegenwart* (Munich 1999), 13–70.

Kaschuba, W., *Die Überwindung der Distanz. Zeit und Raum in der europäischen Moderne* (Frankfurt am Main 2004).

Mühl, A. and Klein, J., *Reisen in Luxuszügen. Die Internationale Schlafwagen-Gesellschaft. Die großen Expresszüge und Hotels: Geschichte und Plakate* (Freiburg im Breisgau 2006).

Nabokov, V., *Speak, Memory: An Autobiography Revisited* (London 1999).

Osterhammel, J., *Die Verwandlung der Welt. Eine Geschichte des 19. Jahrhunderts* (Munich 2009).

Piątkowski, A., *Kolej wschodnia w latach 1842–1880. Z dziejów transportu kolejowego na Pomorzu Wschodnim* (Olsztyn 1996).

Przegiętka, M., 'Der Transitverkehr durch Polen nach Ostpreußen in der Zwischenkriegszeit. Anlass für eine verstärkte Zusammenarbeit oder Ursache für den Zweiten Weltkrieg?', in Institut für angewandte Geschichte (ed.), *Die Ostbahn im Spiegel der Zeit. Eine Reise von Berlin nach Königsberg* (Frankfurt (Oder) 2010), 22–3.

Ramm, W., 'Der Bau und das bewegte Schicksal der Dirschauer Brücke', in W. Ramm and C. Groh (eds), *Zeugin der Geschichte: die alte Weichselbrücke in Dirschau. Świadek przeszłości: Dawny most przez Wisłę w Tczewie* (Kaiserslautern 2004), 61–77.

Razvozjaeva, E., 'L'Histoire du tourisme russe en France 1885–1914', *Bulletin de l'Institut Pierre Renouvin*, 25, 2007, 5–7.

Roth, R., *Das Jahrhundert der Eisenbahn. Die Herrschaft über Raum und Zeit 1800–1914* (Ostfildern 2005).

Schivelbusch, W., *Geschichte der Eisenbahnreise. Zur Industrialisierung von Raum und Zeit im 19. Jahrhundert* (Frankfurt am Main 1989).

PART II
Under Russian Protection

Chapter 7

1918, 1945 and 1989: Three Turning Points in the History of Polish Railways in the Twentieth Century

Marcin Przegiętka

Introduction

In my chapter I would like to describe three turning points in the history of the Polish state railways in the twentieth century. Three dates – 1918, 1945 and 1989 – are essential for understanding the history of modern Poland: they mean political, economic and social changes. This contribution shows that these turning points impacted the railways too. The history of transportation is interconnected with the history of politics.[1]

In the middle of nineteenth century, when the railways were being built all over Europe, there was no independent Polish state. After the partitions of Poland at the end of eighteenth century, Polish territories were under the 'protection' of three countries: Russia, Germany and Austria. The lack of independence had not only political results but economic ones too. Polish provinces were borderlands of three monarchies. None of them wanted to allow the Polish territories to develop economically. Consequently, the development of railways was very limited, and depended on the economic and strategic needs of Moscow, Berlin and Vienna.[2]

The first railway built by Poles was the Warsaw–Vienna Railway (Droga Żelazna Warszawsko-Wiedeńska). In fact this line have not directly reached Vienna but ended in Maczki, on the border between Russia and Austria. It was a private initiative by Polish capitalists, and it opened in 1845, in the part of Russian domination.[3] Building of this line was initiated by two bank experts, Henryk Lord Łubieński

---

[1] M. Jarząbek and D. Keller, 'Rozdział wprowadzający', in D. Keller (ed.), *Dzieje kolei w Poslce* (Rybnik 2012), 13–59, here 13–14.

[2] See N. Davies, *Boże igrzysko: historia Polski*, 2 vols (Kraków 1996), vol. 2, 191. This book is available in English too: N. Davies, *God's Playground: A History of Poland*, vol. 2: 1795 to the Present (Oxford 2005).

[3] See S. Faecher and S. Peters, 'Początki polskich kolei', in S. Faecher and S. Peters (eds), *20 lecie komunikacji w Polsce odrodzonej* (Kraków 1939), 123–40, here 125.

and Piotr Steinkeller, the main engineer was Stanisław Wysocki.[4] At the time of the partitions Poles underlined the significance for this enterprise because in this way they were able to show the need of independence at least in the economic sphere. The next railways, which were built in the western part of Russian domination were mostly constructed by Poles, but all them were nationalised a few years before World War One. However, it was thought of as the first railway in Poland only until 1945. After World War Two, the Polish state acquired the formerly German territory of Lower Silesia, where the first railway line from Wrocław to Oława had been built in 1842, three years before the Warsaw–Vienna Railway. Nowadays this line is thought of as the first railway in Poland, i.e. the Poland within the borders which were established after 1945, whereas the Warsaw–Vienna railway was the first railway built and operated by a Polish public company.[5]

The development of railways in Polish territories was uneven. The highest density of railways was in the Polish territories under the hegemony of Germany and the lowest in the area under the hegemony of Russia. The Russian government did not allow the construction of many railways because of strategic considerations: the territory of West Russia was to be a 'communications desert', which in the event of war was intended to stop a potential offensive by the German army. Many cities were not linked by rail with the outside world. A good example is Płock, an administrative centre with a population of 30,000 people, which until 1925 did not have any rail connection. Another setback was the fact that two different gauges had been used for the main lines. In Austrian and German zones of Poland, only the standard gauge (1435 millimetres) was used. But in the Russian part of Poland, most of tracks were broad gauge (1524 millimetres), and the standard gauge was used only in a few lines on the west bank of the Vistula River.[6] Polish territory had been partitioned, and only a few lines crossed the borders between its separated parts. For example, Galicia (under the protection of Austria) had only two railway connections with the Kingdom of Poland (under the protection of Russia), but as many as eight with the rest of the Austrian Monarchy. There was a similar shortage of links between the Grand Duchy of Poznań (part of Poland under the protection of Germany) and Kingdom of Poland.

During World War One, a fairly large part of Poland was destroyed. The armies of Russia, Germany and Austria blew up many bridges (41 per cent of the total), viaducts, railway stations (61 per cent), locomotive sheds (48 per cent) and water towers (81 per cent). Some of these were rebuilt during the war, mostly out of

---

[4]   See H. Hilchen, *Historya drogi żelaznej Warszawsko-Wiedeńskiej 1835–1848–1898. Przyczynek do historyi kolejnictwa w Królestwie Polskiem* (Warszawa-Kraków 1912), 14–15.

[5]   See S. Koziarski, *Sieć kolejowa Polski w latach 1842–1918* (Opole 1993), 13.

[6]   See M. Krzysica, 'Rola czynników wojskowo-politycznych w budowie kolei żelaznych w Królestwie Polskim', in R. Kołodziejczyk (ed.), *Studia z dziejów kolei żelaznych w Królestwie Polskim (1840–1914)* (Warszawa 1970), 9–44, here 13–15, and M. Przegiętka, 'Historia kolei w Płocku', *Świat kolei*, 5, 2006, 17–23, here 17–20.

wood. But some still remained ruined after the war or needed reconstruction.[7] At the time of offensives in Kingdom of Poland, the German and Austrian armies built military railways with total length of about 2,000 kilometres.[8] Most of them were narrow gauge (mainly 600 and 750 millimetres). They were necessary to supply military units, and were constructed very quickly and provisionally: the station buildings and the bridges were wooden.[9]

1918: Poland Regains Its Independence and the Railway System Becomes Unified

The collapse of Germany, Austria-Hungary and Russia at the end of World War One created a situation in which an independent Polish state was reborn. Independence was declared on 11 November 1918, the same day the armistice was signed, and the Polish state started creating its own institutions, such as the Polish State Railways, Polskie Koleje Państwowe (PKP).

The Polish railways needed unification: there were three poorly interconnected networks of railways. Every separate part of Poland had different railway traffic regulations, because, for example, unlike other railway administrations in Central Europe, the Austrian ones mandated left-hand traffic.[10] In independent Poland, there were as many as 165 different types of locomotives and 66 types of rails. The railways and their unification was an extremely serious issue, because other systems of transport did not count at that time. The road transport was less developed because of shortage of paved roads and the river navigation has a secondary meaning because only a few sections of Polish rivers were navigable. As a result of the partitions, it was not only the railways that needed rapid unification: the newly united parts of Poland had different taxes, currencies, economic guidelines and laws. The borders had to be delineated, the structures of administration had to be created, the army had to be organised. These tasks had to be carried out under extremely difficult conditions, because the Polish–Soviet War lasted until 1920, and minor border conflicts persisted until 1921.[11] Between 1915 and 1920, the gauge of railways in eastern Poland was changed three times: first by the Germans after their offensive during World War One, second by the Soviets during the Polish–Soviet War and third by Poles after defeating the Soviets.[12] The reconstruction and development of

---

[7]   See B. Hummel, 'Odbudowa i utrzymanie kolei', in S. Faecher and S. Peters (eds), *20 lecie komunikacji w Polsce odrodzonej* (Kraków 1939), 141–62, here 141–43.

[8]   See B. Pokropiński, *Koleje wąskotorowe PKP* (Warszawa 1980), 18.

[9]   See B. Pokropiński, *Kujawskie Koleje Dojazdowe* (Poznań 1994), 15–21.

[10]   See Koziarski, *Sieć kolejowa 1842–1918*, 167.

[11]   See N. Davies, *Orzeł biały, czerwona gwiazda. Wojna polsko-bolszewicka 1919–1920* (Kraków 2000). It has been also published in English before: N. Davies, *White Eagle, Red Star: The Polish–Soviet War, 1919–20* (London 1972).

[12]   See Z. Taylor, *Rozwój i regres sieci kolejowej w Polsce* (Warszawa 2007), 47.

railway transport had a huge importance for the economic integration of the country, as the damage caused by the wartime destruction needed to be repaired. About 600 station buildings were reconstructed.[13]

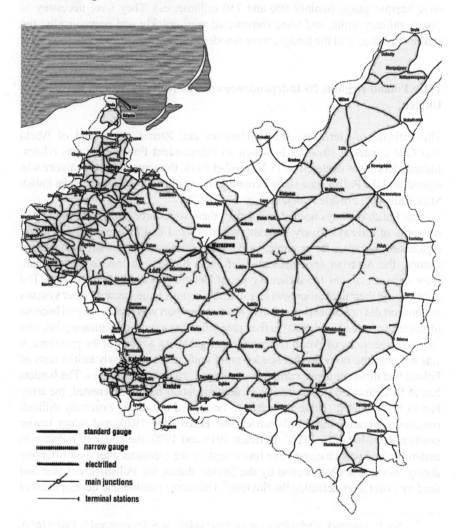

Figure 7.1   Map of the Polish railways, 1939

Source: UIC Documentation Centre, Paris. Also reproduced in Kolejowa Oficyna Wydawnicza KOW), *150 Lat Kolei na Ziemiach Polskich* (150 years of railways in Poland) (Warszawa 1995).

---

[13]   See J. Żarnowski, *Polska 1918–1939. Praca, technika, społeczeństwo* (Warszawa 1999), 181.

The structure and the directions of the main lines of the existing railways were not in accordance with needs of Poland.[14] The first railway built by the new Polish government was a short line from Kokoszki to Gdynia that opened in 1921. Near the coast of the Baltic Sea; this connection facilitated transport to the new Polish harbour in Gdynia. A few lines in central Poland, which were to connect the three original railway networks, had been under construction since 1919. The plan was imposing: the projected tracks were to total 4,258 kilometres. But money was short, and the construction schedule was disorganised: it was not clear when each line should be built. The order changed often. As a result, many of the railways were started but not finished, or were finished after 10 or 15 years. Only after 1934 did the construction of railways gain speed and organisation.[15]

In the middle of the 1920s, the Polish government realised that the state was not able to finance the growth of the railway network, and sought foreign capital. It was successful only in one case.[16] The construction of the railway from Herby to Gdynia – 458 kilometres long, built from 1925 to 1933 – which is considered the greatest achievement of the Polish railways during the interwar period, was in part possible thanks to French loans. This line had great economic importance, linking the great industrial and coal mining areas in Upper Silesia with Polish harbours.[17] Between 1918 and 1939, a total of 1,945 kilometres of railway track was laid. Many other railway projects could not be realised before World War Two.[18]

The Polish State Railways had a shortage of rolling stock after 1918. At the beginning of interwar period, the Polish state had hardly any rolling stock industry. There were only a few factories that produced wagons, and none that made locomotives. The first locomotive factory was founded in 1919 in Chrzanów. It was named The First Factory of Locomotives in Poland, Pierwsza Fabryka Lokomotyw w Polsce, and called FABLOK, short for Fabryka Lokomotyw. Its first steam engine went into service in 1924.[19] During the 1920s, two more factories started producing locomotives: H. Cegielski – Poznań S.A. in Poznań

---

[14]   See B.A. Barber, *Report of European Technical Advisers Mission to Poland 1919–1922* (New York 1923), 14.

[15]   See M. Przegiętka, 'Między ambicjami a rzeczywistością. Polskie plany rozbudowy sieci kolejowej i ich realizacja w Drugiej Rzeczypospolitej', in W. Marciniak (ed.), *Księga pamiątkowa XV. Ogólnopolskiego Zjazdu Historyków Studentów* (Łódź 2008), 101–13, here 102–103.

[16]   See W. Jakubowski, 'Pierwsza wielka koncesja kolejowa w Polsce', *Inżynier kolejowy*, vol. 4, 1925, 77–80, here 77.

[17]   See M. Widernik, 'Magistrala węglowa Śląsk – Gdynia i jej znaczenie w okresie międzywojennym', *Zapiski Historyczne*, 49, 1984, 31–52.

[18]   On the time before World War Two, see Przegiętka, 'Między ambicjami', 112.

[19]   See J. Piwowoński, *Parowozy kolei polskich* (Warszawa 1978), 23.

Figure 7.2   Streamlined steam locomotive Pm36

Note: One of the greatest achievements of Polish railway industry of the interwar period was the Pm36 streamlined steam locomotive, constructed by FABLOK in 1937. It received an award at the Paris International Exhibition. This locomotive headed prestige passenger trains for only two years, until the German attack on Poland – the beginning of World War Two in 1939.

Source: Collection of Narodowe Archiwum Cyfrowe w Warszawie.

and Warszawska Spółka Akcyjna Budowy Parowozów in Warsaw.[20] Earlier, at the beginning of 1920s, the locomotives had to be purchased abroad.

Before World War Two, the modernisation of Poland's rolling stock was only just beginning, even if in 1937, the Polish railway industry built a streamlined locomotive able to reach the speeds of 140 kilometres per hour. The problem was that there were no tracks for such a high-speed train.[21] The greatest achievement of the Polish State Railways in the area of motorisation was a motor-driven car called *Lux-torpeda* ('luxury torpedo'), used starting in 1936 as an express train between the largest cities and holiday resorts.[22] Electrification had also begun before World War Two. In 1936, the first sections of railway lines in the junction at Warsaw were

---

[20]   See I. Hütter and R. Holzinger, *Die Lokomotiven der PKP (1918–1939)* (Werl 2007), 57.

[21]   See Piwowoński, *Parowozy kolei*, 68–9.

[22]   See B. Pokropiński, *Lux-torpeda PKP* (Warszawa 2007), 47–9.

electrified.[23] Although its performance during the interwar period was criticised after 1945, there is no doubt that the PKP would have been up to the challenge of modernising itself. The government had large scale plans to develop the railway network and rolling stock, which would have played a great part in improving the economic life of the country. Unfortunately, the German invasion in 1939 put a brutal stop to the realisation of these plans for several years.

During World War Two, the Polish railways and all of the bridges over the Vistula River were destroyed two times: first in September 1939, when Germany attacked Poland, and second as the German Wehrmacht withdrew before the Red Army in 1944–45.[24] During wartime, the railways served the German army and became a target of partisan attacks. Railways which had once signified travel and modernity came to mean the road to Auschwitz and death. In central and Eastern Europe, even apart from the Holocaust itself, there were many forced resettlements during and after the war involving exhausting rides on the train.[25]

1945 Poland behind the Iron Curtain: The Railways in the Service of State Socialism

The second date, 1945, was the end of the Second World War. Poland was liberated by the Red Army and became part of the sphere of influence of Soviet Russia.[26] Poland's borders shifted westwards: the Eastern Borderland (Kresy Wschodnie) was lost and Poland received some of the eastern part of Germany.

To satisfy its strategic and wartime needs, the Red Army had hurriedly converted some of the main lines to broad gauge. After the end of the war, these lines were restored to normal gauge. In the West, in the ex-German areas of Silesia, West Pomerania, and the southern part of East Prussia, about 2,500 kilometres of railways had been disassembled by Soviets. Many station buildings were also burned or demolished. The rails, overhead cables and workshop machines were taken eastwards as part of the spoils of war. Such removals went on even until 1948.[27] People used to say ironically, 'The rails were taken to nickel-plate.'[28] In fact the rails were taken to the Soviet Union as the spoils of war. In some cases, the second tracks were disassembled. As a Polish engine driver recalled:

---

23 See F. Frontczak, *50 lat elektryfikacji PKP* (Warszawa 1989), 78–9.

24 See B. Chwaściński, *Mosty na Wiśle i ich budowniczowie* (Warsaw 1997), 200–21.

25 See W. Tomasik, *Ikona nowoczesności. Kolej w literaturze polskiej* (Wrocław 2007), 256–66.

26 Polish historians are still debating if the year 1945 meant liberation or the beginning of a second occupation.

27 See S. Bufe, *Eisenbahnen in Schlesien* (Egglham 1993), 256, K. Soida, *Kolej Gliwice Trynek – Rudy – Racibórz* (Łódź 1994), 34–5, and Taylor, *Rozwój i regres*, 106–32.

28 See R. Sternciki, 'Łobeskie bułeczki', *Łabuź. Klubowy okazjonalnik literacki*, 15, 1995, 12–15, here 12.

The drive from Iława to Olsztyn (in the former East Prussia; M.P.)] at that time was possible only on a single track. The other had been demolished in a special way: from one station to another the train ran on the left track, then to the following station on the right track.[29]

Although there was no good economic reason for inflicting such damage on the rail network, it was only possible to repair some of it in the years that followed. These Soviet acts of lawlessness in Polish territory were possible because beginning in mid 1944, the administration of Polish railways was carried out by the Red Army.[30] The Polish government got the administration of its own railways back only in July 1945. Although by the agreement signed then, 'the government of Soviet Union immediately gives up dismantling of workshops, locomotive sheds, means of communication, and signalling systems in Poland', in fact the disassembling was not stopped until 1948.[31] The topic was taboo for decades, and was not researched until 1989. Almost no information about it was published before the fall of the Iron Curtain.[32]

At the same time, rebuilding of destroyed railways, stations and bridges began. The level of war damage was much bigger than after World War One. In 1944 and 1945, all the bridges over the Vistula were completely destroyed. The reconstruction required a massive effort and lasted about 12 years. Railways destroyed in the war continued to be reconstructed until about 1956, when the last railway bridge over the Vistula River (in Fordon, near Bydgoszcz) was completed.[33]

In Poland, the period of state socialism began. The Soviet economic model was applied to Polish railways as it was to so much else in the country.[34] As a feature of the planned economy, the Polska Partia Robotnicza (PPR) (Polish Workers Party, i.e., the Communists) started supporting competition among railways workers (for example engine drivers and workshop workers). In December 1947, during the Polish State Railways workers' convention, it was decided that competition would begin. The engine drivers pledged to save up coal and haul trains that were heavier than had been planned in the timetable, while builders of bridges and stations pledged to complete their work before the deadline. The model for this competition

---

[29]   A. Liegmann, *Szlaki pomorskich kolejarzy* (Toruń 1978), 86.

[30]   See Umowa między PKWN a Rządem ZSRR o trybie eksploatacji i zarządu kolejami Polskimi na czas wojny. 11.05.1944. http://www.traktaty.msz.gov.pl/ fd.aspx?f=P0000012666.pdf (last accessed 10 September 2010).

[31]   See Umowa między Polskim Tymczasowym Rządem Jedności Narodowej i Rządem ZSRR o przekazaniu Ministerstwu Komunikacji RP zarządu nad kolejami żelaznymi w Polsce, 11.07.1945. http://www.traktaty.msz.gov.pl/fd.aspx?f=P0000012671. pdf (last accessed 10 September 2010).

[32]   See Taylor, *Rozwój i regres*, 106.

[33]   See J. Pawłowski, *150 lat kolei w regionie kujawsko-pomorskim 1851–2001* (Bydgoszcz 2001), 36.

[34]   J. Kaliński, *Gospodarka Polski w latach 1944–1989* (Warszawa 1995), 33 and 35.

originated in Soviet Russia.[35] In fact, the ostensible technological progress and modernity were only a matter of propaganda, and the real economic value of the programme was not high.[36] Also the numbers of passengers carried and the amount of freight shipped was planned for next 5 or even 20 years by government, and every year the planned figures were too low.[37] The railways played their part in the industrialisation of the newly Communist country. According to the new guidelines, everything had to be made cheaper, faster or in a larger quantity. But that did not mean that it should be made better. Lower quality in work, products and services is a legacy of the socialist state.[38]

During the Cold War, the railways in Poland were strategically important. They were used to transport Soviet forces, because the People's Republic of Poland (*Polska Rzeczpospolita Ludowa*), like other countries in Eastern Europe, was a signatory to the Warsaw Pact, the defence treaty signed in 1951. The Red Army stayed in Poland and the German Democratic Republic until the beginning of 1990s.[39] Everything connected with transport was secret and it was forbidden to take photographs of trains, bridges and stations. Ordinary people were supposed to watch out for spies.[40] The obsession with secrecy was one of the reasons for the low level of interest in railways in Polish society. Economic cooperation in the Soviet bloc started with the Council for Mutual Economic Assistance (COMECON) in 1949. In Poland this cooperation was seen from the angle of trains that were transporting Polish goods (grain and coal) to the Soviet Union, but without payment. These trains were called 'friendship trains'.

After 1945, the railways were still the most important means of transport. The main lines were electrified, and steam locomotives were replaced with diesel and electric engines. Modernisation moved forward very slowly, because of the economic problems of socialism. A huge achievement was the electrification of 11,016 kilometres of railways by 1989.[41] New railway connections and second tracks on existing lines were also built. The largest investment of the 1970s was the

---

[35] See Pawłowski, *150 lat kolei*, 27.

[36] A dramatic conflict between an older engine driver who was sceptical about the new economy of railways, and a younger one who was a party activist, was shown in Andrzej Munk's 1956 movie *Człowiek na torze* (Man on the Tracks).

[37] Archiwum Akt Nowych w Warszawie, Ministerstwo Kolei, 229, Projekt założeń planu perspektywicznego pracy taboru na lata 1956–1975, 1–25; 241, Sprawozdnie z wykonania Narodowego Planu Gospodarczego przez Ministerstwo Kolei, 1953, 5.

[38] See B. Orłowski, *Technika* (Wrocław 1999), 154–59, and M. Przegiętka, 'Dzieje kolei normalnotorowych na obszarze Warmii i Mazur', in D. Keller (ed.), *Dzieje kolei w Poslce* (Rybik 2012), 305–26, here 321.

[39] Z. Tucholski, *Polskie Koleje Państwowe jako środek transportu wojsk Układu Warszawskiego. Technika w służbie doktryny* (Warszawa 2009), 5–9.

[40] See T. Suchorolski, 'Czyżby znów powtórka z historii', *Koleje małe i duże*, 4, 2001, 14.

[41] See S. Koziarski, *Sieć kolejowa Polski 1918–1992* (Opole 1993), 170.

Figure 7.3   An ex-German war locomotive (*Kriegslokomotive*) leads the train
                from Warsaw to Moscow with gifts for Stalin's birthday, 1950

Note: After 1945, Poland belonged to the Soviet Union's sphere of influence. Even the
railways were supposed to worship Josef Stalin.

Source: Collection of Polska Agencja Prasowa (PAP).

Central Main Railway Line, which connected Warsaw with Katowice and Cracow. It opened in 1977. The extension of this railway to Gdańsk and Gdynia (on the coast of the Baltic Sea) was not accomplished because of crisis of the 1980s. This line, though, is still the most modern railway in Poland. On it, trains of the highest standards reach speeds of 160 kilometres per hour. After it was opened, the length of the Polish railway network became the greatest in its history: 27,271 kilometres.

Starting at the end of the 1960s, a process began of closing down narrow-gauge and local railways. The reason was competition from road transport (passenger and freight) and a shortage of light diesel rail motors for operating the local non-electrified connections.[42] Although in the 1970s two new central stations buildings were opened (Katowice in 1972 and Warsaw in 1975), the quality of passenger traffic did not get better.[43] The economic crisis of the 1980s and the Solidarity (*Solidarnosc*) movement caused the political transition of 1989.

1989: Free Market Reforms and the Contraction of Railway Network

In 1989, the first free elections after the end of World War Two initiated the process of transforming the socialist state into a democratic and market-oriented one. In the 1990s, the domination of rail transport came to an end. Road transport increased despite the poor network of roads. Many regional railways were closed. Thefts of rails and overhead cables also caused great problems.

Although Poland is situated in Central Europe between the East and the West and includes four of the most important trans-European transport corridors, the country does not make good use of its location. Only a few main lines allow journeys at speeds up to 160 kilometres per hour. The timetables of passenger trains are not adjusted to the needs of the customers. The railways have not dealt with their own backwardness. The rolling stock is mainly old, obsolete and not economical. Until the end of 1990s, there were almost no light motor cars to service the local railways with low numbers of passengers. Instead, heavy, powerful engines that were expensive to run served these lines. The liberalisation of the bus market and passive marketing policy of the Polish State Railways resulted in a huge decrease in the numbers of passengers carried and in the freight shipped in the 1990s. In 1989, there were 951 million passengers, and in 2004, only 272 million. The freight traffic is also smaller: in 1989, 388 million tons of goods were carried, and in 2004, only 282 million tons.[44] One of the biggest problems of the last 20 years is the unsatisfactory financing of railway infrastructure from the state budget. Also

---

[42] See A. Dychtowicz, 'Regres sieci kolejowej w Polsce – reguła czy wyjątek?', *Świat kolei*, 11, 2001, 12–15, here 12–13.

[43] See Kaliński, *Gospodarka*, 167.

[44] Z. Taylor, 'The Transport System of Poland in a Period of Transition', in M. Degórski (ed.), *Natural and Human Environment of Poland: A Geographical Overview* (Warsaw 2006), 275–96, here 284.

subsidies for passenger trains were not sufficient.[45] The provincial authorities of the voivodeships were supposed to take care of local rail transport. As a result for about five years, the situation of railways has been different in each province. The process of railway closure stopped in 2003 and since 2004 a few connections have reopened. Today's railway network is about 19,000 kilometres long and the local, closed railways are still being demolished. The process of restructuring and privatising the Polish State Railways is not unpopular and seems to have met with failure.[46] The reason is the lack of a consistent transportation policy. Every government has changed the guidelines. For most of them, the absolute priority has been building highways, another process that moves at a snail's pace. The customers judge the quality of the railways' service to be poor. Widespread high-speed rail service continues to be an elusive dream. Polish railways are thought of as technologically backward in terms of infrastructure, rolling stock, staff and management: for many years they have had bad press.[47] There are also some drawbacks to the modernisations of the last 20 years. In many cases the tracks were upgraded to serve a speed of 160 kilometres per hour. But such a speed is not allowed when a train passes a station. In many cases, the distances between two stations are too short to run the trains at maximum speed. This is one example of how the traffic capacity became diminished as a consequence of modernisation.[48]

In May 2010, the owner of the infrastructure, Polskie Linie Kolejowe S.A. (PKP), closed down the tracks for several dozen trains of the railway carrier Przewozy Regionalne because some passenger railway companies, beside Przewozy Regionalne also PKP Intercity, did not pay their fee for getting access to rail infrastructure. This scandalous situation has a strong impact on the passengers and was a sensation in the mass media. Although the trains returned to service after a few weeks, unfortunately no one knows what kind of future the railways in Poland can have. Is the losing streak over? One hopes that the investments in railways and stations of the biggest cities, which are connected with preparations for Euro 2012, will change the situation and open a new page in the history of Polish railways.

Conclusion

Polish territory is situated in the middle of Europe and since the Middle Ages it has drawn extensively on the trade between the East and West. As a result

---

[45]   *Raport roczny grupy PKP 2003 / Annual Report of PKP Group 2003*, 12.

[46]   See I. Książkiewicz, 'Uwarunkowania procesu restrukturyzacji PKP w latach 2003–2004', in L. Gilejko (ed.), *Aktorzy restrukturyzacji – trudne role i wybory* (Warsaw 2006), 163–85, here 172.

[47]   P. Faryna, 'Kolejowa biała księga', *Rynek kolejowy*, 2, 2010, 10–11.

[48]   R. Wyszyński, 'Modernizacje czy partactwo?', *Rynek kolejowy*, 2, 2010, 56–9, here 56–7.

of political and economic conditions in the nineteenth and at the beginning of twentieth centuries, it became almost a desert in the area of transportation lines. This unfavourable situation started to change between the First and Second World Wars with the unification of railways, but this period was too short and many malfunctions were not removed. The damage during the war and the special development of Communist system made it impossible to modernise as fast as countries of Western Europe. Today, the Polish railways are backward in many areas: infrastructure, rolling stock and management. Without a state transportation policy, the Polish railways will lose their chance to be competitive both externally and internally. Will Poland be the missing link on the railway map of Europe for a second time?

Bibliography

Barber, B.A., *Report of European Technical Advisers Mission to Poland 1919–1922* (New York 1923).

Bufe, S., *Eisenbahnen in Schlesien* (Egglham 1993).

Chwaściński, B., *Mosty na Wiśle i ich budowniczowie* (Warsaw 1997).

Davies, N., *Boże igrzysko: historia Polski*, 2 vols (Kraków 1996).

Davies, N., *God's Playground: A History of Poland, vol. 2: 1795 to the Present* (Oxford 2005).

Davies, N., *Orzeł biały, czerwona gwiazda. Wojna polsko-bolszewicka 1919–1920* (Kraków 2000).

Davies, N., *White Eagle, Red Star: The Polish-Soviet War 1919–1920* (London 1972).

Dychtowicz, A., 'Regres sieci kolejowej w Polsce – reguła czy wyjątek?', *Świat kolei*, 11, 2001, 12–15.

Faecher, S. and Peters, S., 'Początki polskich kolei', in S. Faecher and S. Peters (eds), *20 lecie komunikacji w Polsce odrodzonej* (Kraków 1939), 123–40.

Faryna, P., 'Kolejowa biała księga', *Rynek kolejowy*, 2, 2010, 10–11.

Frontczak, F., *50 lat elektryfikacji PKP* (Warszawa 1989).

Hilchen, H., *Historya drogi żelaznej Warszawsko-Wiedeńskiej 1835–1848–1898. Przyczynek do historyi kolejnictwa w Królestwie Polskiem* (Warszawa-Kraków 1912).

Hummel, B., 'Odbudowa i utrzymanie kolei', in S. Faecher and S. Peters (eds), *20 lecie komunikacji w Polsce odrodzonej* (Kraków 1939), 141–62.

Hütter, I. and Holzinger, R., *Die Lokomotiven der PKP (1918–1939)* (Werl 2007).

Jakubowski, W., 'Pierwsza wielka koncesja kolejowa w Polsce', *Inżynier kolejowy*, 4, 1925, 77–80.

Jarząbek, M. and Keller, D., 'Rozdział wprowadzający', in D. Keller (ed.), *Dzieje kolei w Poslce* (Rybnik 2012), 13–59.

Kaliński, J., *Gospodarka Polski w latach 1944–1989* (Warszawa 1995).

Kolejowa Oficyna Wydawnicza (KOW), *150 Lat Kolei na Ziemiach Polskich* (150 years of railways in Poland) (Warszawa 1995).

Koziarski, S., *Sieć kolejowa Polski 1918–1992* (Opole 1993).

Koziarski, S., *Sieć kolejowa Polski w latach 1842–1918* (Opole 1993).

Krzysica, M., 'Rola czynników wojskowo-politycznych w budowie kolei żelaznych w Królestwie Polskim', in R. Kołodziejczyk (ed.), *Studia z dziejów kolei* żelaznych *w Królestwie Polskim (1840–1914)* (Warszawa 1970), 9–44.

Książkiewicz, I., 'Uwarunkowania procesu restrukturyzacji PKP w latach 2003–2004', in L. Gilejko (ed.), *Aktorzy restrukturyzacji – trudne role i wybory* (Warsaw 2006), 163–86.

Liegmann, A., *Szlaki pomorskich kolejarzy* (Toruń 1978).

Orłowski, B., *Technika* (Wrocław 1999).

Pawłowski, J., *150 lat kolei w regionie kujawsko-pomorskim 1851–2001* (Bydgoszcz 2001).

Piwowoński, J., *Parowozy kolei polskich* (Warszawa 1978).

Pokropiński, B., *Koleje wąskotorowe PKP* (Warszawa 1980).

Pokropiński, B., *Kujawskie Koleje Dojazdowe* (Poznań 1994).

Pokropiński, B., *Lux-torpeda PKP* (Warszawa 2007).

Przegiętka, M., 'Dzieje kolei normalnotorowych na obszarze Warmii i Mazur', in D. Keller (ed.), *Dzieje kolei w Poslce* (Rybik 2012), 305–26.

Przegiętka, M., 'Historia kolei w Płocku', Świat *kolei*, 5, 2006, 17–23.

Przegiętka, M., 'Między ambicjami a rzeczywistością. Polskie plany rozbudowy sieci kolejowej i ich realizacja w Drugiej Rzeczypospolitej', in W. Marciniak (ed.), *Księga pamiątkowa XV. Ogólnopolskiego Zjazdu Historyków Studentów* (Łódź 2008),101–13.

Soida, K., *Kolej Gliwice Trynek – Rudy – Racibórz* (Łódź 1994).

Sterniciki, R., 'Łobeskie bułeczki', Łabuź. *Klubowy okazjonalnik literacki*, 15, 1995, 12–15.

Suchorolski, T., 'Czyżby znów powtórka z historii', *Koleje małe i duże*, 4, 2001, 14.

Taylor, Z., 'The Transport System of Poland in a Period of Transition', in M. Degórski (ed.), *Natural and Human Environment of Poland: A Geographical Overview* (Warsaw 2006), 275–96.

Taylor, Z., *Rozwój i regres sieci kolejowej w Polsce* (Warszawa 2007).

Tomasik, W., *Ikona nowoczesności. Kolej w literaturze polskiej* (Wrocław 2007).

Tucholski, Z., *Polskie Koleje Państwowe jako* środek *transportu wojsk Układu Warszawskiego. Technika w służbie doktryny* (Warszawa 2009).

Widernik, M., 'Magistrala węglowa Śląsk – Gdynia i jej znaczenie w okresie międzywojennym', *Zapiski Historyczne*, 49, 1984, 31–52.

Wyszyński, R., 'Modernizacje czy partactwo?', *Rynek kolejowy*, 2, 2010, 56–9.

Żarnowski, J., *Polska 1918–1939. Praca, technika, społeczeństwo* (Warszawa 1999).

Chapter 8

Transport under Socialism: The Case of the Czechoslovak State Railways 1948–1989

Ivan Jakubec

Just as in the case of road transportation, the development of railway transportation in Czechoslovakia after 1948 is closely associated with changes in political power, military strategy and ideology. After the damage of the war was successfully overcome, transportation was affected by the new political and economic system, that is, the association with Moscow and the other so-called people's democratic countries of the Eastern Bloc.

Let us look at the complex of questions that were projected onto railway transportation. The article will focus on the political level – the Soviet political model, the orientation of foreign policy to Moscow – and on the economic level: the Soviet-style planned economy, the Eastern economic bloc, the dependence on the import of raw materials from the Soviet Union, and the creation of the material and technological basis of Communism. It would have been of interest to include a third dimension of the problem, the military-strategic level relating to Czechoslovakia's membership in the Warsaw Pact. This level primarily relates to the strengthening of the carrying capacity of the railway infrastructure, the attachment to steam traction (which ended in 1980), and so on. The Czechoslovakian transport network, and hence the Czechoslovak State Railways, was a part of the military-strategic plans of Moscow and its allies. The formal expression of transport as an integral part of the military was the name derived from the colour of the uniforms: railway workers were known collectively as the Blue Army. A spectacular annual festival called the Day of Railway Workers celebrated them every September. But less research has been done on this level, and we must consider it as open to investigation.[1]

In the Soviet economic model, the railway system was the main transport system, but in interwar Czechoslovakia, the road system had been developed too. After 1948 in Czechoslovakia, the railways gained support from political, economic and military representatives. The too-high traffic demand (economic, military) for railways stimulated both the development of the state trucking company, and company transport by individual companies (see below).

---

[1] The military-strategic level waits for its researchers. See the book about Soviet military strategy in Czechoslovakia: Petr Luňák (ed.), *Plánování nemyslitelného. Československé válečné plány 1950–1990* (Prague 2007).

The Political Level

The development after 1948 can be categorised as interference with the management and operation of railways by incompetent political party and government institutions, the absence of a clear concept, and a continuous period of changes. Despite the proclaimed importance of the transportation infrastructure, including railway transport, and its support within the framework of building the so-called material-technical basis of Communism (a programme that emphasised raw materials, energy, heavy industry and weapons manufacture), in actuality, its importance was underestimated. It was demoted to the position of a servant of industry and the military, and it received insufficient investment. The reported growth of (often unnecessary) transportation activities did not automatically mean an increase in production or labour productivity. In the area of transportation, including railway transportation, regularity, speed, power and safety were the basic goals, but they were often unattainable. The railway rolling stock was obsolete, and was renewed too slowly. New transportation trends and technologies were introduced too late. The Soviet management models were mechanically adopted, as were the technical parameters and equipment of Soviet railways. In a number of cases, the state of transportation, including railway operation, limited the national economy.

Period comparisons of Czechoslovak transportation with that of developed economies can be misleading: for example, in the carrying capacity of the Czechoslovak State Railways for one kilometre of operating distance, the average number of journeys and passenger kilometres travelled per resident, etc. The seemingly comparable maturity of Czechoslovakia, expressed quantitatively, did not correspond to a comparable level in manufacturing, labour productivity, quality, speed, efficiency and safety. The mere fulfilment of transportation plans without adequate improvement of their technical basis led to a lowering of quality. Above all, the pressure of growth in manufacturing volume demanded an increase in the number of freight cars, which manifested itself in disproportions among the number of cars vis-à-vis the traffic-carrying capacity of the lines and stations. The inefficiency of the operation of the Czechoslovak State Railways necessitated large state subsidies.

Forms of ownership other than state and cooperative were abolished. The transport market was liquidated. All transport companies, including private railway companies, were nationalised. Czechoslovak State Railways became a state-owned company.[2] The railway connections with Western and Eastern Europe was curtailed, i.e., some railways that crossed borders were taken out of service in order to support increased surveillance of goods and people, and not all of the pre-war border crossings were renewed. Decision-making processes were influenced not only by experts, but often and primarily by incompetent political workers, including

---

[2]   Law no. 311/1948 Coll., Sbírka zákonů ČSR (The Collection of Laws of the Czechoslovak Republik) (Prague 1948).

Figure 8.1   Title page of the theory of command economy by František Tabery, 1959

Source: František Tabery, *Plánování a organisace dopravy. Část I* (Prague 1959).

through planning, meetings and resolutions of the Czechoslovak Communist Party. Railway managers and professionals who did not respect the new political line were removed. Efficiency and quality alone were not decisive, but instead the fulfilment of quantitative indicators. This was true both for freight and passenger railway transportation.

At the end of the 1950s and the beginning of the 1960s, František Tabery of the University of Economics in Prague (Praha) stated in a college textbook on planning railway transportation:

> The task of railway transportation is, by means of systematic improvement
> of organisation, technology and equipment, and the growth of the economy,
> to ensure the full operation of the principal economic law of Socialism (...)
> Railway transportation therefore must fully ensure the uninterrupted growth of
> socialist manufacturing by a continuous increase of productivity and quality of
> work and an increase in comfort in passenger transportation, and, by a continuous

lowering of its own expenses, it must help to maximise the satisfaction of the continuously growing material and cultural needs of the people.[3]

The planning and approval phases for investment, along with the irregularity in passenger and goods transportation, were amongst the chronically recurring problems. Resolutions by the Central Committee of the Communist Party of Czechoslovakia (*Ústřední výbor Komunistické strany Československa*, ÚV KSČ), Conferences of Communist Party of Czechoslovakia, and resolutions by the government – for example in the years 1951, 1955, 1958 and 1961 – reacted to the often-critical situation. An analysis of the structuring of investments into transportation infrastructure shows that these were not investments for the development of the infrastructure itself, but investments that supported the development of other branches of the national economy. Despite this, the Czechoslovak State Railways attempted, within the framework of its financial possibilities, to react positively to pan-European technical trends such as the electrification of railways, the switch to diesel traction for freight transportation, the modernisation of rolling stock, speed increases, the introduction of computers, the renovation of the railway network, work development, the introduction of intermodal transport, container transport and so on. Of course, the expanded resources were not enough for a qualitative change in the short term. Delays became regular, as did other problems such as damage to cars, high prices and a too-great emphasis on freight transportation. These inadequacies became unavoidable attributes of the extensive expansion of the national economy.

A year before 1989 (14 October 1988), the daily *Rudé Právo* (The Red Right) carried an article by Miroslav Zeman on transportation, in which the author materially evaluated the development to date of the transportation infrastructure in the nation:

> While more developed industrial nations have invested in railways, built new routes and hubs, and constructed modern vehicles, we have devoted ourselves only to using, maintaining and improving that which was already here. This cannot go on forever, however. Today we have no other choice but to build. As long as we want to speed up railway transportation – and that we must – it is necessary to build new lines and especially to strengthen the main routes; we must build new stations, hubs, and change over to electronic safety equipment. This will, however, be very expensive.[4]

So in the 1980s the real situation in the railway transport was even being discussed publicly. The improvement of the rail system was linked to higher financial resources, which were not available.

---

[3]   František Tabery, *Plánování a organizace dopravy.* Část *I.* (Prague 1959), 10.

[4]   Miroslav Zeman, 'Budeme cestovat rychleji?', *Rudé Právo* of 14 October 1988, 4.

The Economic Level

Demands on railway transportation grew disproportionately, in particular as a result of an increased orientation to the build-up of the material-technological base of Communism. In accordance with the Soviet model, the Czechoslovak State Railways (Československé státní dráhy, ČSD) became an essential mode of transportation. Despite this, the share of ČSD in volume indicators continued to decrease. The Czechoslovak State Motorcar Transport (Československá státní automobilová doprava, ČSAD), a state agency that ran motorbuses and trucks, competed with ČSD, as did the internal transportation systems of individual companies. While the volume of goods carried by the ČSD more than doubled in the period of 1952 to 1989, the volume carried by the ČSAD grew more than sevenfold, and the volume moved by individual companies grew more than eightfold. The situation is illustrated in Table 8.1.

Table 8.1　Freight transport of the Czechoslovak State Railways (ČSD), Czechoslovak State Freight Car Transport (ČSAD), and company transport 1952–1989 (in thousand tons)

Year	ČSD	ČSAD	Company transport
1952	118,888	44,816	114,688
1960	194,077	131,562	296,839
1970	236,876	226,011	477,281
1980	286,027	337,162	898,123
1989	283,674	328,984	929,134

Sources: Anonymous, *Historická statistická ročenka ČSSR* (Prague 1985), 310–11, anonymous, *Statistická ročenka Československé socialistické republiky 1986* (Prague 1986), 418, and anonymous, *Statistická ročenka České a Slovenské federativní republiky 1990* (Prague 1990), 438.

ČSD maintained its leading position in mid- and long-distance transportation of large-volume freight. Between 1952 and 1989, the number of ton-kilometres grew threefold for the state railways, for state road transport it grew more than 21 times, and for company transport more than eight times (see Table 8.2 below).

Table 8.2   Freight transport of the ČSD, ČSAD and company transport
1952–1989 (in million ton-kilometres)

Year	ČSD	ČSAD	Company transport
1952	24,404	620	1,292
1960	47,407	2,422	2,686
1970	60,995	4,838	5,255
1980	72,640	10,802	10,533
1989	71,985	13,246	10,579

Sources: Anonymous, *Historická statistická ročenka ČSSR* (Prague 1985), 310–11; anonymous, *Statistická roèenka Československé socialistické republiky 1986* (Prague 1986), 418; anonymous, *Statistická ročenka České a Slovenské federativní republiky 1990* (Prague 1990), 438.

Finally, let us consider the interesting comparison of the performance of the freight transport of the Czechoslovak State Railways, the Deutsche Reichsbahn and the Österreichische Bundesbahnen in the years from 1950 to 1989. All three were approximately of the same size. Table 8.3 shows a substantially higher loading of both the railway companies of the Eastern bloc.

Table 8.3   Freight transport of the ČSD, Deutsche Reichsbahn/GDR and
Österreichische Bundesbahnen 1950–1989 (in million metric tons)

Year	ČSD	DR/GDR	ÖBB
1950	96	129	35.9
1960	194	238	45.4
1970	237	263	50.0
1980	286	312	51.6
1989	284	339	58.6

Sources: Anonymous, *Historická statistická ročenka ČSSR* (Praha 1985), 310–11; anonymous, *Statistická ročenka Československé socialistické republiky 1986* (Praha 1986), 418; anonymous, *Statistická ročenka České a Slovenské federativní republiky 1990* (Praha 1990), 438.

Table 8.4 shows the number of ton-kilometres performed. This shows that the significant increase is similar for both the Eastern European railway companies.

Table 8.4   Freight transport of the ČSD, Deutsche Reichsbahn/GDR and Österreichische Bundesbahnen 1950–1989 (in million ton-kilometres)

Year	ČSD	DR/GDR	ÖBB
1950	18,634	15,100	18,820
1960	47,407	32,900	26,685
1970	60,995	41,500	32,971
1980	72,640	56,400	38,966
1989	71,985	59,000	44,048

Sources: Anonymous, *Historická statistická ročenka ČSSR* (Prague 1985), 310–11; anonymous, *Statistická ročenka Československé socialistické republiky 1986* (Prague 1986), 418; anonymous, *Statistická ročenka České a Slovenské federativní republiky 1990* (Prague 1990), 438.

The following two tables devoted to passenger traffic of the Czechoslovak State Railways, the East German Deutsche Reichsbahn and the Österreichische Bundesbahnen in the period from 1950 to 1989 show further interesting results. While the ČSD transported most people in 1960 and then showed a decreasing trend, the Deutsche Reichsbahn shows a steady decrease in people transported. Over the same period, the performance of the Österreichische Bundesbahnen is characterised by a 50 to 60 per cent increase. Regarding the parameter of passenger kilometres, for all railways, this figure jumped, dipped, then rose again in the case of both the Eastern European railway companies, and increased steadily in the case of the Österreichische Bundesbahnen (see Table 8.5 and 8.6 below)

The ČSD was located at the boundary of two political, economic and military systems. It had to join the newly established Moscow transport and rail structures, and, following World War Two, it restored its membership in the most significant Western organisations. This way, the ČSD maintained contact with Western Europe. It was in the self-interest of the state railways to keep the international contacts intact, in part due to the fact that the transit meant a significant inflow of foreign currency.

Table 8.5   Passenger transport 1950–1989 (in million)

Year	ČSD	DR/GDR	ÖBB
1950	441.5	954	115.2
1960	580.6	943	163.7
1970	486.1	626	170.2
1980	352.1	607	184.3
1989	411.0	592	178.7

Sources: Brian Mitchell, *International Historical Statistics: Europe 1750–2005*, 6th edn (New York et al. 2007), passim.

Table 8.6   Passenger transport 1950–1989 (in million passenger kilometres, excluding the Grand Duchy of Finland)

Year	ČSD	DR/GDR	ÖBB
1950	15,615	18,576	4,288
1960	19,335	21,288	6,840
1970	16,884	17,666	6,478
1980	15,402	22,027	7,586
1989	19,699	23,588	8,445

Sources: Brian Mitchell, *International Historical Statistics: Europe 1750–2005*, 6th edn (New York et al. 2007), passim.

Technical obsolescence in comparison to Western Europe led to a reduction in transit from Southeastern Europe to Western Europe through Czechoslovakia. This was felt from the point of view of losses of part of the revenue for transportation. In correlation with the political, economic and the military situation after 1948, a re-orientation of the direction of Czechoslovakia's foreign trade took place, away from Western Europe and primarily towards Eastern and Southeastern Europe.

Frequent structural changes in the administration and management of transport (formerly of railways only) did not produce the intended results. In 1949, a tried-and-true structure had been dismantled – the Directorate of State Railways. It was replaced by the so-called regional directorates (Plzeň, Prague, Olomouc, Bratislava), which were guided by the Central Directorate. At the same time, the Ministry of Railways was reorganised as Ministry of Transport (in Slovakia, the

'Transport Committee' took on the role of a de facto Slovak Ministry of Transport). In 1952, some reforms were initiated by the Ministry of Railways, and the regional headquarters were replaced by the directorates in Prague, Ústí nad Labem, Plzeň, Ostrava, Bratislava and Košice. In 1960, a further change occurred: the Ministry of Transport and Communications was established and the Transport Committee was abolished. In 1963, things shifted again: the Ministry of Transport was re-established and the number of directorates was reduced to the North-Western, Central, South-Western and Eastern. The establishment of the Czechoslovak Federation in 1968 meant the creation of two Ministries of Transport for both republics and the Federal Coordinating Committee for Transport and the central management of railways.[5] However, two years later, the Federal Ministry of Transport was created. In 1988, the Central Directorate was renewed. A year later, the regional headquarters (Plzeň, Prague, Olomouc and Bratislava) were created. Other changes came in November 1989 and when the federation dissolved in 1992.

Great and unrealistic hopes were placed in technical renovation during the third five-year plan (1961–65). Within the plan were hidden a number of unrealisable assignments: for example, the reduction of steam traction to 25 per cent of the total transportation performance by 1965 and its complete elimination by 1968; 90 per cent mechanisation of loading and unloading; the electrification of 1,044 kilometres of lines by 1965; the mechanisation and gradual automation of operations safety at railway yards; and the achievement of a decisive proportion of large capacity cars in the fleet.[6] The conversion of narrow-gauge tracks, also called for in the third five-year plan, was intended to facilitate a number of changes – even there did not exist very much narrow-gauge lines. It would increase the carrying capacity of the railway infrastructure. It would make doubling and even tripling of tracks possible. It would support the construction of new routes, plus electrification, mechanisation and automation. It would make it possible to shift over to Soviet methods of operation, in particular to the 'heavy tonnage movement' (which proved none too successful), and to Soviet equipment for traffic safety and automatic block system. In the 1970s, it would support the switch to diesel traction, which, however, proved uneconomical. Increased mining of black and brown coal required the re-laying of a number of railway lines, especially in northern Bohemia and northern Moravia.

The attempt at increasing the work of railways in transportation naturally found its limits. The financial limits led to low standards: for passenger transportation, this meant regular delays and unreliability – though on the positive side, the fares were low; for freight transportation, this meant frequent delays though freight

---

[5]   Act No. 143/1968 Coll. Sbírka zákonů ČSR (The Collection of Laws of the Czechoslovak Republik), Praha 1968.

[6]   Anonymous, 'Usnesení Ústředního výboru Komunistické strany Československa k zabezpečení dalšího rozvoje železniční dopravy', *Rudé právo* from 15 April 1961, 4, and Národní archiv Praha, Ústřední výbor KSČ, Fond 60, vol. 8, Archiv-No. 77, Základní směry rozvoje železnic do roku 1970 (top secret).

had priority over passenger transportation. The transportation limits meant that small parts of the network were disproportionately burdened, leading to increased vulnerability to all sorts of problems, including delays being transmitted to the entire network. The political – and ideological – limits of transport which led to low fares and more support for the railways than for automobile mobility meant low quality of mobility. Political decisions took priority over professional decisions. This led to unnecessary and inefficient transportation on long routes and the maintenance of unprofitable routes. Also, we cannot forget the evening out of the economic and cultural level between the Czech lands and Slovakia; in the case of economy, it was a continuation of the industrialisation of Slovakia, i.e. new factories, new railways lines, new urban settlements.

High transport demand for long distances resulted from the separation of locations of raw materials and the places where they were processed, the distribution of goods over large distances, and the import of raw materials, mainly from the Union of Soviet Socialist Republics (USSR). The problem of disproportionate distribution of load flows and simultaneously the uneven use of the railway system afflicted the ČSD up until 1989. A total of 8 per cent of all railway transport was concentrated on the Most–Ústí nad Labem route (1.33 per cent of the area of the network) and 51 per cent of railway transportation on the Most-Ústí nad Labem-Česká Třebová-Čierna nad Tisou section (1 per cent of the network area). In the event of disruption of one of the hubs, the transport of coal was especially threatened. Almost the entire loading which amounted to 45 per cent of goods transport in total came from only four places. Those were Sokolov with a share of coal to all goods transport reached 83 per cent, Ústí nad Labem with a share of coal of 78 per cent, Ostrava region with a share of coal and coke of 60 per cent and Čierna nad Tisou where as well as ore as coal came from.[7] Not adhering to the plan and an excessive concentration of freight loads on a fraction of the railway network caused tension and a tendency to disruptions.

During the whole lifespan of Czechoslovakia, a total of 298 kilometres of track were newly constructed. Railway junctions were renovated, for example at Česká Třebová, Brno, and Prague. In 1984, a standard gauge border crossing for freight transportation was added between Maťovce and Užhorod at the Czechoslovak-Soviet border. Re-laying of tracks took place in industrial regions such as Ostrava, Most and Teplice.

Although the first steps were realised in the Monarchy and the first Czechoslovak Republic, the electrification of the Czechoslovak railway network officially began in 1949. It was a 3,000-volt direct current system. By 1960 the line from Ústí nad Labem via Nymburk, Prague and Česká Třebová to Košice was electrified. Based on the positive experiences especially of France, Great Britain, Japan and the Soviet Union with alternating current of 25 kilovolt and 50 Hz, it was decided

---

[7]   NA Praha, ÚV KSÈ, Fond 60, vol. 4, Archive-No. 50, Celková zpráva o plnìní usnesení Politického byra ÚV KSÈ z 19. listopadu 1956, p. 8; NA Praha, ÚV KSÈ, Fond 60, vol. 20, Archive-No. 190, Nìkteré poznatky ze situace na železnici, p. 2.

in the mid 1960s to electrify lines with this type of power system in the southwest of Czechoslovakia: Cheb-Plzeň-České Budějovice and Kolín-Havlíčkùv Brod-Brno-Bratislava – Štúrovo. By the mid 1980s the share of electric traction of both systems was about 25 per cent in kilometres, and 66 per cent of the output.[8]

The technical trends such as the electrification of railways, renovation of the railway network, container transport and so on did not improve the position of railway transportation. The gap between the levels of transport in the West and East only increased.

Conclusion

The state enterprise Czechoslovak State Railways underwent very inconsistent development after World War Two. On the one hand, it continued as a state enterprise, and thus as a stabilising element in the political, economic, military-strategic, social and cultural fields. On the other hand, the ČSD was fully pulled into the transformation of Czechoslovak society and economy in accordance with the Soviet model. This situation led to plans that were difficult or impossible to fulfil, neither from Czechoslovakia nor from the Council for Mutual Economic Assistance, COMECON: unnecessary transport of raw materials and intermediate products and goods over long distances; the securing of a material-technical base for socialism/communism; the inefficient use of rolling stock; disproportionately increasing demands for transport in connection with the tasks of the five-year plans; and strengthening the defence system of the country and preparing for war. Only partially and in limited form (according to the financial possibilities) did the technological development reflect international trends in transport such as AC and DC electrification, diesel power in cargo transport and automatic block system. Limited funds invested in the rail infrastructure in connection with weather conditions frequently limited the operation of the national economy (most recently in 1979). At the same time, the ČSD was subject to political decisions that took precedence over professional decisions. Passenger rail travel was primarily focused on providing a means to reach school, work and domestic recreation destinations. The low cost of the fares could not compensate for the slow speed and low quality of travel.

Bibliography

Anonymous, *Rozvoj dopravy v ČSSR* (Praha 1981).
Anonymous, *Statistická ročenka Československé socialistické republiky 1986* (Prague 1986).

---

[8] See František Jansa, 'Z dějin vývoje elektrizace železnic', *Dějiny věd a techniky*, 4, 1988, 224–38, here 230 and 235, and *Historická statistická roèenka*, 309–10.

Anonymous, *Statistická ročenka České a Slovenské federativní republiky 1990* (Prague 1990).

Anonymous, *30 let socialistické dopravy* (Prague 1975).

Anonymous, 'Usnesení Ústředního výboru Komunistické strany Československa k zabezpeěení dalšího rozvoje železniční dopravy', *Rudé právo* from 15 April 1961.

Anonymous, *Z historie elektrizace železnic, Příloha dvojmagazínu Grand expres a ČD pro vás*, únor 2008.

Anonymous, *Železnice Čech, Moravy a Slezska* (Prague 1995).

Boyer, Christoph (ed.), *Sozialistische Wirtschaftsreformen. Tschechoslowakei und DDR im Vergleich* (Frankfurt am Main 2006).

Jakubec, Ivan, *Česko-slovenské vztahy zhlediska dopravní infrastruktury 1948–1967*, in *Česko-slovenská historická ročenka* (Brno 1988).

Jakubec, Ivan, 'Dopravní infrastruktura České republiky vsouvislosti spřipravovaným vstupem do EU – historické zamyšlení', *Ekonomická revue*, 3, No. 1, 2000, 69–78.

Jansa, František, 'Z dějin vývoje elektrizace železnic', *Dějiny věd a techniky*, 1988, 224–38.

Jirásek, Zdeněk, 'K otázce sovětských vlivů na československé hospodářství v letech první pětiletky', in Jan Hájek, Jiří Kocian and Milan Zítko (eds), *Fragmenty dějin. Sborník prací k šedesátinám Jana Gebharta* (Prague 2006), 587–92.

Luňák, Petr (ed.), *Plánování nemyslitelného. Československé válečné plány 1950–1990* (Prague 2007).

Mitchell, Brian, *International Historical Statistics. Europe 1750–2005*, 6th ed. (New York et al. 2007).

Průcha, Václav, 'Hospodářský vývoj v letech 1945–1992', in Jaroslav Folta (ed.), *Studie o technice v českých zemích 1945–1992*, 2 vols (Prague 2003).

Urban, Rudolf, *Die sudetendeutschen Gebiete nach 1945* (Frankfurt am Main 1964).

Tabery, František, *Plánování a organizace dopravy. Část I.* (Prague 1959).

Zeman, Miroslav, 'Budeme cestovat rychleji?', *Rudé Právo* of 14 October 1988.

Chapter 9
The Modernisation of Railways in Slovakia after 1945

Milan Klubal

The Long and Winding Road of Slovakia from the Days of the Austro-Hungarian Empire up to World War Two

Even before achieving independence in 1993, Slovakia had a complex history. It is useful to go over it briefly in order to understand the role that railways play today in this nation. At the time of the Austro-Hungarian empire, Slovakia was not a province, as was, for instance, Galicia, but a geographical region, often called 'Upper Hungary' (Hungarian: Felső-Magyarország, Slovak: Horné Uhorsko) because it coincided mainly with the high Tatra range. This region, composed of 17 *comitats* (counties), was named Slovakia because it was mainly inhabited by Slovaks, who spoke a Slavic language, close but distinct from Czech and totally different from Hungarian.

In the far west, Slovakia is separated from Moravia (today part of the Czech Republic) by the Morava River, and then, more to the northeast, by the White Carpathian and the Beskid ranges. In the north, the border with Galicia (now part of Poland) mainly follows the summits of the Tatra Mountains. In the east, Slovakia is separated by the Tisza River from Sub Carpathian Ruthenia (now part of Ukraine). In the south, the limit with the Hungarian plain is clearly delimited on the west side by the Danube from Bratislava (German: Pressburg, Hungarian: Pozsony) to the place where it curves towards Budapest, in the centre by the first hills announcing the Tatra range, and on the east side by the Tisza River.

Most of the first railways built in the Austro-Hungarian empire, from Vienna to Bohemia and to the Adriatic (Trieste), in Galicia along the Russian border, and from Budapest towards Transylvania, totally bypassed Slovakia. There was only one minor exception: the line built in the 1850s from Vienna to Budapest along the Danube.

The Austro-Hungarian Compromise of 1867 (German: *Ausgleich*, Hungarian: *Kiegyezés*) awarded Slovakia to the Hungarian part of the Double Monarchy. Budapest was then responsible for its railway policy. Immediately, the construction of railways started in Slovakia, with two objectives. First, the county had an eye toward exploiting the mineral resources of this region. This concept led to the construction by the private Košice–Bohumin Railway of a main transportation artery connecting the iron ores of Košice to the Silesian coalfields. Second the planners wanted to connect Budapest to the strategic Galician line through the Lupkov and Leluchów Passes.

Up to 1890, the construction of railways was mainly pushed forward by the Hungarian State Railways (Magyar Államvasutak, MÁV), and by private companies which were step by step nationalised and incorporated in the MÁV. All in all up to 1918 this company alone created a network of 2,039.7 kilometres length on Slovak territories. But MÁV was not alone in that field. Starting in 1890, railways were mainly built by 57 different private companies, each of which contributed an average length of 41 kilometres to the system to make up a total length of 2,333.5 kilometres by 1918. Out of these companies, 32 exploited dead end lines serving isolated mountainous valleys and mines; these comprised one-third of the total length.

In 1918, Slovakia was served by a well ramified network of 4,410 kilometres, which was concentrated around three centres: Budapest, Bratislava (until 1919 known by its Hungarian name, Pozsony) and Košice (then called Kassa). The connections with the Austrian part of the empire were few. There were five lines directed to Moravia, namely four along the Morava River, and only one through the Little Carpathians through the Vlara Pass. Then there existed four connections between Slovakia and Galicia, but only one with Ruthenia through Chop. With the rest of Hungary, there were some more lines, nine in all, but only in Komarom was a bridge built to cross the Danube, between Pozsony and Budapest.

After the split of the Dual Monarchy, Slovakia was incorporated into the new state of Czechoslovakia, which was composed of the three former Austrian provinces of Bohemia, Moravia and Silesia and of the former Hungarian region of Ruthenia. At the peace conference in Paris, though, Hungary spoke of the necessity to avoid cutting the main railway lines, and, after long discussions, retained the southern part of six Slovakian counties situated between Danube and Tisza, each of which contained a strong Hungarian minority. Altogether, Slovakia inherited 3,360 kilometres of the former railway network and left 1,049 kilometres to Hungary. The Slovakian network had to be adapted to a new political and economic space that stretched 1,000 kilometres from west to east.

Slovakia was well equipped with north–south railway lines oriented towards Budapest, Bratislava and Košice, the main city of the eastern part. But it lacked east–west lines that would have been able to support the traffic with the Czech provinces and with Ruthenia. For these purposes there was only one connection, the Košice–Bohumin line. But this line led only to Silesia and had no connection with Moravia and Prague.

A number of new lines were built to cure this situation. From 1921 onwards, a line was put into service between Bánovce and Vajany (18.4 kilometres) that partially doubled the single line from Slovakia to Ruthenia. Between Slovakia and Moravia two lines were built across the Little Carpathians range. One led from Veselí nad Moravou on the Moravian side to Nove Město nad Vahom on the Slovakian side (42.3 kilometres) and was opened in 1929. Another one, opened in 1937, was built from Horni Lideč (Moravia) to Puchov nad Vahom (20.4

kilometres). These two lines reached the main Bratislava–Žilina line along the Váh valley, which connected with the Košice–Bohumin line in Žilina. Several short connections permitted the creation of a second east–west axis that ran parallel to the Košice–Bohumin line, about 100 kilometres south of this line. From west to east, the line from Zbehy–Zlatne Moravce railway (1938) reached a length of 32.1 kilometres, and the line from Handlova to Horna Štubla, 17.6 kilometres; the latter one was set into business in 1931. Moreover in 1936 the Cervena Skala–Gelnice railway was constructed, a network of 68.4 kilometres. A number of private companies were nationalised in 1921, among them the Košice–Bohumin.

After the First Vienna Arbitration of 2 November 1938 Slovakia was deprived of one third of its territory, a stretch of 50 to 100 kilometres north of the 1919 border with Hungary, as well as the whole eastern part beyond the Lupkov Pass and its associated railway line inclusive a tunnel. It lost 20 per cent of its population, and 1,069 kilometres of railway lines from its former network of 3,554 kilometres, retaining 2,484 kilometres. The new border cut straight across many railway lines. Hungary annexed Košice, the main city of Eastern Slovakia, and Slovakia was left without any connection with Ruthenia, except through Hungary.

On 14 March 1939, while Monsignor Jozef Tiso was premier of the autonomous Slovak region, the Slovak Parliament voted for the independence of Slovakia. But the State of Slovakia was created under the presidency of Monsignor Tiso, an entity that in practice was dependent on Germany. The Slovakian Railways (Slovenske Železnice, SŽ) were created. The war provoked a sharp increase in freight transport. The export of raw materials, agricultural and food products played key roles. Passenger transport was characterised by extensive seasonal movements of agricultural and industrial workers from Poland, Slovakia, Ukraine and Russia on their travels to Germany. In order to alleviate the lack of east–west connections, two railway lines were built during the war. One led from Dolna Štubna to Harmanec, a distance of 27.8 kilometres, and was finished in 1940. The other one connected Kapušany pri Prešove with Stražske and reached its total length of 49.8 kilometres in 1943.

Technical Status of Railways after World War Two

In May 1945, Slovakia recovered the territories it had lost in 1938, except for the eastern part that included the main railway hub of Chop, which was annexed by Union of Socialist Soviet Republics (USSR). At this time Slovak railways measured 3,506 kilometres. Of this total length, 398 kilometres were double tracked. On these railways there were more than one thousand bridges with a width over five metres, with a total length of 28.9 kilometres, 71 tunnels with a total length of 33.9 kilometres, 2,834 buildings, with a territory of 754,000 square metres, including 372 station buildings and 94 buildings for the maintenance of locomotives and wagons. Water for steam locomotives was supplied from 222 water reservoirs in warming facilities and railway stations.

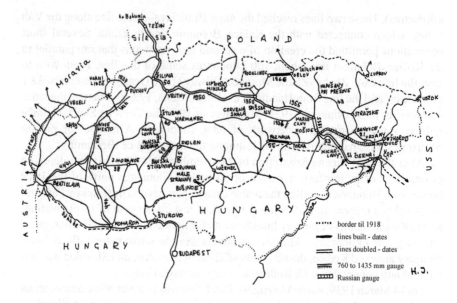

Figure 9.1   Railway map of Slovakia showing its development between 1945
               and 2011

Source: Map created by Henry Jacolin.

Officially, Slovak Railways possessed 665 steam locomotives, 131 motor trains, 1,550 passenger cars and 15,245 cargo wagons. But these figures did not show the reality, which was much worse. After the liberation there were only 22 steam locomotives that worked. Most of the wagons had been taken away and were gradually returned after the war. In the last months of the war, the retreating German army had systematically destroyed the railway infrastructure. Almost three-quarters of the tracks were destroyed and those which remained intact were cut off from the network and could not be set into business. Buildings fared similarly: only 29 were not destroyed. Rail switches, security and signal devices, waterworks and lighting systems were also destroyed. Some railways had been repaired by the advancing Soviet army during wartime. But the main responsibility for the repairs lay on the shoulders of railway workers and local building companies. It were especially workers in Podbrezova and Prakovce, and of the arms factory in Povazska Bystrica, as well as a lot of Czech engineering companies who helped to repair the bridges. By March 1946, the whole Slovak railway network had been reconstructed as a part of the Czechoslovakian railway network. One must keep this situation in mind to understand the problems with which the region of Slovakia was confronted after Second World War.[1]

---

[1]   P. Puraš, *Rozvoj železníc Slovenska od roku 1945 do roku 1970* (Časopis 1970), 1–6.

The establishment of a Communist regime in 1948, with a constitution defining Czechoslovakia as a socialist state, led to the nationalisation of all remaining private railway companies. The Czechoslovak Railways became part of the state administration in 1950. The new regime had a twofold influence on the railways of Slovakia: First, the industrialisation in Slovakia, marked by the Stalinist concept of 'iron and steel', imposed a huge increase of transportation. There was a strong concentration in transport of raw materials, building materials, fuels and food. Industrialisation had even a significant impact on the growth of passenger transport: people travelled long distances for work and school. The growth caused an imbalance between demand and technical capabilities. Heavy industries and companies for building materials were created. In 1937, 12.8 million tons were transported. In 1950 it was 18.5 million tons, and five years later, 56.3 million. These achievements must be seen in the context of improved technology, for example the increase in traction power of locomotives freight cars and loading facilities at the station.

Secondly, the reorientation of the foreign trade towards the Soviet Union increased significantly after 1948. Czechoslovakia depended fully on Soviet natural resources and was fully engaged in weaponry and heavy industry in the framework of the Council for Mutual Economic Assistance (COMECON). In the 1970s, each day 29,000 tons were moved through its territory. All oil had to be transported only by train before there was a pipeline. Because of low quality of Soviet wagons, oil was often spilled, which caused serious damage.

First Steps to Progress

The single-track line from Čierna nad Tisou over Košice and Žilina to Ostrava (Bohumin) could not cope with the huge amount of transported goods and was soon overloaded. In this situation the government decided to create a stronger railway corridor from Bohemia and Silesia in the west to the Soviet border in the east. The modernisation of this line included three main points.

First, the line would be double. The line between Bohumin and Žilina had been equipped with a double track since World War One. In the beginning of World War Two the construction of a double track started between Žilina and Vrutky. From Markušovce via Spišská Nová Ves to Žilina the line was also doubled in 1950, and from Michalany to Čierna nad Tisou in 1951. The second rail was 300 kilometres long.

This doubling necessitated the construction of the 3,410-metre-long Bujanov Tunnel. In some places, the necessity of enlarging the curve radius sometimes enforced a new routing. Around the Ruzinska Dam it was necessary to stop working for a while because of the new water work. This project was connected with the modernisation of the Margecany Station. For the reconstruction of the railway, the state used a respectable portion of its resources: 7.5 million cubic metres of soil were moved and 200,000 cubic metres of cement were installed.

Secondly, a broad-gauge line from the Soviet border to Košice was constructed. The transfer of iron ore in Čierna nad Tisou was slow and not very productive. For that reason it was necessary to find out how to increase reloading and how to manage the increasing demands of East Slovakian furnaces and companies in the Ostrava region. There were not only economic problems to solve but also military ones: the Soviet Army had its demands. The Soviet Union communicated through the representative of Hungarian Communist Party, Mathias Rakosi. In 1949, he sent a letter to Klement Gottwald, who was at this time president of Czechoslovakia and head of the Czechoslovak Communist Party, with a project to coordinate transport from the Soviet border to the west through Czechoslovakian and Hungarian territories. As consequence of this letter, the Budapest Conference was convened in October 1949. At the conference, high representatives of the army and command bodies of the two nations took place. The report of the conference, on 24 October 1949, requested the construction of second track from Čierna nad Tisou to Slovenske Nove Město, and a broad-gauge line to Kralovsky Chlumec which was to be realised in 1950.[2] The achievements were clearly visible. In 1924, the station Štrba registered only 8,400 tons per day in both directions. By 1937, this volume had increased to 16,100 tons. But in 1953, it was nearly 40,000 tons per day.[3]

These plans were worked out with involvement of the Soviet army. To camouflage real motive of building a broad-gauge line from Soviet border to the west, it was said that Hutnický kombinát (HUKO), the metallurgical complex in Košice, needed to be supplied with ore and coal. Especially for this problem a conference was arranged between the Ministers of Transport of the Soviet Union and Czechoslovakia in 1963. In this conference it was proclaimed that transport between USSR and Czechoslovakia would have to go through Čierna nad Tisou and Kapušany. The work took 22 months and was finished in November 1965. But the service did not start until May 1966. The railway is now 88 kilometres long and was built for a speed of 80 kilometres per hour. At first, there were diesel motor trains, but this changed later to electric trains.[4]

A third field of innovation was the electrification of the east–west corridor. The section from Žilina to Spišská Nova Ves was electrified in 1956. Then the line from Spišská to Košice followed in 1961, and the line from Košice to Čierna nad Tisou in 1962.

Some Further Projects

As Slovakia already had a rather well-developed network, only a few railway lines were built from 1945 onwards. Some sections of main lines had to be re-routed because of the construction of hydroelectric plants. This was the case in the

---

2   See Milan Klubal, *Stručné dejina* železničnej *dopravy Slovenska* (Bratislava 1988).

3   Puraš, *Rozvoj železnic Slovenska*, 1–6.

4   See Vladimír Hajko (ed.), *Encyklopédia Slovenska* (Bratislava 1982).

Váh valley. A line had to be built that led from Puchov to Povazska Bystrica (13 kilometres). Near Hydrocentrál Hricov a track was built from Hricov to Turany, and the construction of the Krpelanska Dam necessitated a line from Sutovo to Turany (six kilometres). The longest track for hydraulic structures at the River Váh led from Liptovska Tepla to Liptovsky Mikulas and was 18 kilometres long. The project of a hydroelectric plant on the River Hornad required also a conversion of the station of Margecany, of the Ruzinsky Viaduct, of the Bujanov Tunnel and also at the railway line from Margecany to Kysak. During the construction of the dam in Hnilec, a stretch of the length of four kilometres near Dedinky was reconstructed.[5]

A further three totally new lines were built. The line from Roznava to Turna nad Bodvou (31 kilometres) was the last section which remained to be completed to create a new east–west direct connection between Zvolen and Košice. It was necessary to bore a 3,186-metre tunnel through the calcite mountain. Alone this work took three and a half years and was finished on 25 January 1955.

The presence of brown coal in the sector of Modry Kamen had been previously known, but significant mining first started after 1945. Because the volume of transportation increased, it became necessary to build a railway line. To avoid the construction of a long line, as the mine was close to the Hungarian border, an agreement with Hungary permitted building only a short section of 12 kilometres from Bušince to Male Straciny. This opened on 12 September 1951. This line was prolonged to Velky Krtiš on 24 November 1978. The total distance from Velky Krtiš to Lučenec is 41 kilometres, including 19 kilometres in Hungary. Personal transport on the railway going through Hungary to Male Straciny was cancelled.

In 1873 a 20.3 kilometre narrow-gauge railway had been built from Hronska Doubrava to Banska Stiavnica. In the late 1930s it was no longer suitable for the increasing demands of transport. This was why the Slovak state decided during the war that the line should be rebuilt with normal gauge. The reconstruction began in 1943. The events of the war stopped the construction work when only 40 per cent of this railway had been renewed. Czechoslovakia took up the reconstruction in 1947 and mobilised for that purpose the Communist Czechoslovak Union of Youth (ČSM), which organised mandatory participation of students for manual work. That was why this railway was called the 'youth construction' or 'youth railway'.

The construction of the 31 kilometre railway from Orlov via Plavec to Podolinec began in 1943. After the World War, the work continued from 1946 until 1949, and then stopped again. In 1961 construction started again. The whole railway began to operate on 26 November 1966. Today it is rarely used and there is an ongoing discussion about closing some stations.

In 1949, on the basis of Paragraph 311 of the body of law about nationalisation of property, the Tatra Electric Railways (Tatranské Elektrické Železnice, TEŽ), were nationalised, along with the funiculars in Hrebienok and in Lomnicky Stit were nationalised too. The transport system in the High Tatras was destroyed by the retreating German army at the end of the war. Nevertheless already in 1946 the

---

[5]   Kubáček, *Dejinyžezezníc.*

train operation in Skalnate Pleso was successfully modernised, and by 1949 the rest of the network there was also modernised. Before the skiing championship in the High Tatras in 1970, the TEŽ acquired new passenger cars, modernised the higher parts of its network, and built a new forwarding office which was used for a cog rail line from Štrba to Štrbské Pleso. All in all, the TEŽ railways built some new stations and also reconstructed the whole network. At the end of the 1980s, further modernisation took place on the line from Skalnate Pleso to Lomnicky Stit and on the funicular to Skalnate Pleso. Today the TEŽ needs new rolling stock and is being forced to modernise its network.[6]

Electrification and New Railway Stations

The electrification of the railways was considered a landmark in the development of rail transport. The northern part of Slovakia was electrified with a direct current system of 3,000 volts and the southern part of Slovakia with an alternating current system of 25,000 volts and 50 hertz. This caused some problems, later solved by using double current locomotives. The first line that was electrified was the most important routes from Žilina to Spišská Nová Ves. From 1956 onwards, electric trains could operate there. In 1961, the line from Žilina to Košice followed, and, one year later, the line to Čierna nad Tisou. In the 1960s, Czechoslovak Railways successfully electrified all double tracked railways and also some of single lines: a total length of 1,516 kilometres. The last railway which was electrified was the line from Prešov to Plavec. Steam and diesel traction were replaced by new electric engines, which led to an increase of speed and transport capacity of trains. Also in safety, some progress was achieved. Increases in passenger transport necessitated additional capacity at railway stations and a lot of reconstruction and renewal in that area.[7]

Together with electrification, Slovakian Railways achieved some improvements in the safety equipment. Within the modernisation of the railway from Žilina to Čierna nad Tisou, the first part from Žilina to Varin with automatic blocking equipment was installed in November 1953. Safety equipment on double tracked railways functioned only one-way; it was made following a Soviet design. Starting in 1974, the equipment was adapted for both tracks. The first modern automatic train protection system with individual inbuilt relay was from the Ericsson Company and it was installed in Kralova Lehota station in 1951.[8] Afterwards, the

---

[6]　Register and Documents: Central state archives Pratur, fund 100/24 Arch unit 1126/4. SLOVENSKO – zväzok 1. (Dejiny) - Vydavateľstvo OBZOR 1980.

[7]　See Milan Klubal, *Stručné dejiny a súčasnosť železničnej dopravy na Slovensku* (Bratislava 1989).

[8]　The system was called PZB or Indusi and was an intermittent cab signalling system and train protection system used in Germany, Austria, Slovenia, Croatia, Romania and Israel, and on one line in Canada. Developed in Germany the historic short name Indusi

equipment for the automatic train protection system was produced in Slovakia. There it was called 'LS' and LS stands for 'Liniový Systém' which meant the same as automatic train protection system. It was used on all lines where track speed exceeds 120 kilometres per hour of (in the Czech Republic 100 kilometres per hour). This system continuously transmits the next main signal in driver's cabin and when the driver's activity is needed (e.g. reduction of train's speed), it periodically checks the driver's vigilance, i.e. he has to press the 'vigilance' button; else the emergency brake is applied.[9] As a result transport became safer and the demands on the staff decreased.

The growing automobile transport caused some increase of transport crashes on railway crossings. In the beginning of 1960s, automatic barriers and lighting were installed at railway crossings. At first, barriers and machinery were imported from the Soviet Union, but later, domestic products were used. For information to customers public address systems were used, and, after 1980, information systems from PRAGOTRON (today Elektročas s.r.o. in Prague) were introduced. It was a centrally planned system with current information about trains, their arrival time, departures, platforms and also delays.[10] It was a modern product at his time.

There were further expansions of rail transport. The exchange of goods increased gradually between the Balkan countries, Hungary and Eastern Germany, and also between Poland, Czechoslovakia and the Scandinavian countries. This required some improvements at all border stations. At the border between Czechoslovakia and Hungary there were seven border stations. Because of increasing volume of goods, the two states decided to build common stations with infrastructure for the clearance of trains at both sides of the border. On Slovak side, the station at Štúrovo was rebuilt, and the tracks were arranged that way that it became possible to load and reload 30 trains at the same time. Warehouses with cooling systems were installed. The reconstruction also included new offices and social rooms for workers at both sides of the border, rooms for veterinary care, and sheds for locomotives and wagon management. The reconstruction continued in the 1960s and 1980s.

It was necessary to enlarge the capacity of the railway complex of Bratislava, as the population of this city grew up to 350,000 inhabitants, due partly to the growth of the suburbs of Petržalka, situated on the south of the Danube. The line crossing

---

was derived from German *Induktive Zugsicherung* ('inductive train protection'). Later generations of the system were named PZB short of German *Punktförmige Zugbeeinflussung* ('intermittent automatic train running control') as PZB/Indusi is a family of intermittent train control systems and it is a predecessor of the German *Linienzugbeeinflussung* (LZB, 'continuous train protection') system. Originally Indusi provided warnings and enforced braking only if the warning was not acknowledged (similar to traditional automatic train stop) but current developments of PZB provide more enforcement. See http://en.wikipedia. org/wiki/Punktförmige_Zugbeeinflussung (last accessed 16 February 2012).

[9]   On the function of the LS system see http://en.wikipedia.org/wiki/LS_90 (last accessed 16 February 2012).

[10]   See Kubáček, *Dejinyžezeznίc.*

the centre of the city, from Filialka to Petržalka, was closed in 1983 and 1984. It was replaced by a new circle line which was gradually built on the east side of the city from Nove Město to Petržalka. This line was put into service in 1983 after the construction of a new bridge on the Danube which replaced the old bridge (*stari most*).[11] This enforced the construction of five new or fundamental reconstructed stations: Bratislava Nove Město, Bratislava UNS, Bratislava Petržalka, Bratislava Predmestie and Bratislava Main Station (*hlavna*). Built in 1874, this station was for both passenger and freight traffic. In 1983, the freight traffic was separated to absorb an increasing number of passengers.

A totally new station was built in Devinska Nova Ves. The old station was built in 1874 and it was used as well for both passenger service and for cargo transport. Together with the development of industry inside the city, commuters and goods transport increased dramatically. Although in this period a shunting station, railway station and stores for the goods transport was built, infrastructure for passenger transport stayed unfinished.[12]

The modernisation of Zvolen Station began in 1952. A station for passenger transport was built at the location of the original station, Zvolen Castle. Together with this renewal, passenger transport were separated from goods transport and transferred to a location nearby the centre. The construction of the station for personal transport required a new railway link leading to the line from Banska Bystrica to Šahy. In 1996 construction of a new engine house was initiated. Around the rebuilding of the installation station and the container loading station, a lot of projects and studies were conducted.

The lack of capacity of shunting stations in the east–west direction was the reason for a widening of the Žilina Station and the construction of new shunting stations between Žilina and Vrutky. After some obstacles had been surmounted, a new arrangement of lines was built, though some buildings remained unfinished. The resources for investments vanished and the infrastructure and the machinery fell into disrepair. There were also investments in other infrastructure sites, but they did not achieve adequate results. The container terminal in Dobra is an example.

Since World War Two, especially in the 1960s and 1970s, a whole range of new railway stations, sanitary installations, social services for employees, medical facilities, etc., have been reconstructed. As example one can mention the railway stations of Nové Zámky, Komarno, Čadca, Prešov, Krompachy, Roznava, Trnava, Topolčany, and most recently in Michalovce and Bratislava Petržalka. For the construction of these new buildings, the planners experimented with some measurements to minimise 'wet processes' and tried different construction systems with prefabricated elements of the building. The results were mostly negative. The

---

[11]   The circle line was built step by step. First in 1964 from Nove Město to Ustredna Nakladna, then in 1972 from Ustredna Nakladna to the Filialka-Petržalka line (using temporarily the railway lines serving of the harbour), and finally in 1983 from Ustredna Nakladna to Petržalka.

[12]   See Kubáček, *Dejinyžezezníc*.

Figure 9.2　　New railway station at Trnava, constructed in the late 1980s
Source: Photo by Milan Klubal.

Figure 9.3　　Interior of railway station Nové Zámky
Source: Photo by Milan Klubal.

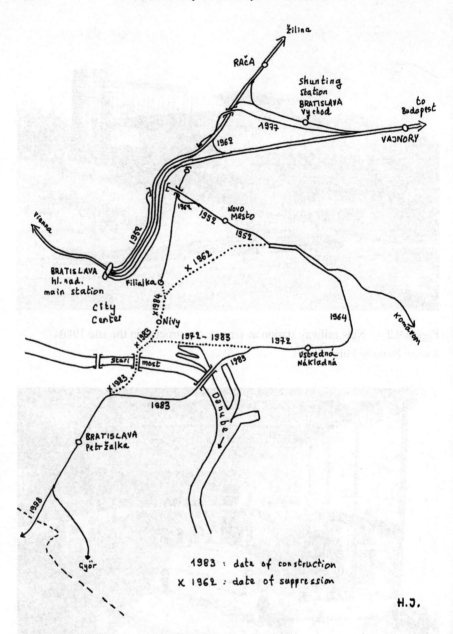

Figure 9.4   Railways around Bratislava, 1945–2011

Source: Map created by Henry Jacolin.

construction time could not be seriously reduced but the costs increased. The flat roofs of the modern buildings were mostly badly constructed, leaky and have had to be reconstructed.

Conclusion

The system of central planning did not work well for railway transport. After 1989 great changes in the world economy took place. The decline of rail transport resulted not only from the gloomy situation on Balkan and in post-Soviet countries, but also from the development of individual motoring. Other factors included changes in technology and in power sources. Coal was replaced by gas and this affected transport demands. At this stage of decline of passenger and cargo transport, on 1 January 1993, as the Slovak Republic became independent, the Railways of Slovak Republic was founded.

In the law creating this state-run company, the intention was that the railways should be self-supporting, without state subsidies as before. The single company of ŽSR was split: ŽSR remained responsible for the building and maintenance of the infrastructure, and the subsidiary company ŽZSK was charged with the transportation of passengers, while ŽSSK Cargo/ŽSCS ran the freight services. On their official websites the three companies defined themselves in the following way: Železnice Slovenskej republiky (ŽSR) is the state-owned railway infrastructure company in Slovakia. The company was established in 1993 as the successor of the Československé státní dráhy in Slovakia. Until 1996 it had formal and since then a de facto monopoly on railroad transportation in the country. In 2002 a law divided the company: ŽSR was left with infrastructure maintenance, and transport was moved into company Železničná spoločnosť, a. s. (ŽSSK). In 2005 this new company was further split into Železničná spoločnosť Slovensko, a. s. (ŽSSK) providing passenger services and Železničná spoločnosť Cargo Slovakia, a. s. (ŽSSK Cargo / ŽSCS) providing freight services. ŽSR provides transportation and services that correspond to the interests of state transport policy and market requirements, including related activities.[13]

The main aim of the state is to raise the share of the railways in the general transportation market. However, the unfavourable situation at the beginning of the process necessitated certain cutbacks and closures of lines immediately, reducing the share of the railways. The most important priority was to create conditions for privatisation and to optimise rail activity for business requirements. The strategic objective was to provide access to the European Union trade market and

---

[13]   Slovak rail ŽSSK (http://www.slovakrail.sk/generate_page.php?page_id=113 (last accessed 24 September 2011); ŽSSK Cargo (http://www.zscargo.sk/en/ (last accessed 24 September 2011), and Annual report 2008 (VÝROČNÁ SPRÁVA Železníc Slovenskej republiky (Bratislava 2009).

capitalise on the convenient territory of the Slovak Republic and its attractiveness for tourism.

Bibliography

Commission of Transport and Public Work (ed.), *Reconstruction of Railways in Slovakia* (Bratislava 1964).

Filo, V., *Railway in Bratislava*, ed. by VÚD Žilina (Bratislava 1999).

Hajko, Vladimír (ed.), *Encyklopédia Slovenska* (Bratislava 1982).

Klubal, M., *History of Railway Transport in Slovakia*, (ed.) the Administration of East Railway (Bratislava 1989).

Klubal, M., *Stručné dejina železničnej dopravy Slovenska* (Bratislava 1988).

Klubal, M., *Stručné dejiny a súčasnosť železničnej dopravy na Slovensku* (Bratislava 1989).

Krejcirik, M., *In the Track of Our Railways* (Prague 1990).

Kubáček, J. et al., *Dejinyžezezníc na území Slovenska* (Bratislava 1999).

Kubáček, J. et al., *History of Railway Transport on Slovak Territory*, (ed.) Slovak Railways (Bratislava 1999).

Puraš, P., *Rozvoj železníc Slovenska od roku 1945 do roku 1970* (Časopis 1970).

Chapter 10
The Centrally Planned Economy and Railways in Hungary

Zsuzsa Frisnyák

Almost 17 per cent of all Second World War damage in Hungary involved the transportation system. War damage amounted to 59 per cent of the country's estimated national wealth in 1944.[1] But Hungary did not just lose World War Two. Having ended up in the Soviet sphere, it also lost control for various periods of time over its own communication network. Initially the Soviet army controlled Hungarian railroads for the purpose of war operations and to serve the needs of the Soviet Union. In 1945, 50 per cent of the capacity of the Hungarian State Railway, originally named Magyar Államvasutak (MÁV), measured in freight tons per kilometre, was taken up by services performed for the Soviet Union free of charge. In 1946, the figure was 25 per cent.

Between 1945 and 1948, a post-war reconstruction effort, accompanied by a political campaign, aimed at the rapid reconstruction of the pre-war railway system. This met with the full support of the Hungarian society. The reconstruction was officially completed in 1948, though this was only propaganda; in reality, it was completed in 1953. But from 1948 onward, those in charge of the national economy narrowed down the problem of transportation to that of freight traffic. The railway lost its political priority, in spite of the fact that the national defence and military projects of the period emphasised the development of transportation networks (operational area, staging area).[2]

---

[1] See Iván Pető and Sándor Szakács, *A hazai gazdaság négy* évtizedének *története 1945–1985. I. Az újjáépítés és a tervutasításos irányítás időszaka* (History of four Decades of the Homeland Economy 1945–1985. I. The Period of Rebuild and Central Command Economy) (Budapest 1985), 18, and National Archives of Hungary (*Magyar Országos Levéltár*, MOL), Ministry of Foreign Affers, Peace Preparations Depatment, XIX–J–1. a. 25. III–62. Magyarország közlekedési problémái a békekötéssel kapcsolatban, 1946. június 13 (Transportation problems of Hungary related to the peace treaty, 13 June 1946).

[2] See István Balló, 'Adalékok Magyarország 1949–1953 közötti háborús felkészítéséről, a várható hadszíntér előkészítéséről' (Supplements to the Wartime Preparations of Hungary in 1949–1953, about the Preparation of the Expected Theatre of War), *Hadtörténeti Közlemények*, 4, 1999, 800–23, here 800–809, and Imre Okváth, *Bástya a béke frontján. Magyar haderő és katonapolitika 1945–1956* (A Stronghold on the Frontline of Peace. Hungarian Army and Military Politics) (Budapest 1999), 15.

The origins of the command economy in Hungary go back to 1947. Similarly, even before the introduction of the one-party state in 1949, Hungary began to adopt the Soviet model of transportation. The most important features of the Soviet model of transportation were the following: total state control over transport vehicles, party oversight, the merging of control and implementation, central command, the economy of shortage and Stakhanovite labour competitions.[3] This Soviet model shattered traditional organisational forms, ownership structure, and the regulatory system of the Hungarian transport system, and replaced them with new structures. The important features of the Soviet model were made widely known by the translation of Soviet technical literature and the mass dissemination of Communist propaganda brochures. Propaganda depicted all elements of Soviet transport as good and an example to be followed. All who disagreed were branded as enemies. Slavish copying of the Soviet model reached extremes in the period between 1950 and 1953.

Hungary's Sovietisation resulted in a rapid growth in the performance of cargo shipping. One can analyse rail performance in terms of freight tons per kilometre. In 1937, the figure was 3.044 billion. Rail performance in 1951 was 206 per cent of what it had been in 1937, 312 per cent in 1957, 438 in 1960, 505 in 1963, 608 in 1967 and 700 per cent in 1970. The greatest increases in performance as compared to the previous year occurred in 1950 (119 per cent) and 1952 (119 per cent). However, the forced industrialisation of the 1950s led to an ever more serious and increasing lag in transport capacity. In the 1950s, the centrally planned system and extensive industrialisation changed the country's pre-war production structure without an antecedent. One of the results of the structural changes was that the ratio of transportation expenses in the total cost of one unit of national product became far larger than before 1938.

In Communist Hungary, it was believed that in a Communist-led state, there was no conflict of interest, and therefore the branches of power need not be separated. The application of this logic to railways meant that control, supervision and implementation were merged into a single organisation in 1949.[4] From then on, the managing director of MÁV served as Deputy Minister of Transportation at the same time.[5] Between 1949 and 1956, Lajos Bebrits (1891–1963), a Muscovite

---

[3]   Total state control applied even to individually owned vehicles. Between 1951 and 1957 the state kept record of bicycles. Between 1949 and 1956 it was a special privilege to own an automobile. The state had a priority of purchase for horses and carts.

[4]   See Vilma Alföldi, 'A közlekedés és posta irányítási rendszere 1945–1955' (The Management System of Transportation and Post 1945–1955), *ÚMKL Közleményei*, 2, 1985, 146–89, here 146 and 188.

[5]   Defence Authority took MÁV president László Varga from his home. He was condemned to death in a show trial and executed in 1950. The case had no publicity at all. It is typical for the retention of information that in the days of the 1956 revolution some of the railway workers demanded László Varga to head the Hungarian State Railways again, as an uncompromised and credible man. They did not know he had been killed.

functionary who had been incarcerated in Stalin's prisons, was the Minister of Transportation. A passionate railway enthusiast, Bebrits dedicated most of his time to the railway. He was impulsive and rash, but he respected professional competence. MÁV's first managing director was György Csanádi (1905–1974), who was later to become the most successful Minister of Transportation in the Kádár era. Up to 1956, a Soviet adviser operated in the Ministry of Transportation. The Soviet adviser was always treated with respect. His Hungarian colleagues listened to his recommendations politely and followed them, even when their implementation in Hungary was tantamount to a regression from a more advanced structure to a more rudimentary one. Only Bebrits dared say no to the Soviet advisers now and again. And the leaders of the railway company pretended to agree with the Soviet advisers but tacitly backed Bebrits.

In 1949, for the sake of party oversight, the Hungarian Workers Party (Magyar Dolgozók Pártja, MDP) established Railway-Political Departments, which were party units delegated to the railways. Functionaries working at the Railway-Political Departments were paid by the party. The Railway-Political Departments were in charge of agitation, repression and political cleansing (from intimidation to sacking). Members of the Railway-Political Departments were in close contact with the feared State Defence Authority. They knew next to nothing about railways and acted as commissars. Their behaviour was characterised by brutality and scandal. Even before the outbreak of the revolution, the party disbanded the Railway-Political Departments in 1956.

The Railway in the 1950s

Hungary's leaders in the 1950s were not people who thought in terms of long-term problems of transport policy or geopolitical strategy. Instead, they had daily problems and daily solutions on their minds. The five-year plan for transport was compiled along the perspectives of branches and territories. The cargo shipment plan constituted the most important element of the transportation plan, which summed up the shipping indicators for industrial, agricultural, mining and other sectors.[6] Shipping indicators were constantly adjusted to the ever-changing five-year plans. Hence, for example, in 1952, the transport-related indicators of the five-year plan were modified 113 times. Shipping plans were made for each individual type of commodity.

Established in 1948, the Central Transportation Council was in charge of working out and implementing shipment plans; its work was marked by bureaucratic coordination and the economy of shortage. The Council was in

---

[6] MOL, Ministry of Transport and Post (KPM) XIX–A–16a. 167. 78/903/950. Részletes utasítás a közlekedési ágak dolgozói és az összes tervkötelezettek részére szállítási tervek készítésére, 1950 (Detailed instruction to the transportation workers about transportation planning, 1950).

charge of bringing the indicators appearing in the Hungarian five-year plans in line with the shipping capacity at the disposal of rail and road transport companies. This proved to be all but impossible, because the five-year plans were not in line with transportation capacities at all. In order to bridge the gap, in 1950 the Council established an optimal shipping distance for each and every commodity. Producers were charged extra for commodities that had to be shipped longer than the optimal shipping distance. In addition, the Council prepared operative plans every three months that established the quantity of goods each company was allowed to ship by rail or road in any given month. Almost incredibly, this system of transportation worked to some extent, although not the way the members of the Council had imagined. In order to keep the system in motion, they came up with many creative ideas (labour competitions, centralised allocation of commodities, limiting the delivery of certain kinds of commodities) in addition to loads of office work and even the intensification of repression. It was just its original objective that the new system was unable to meet, namely, to assure economical transportation. In fact, the elimination of direct contact between the producers resulted in the growth of the distance commodities had to be shipped.

By 1953, the divergence between reality and the indicators given in the transportation plans was so wide that the Council of Ministers decreed that producers were required to ship the quantity of goods laid down in the monthly plan. And what is to say about the consequences? The transportation system became overcrowded from companies delivering half-finished products to each other, back and forth.

Why was all this necessary? According to the Soviet model, there was no competition in transportation under socialism, because the state was able to organise transportation in the most efficient way possible. In socialist Hungary, the gap between the demand for transportation and the capacity concealed the existence of competition in transportation. In reality, competition continued to exist, only on the level of state administration. Companies – trying to shift assignments to each other, instead of being interested in obtaining new ones – did not compete with each other anymore; rather, it was the ministries that fought each other for the possession and control of transport capacities. In this system, victory did not depend on who offered the fastest and least expensive service, but on relations of power. There were informal rankings, and privileges appeared even in the world of transportation.

Labour competitions were a spectacular and frequent feature of socialist railways. The most important and best known competition was one called the 500 Kilometres Movement. It aimed at making sure that locomotives performed their daily service duty of 500 kilometres. This goal was never attained. The average daily performance of locomotives taking part in the movement was 160 kilometres in 1950 and only 108 kilometres in 1952. Locomotives that did not participate in the competition ran 104 kilometres daily. There were 13 different labour competitions underway in the field of rail transportation at the end of 1952.

Figure 10.1   Communist propaganda. A peasant, a soldier and a worker looking
              into the cargo traffic plans

Source: Hungarian Museum of Science, Technology and Transport.

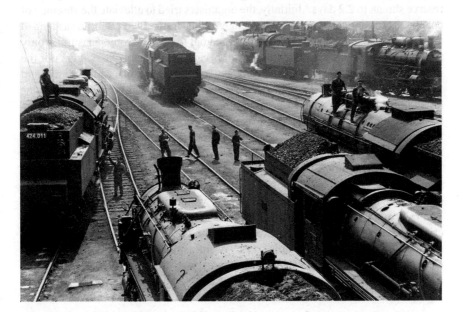

Figure 10.2   Steam engines waiting for the train in Budapest, 1950s

Source: Hungarian Museum of Science, Technology and Transport.

Propaganda of the Stakhanovite movement proclaimed that the wisdom and cleverness of popular cadres could surpass the technical expertise of Hungarian engineers and the restrictions imposed by technological regulations. According to the propaganda, labour competition was a high-standards method of building the socialist railway. But labour competitions were at odds with the very essence of the railway. Railways are not built on competition but on cooperation: the rhythmic operation of a complex system is guaranteed by the coordinated cooperation of the participants. Railways have always required the temporal and spatial collaboration of tens of thousands of people. The competitions created a hitherto unknown phenomenon: a lack of cooperation between the service branches of traction and traffic. Some examples may illustrate that: a crew of traffic workers offered to start more freight trains than earlier thus increasing the utilisation of wagons, even at the price of starting empty ones. At the same time another crew of traction workers offered to carry heavier trains. Engine drivers offered to take fewer engines to the repair workshop by doing some repair tasks by themselves, while the servicemen offered to repair more engines. This contributed to the rail traffic crisis and was one reason why Hungarian railway traffic collapsed in 1952.[7] This was unprecedented. Nothing like it had happened before in Hungarian history. First, in the fall of 1952, the traffic broke down between the Hungarian and the Soviet railways. Goods had to wait an average of 30–35 days on the Hungarian-Soviet border crossing (Záhony) in the wide-gauge Soviet wagons. The shortage of wagons was made even worse by the general shortage of coal. The railway's coal reserve shrank to 2.2 days.[8] Initially, the organisers tried to alleviate the shortage of coal by decreasing the number of passenger trains. Later, Lajos Bebrits suspended timetable based passenger traffic. This turned out to be the wrong measure: it only served to increase the chaos in rail traffic, because neither the passengers nor the railway workers knew what to do. More and more freight trains carried fewer and fewer goods. In the last four months of 1952, the huge number of freight trains (124,000!) overloaded the rail network. Insufficient transport capabilities, wrong traffic measures and work competitions all contributed to the growth of the huge traffic jams. There were days when 87 per cent of the freight trains were cooped up, loaded, in small areas of the railway network.

The general opinion of the experts was that by the end of 1952, traffic had reached the upper limit of the railway's capacity. In early 1953 it was clear that the railway collapse that had taken place in 1952 would not remain an isolated event. The railway leadership did their best to warn the political leadership that a new crisis in transportation could be expected in the fall of 1953, and that investment was needed. However, developing railway infrastructure was not on the state's economic agenda. The party had to find another way to avoid or alleviate the next traffic crisis. This turned out to be the intensification of repression.

---

[7]   Frisnyák, 'A hazai vasúti közlekedés jellemzői és válsága 1949–1953 között', 270–90.

[8]   At the end of the nineteenth century, MÁV had a coal reserve that would last about two months. Half of it was the so-called military coal supply.

In order to intimidate railway workers, the State Defence Authority carried out a coordinated action in March 1953 and carried off 239 railway men from their homes with the charge that prior to 1945 they had been involved in counterespionage in MÁV's military cargo department.[9] But the party, however, did not have the political strength anymore to carry out a massive show trial, as Stalin died in March 1953. Therefore the terror eased in the country. Repression in the workplace, politically motivated layoffs and transfers gradually diminished after peaking in 1953. The relaxation of political terror did not mean any change in the system-specific features of the Soviet model.

The Elimination of the Soviet Model

The elimination of the Soviet model was a piecemeal process that took place over the course of almost two decades.

In Kádár's Hungary, in line with the doctrines of the Soviet model, the existence of competition between rail and road transport was denied. This went on until the beginning of the 1980s. The existence of freight competition between the two branches of transport seemed to be irreconcilable with the planned economy, and its presumed absence seemed to prove the superiority of the socialist state. The Central Transport Council continued to function even after 1956, and the railway suffered from periodic crises.[10] Investment in the railway sector increased only when tensions in transportation increased to an extent that the leading organs of the Hungarian Socialist Workers Party were forced to deal with the issue.[11] Significantly, after 1968, transport plans no longer had to be sent in, and from then on the Central Transport Council functioned without a scope of authority. They produced reports, and not much more.

Just like its predecessor, the Kádár system regarded railway tariffs (railway rates) as a political question. Despite the increased charges and inflation, tariffs for long-distance passenger transport hardly changed between 1952 and 1982. The situation was similar in the field of freight transport. Market prices applied for loading and other services only. All this meant that the shipping needs of different producers were not met by any limit and the real costs of shipping were

---

9 Frisnyák, 'Az ÁVH és a vasúti kémelhárítók, 1953', 253–69.

10 Major, 'Szállítási feszültségek Magyarországon, a vasúti közlekedés példája alapján', 101.

11 Between 1950 and 1967, over 100 billion forints (at 1968 levels) of investment were missing from the transportation sector, which approached the value of two years of average investment in the 1960s. Between 1968 and 1980, the amount not invested in the development of transportation grew by another estimated 250 billion forints. Between 1960 and 1985 the share of transportation in fixed assets, i.e. the total wealth of the country, fell from 20.4 to 17.6 per cent.

not covered by the users. The producers had to pay only a fraction of the real transportation cost.

It was György Csanádi who pushed through the transportation modernisation programme. The 1960s and 1970s brought about the best period in Csanádi's career. It was clear to Csanádi that Hungarian national interests were connected to the transportation network (strengthening links with international transport, elevating the standards of transit routes, etc.), and he used his ministerial powers to push toward these goals. In cabinet meetings he submitted interesting proposals that were, however, rejected. The proposals tested the limits of the existing political and economic system. He argued, for instance, that the traffic corridor between Budapest and Vienna should be developed, and that private ownership of trucks should be permitted. He had prestige as a 'man of science', but he had no influence in the highest echelons of the Hungarian Socialist Workers Party (HSWP). Csanádi, who viewed developments in a European context, surrounded himself with well-trained advisers. They were the ones who drafted the reform concept in transport politics in 1968.

The aim of this concept was to bring the country's railway network (built in the nineteenth century) and the road network (that complemented the railway network) in line with the needs of twentieth century motorisation. The rail and road network, which carried the country's export, import and transit freight traffic, began to be prioritised once again. The new transportation concept broke with the investment policy inherited from the 1950s, and concentrated on cooperation between rail and road transport. The social reception of some of the provisions of the reform that parliament passed in 1968 was somewhat ambivalent (some people were unhappy that lines with small traffic had been closed), while other provisions received unequivocal support (railway electrification, modernisation of the railway trunk lines).[12] The 1968 reform programme no longer relied on a central logistical organisation being in charge of planning transportation (let us remember the activity of the Central Transport Council in the 1950s) but on the transformation of the rail and road network instead. Under the programme, freight and passenger lines were closed when the traffic was too low, and trucks and buses went into service in their stead. Between 1968 and 1982, 634 kilometres of normal lines, 360 kilometres of narrow-gauge lines and 672 kilometres of private industrial railway lines dedicated to a certain factory were closed down in Hungary. By 1970 10 per cent, by 1980 20.6 per cent, by 1985 25.8 per cent and by 1990 28 per cent of MÁV's lines were electrified. All in all, in Hungary the proportion of electrified lines within the network grew more rapidly as compared to the 1960s than anywhere else in Europe except Finland. This relative speed of railway electrification lost some of its momentum after 1980.

Csanádi was able to push through the idea that Hungary's transportation-strategic position was a valuable asset of such importance that it had to be put into

---

[12]   Erdősi, 'A magyarországi normál nyomtávú vasúthálózat megritkításának következményei', 655.

the service of the national interest. It was Csanádi who explained to the leadership socialised in the 1950s what transit traffic was. In his opinion it meant a way to earn hard currency. In the 1950s, transit traffic brought no profit. In 1951 a unified railway tariff was introduced for all railway traffic among the socialist countries based on the assumption that all socialist states shared a common interest. In reality, though, this measure served the interests of the Soviet Union. Not only did Hungary lose money because of this measure, it was also deprived of an important tool of economic policy. It took decades for Hungary to be able to back out of a system that was contrary to its national interest. For two decades, the Council for Mutual Economic Assistance (COMECON, an economic organisation of socialist countries) struggled to resolve two financial issues related to transportation: tariffs and financial settlement. In 1951, when the Soviet bloc established its new railway regime, the Soviet Union had not figured in railway cargo traffic between the socialist and the Western countries; therefore, in the 1960s, Western transport companies also benefited from the low tariffs.

In 1964, because of conflicts of interest among the COMECON member states, tariffs were raised provisionally to a different extent for each country group, by 17.5 per cent (Bulgaria and Romania) and 35 per cent (Czechoslovakia, GDR, Poland and Soviet Union), respectively. Hungary did not take part in the raising of tariffs.[13] The COMECON countries could only reach a provisional agreement in two railway-financial issues, because of their opposing interests. The first issue was the increase of tariffs. The second was the rules of financial liquidation between each other. Hungary did not raise the tariffs, being afraid – as it later turned out unfounded – that raising tariffs would weaken its position of negotiation in the second issue, which was more important for Hungary. By the mid seventies, COMECON's provisional tariffs became untenable: Western European railways were charging three to four times as much.

The debate on railway tariffs that had taken place largely in the framework of COMECON for two decades reached its climax in 1980. In 1976, Poland rescinded the 1951 agreement governing railway tariffs among socialist countries and all the other amending agreements. In 1980, Czechoslovakia and Hungary did the same. In 1980, too, the Hungarian State Railway carried the most transit cargo in Europe with 19.7 million tons. Starting in 1981, Hungary raised its tariffs annually: by 92 per cent in 1981, 16 per cent in 1982, 4 per cent in 1983 and by 4 per cent again in 1984. Rise in transport prices re-established transport competition among the railway companies in Central Europe. In this field, MÁV competed with the Yugoslav, the Austrian and the Czechoslovak railways. In 1983 MÁV gave 50 foreign companies 150 individual discounts for them to use its lines for their transit traffic.

In contrast to the 1951 unified tariff system, the establishment of the Common Goods Wagon Park in Russia named *Obschtchij Park Wagonow* (OPW) turned out to be advantageous for Hungary. The OPW was based on a concept developed

13   MOL, XIX–A–83a. 238. Record of Council of Ministers, 8 August 1964.

by György Csanádi. The Central Railway Wagon Pool held 100,000 wagons from seven COMECON countries in such a way that the wagons placed in the common reserve remained in the possession of the railway company that owned them. The benefit of the new accounting system was that a wagon did not have to be returned immediately to the owner's line – even when empty – but, with certain restrictions, it could be used in COMECON traffic. MÁV conducted a large quantity of transit traffic but suffered from a shortage of wagons: hence, it was interested in making use of the wagon pool as much as possible. As for the structure of MÁV's hard currency income and costs, income came from transit while the majority of the expenditures came from leasing from the common pool.

According to Hungarian propaganda, while capitalist transportation relationships exclusively protected the interests of their participants, socialist transportation relationships reflected the common interests of the fraternal countries. Hence the agreements concluded by the socialist countries represented the diverse interests of the community of allied countries on a higher, general plane. This of course was not exactly true. Hungary did not copy the Soviet Union in this case. So it was a sober decision for Hungary to remain a member in the Union internationale des chemins de fer (UIC) in 1945. In 1956, the transport ministers of eight European and four Far Eastern socialist countries founded the Organisation of Railway Cooperation which was named in Russian ОРГАНИЗАЦИЯ СОТРУДНИЧЕСТВА ЖЕЛЕЗНЫХ ДОРОГ (OSZhD). COMECON's Permanent Committee for Transport was set up in 1958, but its work was fundamentally hampered by the fact that the recommendations and resolutions had to be passed unanimously. Until the middle of the 1960s Hungary neglected the sub-committees of the European Economic Commission in charge of transport. In 1971, the idea that Hungary could join the European Conference of Ministers of Transport (ECMT) was raised, but it was rapidly dismissed as not timely.

Conclusion

In Hungary the questions of international transport relations and the national interests related to them were hardly ever mentioned during the Kádár years. The public knew nothing of the conflict of interest in international transport among the members of the COMECON. After 1945, Hungary was integrated into the Soviet sphere of interest and subordinated its international transport relations to the Soviet Union's interests. In 1950 the capitals of Hungary and Yugoslavia were connected by only two express trains. In 1950, 13 European destinations were directly linked to the Hungarian railway system. In 1960, the number had risen to 25, and in 1970, 49.

Throughout the Kádár years, Hungary participated in the evolving European transport system and followed the (Western) European trend only to a limited extent, because for a long time the country defined itself primarily as part of the socialist community and only secondarily as a European country. Hungary usually did not take the initiative: when representing its transport interests within the COMECON, it was open to agreements, it searched for compromises and allies. Hungary strove to keep the socialist countries' conflicts of interest hidden from public eyes.[14] In response to the intensification of links between Western countries (InterCity, EuroCity), the socialist countries also expanded their railway contacts, for example through Inter-express. Out of the 30 trains that operated in the Inter-express network only 3 involved Hungary. As time went by, socialist Hungary's foreign policy and foreign economic orientation had less and less influence on its foreign transport relations.

In the final years of the Kádár system, the state apparatus redefined Hungary's interests in transport and the state's role in it. The state broke with the remnants of the Soviet model in 1983. Then they eliminated the structure that had come about after MÁV's reorganisation in 1949. State and company authorities were separated once again. After the elimination of the last remnants of Sovietisation, there was no more room for development within the framework of the existing political system. Transport policy in the last years of the Kádár period was characterised by a tactic of minimising loss and fence-sitting. The public failed to notice an event of symbolic importance: in late May 1988, the first Vienna-bound EuroCity Express departed from Budapest. This meant that Hungary was the first socialist country to join the EC network that so spectacularly embodied the unity of European transport.

Some historians interpret the history of socialist Hungary as an experiment in modernisation. Perhaps this paper has made it clear that the post-1945 history of the Hungarian railway would be difficult to interpret within the framework of this approach. It is not that those who worked in this area did not do their best to modernise the country's transportation and were not devoted to their profession. It is that most of what was done was damage control in the sense that it tried to solve the problems that arose out of the planned economy, the mechanism of the economy. A great deal of inventiveness and lots of energy was required to find the limited number of solutions within the framework provided by the political system.

Bibliography

Alföldi, Vilma, 'A közlekedés és posta irányítási rendszere 1945–1955' (The Management System of Transportation and Post 1945–1955), *ÚMKL Közleményei*, 2, 1985, 146–89.

---

[14] The reloading of normal and wide-gauge freight wagons caused constant tension in the transport relationship between Hungary and the Soviet Union. In 1979–1980 the Soviet Union's crisis in railway transport had an impact on Hungary. There were similar traffic problems in 1981, 1984 and 1985, MOL, KPM. XIX–H–1 pp. 446. d. and XIX–H–1 rr. 1. 38. d. Iratok a magyar-szovjet áruszállítás helyzetéről, és a forgalmi válságról (Papers about the status of the Hungarian–Soviet goods transportation, and about the traffic crisis).

Balló, István, 'Adalékok Magyarország 1949–1953 közötti háborús felkészítéséről, a várható hadszíntér előkészítéséről' (Supplements to the Wartime Preparations of Hungary in 1949–1953, about the Preparation of the Expected Theatre of War), *Hadtörténeti Közlemények*, 4, 1999, 800–23.

Erdősi, Ferenc, 'A magyarországi normál nyomtávú vasúthálózat megritkításának következményei' (Consequences of Downsizing the Normal-Gauge Railways in Hungary), *Területi statisztika*, 6, 1985, 650–60.

Frisnyák, Zsuzsa, 'A hazai vasúti közlekedés jellemzői és válsága 1949–1953 között' (Features and Crisis of Railway Transportation between 1949–1953), in István Mezei (ed.), *Vasúthistória Évkönyv 1997* (Budapest 1999), 263–301.

Frisnyák, Zsuzsa, 'Az ÁVH és a vasúti kémelhárítók, 1953' (The State Defense Authority and the Counter-Espionage of the Railway), in István Mezei (ed.), *Vasúthistória Évköny 2001* (Budapest 2003), 253–69.

Major, Iván, *Szállítási feszültségek Magyarországon, a vasúti közlekedés példája alapján* (Transportation Stress in Hungary, Based on the Example of Rail Transportation) (Budapest 1981).

Okváth, Imre, *Bástya a béke frontján. Magyar haderő és katonapolitika 1945–1956* (A Stronghold on the Frontline of Peace: Hungarian Army and Military Politics) (Budapest 1999).

Pető, Iván and Szakács, Sándor, *A hazai gazdaság négy évtizedének története 1945–1985. I. Az újjáépítés és a tervutasításos irányítás időszaka* (History of Four Decades of the Homeland Economy 1945–1985: I. The Period of Rebuilding and Central Command Economy) (Budapest 1985).

Chapter 11
The Railways of the Ukrainian Soviet Socialist Republic: 1920–1990

Ihor Zhaloba

In 1991, Ukraine inherited from the Soviet Union six railways: Odeska, Pivdenno–Zakhidna, Pivdenna, Donetska, Prydniprovska and L'vivs'ka. The main lines of most of these railways were built in the second half of the nineteenth century and in the early twentieth century within the territories of the largest empires in Europe, the Austro-Hungarian and the Russian. How did these railways develop after the collapse of the states that gave birth to them? What factors influenced this development? What was the condition of these railways when independent Ukraine took them over in 1991? Lines that are part of the L'vivs'ka Railway today formerly belonged to the Kingdom of Romania and to two newly established states – Poland and Czechoslovakia. Their development was quite different from the processes in the Union of Soviet Socialist Republics where the other five railways were situated.

Ukrainian Railways in the Transition Period from Free to Socialist Industry (1920–1941)

The USSR's official historiography divided the time after the Ukrainian War of Independence (or Civil War) and before World War Two (also known as the German–Soviet War, or, in Soviet terminology, the Great Patriotic War) in June of 1941 into the following periods: the period of the restoration of national industry (1921–25), the period of the establishment of the basis of socialism (1926–32), the period of the completion of the socialist reconstruction of national industry (1933–37), and the period before the Great Patriotic War (1938–June 1941). These impressive, positive-sounding words mask the drastic, violent and often bloody transformation of public life in every sphere, from culture in its broadest sense to industry and railways.

After the War of Independence from 1918 to 1920 when, after all attempts, the Ukrainians failed to defend their own independent state, the Ukrainian Soviet Socialist Republic was established in the Ukrainian part of the former Russian empire. It was very closely connected with the Bolshevik regime in Moscow and consequently in 1922 it announced itself as part of the newly founded Union of Soviet Socialist Republics. In 1920 in the Ukraine Soviet Socialist Republic

(UkrSSR), the railways retained the names they had received in the Tsarist times: the Pivdenno–Zakhidna Railway, with its centre in Kiev; Pivdenna Railway, with its centre in Kharkiv, which, incidentally, was the capital of the UkrSSR from 1919 to 1934; the Donetska Railway, renamed Donetski Railways in 1921; and the Yekaterininskaja Railway, with its centre in the city Katerynoslaw (Ekaterinoslaw in Russian, since 1926 the city was renamed into Dnipropetrovsk), and has most recently been renamed the Dnipropetrovsk Railway. Under the UkrSSR, all of these railways were nationalised. At the beginning of the 1920s there were formed new administration districts. The existing Odeska and Krymska branches, together with the above-mentioned railways and the Taganrog branch became part of the Pivdennyi district of transportation and communication.[1]

The transport conditions as well as industry as a whole were in a horrible shape in the first years after the War of Independence. In 1920, about 80 per cent of the railway network was damaged. More than 4,000 railway bridges were destroyed or damaged, including two important bridges in Kiev (960 metres and 2,300 metres respectively), one in Cherkasy (1,088 metres), one in Kremenchug (880 metres) and one at Dnipropetrovsk (1,070 metres) across the Dnieper and at Mykolayiv one across the Pivdennyi Bug. About 60 per cent of the engines and 23 per cent of the rolling stock were in bad condition and required repairs. Ivan Gronskij, a delegate to the All-Russian Congress of Soviets, remembered that in December of 1922, one could see 'graveyards of broken engines and wagons' at locomotive depots and railway stations.[2] During the times of the War of Independence, the railway losses amounted to more than one billion gold roubles in the prices of 1920.[3]

Among the Ukrainian railways, the one in the worst condition was the Pivdenno–Zakhidna Railway. At the beginning of the 1920s, it was the longest

---

[1]   At the start of the 1920s in the Soviet State for the centralised management of railways there were created regions (boroughs) of communication lines, namely Petrogradskij Kavkazky (Caucasus), Turkestan. The existing railways were managed by the Pivdenny (Southern) region of communication lines and were divided into the four above-mentioned railways. Besides this there also existed three line departments – Odessa, Crimea and Taganrog, that were in their turn, parts of South-Western, Kateryninska and Donetsk Railways respectively, but with a certain portion of autonomy in management. All of them were built in the second half of nineteenth and the beginning of twentieth century. See Г.М. *Афонина, Краткие сведения о развитии отечественных железных дорог с 1838 по 1990 гг.* (Москва 1995), 95–101. On 4 March 1919, by decree of the People's Commissars Soviet of UkrSSR, the People's Commissariat of Connection Ways of Ukraine was established. However, this body had little importance in the running of the railways, as it was subordinated to the centre in Moscow. See Б.С. Олейник (ed.), *Юго-Западная железная дорога. Вчера. Сегодня. Завтра* (Киев 1995), 63.

[2]   See А.А. Зайцев, В.Е. Павлов and М.М. Уздин, 'Восстановление и начало реконструкции железных дорог (1921–1928)', in В.Е. Павлов and М.М. Уздин (eds), *История железнодорожного транспорта России и Советского Союза: 1917–1945 гг.* (Санкт-Петербург 1997), 25.

[3]   Ibid.

railway of the country, totalling 4,820 kilometres. But during the war 58 large bridges were blown up, and 70 per cent of the engines and 30 per cent of the rolling stock were out of use. In 1920, this railway transported only one-nineteenth of the freight volume and one-ninth of the number of passengers of 1915.[4]

There was also a serious shortage of technical experts, qualified workers and clerks. In Kharkiv the locomotive and wagon plants were damaged and out of use and the shops in Luhansk operated only irregularly. The supply of locomotive fuel was most irregular and that caused all movement to come to a complete standstill on 31 lines in February 1921.[5] As early as in 1919 at a meeting in Lenin's office, the experts explained the sad state of transportation to the Soviet authorities. At this meeting Lenin authorised Leon Trotsky, at that time People's Commissar of Army and Navy Affairs and chairman of the Supreme Military Council, to head the People's Commissariat of Transport and impose order on the railways by means of extreme measures.[6] The most important of these measures were the involvement of specialists, the creation of workers' armies, and the founding and active use of a transportation tribunal in accordance with the policy of 'military communism' which the Bolsheviks were following then, plus three new principles of Bolshevik policy: management centralisation, personal responsibility of all authorities and strict discipline.

In 1921, the Communist Party announced a change in the policy, the so-called transition to a 'New Economic Policy' (NEP) which was supposed to allow market elements in the economy. Naturally, the Party was to control the process. This was especially evident in the transportation sphere where a new chief was appointed. This was Feliks Dzerzhynskyi, who simultaneously stayed on as head of the All-Russia Extraordinary Commission to Combat Counter-revolution and Sabotage (known as Cheka for its initials in Russian), which was the main repressive body of the Bolsheviks. At the same time he also remained in charge of the People's Commissariat of Internal Affairs, i.e. Narodnyy komissariat vnutrennikh del (NKVD).[7] Strict measures, reorganisation of the administration, broad propaganda and agitation had their positive results: by 1925 almost all planned repairs of engines and rolling stock had been finished, freight traffic reached 104.8 per cent of the volumes of 1913, and in 1925/1926 the total length of the USSR railway

---

[4]   See Олейник, *Юго-Западная железная дорога*, 65.

[5]   See Е.П. Муравьева, 'Железнодорожный транспорт в период восстановления народного хозяйства (1921–1925)', in А.Г. Мушруб (ed.), *Развитие советского железнодорожного транспорта* (Москва 1984), 45–6.

[6]   В.И. Голубев and М.М. Уздин, 'Железные дороги в годы гражданской войны и военной интервенции', in Павлов and Уздин, *История железнодорожного транспорта России и Советского Союза*, 16, 18.

[7]   See Б.М. Николаев, 'Нарком Дзержинский', *Электрическая и тепловозная тяга*, 10, 1987, 22–4, here 23.

lines was 74,600 kilometres as compared with 58,500 kilometres in 1913.[8] The network of vocational schools was also founded in these years.[9]

However, despite all efforts, the railways in the Ukraine were in quite a bad shape at the beginning of the 1930s. The cause of the problem was the establishment of the totalitarian regime in the USSR. This became manifest in the transition from the NEP, with its liberal approaches to economic process management at the end of 1920s, to the more authoritarian and non-economic methods of running the national economy. At the beginning of the 1930s there was a return to the bankrupt policy of 'military communism', which was based on the idea that commodity-money relations were dying out. Now, administration by force became the determining factor in the USSR's economic policy.

Scanty investment, and, in some years direct withdrawal and redistribution of railway profits to other sectors of the national economy resulted in the basic assets of the Ukraine railways becoming extremely dilapidated. Chaotic attempts from the country's top political authorities to implement elements of economic accounting and increase work efficiency by offering rewards to railway workers resulted in even more centralisation in the management of transportation. It also curtailed the initiative both of workers and of branch top managers.

A string of problems – poor work discipline, high labour turnover, spontaneous strikes, the famine of 1932 and 1933, frequent accidents and insufficient financing and supply – meant that only 50 to 60 per cent of the annually planned transportation actually took place.[10] Looking for reasons for these problems, the Soviets found many 'enemies' and started to repress them. These 'enemies' became a simplified and clear explanation of the accidents at work, the lack of consumer goods, the difficulties with the supply of products etc. At the end of 1920s and in the 1930s, waves of repression engulfed one by one the Ukrainian railways. First, kurkuls (wealthy peasants) and 'bourgeois experts' were found guilty; then representatives of exploiting classes who 'infiltrated' into certain positions of responsibility; then

---

[8]   See Е.П. Муравьева, 'Железнодорожный транспорт', 65.

[9]   Ibid. 57, 63–5.

[10]   For example, in 1933 at Pivdenna Railways, 89,256 workers came and almost the same number, 76,840, left, taking into consideration the average annual number of 100,494. Also in 1933, 15,384 workers got disciplinary penalties. See Ю.И. Романенко and М.П. Харенко, *Взгляд сквозь годы: Южная железная дорога за 130 лет* (Харьков 1999), 104. See also Ю.П. Бондарчук, 'Залізничний транспорт України в умовах утвердження адміністративно-командних методів управління народним господарством (кін. 20-х-30-ті рр.)', University of Dnepropetrovsk PhD thesis, 1999, 10–11. See Ю.П. Бондарчук, 'Кадрові втрати українських залізниць в ході масових операцій ДПУ-НКВС УСРР 'По очищенню прикордонної смуги'', *Історія України. Маловідомі імена, події, факти*, 2, 1997, 239–46, and Ю.П. Бондарчук, 'Каральні операції органів НКВС України по вилученню "троцькістсько-зінов'євських елементів" на залізничному транспорті', *Історія України. Маловідомі імена, події, факти*, 3, 1998, 125–36.

it was numerous national groups 'recruited' by foreign intelligence services; and finally, Communists who were adherents of Trotsky's ideas.[11] They all suffered.

Alongside show trials of these different 'enemies', where at least a pretence of legitimacy was maintained, non-judicial repression of railway workers became the norm. For example, from 1 January to 1 December 1931, prosecutors of the transportation departments of the State political administration conducted more than 1,500 extrajudicial trials of railway workers during a campaign called 'On cleansing transportation of contra-revolutionary and socially strange and criminal elements'. At least 38 workers were sentenced to be shot, 500 were sentenced to imprisonment in gulags (ГУЛаг), 595 were sentenced to long terms of exile, 72 were sentenced into exile on probation.[12] A remarkable fact of this period is that among the railway workers shot in 1930s, there were 19 directors of Ukrainian railways. These included the first four directors of the Odeska Railway, Pavel Suslov, Lev Milkh, Arkadij Krykhun and Andrej Bodrov, and the directors of the Pivdenno–Zakhidna Railway, Vasilij Obolonnyi, Aleksej Zorin, Feodosij Sljusarenko and Aleksandr Svirikov.[13]

Despite these doubtful sentences, there were considerable achievements in the technical upgrading of the railway machinery at the end of the 1920s and 1930s.[14] A number of changes took place in the mid 1930s. Investments in the Ukrainian railways increased. Fares were reformed and the bureaucratic machine was reorganised. A large number of women were hired to replace the men who had been removed. And technical state examinations were introduced for inexperienced new workers and functionaries; from 1933 to 1936, 259,743 railway workers of the UkrSSR passed this exam.[15] These developments brought some stability to railway transportation, but they could not help achieve the planned development of the railway network or the planned volumes of freight and passenger transportation completely. It was especially obvious that the search for a solution of the problems had never advanced beyond the limits of administration, orders from above and moral and physical intimidation of the workers. One example was the Soviet propaganda that trumpeted about socialist competition, but the

---

[11]   Бондарчук, 'Залізничний транспорт України', 15.

[12]   Бондарчук, 'Каральні операції', 120.

[13]   See Бондарчук, 'Залізничний транспорт України', 16, and В.М. Косьяненко (ed.), *Дорога и люди* (Одесса 1991), 164, Олейник, Юго-западная железная дорога, 93–98, and Л.М. Абраменко, *Постали із забуття: Репресовані залізничники, 1919–1953* (Київ 2001), 120–44.

[14]   See В. Прилуцький, 'Модернізація транспорту Радянської України у міжвоєнний період (1921–1938 рр.)' *Проблеми історії України: факти, судження, пошуки*, 13, 2005, 313–42.

[15]   See Бондарчук, 'Залізничний транспорт України', 11, and Н.А. Захарченко, 'Железнодорожники Украинской ССР на завершающем этапе социалистической реконструкции народного хозяйства (1933–1937 гг.)', University of Dnepropetrovsk PhD thesis, 1988, 10–14.

actual achievements of the Stakhanov–Kryvonos Movement were not as high as claimed in official reports. If they had been, it would have been possible to reach the planning targets.[16]

In 1936 and 1937 the UkrSSR railways were amalgamated. The Ekaterininska Railway was renamed into Stalinska Railway (this name remained until 1961, when it received its current name Prydniprovska Railway) on the basis of Stalinska and Donetska Railways the Pivdenno–Donetska Railway was founded, Donetska Railway was renamed into Pivnichno–Donetska Railway; Pivdenno–Zakhidna Railways (plural) was transformed into Pivdenno–Zakhidna Railway (singular) when Odeska Railway was separated from that body.[17]

In the interwar period, the network of Ukrainian railways increased by 4,000 kilometres of new lines, the majority of which had already been planned before World War One. The main construction took place in the Centre and East of the UkrSSR.[18] The double track main line of the Moscow–Donbas Railway in Ukraine was one of the most important new projects in the entire USSR in the period between the wars.

---

[16]   The man who brought the Stakhanovite movement to Ukrainian railways was Petro Fedorovych Kryvonos, an engine driver of Slov'yansk station of the Donetskaya Railway. In July 1935 he achieved with his locomotive the average speed of 31.6 kilometres per hour and by the end of July he brought it to 37 kilometres per hour by raising the boiler pressure of his engine to 42–45 kilograms, thus outdoing the outdated standards. His triumph caused a wave of Stakhanovism, which spread across every sector in transport. But it should be also mentioned that one of the consequences of the Stakhanov–Kryvonos movement was a 'record mania', where without technical knowledge and with unprepared machines, inexperienced workers tried to break production records. A consequence of this were many accidents with boilers filled with the wrong quality of water which led to damage to the steam pipes and fittings, with the result that the steam engines then needed repairs. Moreover, inexperienced drivers handled heavyweight engines without taking notice of red light signals.

[17]   Афонина, *Краткие сведения*, 117–19 and 164.

[18]   Such railways as the 1925 Chernihiv–Nizhyn (83 kilometres), the 1927 Pohrebyshche-Zhashkiv (77 kilometres), the 1928 Chernihiv-Ovruch (157 kilometres), the 1929 Chernihiv–Novo–Bilytska (106 kilometres), the 1930 Pryluky–Nizhyn (65 kilometres) and the 1930 Fastiv–Novograd–Volynskyi (192 kilometres) were among the most significant projects of Southern-Western railways. In the time between 1936 and 1941 at Odeska Railway, the following lines were built: Artsyz to Izmail (109 kilometres), Vadym to Tsiurupa (78 kilometres), Zolotonosha to Liaplava (43 kilometres) and Monastyryshche to Kooperatyvne (8 kilometres). The Kolosovka–Vodopiy line was being built, intended to connect Odessa with industrial Donbas by the shortest way. On the Pivdenna Railway the following lines were built: in 1921–1926 the Kherson–Apostolove (156 kilometres), which later was extended to Kharkiv; in 1927 the Nyzhnedneprovsk–Kongrad–Merefa (199 kilometres); in 1928–1930, the Apostolove–Lotsmanske; in 1940 the Sviatohirsk–Kup'iansk (70 kilometres) and the Valuiky–Kondrashevska (222 kilometres). See Косьяненко, *Дорога и люди*, 149 and 165–6, and С.М. Слепухин, *Краткая истории строительства и развития Сталинской ж.д.: 1884–1948 гг.* (Днепропетровск 1949), 76. See also Олейник, *Юго-западная железная дорога*, 83 and Зінченко, 112, 120 and 123.

It created a third route for goods from the Donetsk coal basin to the industrial regions of Russia.[19] To become aware of its significance, it should be mentioned that the Donetsk coal basin was the main centre of the USSR for fuel and energy before the war. About 60 per cent of the coal, more than 37 per cent of the cast iron, 25 per cent of the steel, and almost 50 per cent of the coke came from there.[20]

At the end of 1930s, the breath of war was getting hotter and hotter in Germany and also in the USSR, which was getting ready to divide up the European pie with Germany. Under these circumstances, the Soviet Union undertook several administrative measurements to restructure and improve the work of the railways: operation districts were reorganised as traffic departments, engine sectors were changed into transportation sectors, and the former existing 24 railway lines were divided into no less than 51 lines.[21] For example, in 1940 the Vinnytsia Railway was split off from the Pivdenno–Zakhidna Railways; it existed as a separate unit until 1953.[22]

On the eve of war the People's Commissariat of Defence reorganised the defence of the railways. Some specialised troops (road, bridge, operational, and so on) were created and then combined into separate railway brigades. All in all, in the USSR, 14 railway brigades were established. Each consisted of a railway regiment, a battalion of repair workers and a battalion for bridge repairs. The technical equipment and mechanisation of military railway troops were also improved.[23] Such activities were particularly necessary for several reasons. At the beginning of September 1939, when the USSR prepared its military campaign against Poland, the railway transportation proved to be unsatisfactory, and consequently the military's transportation schedules failed.[24] Around the same time, because of the Soviet occupation of Western Ukraine, two additional railways were organised – the L'vivska and the Kovelska Railways.[25] These two covered the territories of

---

[19]   See Л.И. Коренев, 'Магистраль Москва – Донбасс', in Павлов and Уздин, *История железнодорожного транспорта России и Советского Союза*, 75–9.

[20]   Ibid. 79.

[21]   Олейник, *Юго-западная железная дорога*, 103.

[22]   І.Мазило, '3 історії відбудови залізничного транспорту Поділля 1944–1950-х рр. мовою документів', in В.В. Карпов (ed.), *Воєнна історія Поділля та Буковини* (Кам'янець-Подільський 2009), 403.

[23]   Олейник, *Юго-западная железная дорога*, 103.

[24]   See М.И. Мельтюхов, *Упущенный шанс Сталина: Советский Союз и борьба за Европу: 1939–1941 (Документы, факты, суждения)* (Москва 2000). An online version can be found at http://militera.lib.ru/research/meltyukhov/03.html (last accessed 3 August 2010).

[25]   The total length of the Ukraine railways in western regions (L'vivska and Kovelska Railways) and Western Byelorussia (Brest-Lytovska and Bilostotska Railways) that became subordinate to the USSR was 6,700 kilometres, including 4,900 kilometres of single track and 1,800 kilometres of double track lines. See І. Мазило, 'Відновлення роботи і розвиток залізничного транспорту в західноукраїнських областях 1944–1950 рр. (на

Halychyna and Volyn, which had been owned by Poland in the period between the wars. In Halychyna, the construction of the railway network had been executed by the Austrian empire, and in Volyn by Russia in the second half of the nineteenth and the beginning of the twentieth centuries.

In the interwar period, the only addition to the existing railway network of the aforementioned regions was the August 1928 completion of the line from L'viv via Stoianiv to Lutsk, a line whose construction had started in 1914.[26] To make them compatible with the new Soviet railways, the Soviet workers began to pull up the standard-gauge tracks of their new acquisitions and spike them back in place according to the Soviet standard of 1520 mm. To meet the needs of the Soviet Army it was necessary to increase the traffic capacity, especially of the L'vivska Railway. That is why a lot of money was invested in the rebuilding of the Western Ukrainian and Byelorussian railways. To implement these large scale works, the 1st, 4th and 5th Railway Brigades, a special corps of railway troops, were transferred to the western regions. One of their tasks was to construct a second track on the section from Iarmolyntsi via Kopychyntsi to Bila (Chortkivska) and the continuation from Buchach via Monastyrsk to Stanislaviv (today, Ivano-Frankivsk). The line from Ostriv via Potutory to Khodoriv was also slated for this improvement. The construction of a second track allowed the creation of new transport corridors to the west.

In June, 1940, the USSR's troops occupied the territories of Bessarabia and Northern Bukovyna. And though the territory of Bukovyna was not covered under the secret clauses of the Molotov-Ribbentrop Pact of 23 August 1939, the Soviets insisted on invading the northern part of Bukovyna. They were interested in controlling the railway to Chernivtsi, which facilitated direct railway communication from Bessarabia to L'viv through Chernivtsi. The proof of such interest is that it took Soviet specialists only 24 hours to regauge the main L'viv–Chernivtsi line.[27] However, the railway sectors between the rivers Dniester and Danube were temporarily subordinate to the Kyshynivska Railway formed in

---

матеріалах Галичини і Закарпаття)', in В.В. Карпов (ed.), *Воєнна історія Галичини та Закарпаття* (Київ 2010), 549–52, here 549.

[26]   П. Гранкін, П. Лазечко, І. Сьомочкін, Г. Шрамко, *Львівська залізниця. Історія і сучасність* (Львів 1996), 103–5.

[27]   С.М. Гакман, Ю.І. Макар, 'Радянсько-румунсько-німецькі відносини і приєднання північної частини Буковини та Хотинського повіту Бессарабії до Української РСР у складі СРСР', in В.М. Ботушанський (ed.), *Буковина в контексті європейських міжнародних відносин (з давніх часів до середини XX ст.)* (Чернівці 2005), 611–12. The railways in Bukovyna were built when the area belonged to the Habsburg monarchy, and they did not change much in the period between wars, when the region was part of the Kingdom of Romania. See I. Zhaloba, I. Piddubnyj, 'Verkehrs- und Kommunikationsnetze in Czernowitz in der Zwischenkriegszeit (1918–1940)', in R. Roth (ed.), *Städte im europäischen Raum: Verkehr, Kommunikation und Urbanität im 19. und 20. Jahrhundert* (Stuttgart 2009), 63–86.

1940.[28] This was because they were within the UkrSSR's Akkermanska Oblast, formed on 7 August 1940, and renamed Izmail Oblast on 7 December of the same year. These railway sectors included the line from Akkerman to Artsyz. A line from Artsyz to Izmail was constructed later to achieve direct railway communication between the Moldavian SSR and the UkrSSR. The Bukovynian Railways were also subordinated to the Kyshynivska Railway, though Northern Bukovyna – which was within the borders of Chernivtsi Oblast formed on 7 August 1940 – was included within the UkrSSR. On the whole, together with the above-mentioned changes in 1940, the total railway network of Ukraine had reached a length of 20,100 kilometres, 7.1 per cent of the total in the USSR. In 1913, by contrast, the Ukrainian railways had a network of only 10,900 kilometres.[29] In 1913 they had shipped 61.7 million tons of freight and 49 million passengers; in 1940, these figures rose up to 200 million tons of freight and 243 million passengers.

The Ukrainian Railways in the Times of the German–Soviet War (1941–1945)

On 22 June 1941 the German–Soviet War began. At once the Soviet authorities determined the main priorities in railway transport work under the conditions of war. The railways had to change over to a military schedule, discipline had to be strengthened and traffic capacity had to be increased. Since the beginning of the war, the territory of the UkrSSR was a battleground, and the most important task of the railway workers was to provide transportation for the Red Army: 85 per cent of this traffic was directed over the Moskovsko–Kievska, Pivdenno–Zakhidna and Pivdenna Railways. During the first months of the war, 291 divisions, 94 brigades and more than 2 million soldiers were sent to the front, mainly by rail. The percentage of military transportation on the UkrSSR's railways was 72.6 per cent in the first six weeks of the war.[30]

Alongside with the manpower to run the trains to the front, fighting battalions and people's volunteer corps were organised and recruited from the railway personnel, which meant a great help. They guarded railway lines and station buildings and provided security in the rear of the Soviet troops. The people's volunteer corps even participated in the actual fighting. As a considerable section of railway workers were drafted into the army, it became necessary to replace them with women and young people who had no corresponding qualification and whose training took place at an accelerated pace. Pensioners also returned to their old positions.

---

28   Косьяненко, *Дорога и люди*, 165.

29   А.Г. Яремчук, 'Развитие железнодорожного транспорта Украины (1951–1964 гг.)', Kiev Institute of National Economy PhD thesis, 1965, 8.

30   И.В. Мазыло, 'Железнодорожники Украинской ССР в годы Великой Отечественной войны (1941–1945)', Institute of History of Academy of Science of UkrSSR PhD thesis, 1988, 7–8.

Despite all difficulties, in June 1941 almost all the railways of Ukraine exceeded their average daily loading quotas. Along with the increasing transportation needs of the army and the national economy, as the enemy moved deeper into Soviet territory, it became vital to preserve the UkrSSR's industrial equipment, agricultural produce, cultural treasures and qualified labour force. With almost incredible efforts, the Ukrainian railway staff moved the equipment of 550 large industrial enterprises, part of the local industrial plants, the property of collectives and Soviet farms, the property of scientific institutions, and more than 3.5 million citizens to distant regions of the USSR. The significance of such heroic work in preserving and increasing the USSR's military production is difficult to overestimate. On the way a lot of difficulties had to be overcome and railway personnel worked under extremely difficult conditions. Some of these industrial enterprises had been involved in supplying the front up to the last possible moment. Orders for their evacuation were given only at the time of the greatest danger. Under such circumstances, the People's Commissariat of Communication Ways could not fully complete the registration and stock-taking of everything that had been moved. That is why railway workers were additionally able to evacuate a considerable amount of so-called 'undocumented freight'. This included the production assets of mid-size and small enterprises, the property of the so-called machinery-tractor stations, and collective as well as Soviet farms.[31]

According to incomplete data, by 1 October 1941 the total number of evacuated workers of the nine railways of the republic was 75,590. Consequently many industrial enterprises in the Soviet hinterland were released from the task of providing the railways with equipment and were instead asked to concentrate their efforts on the production of military equipment. As the Soviet Army retreated, the railway staff collaborated with field engineer companies of the railway troops to destroy the roads, the water supplies and the large bridges, thereby causing great difficulties for the enemy as he advanced into the territory. However, a considerable number of railway workers stayed with their families in the occupied territories and many of them joined the partisan movement against Nazi Germany. The workers' most important work in this respect was sabotage of the invaders' attempts to restore and operate the railways. Such sabotage affected a much larger portion of the supply lines of the enemy than did the subversive acts of the chief groups of partisans, whose actions were generally confined to the northern forest regions of Ukraine.

The liberation of the UkrSSR by the Soviet Army began in 1943 and by 14 October 1944, its territory was free of German troops. The restoration of the economy started in Ukraine with the railway sector, as workers restored the damage caused by the retreating *Wehrmacht*. Without restoration of the railways, which carried 83.5 per cent of all traffic, including 70.5 per cent of military freight, it would have been impossible to provide the armies at the front with all they needed, or to reinstate more or less normal conditions of life and economic

---

[31]   Мазыло, 'Железнодорожники Украинской', 8–9.

activity of the population. River transportation made up only a small percentage of the military and national economic needs. For a short period of time waterways replaced road transportation, but to a very limited extent only. After a considerable loss of cargo ships the waterways only had any importance for the supply of a small portion of the Soviet–German front. The role of automotive transport was even more limited to the areas close to the front line. It was impossible to use roads for military purposes over distances of several thousands of kilometres away from the front line because they had been poorly developed in the pre-war period and subsequently destroyed during the battles in the civil war. That is why all available forces were directed to the rebuilding of the railway network. The main problem lay in the fact that it had to be done very close to the front line, with extreme efforts and at high speed.[32]

The accelerating pace of the reconstruction work on the main lines that secured the needs of the front could be seen in the fact that from an average of eight kilometres per day, the speed of the rebuilding on Right Bank Ukraine reached 11 to 12 kilometres and occasionally 14 to 15 kilometres per day. In other regions of the republic, the reconstruction of bridges, station buildings and the rest of the railway infrastructure were being done at a high speed too. Railway workers, their families and residents of the nearby communities were all involved in the rebuilding of the railways of Ukraine. The Soviet People's Commissariat of the USSR and the Central Committee of the All-Union Communist Party (of Bolsheviks) sent a letter titled 'On providing assistance to the railways' to the secretaries of the regional committees, land committees, Central Committees of the Communist Parties of the Socialist Republics and regional executive committees, in which they called upon workers to take an active part in the restoration of railway transportation and in such a way give help to the Red Army in the total defeat of the German Fascist invaders and the rebuilding of the national economy.[33] The following fact reveals the letter's practical consequences: 16,906 citizens from the territory of Vinnytsia Oblast were recruited for the reconstruction of the railways of Vinnytsia and Kamianets–Podilskyi Oblasts on the territory of Right Bank Ukraine in 1944.[34] German prisoners of war were also involved in the reconstruction work of the infrastructure. On the Vinnytsia main line, they rebuilt the water supply of the stations Koziatyn, Zhmerinka, Rakhny, Nemerchi, Sukhovate, Viktoriia and Starokostiantyniv.[35]

Hard work facilitated the rapid restoration of the network in Ukraine, which made it possible to supply the Red Army effectively. In January and February 1944, just to facilitate the offensive of the Soviet troops on the territory of the Right Bank Ukraine, 78,000 wagons with men and military supplies were run by the Stalinska Railway, and 100,000 wagons by the Pivdenno–Zakhidna main line. From March to April 1944, 200,000 wagons went by the Vinnytsia, Pivdenno–Zakhidna and

---

32   Мазыло, 'Железнодорожники Украинской', 9–12.

33   Мазило, 'З історії', 404.

34   Ibid.

35   Ibid.

Kovelska Railways. To help operations in the liberation of the Crimea, 33,000 wagons were sent to the front line. While the Soviet troops were liberating the western regions of Ukraine, railway workers of the Kovelska, L'vivska and other lines brought 140,000 wagons with men and military supplies to the front.[36] The Commander-in-Chief of the Ukrainian front, Nikolaj Vatutin, admitted that 'without rapid restoration of the ruined railways it would have been much more difficult and sometimes even impossible to solve the most important offensive duties'.[37]

Thus, during the German–Soviet war of 1941–45, the Ukrainian railways were destroyed twice – once when the Red Army retreated, the second time when the Wehrmacht retreated. Partisans' actions, bombs and artillery fire made their contribution as well. As a result, 10 main railway lines, 29,800 kilometres of railway tracks, 1916 stations, and 5,600 bridges were damaged; 6,700 engines and more than 181,000 wagons and carriages were damaged or missing.[38] The total loss caused by the war to the UkrSSR national economy was estimated at 285 billion roubles (in 1942 prices), of which more than 10 billion was the loss to the UkrSSR railway system.[39] By the end of 1945, at the expense of much self-sacrificing work, 88 per cent of the Ukrainian railway network was restored and traffic in all main directions was resumed. In the following two years after the war, the reconstruction continued. The network was fully rebuilt by the end of 1947.[40] This work had been a great strain on the strength of the population.

From Reconstruction through Development to Stagnation: the UkrSSR Railways between 1946 and 1990

According to the fourth five-year plan, adopted by Verkhovna Rada of the USSR in March 1946, the Ukrainian railway workers' objective was to increase transportation capacity from Donbas to the centre of the USSR, from Donbas to

[36]   Мазыло, 'Железнодорожники', 15.

[37]   Cited from В. М. Литвин, *Україна в Другій світовій війні (1939–1945)* (Київ 2004), 414.

[38]   І.Г. Вєтров, *Економічна експансія третього рейху в Україні 1941–1944 рр.* (Київ 2000), 90 and Мазило І. 'Залізничний транспорт України в забезпеченні фронту під час наступальних боїв Червоної Армії (1943–1944 рр.)', in В.М. Ботушанський (ed.), *Матеріали V Буковинської Міжнародної історико-краєзнавчої конференції, присвяченої 130-річчю заснування Чернівецького національного університету імені Юрія Федьковича*, 2 vols (Чернівці 2005), vol. 1, 244.

[39]   See Вєтров, *Економічна експансія*, 93, and Яремчук, *Развитие железнодорожного транспорта Украины*, 9.

[40]   See В.М. Литвин, *Україна у першому повоєнному десятилітті (1946–1955)* (Київ 2004), 126, and Яремчук, *Развитие железнодорожного транспорта Украины*, 9.

Kryvyi Rih and from Donbas to Povolzhia.[41] It was possible because the railways were acquiring new and more powerful steam engines, and industry started to deliver diesel locomotives of the types TE-1 and TE-2. As a result, in 1950, freight transportation on the Ukrainian railways was 17 per cent higher than it had been before the war.[42] At that time, the railway network of Ukraine could be divided into three distinct regions:

- the railways of Donbas and Kryvyi Rih
- Central and Left Bank Ukraine
- railways in border regions.

The railways of the first region were the most important in the network of the USSR.[43] These lines were the Prydniprovska, the Pivdenna and the two that made up the Donetska – in 1953 Pivdenno–Donetska and Pivnichno–Donetska were amalgamated into the Donetska Railway. The main lines of these railways connected the industrial regions of Ukraine with all parts of the USSR. Here was the most densely network in Ukraine, 6.5 kilometres of track per 100 square kilometres.[44] The railways of the second region were Pivdenno–Zakhidna and Odeska. The latter was united with the Kyshynivska between 1953 and 1979, and was then called the Odesko–Kyshynivska Railway.[45] They served Ukrainian regions where light industry, food industry, machine-building, and the production of building materials were developed, and which were also famous for their plentiful agricultural production. The Odeska Railway also connected the Black Sea ports with ports on the rivers.[46] The railway of the third region was the L'vivska and in the period of 1945–53 it underwent some definite structural changes. On 10 December 1945, some lines in Zakarpattia became part of it when Zakarpattia was included into the UkrSSR; on 22 January 1946, the present Zakarpatska Oblast was formed.[47] In October 1944, at the time of its liberation from the German invaders by the Soviet troops, Zakarpattia's railway network counted some 700 kilometres, consisting of all gauges – narrow, Western European, and Russian broad gauge.[48]

---

[41]   А.Н. Давыдов, 'Восстановление железнодорожного транспорта и повышение его технической оснащенности', in Мушруб, *Развитие советского железнодорожного транспорта*, 151.

[42]   Литвин, *Україна у першому*, 126 and Яремчук, *Развитие железнодорожного транспорта Украины*, 9.

[43]   Афонина, *Краткие сведения*, 147.

[44]   В. Кубійович (ed.), *Енциклопедія українознавства* (Львів 1993), т. 2, 732.

[45]   In 1979, the Kyshynivska Railway was again separated from the Odeska, and was renamed the Moldovska Railway. *Афонина, Краткие сведения*, 147, 196.

[46]   See Яремчук, *Развитие железнодорожного транспорта Украины*, 9, 9–10.

[47]   Between 1920 and 1939 Zakarpattia was a part of Czechoslovakia. From 1939 to 1944 it was occupied by Hungarian troops.

[48]   See Мазило, 'Відновлення роботи', 551.

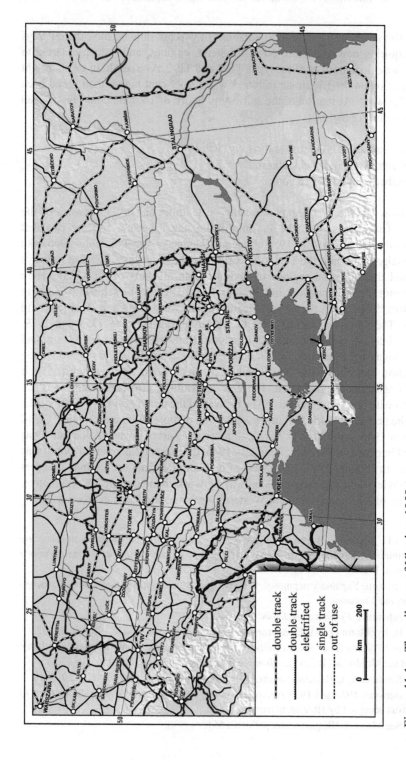

Figure 11.1   The railways of Ukraine, 1958

Source: Created by the author on the model of a map in В. Кубійович (ed.), *Енциклопедія українознавства* (Львів 1993), т. 2, 733.

For some time, the creation of a separate Zakarpatska Railway was considered. It was supposed to include 800 kilometres of broad-gauge, 140 kilometres of narrow-gauge tracks in the lowlands, and also standard-gauge mountain lines which were situated in the territories of Drohobytska, Stanislavska, Ternopilska and Chernivetska Oblasts, with a total length of 1,740 kilometres. The railway administration was to be situated in the former Directorate of Polish railways in Stanislav. This project was never implemented.[49] In 1953 the Ministry of Communications consolidated the railways, not only to cut expenses of administrative staff, but to eliminate delays at the junctions. The Kovelska Railway, consisting of its Kovelskyi, Sarnenskyi and Zdolbunivskyi sectors, was incorporated into the L'vivska Railway.[50] The Chernivetskyi sector of the former Kyshynivska Railway was also made part of the L'vivska.[51] At that point, the L'vivska Railway began serving all the western regions of Ukraine. However, it was mostly of local significance, and only later, when trade ties between the USSR and Central European countries were developed, did it attain international importance, in particular for shipment of freight.

In the 1950s and 1960s, a lot of work was done on technical upgrading, modernising and electrifying the UkrSSR railways. In 1956 steam engines were still built in great numbers in Voroshylovgrad (today Luhansk) and Kharkiv. The following year the two Ukrainian plants as well as other USSR plants stopped the construction of steam engines, and soon the share of steam traction in railway transportation began to decrease very quickly. The use of internal combustion and electric traction removed the railways from the list of the biggest consumers of coal.[52]

In Ukraine, by 1965, 3,250 kilometres of railway lines had been electrified, and a further 8,300 kilometres had been given over to diesel traction.[53] In 1960s, probably the most important electrified main line crossing Ukraine was the line which connected the cities of Leningrad (today: St Petersburg), Moscow, Kharkiv, Rostov, Tuapse, Sukhumi, Tbilisi and Leninakan. All in all, this line has a length of 3,500 kilometres. The second most important electrified main line was the one that stretches from Moscow via Kiev and L'viv to Chop, and has a length of 1,642 kilometres including a branch to Mostiska. This branch connected the railway network of the USSR with the railways of the Czechoslovakian Socialist Republic

---

[49]   See ibid., 552.

[50]   See Гранкін, Лазечко, Сьомочкін and Шрамко, *Львівська залізниця*, 108.

[51]   See Ю.С. Линюк, *Сторінки історії Одеської залізниці: 1865–2005* (Одеса 2005), 170.

[52]   See В.М. Литвин, *Україна у другому повоєнному десятилітті (1956–1965)* (Київ 2004), 115, and А.Г. Мушруб, '*Коренная техническая реконструкция на основе Генерального плана электрификации железных дорог*', in Мушруб, *Развитие советского железнодорожного транспорта*, 173.

[53]   Яремчук, Развитие железнодорожного транспорта Украины, 10.

Figure 11.2   The meeting of high-ranking delegation at Kiev railway station, 1973

Note: In the first line from the right to the left: Petro Kryvonos, chief of the Pivdenno–Zakhidna Railway from 1953 to 1980; Leonid Brezhnev, General Secretary of the Central Committee of the Communist Party of the Soviet Union; and Vladimir Shcherbytskyi, First Secretary of the Central Committee of the Communist Party of Ukraine.

Source: Donation of Kryvonos family to Scientific Institute of Ukrainian Railway, Kiev.

and the Polish People's Republic. Its last stretch of electrification was dedicated to the fiftieth anniversary of the Great October Socialist Revolution in 1967.[54]

The 1970s saw a gradual decline of the UkrSSR railways which reached its lowest point in the 1980s. At the end of 1980s Ukraine owned the above-mentioned six railways with 900 subsidiaries. The operational length amounted to 22,700 kilometres, of which 7,800 kilometres were electrified.[55] But the capacity and the reserves of the Ukrainian lines were exhausted. The figures for freight in 1986 were 3.52 times of what it had been in 1955. But at the same time the operational length of the railways increased only by 11.3 per cent. The modernisation and maintenance of the railways slowed down. In the years from 1981 to 1985 the

---

[54]   А.В. Воронин, 'История электрификации железнодорожного транспорта в СССР', in С.М. Сердинов (ed.), *50 лет электрификации железных дорог СССР* (Москва 1976), 29–30.

[55]   В.І. Букін, *Транспорт республіки в умовах перебудови* (Київ 1989), 10.

production of about 70,000 freight wagons was planned, but 463 electric engines, 185 shunting locomotives and 1,240 passenger carriages failed to be delivered. The time intervals between trains were shortened between six and seven minutes, which caused difficulties in movement management and in the whole operation of the railways. This led to numerous accidents with casualties and material losses.[56] The goals of the plans were not reached. In the 1970s, the railway industry met the USSR national economy demands only by 88 per cent and in the 1980s by 94 per cent. The population's demands were met only by 80 to 92 per cent.[57]

Not only material and technical factors aggravated the position of the railways; the labour discipline also got worse. In 1987, the People's Control Commission of the USSR came to the following conclusion:

> The majority of accidents, collisions, train crashes, derailments, and other violations of road safety regulations took place because of the low level of operational and technological discipline.[58]

For example, in 1987, more than 4,000 passenger and local trains were late on the lines of the Odeska Railway. 19,000 freight trains departed from Odessa late, 14,000 arrived at this station far behind the schedule. All together this caused great material and social losses. Failures in the running of freight trains alone caused Odeska Railways 2.2 million roubles in losses, while other branches lost from 1.5 to 6 million roubles. The locomotive stock was used in an extremely unsatisfactory way. None of the railway departments fulfilled the plan regarding efficiency and daily running of the engines. In 1987 the overloading of engines caused 1.5 million roubles in losses. On the whole, lack of organisation and the absence of strict technological discipline in the sector of traction cost 6 million roubles.[59] The data given by the newspaper *Pravda* on 7 February 1988 were also significant for that time. They characterised the stability of the labour force in different branches of the national economy. The lowest fluctuation of workers (0.1 per cent) was in railway work.[60] Ten years before the railways had been among the branches with the highest turnover. The Communist Party of the Soviet Union (CPSU) tried to improve the situation. The problems of the railway industry were discussed at one of the meetings of Political Bureau of the Central Committee of CPSU

---

[56]   Букін, *Транспорт*, 10 and 16.

[57]   See И.Г. Черната, 'Перспективы развития транспортного комплекса Украинской ССР', in Н.Е. Гончаров (ed.), *Региональные проблемы развития транспортной системы Украинской ССР* (Москва 1988), 9.

[58]   Quoted from Косьяненко, *Дорога и люди*, 254.

[59]   See Косьяненко, *Дорога и люди*, 254–5.

[60]   See *Правда* of 7 February 1987.

in December 1987. The decision was taken for a comprehensive modernisation scheme of the railways between 1991 and 2000.[61] But it was too late.

Conclusions

Due to the forceful activities of the Bolsheviks, some order was brought to the railway industry until the mid 1920s. But Lenin's words, spoken when he was already ill, 'We must learn to manage', did not find a corresponding response and understanding among the majority of Bolsheviks, who were more inclined to violence than to economic stimuli, as this had brought success in the times of the War of Independence. This type of mentality revealed itself fully in the 1930s, when the planned targets could not be attained and it caused repression. In the late 1930s, the railways improved as a new generation of railway staff trained by the Soviet system went to work. These changes, as well as increased pressure on the staff, caused the Ukrainian railway system to perform well during the Second World War.

In post-war times, the railways of Ukraine were rapidly rebuilt and the 1950s and 1960s were known for good technical progress in the railway world. Economic problems that surfaced in the 1970s were in full swing in the 1980s, and they influenced the railways of Ukraine negatively. The Soviet authorities began to take measures to improve the situation, but these measures came too late when a new political era dawned.

Bibliography

Абраменко, Л. М., *Постали із забуття. Репресовані залізничники* (1919–1953) (Київ 2001).

Афонина, Г.М., *Краткие сведения о развитии отечественных железных дорог с 1838 по 1990 гг.* (Москва 1995).

Бондарчук, Ю.П., 'Залізничний транспорт України в умовах утвердження адміністративно-командних методів управління народним господарством (кін. 20-х–30-ті рр.)', University of Dnepropetrovsk PhD thesis, 1999.

Бондарчук, Ю.П., 'Кадрові втрати українських залізниць в ході масових операцій ДПУ-НКВС УСРР "По очищенню прикордонної смуги"', *Історія України. Маловідомі імена, події, факти*, 2, 1997, 239–46.

Бондарчук, Ю.П., 'Каральні операції органів НКВС України по вилученню "троцькістсько-зінов'євських елементів" на залізничному транспорті', *Історія України. Маловідомі імена, події, факти*, 3, 1998, 125–36.

Букін, В.І., Транспорт республіки в умовах перебудови (Київ 1989).

---

[61] See Б.Н. Зимтинг 'Железные дороги: достижения, проблемы и перспективы (интервью с заместителем министра путей сообщения В.П. Калиничевым)', *Электрическая и тепловозная тяга*, 10, 1987, 2–4.

Вєтров, І.Г., *Економічна експансія третього рейху в Україні 1941–1944 рр.* (Київ 2000).

Воронин, А. В., 'История электрификации железнодорожного транспорта в СССР', in С.М. Сердинов (ed.), *50 лет электрификации железных дорог СССР* (Москва 1976), 8–31.

Гакман, С.М. and Макар, Ю.І., 'Радянсько-румунсько-німецькі відносини і приєднання північної частини Буковини та Хотинського повіту Бессарабії до Української РСР у складі СРСР', in В.М. Ботушанський (ed.), *Буковина в контексті європейських міжнародних відносин (з давніх часів до середини ХХ ст.)* (Чернівці 2005), 586–642.

Голубев, В.И. and Уздин, М.М. 'Железные дороги в годы гражданской войны и военной интервенции', in В.Е. Павлов and М.М. Уздин (eds), *История железнодорожного транспорта России и Советского Союза: 1917–1945 гг.* (Санкт-Петербург 1997), 12–21.

Гранкін, П., Лазечко, П., Сьомочкін, І. and Шрамко, Г. (eds), *Львівська залізниця. Історія і сучасність* (Львів 1996).

Давыдов, А.Н. 'Восстановление железнодорожного транспорта и повышение его технической оснащенности', in А.Г. Мушруб (ed.), *Развитие советского железнодорожного транспорта* (Москва 1984), 149–62.

Зайцев, А.А., Павлов, В.Е. and Уздин, М.М. 'Восстановление и начало реконструкции железных дорог (1921–1928)', in В.Е. Павлов and М.М. Уздин (eds), *История железнодорожного транспорта России и Советского Союза: 1917–1945 гг.* (Санкт-Петербург 1997), 25–46.

Захарченко, Н.А., 'Железнодорожники Украинской ССР на завершающем этапе социалистической реконструкции народного хозяйства (1933–1937 гг.)', University of Dnepropetrovsk PhD thesis, 1988.

Зимтинг, Б.Н., 'Железные дороги: достижения, проблемы и перспективы (интервью с заместителем министра путей сообщения В.П. Калиничевым)', *Электрическая и тепловозная тяга*, 10, 1987, 2–4.

Зінченко, В.І., *Розвиток залізниць і залізничного транспорту в датах* (Київ 1998).

Коренев, Л.И. 'Магистраль Москва – Донбасс', in В.Е. Павлов and М.М. Уздин (eds), *История железнодорожного транспорта России и Советского Союза: 1917–1945 гг.* (Санкт-Петербург 1997), 75–9.

Косьяненко, В.М. (ed.), *Дорога и люди* (Одесса 1991).

Кубійович, В. (ed.), *Енциклопедія українознавства*, т. 2. (Львів 1993).

Линюк, Ю.С., Сторінки історії Одеської залізниці: *1865–2005* (Одеса 2005).

Литвин, В.М., *Україна в Другій світовій війні (1939–1945)* (Київ 2004).

Литвин, В.М., *Україна у другому повоєнному десятилітті (1956–1965)* (Київ 2004).

Литвин, В.М., *Україна у першому повоєнному десятилітті (1946–1955)* (Київ 2004).

Мазило, І., 'Відновлення роботи і розвиток залізничного транспорту в західноукраїнських областях 1944–1950 рр. (на матеріалах Галичини і Закарпаття)', in В.В. Карпов (ed.), *Воєнна історія Галичини та Закарпаття* (Київ 2010), 549–52.

Мазило, І., 'З історії відбудови залізничного транспорту Поділля 1944–1950-х рр. мовою документів', in В.В. Карпов (ed.), *Воєнна історія Поділля та Буковини* (Кам'янець-Подільський 2009), 403–5.

Мазило, І., 'Залізничний транспорт України в забезпеченні фронту під час наступальних боїв Червоної Армії (1943–1944 рр.)', in В.М. Ботушанський (ed.), *Матеріали V Буковинської Міжнародної історико-краєзнавчої конференції, присвяченої 130-річчю заснування Чернівецького національного університету імені Юрія Федьковича*, 2 vols (Чернівці 2005).

Мельтюхов, М.И., *Упущенный шанс Сталина. Советский Союз и борьба за Европу: 1939–1941 (*Документы, факты, суждения*)* (Москва 2000) http://militera.lib.ru/research/meltyukhov/03.html (last accessed 12 December 2011).

Муравьева, Е.П. 'Железнодорожный транспорт в период восстановления народного хозяйства (1921–1925)', in А.Г. Мушруб (ed.), *Развитие советского железнодорожного транспорта* (Москва 1984), 43–66.

Мушруб, А.Г. 'Коренная техническая реконструкция на основе Генерального плана электрификации железных дорог', in А.Г. Мушруб (ed.), *Развитие советского железнодорожного транспорта* (Москва 1984), 162–83.

Николаев, Б.М., 'Нарком Дзержинский', *Электрическая и тепловозная тяга*, 10, 1987, 22–4.

Прилуцький, В., 'Модернізація транспорту Радянської України у міжвоєнний період (1921–1938 рр.)' *Проблеми історії України: факти, судження, пошуки*, 13, 2005, 313–42.

Романенко, Ю.И. and Харенко, М.П., *Взгляд сквозь годы: Южная железная дорога за 130 лет* (Харьков 1999).

Слепухин, С.М., *Краткая истории строительства и развития Сталинской ж.д.: 1884-1948 гг.* (Днепропетровск 1949).

Олейник, Б.С. (ed.), *Юго-Западная железная дорога. Вчера. Сегодня. Завтра* (Киев 1995).

Уздин, М. М. 'Государственный план электрификации России и развитие транспорта', in В. Е.Павлов and М.М. Уздин (eds), *История железнодорожного транспорта России и Советского Союза: 1917–1945 гг.* (Санкт-Петербург 1997), 21–4.

Черната, И.Г. 'Перспективы развития транспортного комплекса Украинской ССР', in Н.Е. Гончаров (ed.), *Региональные проблемы развития транспортной системы Украинской ССР* (Москва 1988), 5–21.

Яремчук, А.Г., 'Развитие железнодорожного транспорта Украины (1951–1964 гг.)', Киевский институт народного хозяйства PhD thesis, 1965.

Zhaloba, I. and Piddubnyj, I., 'Verkehrs- und Kommunikationsnetze in Czernowitz in der Zwischenkriegszeit (1918–1940)', in R. Roth (ed.), *Städte im europäischen Raum: Verkehr, Kommunikation und Urbanität im 19. und 20. Jahrhundert* (Stuttgart 2009), 63–86.

Chapter 12
Yugoslavia: The Sub-Savian Magistral

Henry Jacolin

The Sub-Savian Magistral was the name given to a railway project intended to double the main trunk line which runs across Yugoslavia from the Italian border through Ljubljana, Zagreb, Belgrade and Skopje to the Greek border. The line was to be built parallel to the Sava River, about one hundred kilometres to the south – hence its name, Sub-Savian Magistral (in Serbo-Croatian: *pod Savska magistrala*). Planned at the beginning of the 1970s, the project for this railway line was aimed at solving a problem which successively confronted Serbia from 1888 to 1918, the Kingdom of Yugoslavia from 1918 to 1945, and Communist Yugoslavia from 1945 to 1991: the fact that there was only a single railway line that ran across the country from north to south. This main trunk line was the only one that linked the regions of the Kingdom of Serbia, then the provinces of monarchic Yugoslavia, later the Republics of Tito's Federal Yugoslavia. It was also the only feasible route, because the most direct, between Europe on one side, the Balkans and the Orient on the other.

The main trunk line is composed of two sections. The first one connects Belgrade with Salonica (through Niš and Skopje) and Constantinople/ Istanbul (through Bulgaria). It runs through the Morava and Vardar Valleys. Morava River, which flows into the Danube near Belgrade, is only separated from the Vardar River, which flows into the Aegean Sea near Salonica, by the low rise of Preševo, 459 metres. This route is unavoidable. On the east of this Morava–Vardar corridor, the route, running across Hungary, Romania and Bulgaria, is longer, because it must cross the Danube at the Giurgiu-Ruse bridge, and is more difficult, because it climbs through the Balkan range. Its capacity is low: the railway infrastructures of the countries involved have never been prepared for transit traffic, as the Morava–Vardar route always seemed to be the most natural access to the Balkans.

The second section north of Belgrade divides into two branches. The first one leads toward Central Europe, via Budapest and Vienna, through the Pannonian Plain, crossing the Danube at Novi Sad. The second branch runs toward western Europe along the Sava Valley, passing through Zagreb and Ljubljana before reaching Trieste and the Po Valley.

Three recent events have demonstrated the inevitability of the route that the main trunk line follows. At the beginning of the 1980s, Yugoslavia imposed a transit quota on Greece, which had just become a member of the European Community, forcing the Greek trucks to use the sea route between Patras and Italy or the eastern route; both solutions were less practical and more costly than driving along the main trunk line's route.[1] Between 1991 and 1995, the war neutralised the route between Belgrade and Zagreb and diverted transit traffic towards Central Europe, over a route that was longer and more difficult than the route running along the Sava across the Slavonian Plain. Finally, the destruction of the Novi Sad bridge by NATO in 1999 extensively hindered transit traffic in the direction of Central Europe. The uniqueness of this trunk railway line compelled its successive owners to imagine alternative solutions, which this paper will examine.

A Unique and Overloaded Transit Route

In the Days of Serbia (1888–1918)

With the Berlin Treaty of 1878, it was not by chance that the Austro-Hungarians imposed the Morava–Vardar route for the construction of the first railway line intended to connect Vienna and Budapest with Constantinople.[2] By using this route from 1888 onward, the Orient Express, which until then had passed through Bucharest and Varna, using a ferry from Giurgiu to Ruse and a ship from Varna to Constantinople, saved 12 and half hours of its time. However, this international route raised a double problem for the Ottoman and Austro-Hungarian empires: it was the only railway connection between them, and it ran through Serbia, whose Pan-Slavic goals worried them. As a result, they tried unsuccessfully to bypass Serbia in attempting to connect with each other.

Before the Berlin Congress, the Ottoman empire had elaborated a project whereby its railway network would be connected with the European network at the furthest outpost of Bosnia-Herzegovina, near Zagreb. The construction of this line began at each extremity. In the east, the line built from Salonica reached Mitrovica through Skopje in 1874. In the west, the line built in 1872 from Dobrljin, at the Turco-Hungarian border, did not get beyond Banja Luka. The most difficult section, between Banja Luka and Mitrovica, through the Novi Pazar Sandžak and Sarajevo across the mountains of Bosnia, remained to be built. The occupation of Bosnia-Herzegovina by the Double Monarchy in 1878 prevented the realisation of this project.

Due to the worsening of its relations with Serbia after 1903, Austria-Hungary decided to build a railway line that would connect it directly with the Ottoman empire while bypassing Serbia. Two projects were then elaborated:

- The first one, called the 'Sandžak Railway', connecting Sarajevo with

---

[1]   Jacques Marville (alias Henry Jacolin), *Problèmes et perspectives des transports routiers entre la Grèce et la CEE* (in Greek) (Athens 1985), 167–78.

[2]   Henry Jacolin, 'L'établissement de la première voie ferrée entre l'Europe et la Turquie. Chemins de fer et diplomatie dans les Balkans', *Revue d'histoire des chemins de fer*, 35, fall 2006, 5–23.

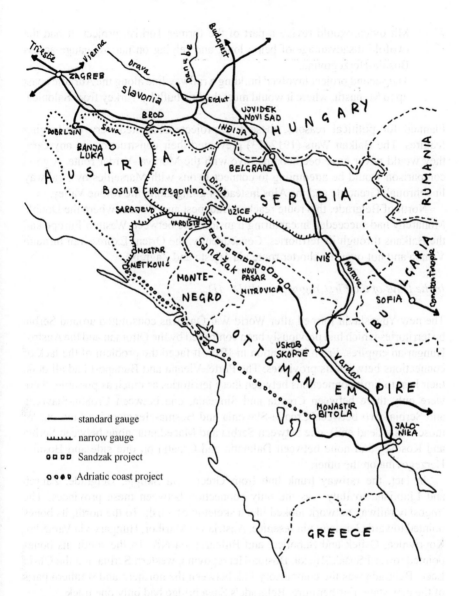

Figure 12.1   Railways of the Balkans, 1912

Source: Map created by the author.

Mitrovica, would revive a part of the former Turkish project. It had the twofold disadvantage of being long, and relying on narrow gauge across Bosnia-Herzegovina.
- The second project involved building a railway line along the Adriatic coast up to Monastir, where it would meet the line built by Turkey from Salonica.

Planned for political reasons, these two projects presented very challenging features. The Balkan Wars (1912–13) prevented their construction. In any case, they would never have been competitive with the Morava–Vardar route. A good comparison would be attempting to connect Lyons with Marseilles by a railway line through Grenoble and the Alps instead of going along the Rhône Valley.

North of Belgrade, this route reached Budapest and Vienna, where the Double Monarchy had succeeded in capturing transit traffic between Western Europe and the Balkans through its territories. Consequently, the Orient Express ran through Vienna and not over the shorter route via Trieste and Zagreb.

In the Days of the First Yugoslavia (1918–41)

The new Yugoslavia formed after World War One was constituted around Serbia by territories which had previously been controlled by the Ottoman and the Austro-Hungarian empires. From its creation in 1918, it faced the problem of the lack of connections between its provinces. The Porte, Vienna and Budapest had all done their best to limit connections between these territories as much as possible: there were only three between Croatia and Slovenia, one between Croatia-Slavonia and Serbia, two between Croatia-Slavonia and Bosnia-Herzegovina (and one of those was a dead end), one between Serbia and Macedonia, none between Serbia and Kosovo, and none between Dalmatia and Croatia on one side and Bosnia-Herzegovina on the other.

In fact, the railway trunk line from Greece via Skopje, Belgrade, Zagreb and Ljubljana to Italy was the only connection between these provinces. The Yugoslav railway network looked like a skeleton of a fish. To the north, its bones pointed toward Germany via Jesenice, Austria via Maribor, Hungary via Varaždin, Koprivnica, Osijek and Subotica, and Bulgaria via Niš. To the south, its bones pointed toward Sušak/Rijeka, Bosnia-Herzegovina, western Serbia and the Ohrid Lake. Belgrade was the compulsory link between the northern and southern parts of the new state. Furthermore, Belgrade's Sava bridge had only one track.

Since it supported the traffic between the provinces of the new state, which had increased thanks to economic development, as well as import and export traffic by sea and transit traffic, this particular railway trunk line was immediately overloaded.[3] Yugoslavia then began to increase the capacity of the 1,183-kilometre line which extended from Italy to Greece.

---

[3] It had only one harbour at its disposal. This was Sušak, associated with Rijeka, situated at the western extremity of Yugoslavia.

South of Belgrade, there was one absolute priority: the creation of a direct connection between Belgrade and Kosovo. When Serbia incorporated Kosovo in 1913 after the Balkan Wars, Kosovo was only connected with Macedonia by the Skopje–Mitrovica line built by the Turks in 1874. The construction of the sections from Kragujevac to Kraljevo in 1929 and from Kraljevo to Mitrovica in 1931 presented the twofold advantage of connecting Kosovo with Belgrade and of creating a route that doubled the Morava–Vardar Railway line from Lapovo to Skopje. The construction in 1924, of a line connecting Belgrade with the Timok region (in eastern Serbia) which crossed a branch of the main line in Mala Krsna, constituted a doubling from Belgrade to Velika Plana. Finally, with the doubling of the short section from Velika Plana to Lapovo, the Belgrade–Skopje line was totally equipped with a double track.

From Belgrade to Italy, the railway line was heterogeneous. From the border to Zidani Most it used the main double track line built by the Austrian *Südbahn* from Vienna to Trieste. From Zidani Most to Sisak via Zagreb it used the branch line built by the same company in 1862 to divert the Hungarian traffic intended for Fiume towards Trieste. Further on, no railway line had been built to connect Belgrade and Zagreb. A line running from Sisak along the left bank of the Sava River, built from 1878 to 1889, connected Slavonia with Budapest via Osijek and the Danube bridge in Erdut. In 1891, starting in Inđija, Hungary built a secondary branch of the Budapest–Belgrade line to serve the Srem region, which was connected with the Erdut line in Vinkovci. When assembled, these sections did not constitute a homogeneous line. There were no direct trains from Zagreb to Belgrade; if there had been, they would have been obliged to turn back in Inđija because there was no direct junction. This railway line was doubled from Zagreb (Dugo Selo) to Novska in 1897 by a section belonging to a private company called Lonjavölgyi. In northern Slavonia, on the right bank of the Drava, the lines of six private local networks, one of which used narrow gauge, could not substitute for the Belgrade–Zagreb line.

Yugoslavia rushed to transform this second class line into a real main trunk line by laying a second track from Belgrade to Novska (1928–29) and building a triangle in Inđija so that the Belgrade–Zagreb trains would not be forced to turn back. With the ownership of this main trunk line, Yugoslavia showed its willingness to play a role in the transit between east and west. In April 1919 the first train, called the Simplon Orient Express, went into service. Instead of speeding to the Balkans via Vienna and Budapest, it went through Milano, Trieste, Ljubljana, Zagreb and Belgrade. The creation of this train was the crowning achievement of the efforts deployed beginning in 1906 (the opening date of the Simplon tunnel) by the Compagnie des chemins de fer de Paris à Lyon et à la Méditerranée (PLM) and the Italian Railways to carry out this project against the opposition of the Austro-Hungarians. Until that time, indeed, the only passable route ran through

Vienna and Budapest. 'The Croatian route, much shorter, was astutely blocked by all means (lack of direct tickets, of connections, of comfortable trains, etc.).'[4]

In 1925 a direct connection was established from Zagreb to the Split harbour in Dalmatia. The connection started from Ogulin on the Zagreb–Rijeka line and ran through the Lika region. This connection increased the overload on the Belgrade–Zagreb line, since south of Split, there were only small harbours served by narrow-gauge lines (Metković on the Neretva river, Dubrovnik and Kotor bay).

In order to solve the problem of the overload on the Belgrade–Zagreb line, the idea of building a line doubling it to the south had emerged after 1918:

> This railway line was first conceived as a third parallel to the Hungarian border, intended for military use in case the railway lines situated between Drava and Sava should be cut off by the enemy. The route finally planned would penetrate deeply inside Bosnia, at the edge of the mountains, in order to be better protected.[5]

In 1922 the government authorised to begin the studies for a railway line from Belgrade via Tuzla and Banja Luka to Una Valley. Several projects were proposed in 1924, 1925 and 1926, with variants, some opting for standard gauge, others for narrow gauge, still others for a combination of both gauges. Another variant tried to fulfil two objectives at the same time, the 'third parallel' and the Belgrade–Adriatic line, by proposing a common route from Belgrade to Tuzla, followed by two branches, one running towards the Una, the second towards Sarajevo and the sea via the Neretva Valley.

One of the projects that were decided on at the Railway Conference in 1926 was the creation of a line running from Belgrade via Obrenovac, Šabac, Bijeljina and Tuzla to Banja Luka. Banja Luka was the point where it would meet the line that had been built by Turkey in 1872. But in 1937, none of this plan had been realised. The government then allocated one billion dinars for studies of the projected Banja Luka–Drina–Valjevo–Čačak line. But by 1941, only some earthworks between Banja Luka and Prisoje (52 kilometres) had been completed.

In the Days of the Socialist Federal Republic of Yugoslavia (1945–1991)

The overloading of the main trunk line was exacerbated by the dramatic increase of the freight traffic, a consequence of the industrialisation implemented by the new Communist regime. To unburden Rijeka and the line serving it, Tito's government then began building railway lines towards other harbours. In 1948, the completion of the Una line between Bihać and Knin created a second access to

---

4   Charles Loiseau, 'Une artère sud-européenne', *Revue de Paris*, of 1 March 1918, 1–17, here 4.

5   Zvonimir Jelinović, *Borba za Jadranske pruge* (The fight for Adriatic lines), Građa za gospodarsku povijest Hrvatske, (ed.) Jugoslovenska Akademija Znanosti i Umjetnosti, vol. 6 (Zagreb 1957), 161.

the Split harbour. In 1966, the commissioning of the standard line from Sarajevo to Ploče, replacing the existing narrow line, opened a new harbour for Yugoslavia. These two new lines relieved the line serving Rijeka. But since they could spread their traffic only by using the main trunk line, of which they were branches, they increased its overload at the same time. Neither the electrification of this main trunk line up to Skopje, as well as the Zagreb–Rijeka and the Vrpolje–Sarajevo–Ploče branches, nor the doubling of the Zagreb–Zidani Most section, nor the construction of a bypass from Batajnica to Resnik allowing the freight trains to avoid Belgrade, succeeded in relieving the main trunk line.

In 1968, the government took out a 50-million-dollar loan for the completion of the Belgrade–Bar line. As a condition for the loan, the World Bank required the construction of a branch from Požega to Čačak, in order to spread its traffic towards southern Serbia and Macedonia. This Požega–Čačak branch suggested a solution to this problem.

In 1971, at the request of the Federal Economic Chamber, the Kirilo Savić Institute conducted a study entitled 'The Optimal Structure of the Yugoslavian Transport System'. The study found that there was 'a need to alleviate the traffic bottleneck in the region of Belgrade by creating a new connection south of the Belgrade–Zagreb line, to be called the Sub-Savian Magistral, from Sunja or Bosanski Novi to Stalač'.[6]

The Construction of the Sub-Savian Magistral

From Sunja, on the Belgrade–Zagreb line, to Stalač, on the Belgrade–Skopje line, the Sub-Savian Magistral line would extend over 618 kilometres. It did not start from scratch, since three groups of railway lines, with a total length of 506 kilometres (82 per cent of the total), already existed. Between these lines, two sections totalling 112 kilometres in length had to be built.

The Utilisation of Existing Railway Lines

The three pre-existing groups of lines in 1971 had been built at different dates, for various reasons which had nothing to do with the new project into which they would be integrated.

The first group connected the railway lines running toward the Split and Ploče harbours. It was composed of three different sections.

From Dobrljin via Bosanski Novi to Banja Luka

As mentioned earlier, this was the first railway line built by the Turks in the region in 1872. It had been intended to meet the line coming from Salonica in Mitrovica

---

    6   Jacques Marville (alias Henry Jacolin), 'L'électrification des chemins de fer yougoslaves', *La vie du rail*, of 2 May 1976.

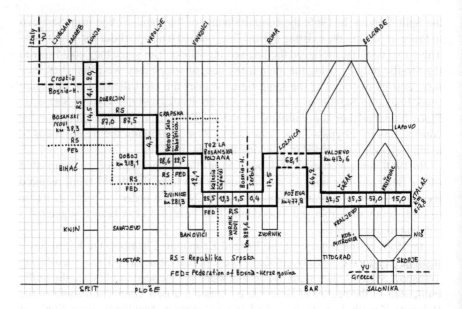

Figure 12.2   Scheme of the Sub-Savian Magistral

Source: Scheme created by the author.

but did not run further than Banja Luka (101.6 kilometres). Abandoned during the Bosnia-Herzegovina Uprising in 1875, it was incorporated by the Austro-Hungarians into the network of Bosnia-Herzegovina in 1879.

From Sunja to Dobrljin

The Dobrljin–Banja Luka line remained isolated until the construction of the Sisak–Dobrljin line by the Hungarian State Railways, Magyar Államvasutak (MAV) in 1882, connecting it to the *Südbahn* network in Sisak. The first part of this line, Sisak–Sunja, later became one section of Belgrade–Zagreb, whereas Sunja–Bosanski Novi constituted the beginning of the Una line serving Split.[7]

From Banja Luka to Doboj

Work began in 1941 in the context of the 'third parallel' project between Banja Luka and Doboj, and was resumed after World War Two, allowing this line to be put into service on 1 January 1953; 87.5 kilometres long, it met the Vrpolje–Sarajevo–Ploče line in Grapska, a few kilometres north of Doboj. This line presented a fourfold advantage: it knitted the Yugoslav network together by connecting the railway lines serving two of the most important harbours; it allowed iron ore

---

[7]   The line from Bosanski Novi to Bihać was put into service in 1924. The section from Bihać to Knin in 1948.

extracted in Ljubija (between Bosanski Novi and Banja Luka) to be transported towards the Zenica (Bosnia-Herzegovina) and Smederevo (Serbia) steel plants, avoiding a detour via Bosanski Novi and Sunja; it relieved the Sunja–Vrpolje section of the main trunk line; it shortened by 48 kilometres the distance from Zagreb to Sarajevo, compared to the route via Vrpolje.

The second pre-existing line connected the Ploče line to the Vinkovci–Banovići line between Doboj and Bosanska Poljana (Tuzla).[8]

On 27 July 1951, it replaced the narrow-gauge line built in 1886 to exploit the Kreka lignite and the François-Joseph Simin Han Salt Mines. It allowed coal from this region to be transported towards the interior of Bosnia-Herzegovina without transferring it from the narrow to the standard gauge in Doboj.

The third group of pre-existing railway lines consisted of standard-gauge lines which progressively replaced the narrow-gauge network serving western Serbia. It is composed of two different sections.

From Stalać via Kraljevo and Čačak to Požega

This line intersects three lines: from Belgrade to Bar in Požega, from Belgrade to Skopje via Kosovo in Kraljevo, and from Belgrade to Skopje via Niš in Stalać. It replaced the narrow track built from 1910 to 1912 up to Užice by the standard-gauge lines of Kraljevo–Čačak in 1955 (35.5 kilometres), Kruševac–Kraljevo in 1958 (57 kilometres) and Čačak-Požega in 1976 (32.5 kilometres).[9]

From Požega to Valjevo

Over a distance of 64.2 kilometres, the magistral uses the Požega–Valjevo section of the Belgrade–Bar line which was put into service in 1972.

The Railway Lines Still to Be Built

Two lines totalling 112 kilometres remained to be built. They represented only 18 per cent of the length of the magistral but were the two most difficult sections.

The line from Živinice to Zvornik

This line breaks off from the Vinkovci–Banovići line 12 kilometres south of Bosanska Poljana. It was designed to transport coal from Tuzla towards the Smederevo (Serbia) steel plant – 5 million tons of traffic were predicted in 1980 – and to supply the Zvornik alumina plant with bauxite from Mostar. It was 44.8 kilometres in length. In Zvornik Novi (a Bosniak city), it met the line Šabac–Zvornik, a Serbian city, which had been built in 1950. It did not shorten the distance between the Tuzla coal field and Belgrade, but allowed the traffic

---

[8]   This line was built in 1946 by the youth brigades to permit the transport of Banovići lignite towards the interior of the country.

[9]   From the beginning, the 15 kilometres from Stalać to Kruševac were equipped with three rails.

Figure 12.3   Railways in Yugoslavia, 1991
Source: Map created by the author.

from this region to relieve the Belgrade–Zagreb trunk line between Vinkovci and Ruma. Its construction began on 19 April 1986 on difficult ground: it included five tunnels with a total length of 5,733 metres, of which one, the *Križevci*, was 4,912 metres long. Completed in 1991, this line was temporarily opened to goods traffic on 30 January 1992, but never officially inaugurated because of the outbreak of the war in Bosnia-Herzegovina. The completion of this line on the eve of the war was interpreted in some Bosnian circles as a plot hatched by the Serbs. Since the Belgrade-Sarajevo narrow-gauge line had been suppressed in 1978, this line was in fact the only railway line that gave Serbia a direct access to Bosnia-Herzegovina.

The line from Loznica to Valjevo
After using the Ruma–Zvornik line over a distance of 19.4 kilometres, the last section, with a projected length of 68.1 kilometres, was to connect Loznica to Valjevo. This was one of the lines that Serbia had planned to build towards the Bosnia-Herzegovina border. A project to construct a line reaching Loznica had been presented to the Parliament of Serbia in 1886 (the Šabac–Zvornik line did not exist at that time). The 1914 Serb railway network law had provided for the construction of a narrow-gauge Valjevo–Drina line, which World War One

suspended.[10] Within the framework of the 'third parallel' project, some earthworks were undertaken before World War Two: a tunnel was bored, but then shut up because of cave-ins. The war once again suspended works.

New studies were undertaken in 1979–80 for the construction of this difficult line, comprising 19 tunnels with a total length of 9,759 metres. The boring of one of them, the Trifković Tunnel, was begun on 12 November 1991, but suspended by the war. Work has not been resumed since that time.

Conclusion

The construction of the Sub-Savian Magistral suffered the same fate as a number of other projects elaborated between 1918 and 1991. The Yugoslav Kingdom was not able to complete the great project of an 'Adriatic line', which intended to connect Belgrade with the sea.[11] Torn between the conflicting demands of its provinces, it never succeeded in setting up a clear hierarchy of priorities and adhering to it.

Tito's Yugoslavia began too many projects simultaneously without the financial resources to complete them: the creation of new harbours (Ploče and Bar) and their connection to the interior of the country to relieve Rijeka; the unlocking of isolated regions (eastern Serbia, Kosovo, Macedonia); the construction of the Sub-Savian Magistral. This last project, however, presented a fourfold advantage: for a relatively small amount of money (there were only approximately 100 kilometres of railway lines to build), it would have doubled the main trunk line that ran across the whole country and relieved it of part of its transit traffic; it would have avoided the congested passage through Belgrade; it would have created connections which did not formerly exist between the republics (Serbia-Bosnia Herzegovina, Croatia-Bosnia Herzegovina); it would have integrated a network which was far too skeletal. The Sub-Savian Magistral would have deeply transformed and improved the geography of transportation in Yugoslavia. Unfortunately this project suffered because it was not a priority: in the 20-year period from 1971 to 1991, only one section was constructed, representing 40 per cent of the length that was supposed to be built.

The incompleteness of the last section from Loznica to Valjevo, which was key to allowing traffic crossing Yugoslavia to avoid Belgrade, deprived the Sub-Savian Magistral project of most of its interest. With the dissolution of Yugoslavia in 1991, the need for this project also disappeared.

The Sub-Savian Magistral is now divided into five sections belonging to four owners: the Croatian Railways from Sunja to Dobrljin (20.7 kilometres), the Railways of the Republika Srpska from Dobrljin to Doboj and from Doboj to Petrovo Selo (226 kilometres), the Railways of the Federation of Bosnia-Herzegovina from Petrovo Selo/Dabostica to Kalesia (60.1 kilometres), the

---

[10] Valjevo had been reached in 1908 by a narrow line coming from Belgrade.

[11] See Chapter 3 of the present book: Henry Jacolin, 'Serbia's Access to the Sea'.

Railways of the Republika Srpska (again) from Kalesia/Capardi to Zvornik Novi (20.8 kilometres) and the Railways of Serbia from Zvornik to Stalač (222.1 kilometres built and 68.1 kilometres remaining to be built).

Each section that would have been part of the Sub-Savian Magistral has taken up, more or less, the task for which it was originally built. But within the framework of the new states, some of these sections acquired new functions. The Bosanski–Doboj line, which permitted Bosnia-Herzegovina to establish a direct liaison between the Bosna Valley (Sarajevo) and the Una Valley, thereby avoiding Croatia, now constitutes the backbone of the western part of the Republica Srpska. The short section from Daboštica to Kalesia (60.1 kilometres), owned by the Federation of Bosnia-Herzegovina, emphasises the railway isolation of the Bosniak Tuzla region, which must use the tracks of the Republica Srpska to reach Sarajevo. The Tuzla–Zvornik line, which was finally opened to freight traffic on 8 June 1999, now plays an international role, exporting coal from Tuzla to Serbia. This line was rehabilitated in 2004 thanks to credit received from the European Investment Bank.

It is unlikely, at least for the moment, that Serbia will build the Valjevo–Loznica line. This difficult and costly project would serve only Zvornik, which is already connected to the Belgrade–Zagreb trunk line by the line running along the Drina. Reviving the Sub-Savian Magistral would deprive Serbia – as well as Croatia – of transit traffic between east and west for the benefit of Bosnia-Herzegovina. It is no longer a priority for Serbia, whose economic crisis in the aftermath of the war has dramatically reduced traffic on the main trunk line and relieved its overload.

Bibliography

Jacolin, Henry, 'L'établissement de la première voie ferrée entre l'Europe et la Turquie. Chemins de fer et diplomatie dans les Balkans', *Revue d'histoire des chemins de fer*, 35, fall 2006, 5–23.

Jelinović, Zvonimir, *Borba za Jadranske pruge* (The fight for Adriatic lines), Građa za gospodarsku povijest Hrvatske, ed. by Jugoslovenska Akademija Znanosti i Umjetnosti, vol. 6 (Zagreb 1957).

Loiseau, Charles, 'Une artère sud-européenne', *Revue de Paris* of 1 March 1918, 1–17, here 4.

Marville, Jacques (alias Henry Jacolin), 'L'électrification des chemins de fer yougoslaves', *La vie du rail* of 2 Mai 1976.

Marville, Jacques (alias Henry Jacolin), *Problèmes et perspectives des transports routiers entre la Grèce et la CEE* (in Greek) (Athens 1985).

Chapter 13

Passengers' Railway Identity in Socialist Romania during the 1950s and 1960s

Adelina Oana Ştefan

For the Communist regimes, there was no more powerful image to symbolise modernisation and progress than the locomotive.[1] This statement, true for any of the new 'peoples democracies' that emerged after 1948 in Eastern Europe undoubtedly refers to the Romanian regime from the 1950s to the 1980s. Although the issue of passenger train transportation was not at the core of the Communist party's policies, it was one of the most important means of showing the regime's strength and empathy towards the ordinary people's style of living. At the same time railways had a significant role in connecting various regions of the country in the attempt to overcome local distinctiveness and construct a new socialist identity. In order to understand how a passenger railway system functioned in a socialist society, a short introduction on the nature of socialist regimes in Eastern Europe is required. The interpretation of these regimes varies. They may be called totalitarian, or they may have followed an 'institutional interest group' or corporatist model, as Arfon Rees, a historian of Soviet railways, puts it.[2] Whereas during the 1960s, political scientists such as Carl J. Friedrich and Zbigniew K. Brzezinski labelled the socialist regimes of Eastern Europe totalitarian, a more moderate perspective appeared beginning in the 1970s and 1980s when it became possible for Western researchers to gain access to the Soviet Union's archives.[3] A new wave of researchers, among them Moshe Levin, argued that total control over these societies was impossible, given the limited resources of the Communist regimes, especially in their early years, as well as the often-inefficient allocation of supplies.[4]

---

[1]   Arfon Rees, *Stalinism and Soviet Rail Transport, 1928–1941* (Basingstoke and New York 1995).

[2]   Ibid.

[3]   Carl J. Friedrich and Zbigniev K. Brzezinski, *Totalitarian Dictatorship and Autocracy* (Cambridge 1956). See also Shella Fitzpatrick, 'New Perspectives on Socialism', *Russian Review*, 45, 1986, 357–63. For a complete discussion on revisionism regarding the Soviet regime, see *Russian Review*, vol. 45, 1986, and vol. 46, 1987.

[4]   Ibid. and János Kornai, *The Socialist System: The Political Economy of Communism* (Princeton 1992), Katerine Verdery, *National Ideology under Socialism: Identity and Cultural politics in Ceausescu's Romania* (Berkeley and Los Angeles 1991).

This was as true for the Communist regimes in Eastern Europe as it was for the Soviet Union itself. Although each had its own temporal and structural dynamic, they all followed the Soviet model (party-state, planned economy, collectivisation of agriculture, focus on heavy industry, etc.) with its strengths and limitations, especially during early 1950s. However, towards the end of the 1950s, these regimes underwent reforms as a consequence of both domestic political consolidation and various social movements (as in East Germany and Hungary) that demanded for a liberalisation of society and a break with the Soviet model. One of the results was that Communist officials started to pay increased attention to consumption and services in the attempt to become appealing to ordinary citizens as Mark Pittaway puts it.[5]

Romania fits into this model, but it delimitates itself from this temporal pattern in that from the end of 1970s to the beginning of 1980s, a regression toward harsh dictatorial conditions took place even as the neighbouring socialist countries took the path of liberalisation.[6] Moreover, the political regime in Romania offered only limited access to consumer goods and services, this situation getting worse in the 1980s. The main consequence of this policy was the deepening of smuggling practices and of bargaining, phenomena that became part of the socialist system in itself. The incapacity to reform led in the end to the downfall of the regime. However, things were not so clear at the end of the 1940s – beginning of the 1950s when the Communist regime came into power in Romania.

Back to the 1950s, despite the constant limitations which the ordinary citizens had to deal with in their everyday life, the socialist regime in Romania attempted to gain support from its citizens by promoting certain social services. I mention among these services housing, medical care, jobs, vacations and, last but not least, transportation, all of which were offered within the framework of an ongoing modernisation process. Passenger transportation via railways was intended to be part of this large project of modernisation by playing a significant role in both the building of new socialist identity and the improving of ordinary people's living standards. The questions that arise here are what sort of identity people travelling by train during the 1950s and 1960s gained, and to which extent this was politically and socially conditioned. I argue in this chapter that although the passengers in socialist Romania of the 1950s

---

[5]   Mark Pittaway, *Eastern Europe, 1939–2000: Brief Histories* (Oxford 2004).

[6]   The historiography on Romanian Communism tends to agree that three sub-periods can be delimitated for the Communist regime in Romania. The first, between 1948 and 1962, was characterised by strong political and economic restrictions, including political detentions, the collectivisation of agriculture, and a lack of consumer goods; the second, between 1962 and 1971, was a time of continuous liberalisation in almost all aspects of life; during the third, which started around 1971 and went until 1989, there was a return to ideology and limitations. For more on this topic, see William E. Crowther, *The Political Economy of Romanian Socialism* (New York et al. 1988), Vladimir Tismăneanu, *Stalinism for All Seasons: A Political History of Romanian Communism* (Berkeley, CA 2003) and Pavel Câmpeanu, *Ceauşescu. Anii numărătorii inverse* (Iaşi 2002).

and 1960s had to face various political and economic limitations, the experience of railway travel changed their perception of time and space, and played a major factor in their increasing geographical and ultimately their social mobility.

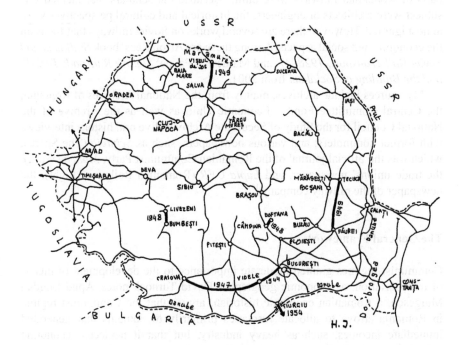

Figure 13.1   Railway Map of Romania, 1960s
Source: Map created by Henry Jacolin.

This project will develop on two levels of analysis: the first level will look at the official policies of the Communist regime regarding railways, paying attention to legislation, official directives and practices, while the second level of analysis will look at the way passengers remember the experience of the everyday use of railways. My aim is to investigate the role of passenger transportation within the railway system, the passengers' use of railway lines, the conditions provided by various types of trains, and last but not least the cultural and social impact of railways on passengers. I have chosen to research the 1950s and 1960s because these years represent the peak of railway use as a main means of transportation, and because this period corresponds to the first phase of the industrialisation process in Communist Romania that required a large input of workers from the rural areas, people who usually used trains as the main way to get to the towns.[7]

---

[7]   See *Anuarul Statistic* (Statistical Yearbook) (Bucharest 1990), 550.

This topic has received only little attention in both Romanian and Western historiography. Romanian historiography has focused more on the pre-war period before the outbreak of World War Two, as this was the time when the most important parts of Romanian railways were built.[8] Because the scholars that tackled this subject were architects or engineers, the historical and cultural perspectives were almost ignored. However, there are several works on Soviet railways that focus on the economic and social aspects. Among these are Arfon Rees' book *Stalinism and Soviet Rail Transport, 1928–41*, and Mathew J. Payne' *Stalin's Railroad: Turksib and the Building of Socialism* from 2001.[9]

My sources include archives, mainly from the National Archives of Romania, the Central Committee Fond – Economic Unit, as well as the Archive of the National Council for the Study of Securitate Archives; five oral history interviews with former commuters; and various newspapers, such as *Scînteia* (The Spark), which was the official journal of the Romanian Communist Party, *Munca* (Work), the trade unions' newspaper, and *Lupta CFR* (Romanian Railways' Fight), the newspaper of the railway company.[10]

The General Framework

Communist regimes granted moderate importance to the development of means of transportation, as economic geographer David Turnock notes. Apud Bogdan Murgescu, a Romanian economic historian, argues that the Communist regime in Romania strove to allocate resources primarily to domains that generated immediate incomes, such as heavy industry, but that it neglected economic infrastructures in the long run.[11] Despite these judgements, important investments were made in the railway sector in Romania especially after 1945. Thus, in the 1950s, 14.9 per cent of industrial investments were directed to transportation, while during the 1960s these investments decreased to 7.4 per cent. At the same time the amount of total industrial investment increased by almost four times from 6.3 billion lei to 27.7 billion lei.[12] Hence, the investment in transportation actually

---

[8]   See Radu Bellu, *Mica Monografie a cailor ferate din Romania, vol. 1: regionala Brasov* (Bucuresti 1995), Michel Tanase, 'Railways, Towns and Villages in Transylvania: Impact of the Railways on Urban and Rural Morphology', in Ralf Roth and Marie Noelle Polino (eds), *The City and the Railway in Europe* (Aldershot 2003), 45–59.

[9]   Rees, *Stalinism*, and Mathew J. Payne, *Stalin's Railroad: Turksib and the Building of Socialism* (Pittsburgh 2001).

[10]   CFR is the abreviation for *Căile Ferate Române* (Romanian Railways). Securitate is the informal name for the Department of State Security – the secret police in Romania during Communist times.

[11]   Apud Bogdan Murgescu, *Romania si Europa. Acumularea decalajelor economice 1500–2010* (Bucuresti 2010), 380.

[12]   *Anuarul Statistic* (Statistical Yearbook) (Bucuresti 1990), 524–5.

doubled between 1950 and 1960. The amount of investment was not reflected in the length of railway lines. In 1950, Romania had 10,853 kilometres of railway lines; by 1960, the figure had increased only to 10,981 kilometres; in 1970, it was 11,012.[13] Most of the resources were spent on the reconstruction of railway lines after the war bombardments and for their modernisation. Between 1950 and 1960 not a single kilometre of line was electrified but one-third of the lines were electrified between 1960 and 1989. Notwithstanding the fact that the capacities of the Romanian railways decreased considerably during the war without great progress being made afterwards, the number of passengers was 50 per cent higher in 1950 than it had been in 1938.[14] The main consequence of this shift was the overcrowding of trains and a decrease in the quality of the journey.

Despite this situation, several new railway developments were either finalised or begun at the end of 1940s. One example is the Bumbeşti–Livezeni line.[15] Its construction started during the interwar period and it was inaugurated in 1948. Other examples are the Salva–Viseu and Făurei–Tecuci lines, inaugurated in 1949.[16] These developments were built for economic purposes, but their construction was also widely used for propagandistic reasons.[17] The completion of the Bumbeşti–Livezeni line, despite the difficult engineering and geographical conditions, was required by the increasing importance of coal resources from the Jiu Valley for the underdeveloped Romanian economy. The Salva–Viseu line was also deemed necessary because Maramureş, a province in northwestern Romania close to the Soviet border, had to be connected with the rest of the country as well as with the USSR. These lines' propagandistic role was that they were deemed to be improvements brought by the newly installed Communist regime to the lives of workers and peasants. They were also supposed to show the devotion of the Romanian people to the party's policies, symbolically shown by the unpaid work, voluntarily performed at those sites. These construction sites were supposed to be 'schools of socialism', modelled after the

---

[13]   Ibid., 548.

[14]   Thus, during the 1950s, the situation below the level of 1938. The war and its aftermath were the main reasons for that. In 1938 there had been 11,284 kilometres of track, but in 1950 there were only 10,853 left. There were only 1,042 locomotives in 1950, in comparison with 1,684 in 1938. The number of carriages decreased from 2,959 in 1938 to 2,282 in 1950. Ibid., 548–9. The comparison is somewhat problematic, as the numbers for 1938 include the provinces of Bessarabia, Bukovina and Cadrilater (southern Dobrudja), which no longer belonged to Romania in 1950.

[15]   The Bumbeşti–Livezeni line had to connect Jiu Valley, where important resources of coal were located, with Oltenia, by crossing the Carpathian Mountains. It was 31.4 kilometres long.

[16]   *Arhivele Nationale Istorice Centrale* (ANIC, the National Archives of Romania), Central Committee of the Romanian Communist Party, Economic Fund, file no. 7/1966.

[17]   David Turnock, *An Economic Geography of Romania* (London 1974), 275.

Soviet ones from Magnitogorsk and Turksib.[18] The yard of Bumbeşti–Livezeni was named after the first post-war Romanian Communist Party first secretary, Gheorghe Gheorghiu Dej. Although the yard had been begun in 1921, it was not finished until 1945, and it was entirely presented by the official rhetoric as an accomplishment of the newly installed Communist regime.[19]

Passenger trains were divided into *rapid* (very fast), *accelerat* (fast) and *personal* (less fast but also less expensive), trains, and there were three classes of travel.[20] Undoubtedly, at the end of the 1940s the most crowded means of transportation were the *personal* trains and the third class of *rapid* and *accelerate* as almost 86 per cent of train travellers preferred these types of transportation in 1948.[21] This can tell not so much about the social and economic status of the travellers, how would be the case in a structured society but about the harsh economic conditions of the time with whom the majority of the travellers needed to cope.

The main concern of Communist railway authorities in Romania during the 1950s was not the transportation of passengers, but of goods. Most of the propaganda materials emphasised the importance of increasing railway speed and productivity, measuring the number of tons of goods transported per kilometre.[22] For example, a survey done of *Lupta CFR* (Romanian Railways' Fight), between April and June 1952 shows that thirteen articles on freight transportation were published, and only two on passenger transportation.[23] When focusing on passenger railway travel, propaganda materials of the 1950s stressed the importance of using railways as a way to educate ordinary people in the values and spirit of socialism. So-called 'agitation points' were placed in railways stations or in trains, with agitators distributing materials about various issues of importance for the Communist regime. *Lupta CFR* proudly mentions the 'agitators' that hand out the

---

[18]   Stephen Kotkin, *Magnetic Mountain: Stalinism as a Civilization* (Berkeley and Los Angeles 1995).

[19]   P. Teodorescu, 'Linia Bumbeşti-Livezeni', *Analele CFR*, issue 3, October 1948, 4. Teodorescu, an engineer, wrote in his article, 'The Bumbeşti Livezeni line, which is of major importance for the economy of our country, will not only be one of the most outstanding railway masterpieces, but also will stand as a testimony to the spirit of sacrifice and the devotion of the working people shown to the *Partidul Muncitoresc Roman* (PMR) which leads the working class to the peak.' Ibid., 5.

[20]   P. Zaharia, 'Traficul de calatori' (The passenger railway traffic), *Analele CFR*, issue 3, October, 1948, 4–20.

[21]   Ibid., 10.

[22]   *Lupta CFR*, issue 376, 1952, 380 and 423.

[23]   Figures draw on my personal survey. See *Lupta CFR*, April–June 1952. The existence of a Ministry of Railways shows the importance of this sector for the Romanian economy and Communist modernisation project in the discussed period. The Ministry of Railways was set up between 1953 and 1957, being abolished afterwards. See Stelian Neagoe, *Istoria Guvernelor României de la* începuturi *1859, până* în *zilele noastre, 1995* (Bucureşti 1995).

new Communist organic laws – the legal fundaments of the new society – to the train travellers:

> Seven o'clock. The train for Galaţi from the Northern Railway Station prepares for departure. There are only a couple of minutes left and the last travellers hurry to take their seats. Near the train, the ticket controllers Dumitra Gardaru and Elena Tudose wait for the train departure and they seem to carefully watch every passenger that steps before them. Today, apart from their usual work, they will have an additional job. And immediately after the train's departure they start to hand out propagandistic brochures to the travellers. Although the majority of the passengers have read the project of the new organic law, they are eager to read it one more time: they are very fond of the document that mirrors the great changes brought in our country by the socialist regime.[24]

It is certain that the dimension of propaganda discourse regarding trains is overwhelming during the 1950s. This demonstrates the significant interest that the Communist authorities had in raising the railways' efficiency and of using them for building the socialist society.

Travelling Conditions

Behind the propaganda image, and the central authorities' efforts, during the 1950s the passengers' travelling conditions were poor and various mistreatments took place. The archival records of the secret police mention a number of such situations. A report from 1946 drawn up from passengers' complaints states that during the trip from Bucharest to Satu Mare (a town located in the north of the country, at the border with now Ukraine) on 1 March the railway personnel harassed various passengers who did not have proper travel documents, asking them for bribes in order to be left alone. According to the report, the controllers confiscated a total of 25 kilograms of pork and 75 litres of plum brandy (ţuica, a local specialty) and took around 400,000 lei from passengers, but did not submit it to the railway officials or to the militia, keeping both the goods and the money for themselves.[25] On the other side, the habit of riding without a ticket was quite widespread among train travellers. According to a report of the Romanian Railways Direction, it was often that on train routes more than half of the passengers were caught without a ticket while controllers agreed to be bribed.[26]

---

[24] *Lupta CFR*, issue 376, June 1952, 3.

[25] *Arhivele Consiliului National pentru Studierea Arhivelor Securitatii* (ACNSAS) (The National Archives for the Study of Securitate Archives), Documentary Fund, file no. 11815, folio 144. In 1946 a dollar was the equivalent of 179,676 lei see: http://www.leulgreu.ro/istoric_monetar/pe_urmele_leului_nostru (last accessed 6 September 2010).

[26] ACNSAS, Documentary Fund, file no. 11816, folio 6.

Besides these abuses, the quality of railway facilities was also inadequate, the trains being crowded, slow and insufficient. The available statistics show a decrease in the number of passenger trains at the end of the 1940s in comparison with the 1930s. For instance, if in 1936 there were 1,431 daily trains, in 1948 there were only 928 daily trains, while the number of passengers increased.[27] This comparison can help us envision the overcrowdings of train coaches at that time. The slowness of Romanian trains during the 1950s was mocked in a squib published by the *Romanian Railways Fight*:

> Comrades, drive your horses faster as while in the car we cornered, grew up, and now we are going to pine away.[28]

The authorities seemed to be applying themselves to these problems as early as the end of the 1940s, but apparently without much success. An article published in the Romanian National Railways journal of 1949 proposed various solutions for the improvement of the railways services which included:

> Reduction of time the cars spend in back shops, the following of firm itineraries, preserving the carriages in order to decrease the number of those which need repairs, and especially conceiving a management plan to rigorously control the uses of passenger carriages.[29]

The problems were far from being solved even in the 1960s. An archival report of the Ministry of Transportation from 1966 mentioned several actions to be taken in order to improve the passengers' travelling conditions:

> From the analysis of the railways' passenger traffic within recent years and especially in 1965, it can be concluded that due to the characteristics of socialist economy, as well as due to some shortages and difficulties, the railways' capacity has been overloaded. In order to overcome these difficulties and to meet the needs of both socialist organisations and the population in 1966, the Romanian Ministry of Railways aims at continuing the railways modernisation in a systematic way, and to increase its transportation facilities through investments.[30]

In this respect, the Ministry decided to buy 80 diesel-electric locomotives and nine electric locomotives, and in this way to switch almost 50 per cent of the

---

[27]   Zaharia, *Traficul*, 9. It should be noted that in 1948 the territory of Romania was smaller than in 1936, as explained in footnote 14.

[28]   *Lupta CFR*, issue 378, June 14, 1952, 2. 'Tovarasi mana-ti mai repede telegarii ca de cand stam in vagon am incoltit, am crescut si (..) o sa ne si uscam.' Ibid.

[29]   Zaharia, *Traficul*, 16.

[30]   ANIC, CC al PCR, Economic Fund, file 37/1966, folio 15.

transportation capacity to electric and diesel traction.[31] In addition, the Ministry resolved to introduce a new train schedule – which would take into consideration the delays caused by the secondary railway lines and a passengers' number monitoring in order to avoid traffic jams – and to improve travelling conditions.[32] Nevertheless, passenger transportation remained of secondary importance for Communist officials, as the investment plan for the period of 1966–70 planned the purchase of 23,250 freight wagons and only of 2,000 passenger coaches.[33] The consequences of this policy showed during the 1970s, when the Romanian railways system was far from being much improved. A 1978 report of the Maramureş branch of Securitate revealed the impaired functioning of Romanian railways. According to the report, deficiencies such as lack of heating during the winter, dirty carriages, lack of lighting, long delays as well as a general lack of comfort and even safety were among the most frequent problems of Romanian trains during the 1970s. The report also pointed out the inadequate behaviour of train personnel who treated passengers disrespectfully or asked for bribes. Furthermore, certain facilities were lacking. Other common problems led to dangerous situations: overcrowded trains, inadequate inspection of train installations, and the fact that passengers often had to change platforms quickly to get from one train to another, forcing them to cross the tracks in a hurry.[34]

The Communist state policy towards railway transportation during the 1950s was to support investments in order for the railway lines to be rebuilt after the war and to use the railways for propaganda as a symbol of the new regime's economic strength. As we have seen, the freight railways received more attention than did passenger service, leading to important deficiencies in the latter's functioning. Only in the 1960s did the policy become more passenger-oriented, although the results were not at the expected level. This was only partially due to the poor management of the state. Moreover, it was a consequence of smuggling practices of both railways personnel and travellers who in this way voiced their grievances for the lack of proper services.

Last but not least, for a fuller understanding of the passenger railway policies in Romania during socialism, several other aspects should be taken into account. First, the economic underdevelopment, which determined that railways would be the main means of transportation in the framework of a lack of other types of infrastructure. This offered a privileged status to the railway industry and, to a certain extent, its workers. Accordingly, in 1950, railway workers had the highest salaries of any industrial workers, 346 lei per month, at a time when the average was 341 lei.[35] The second important element which should be taken into consideration is the culture of transportation. The political and social transformation that

---

[31]   Ibid.

[32]   Ibid., folio 18.

[33]   Ibid., folio 43.

[34]   ACNSAS, Documentary Fund, file no. 6376, vol. 1, 278–9.

[35]   *Anuarul Statistic* (Statistical Yearbook) (Bucharest 1990), 125.

occurred after the war forced more people to travel long distances to look for a job, especially after the collectivisation of the land in the rural areas, or to study, or for various other reasons that can arise in a society in turmoil. Travel undertaken under such circumstances determined a shift in perspective, not only about the notion of travel itself, but about the train as a material object as well. The train was seen not as a simple means of transportation, but as a way of overcoming geographical isolation, and of establishing one's place in the 'new society.'

Travelling by Train during the 1950s and 1960s: The Passengers' Recollections

The passengers' perspective on railway transportation in Communist Romania of the 1950s and 1960s is brought to light with the help of oral history interviews conducted with five people between the ages of 58 and 90. The interviews discuss the main reasons people used to travel during the 1950s and 1960s, the trains' travelling conditions, as well as the interviewees' thoughts about rail travel. Of the people interviewed three were workers and two were technicians. With the exception of one, Elena R., all interviewees come from rural areas. Among these, two still live in the countryside. Regarding the interviewees' education, one graduated from primary school, three of them finished high school, and one the university. Thus we can affirm that we have a relatively broad array of subjects in terms of age, geographical origin and educational level.

Răstoacă T., born in 1950, used to work in a wood processing factory in Suceava, a town of about 200,000 inhabitants in northeastern Romania. He recalls that he first travelled by train when he was a child, at the age of six or seven, and that the train was hauled by a steam engine:

> I remember when daddy took me with a train that had a steam locomotive, how there were many at that time, and the train was going very – very slowly.[36]

Later on while working as a labourer in a factory in Suceava, he used to return to his home village weekly because after protesting in order to obtain a passport and get medical treatment for his liver disease, he had to prove his presence within the country to the military and the Securitate. This experience is memorable to him, as the only available means of transportation between the town and his village was the train, which used to be very crowded, especially at the end of the week and during school holidays:

> S: And when you got a job in town, how did you travel to your village? R.T.: Trains were more modern then, in comparison to how they were during my childhood, but when the school holidays came it was extremely crowded. All the

---

[36]   Personal interview of Adelina Oana Ştefan, with Rastoaca T., labourer, April 2010.

students of the trade schools used to receive free train tickets and we travelled tightly packed because there were very few trains.[37]

Asked about the possibility of socialising or making conversation in the train, he replied that given his previous experience with the Securitate, he usually avoids talking about 'serious' matters:

> You know, on the train you had to be even more cautious than on the bus, because you didn't know who's staying next to you. You see now I have the courage to speak, but then you had to be very careful when telling a joke, making a wisecrack.[38]

Although it was socially difficult, the train was extremely affordable for Răstoacă T., especially because he rarely had to pay for a ticket:

> S.: How much was a train ticket? Was it expensive?
>
> R.T.: No, the thing is (he smiles) that at that time no one used to buy a ticket. We all travelled without one, you know, by bribing the ticket controllers.[39]

Inquired about the goods travellers carried with them while on the train, he remembers that in the morning, there were women who went to town in order to sell different agricultural products, and in the afternoon, almost everyone used to have a 'full bag', probably filled with small objects or goods taken from their work place. He says this was normal. For Răstoacă T., railways were not ideal, but they were the only available means of transportation to his home village. For him the train was an alienating space as, unlike the local bus, it presupposed the interaction with people who were not part of his community/village. Although he was aware of the poor conditions, he was content with the facilities provided, as he was new to that kind of travel. His testimony shows that people turned the state's incapacity of offering the promised services to their advantage by not paying for their tickets. At the same time they gave up their expectations as well.

George S. was also a worker in a wood processing factory, but from Focşani, a town of about 70,000 inhabitants from southeastern Romania. His train journeys started when he was 14 years old and went to trade school in Sibiu, a historic town situated in the central part of Romania within the Transylvanian depression. He used to travel together with two other schoolmates from his village. The journey was seven or eight hours long, and a distance of about 400 kilometres:

---

[37] Ibid.

[38] Ibid.

[39] Ibid.

We were three colleagues from Buda and we would take the train from Râmnicu Sărat. The train made took two hours until Ploieşti and then another six hours until Sibiu. It was a regional train that stopped in almost every station.[40]

The time of the train journey was used for eating the provisions taken from home, sleeping or playing cards. They did not always have reserved seats.

S.: And how was the train, was it crowded?

G.S.: No, not always, only during the school holidays. Sometimes the train would leave with travellers standing on the stairs for a couple of kilometres.

R.: That means you didn't have a seat, normally?

G.S No, actually I didn't care so much about it. The ticket was without a reserved seat. We got on the train and if there were seats we sat down, if not (...) we didn't![41]

G.S. remembers that passenger wagons were separated into compartments of about eight seats. This offered some privacy to the travellers, especially when the train was not very crowded. Another train journey experience was when G.S. was employed as a worker at the Focşani wood processing factory. Then he used to travel monthly to his home on a shuttle whose main function was to carry local commuters. The trains used to run between two industrial points, Mărăsesti and Buzău, about 100 kilometres from one another. It was the most inexpensive kind of train, usually filled with commuters. He used to travel by himself without other work companions. Although he used to pay for his ticket there were many non-payers on that route. He notes:

As always, the controllers were glad to earn extra money, and the travellers to save some.[42]

Regarding the price of the travel he recalls it as being very affordable, about seven lei, money that one usually paid for two loaves of breads. The opportunity of travelling by train was an important event in G.S.'s life, as he had not had access to that until he went to the trade school. Although the travel conditions were hard, the possibility of seeing the country and of enlarging his geographical and cultural horizon annulled the inconveniences.

Besides the main lines, there were local lines. These were to be found mainly in the mountain areas, and they served industrial purposes. A line of this type was

---

40 Personal interview of Adelina Oana Ştefan with George S., May 2010.
41 Ibid.
42 Ibid.

built after 1948 between Câmpina, a town in the foothills of Southern Carpathians, and the nearby village of Doftana Valley, with the aim of transporting logs to the 'December 21st' wood processing factory.[43] Itself an improvisation, the existence of the 'little train' shows the ability of the Communist state to deal with its own shortages not by providing good services, but by offering a compromise solution. Maria I., an agricultural worker born in 1930, remembers that this line was the only means of transportation to Câmpina, the main town in the area. Otherwise the inhabitants of the villages from the area had to walk ten kilometres to the closest railway station in Comarnic, which was on the main railway line that connected Bucharest and Brasov.[44] On this secondary route, the 'little train' – as it was popularly named – used to run. It primarily transported logs, but it also had a wagon or two for people. According to Maria, the little train ran daily and the travellers were mostly locals who went to town for various administrative issues or workers in the nearby factories. The Câmpina town monograph description shows that during the 1950s and 1960s there were eight main factories in the town, which generally employed workers from outside the town who needed to travel daily to their homes.[45] In the absence of official statistics, one can assume that the number of daily passengers that the little train carried was significant. Regarding the usual price of a ride on the little train, Maria I. does not remember the exact amount that had to be paid, but she recalls that the fare was paid to the driver the same as on a bus.[46]

The passengers' adaptability to the transportation shortages of the 1960s is shown by the recollection of Elena R. She is an accountant from the town of Câmpina, born in 1920. She remembers having travelled with the little train, but mainly for tourist purposes. She recalls that the train's main purpose was to carry logs, but it had a wagon or two that 'looked pretty good' where people could sit.[47] She says that the journey was a memorable one for her, due to the beauty of the area and to the uniqueness of the other travellers:

> The wagons were smaller than the usual ones and the travellers were the inhabitants of the area, a little bit more peculiar, so to speak, and for me, who was travelling for the first time on that route, it was an impressive moment. The little train followed the Doftana River Valley. At that time the valley was very abrupt and winding, and when one looked behind, one could see the whole landscape, which was really beautiful.[48]

43 The factory was named for Stalin's birthday.

44 Maria I. worker, personal interview with Adelina Oana Ştefan, May 2010.

45 Silviu Dan Cratocvil, *Monografia Orasului Campina: Comitetul de Cultura a Judetului* (Prahova 1990), 123.

46 Maria I., unskilled worker, personal interview with Adelina Oana Ştefan, May 2010.

47 Elena R., accountant, personal interview with Adelina Oana Ştefan, April 2010.

48 Ibid.

Her perspective as an outsider of the area was rather romantic but her experience is able to show the multitude of functions that the little train could perform.

Another traveller on the little train was Ana O., technician, born in 1951, who used to take the train when she was a child, before going to high school in Câmpina. She admits that her memories are cloudy, but she says that during her childhood, the little train was her connection with the world. She was also a regular traveller on the little train's descendant after its dismantling in 1965, the van, an even more primitive means of transportation:

> And after I got into high school when I was 14 years old and the construction of
> the dam started, the little train was dismantled and I travelled then with a van, a
> quite primitive one. I remember that it shook us really hard because there were no
> seats in the beginning and we had to hang on to whatever we could, so as not to
> fall. Only later on did they introduce seats, but it was still very uncomfortable.[49]

Her testimony is relevant in telling how important that primitive local railway line was for the region's inhabitants in the framework of a backward infrastructure and of poor passenger transportation facilities. At the same time, one can grasp the ways passengers' identity has been shaped by the use of the train, which was thought of as a more comfortable and more reliable mode of transportation then the van. What is to be noted is that the dismantling of the little train in the context of industrialisation (a dam was to be built in the area) did not bring – in the short term – an improvement of transportation services, but a worsening of them.

These accounts should be seen in the connection with the personal background of the interviewees as well as with the context of socialist and post-socialist Romania. As we know, memories are shaped not only according to past experiences but also in relation with present experiences and contexts.[50] On the one hand, their stories are selection of what they considered relevant to tell in order to build a meaningful story, and on the other hand, these are involuntary collections of images and perceptions they took over from the society they lived in.

Conclusion

The prioritising of automotive means of transportation starting with the 1960s took place in the context of industrialisation, and of the process of the expansion of infrastructure, as shown by the particular example of the little train. This is also connected with the political background of the Communist regime in Romania, which shifted from the influence of the USSR to a more nationalist policy at

---

49   Ana O., technician, personal interview with Adelina Oana Ştefan, April 2010.

50   See Alesandro Portelli, *The Death of Luigi Trastulli and Other Stories: Form and Meaning in Oral History* (New York 1991), and *The Battle of Valle Giulia: Oral History and the Art of Dialogue* (Wisconsin 1997).

the end of the 1950s.[51] This meant that industry had to be developed, especially heavy industry, at the expense of services and agriculture. The development of industry, in turn, made the commuting even more necessary, and spurred the development of a less expensive transportation infrastructure to connect the most remote settlements to towns and cities. Trains could fulfil this demand to a large degree, but as the process accelerated, the use of buses became more economically convenient. The use of trains predominated until the middle of the 1960s, and created a specific identity for their users as they were meant to shape the travellers from both political and social points of view.

According to my interviewees, the main reasons for travelling during the 1950s and 1960s were going to work or school, for shopping or for sightseeing. This is a broad range of motives that could lead a person to depart from her/his home location, regardless of education, social origins or provenance (town or village). This shows a complex society which was becoming increasingly mobile under the political, social and economic pressure. At the same time their testimonies show that a compromise was set up with the Communist regime, which in exchange for poor services, offered citizens the freedom to officially deceive the system by smuggling and creating an underground economy. This helps explain the incapacity of the Communist regime to fulfil its promises of prosperity and good life, and part of the syndrome that eroded them in the end.

The accounts presented are relevant not only in showing the unseen social realities of socialist Romania during the decades between the 1950s and 1970s, but they also tell us about the way people who lived under socialism relate to their own past. Most of my interviewees describe themselves as having been content with the conditions that were provided, although they may not have been pleased with them at the time when they were offered. However, either because these memories are part of their youth, or because they were just unconsciously adopted from the official discourse of Communism, they tend to present this as their own personal recollection. The term that may encapsulate the attitude of my interviewees toward railways and train voyages during Communism is *nostalgia*, a notion often used to denote the physical separation from something – a country, a person, a certain past.[52] This does not show that ordinary people regret the travels during Communism, but rather that they consider this as part of their identity, which cannot be easily removed.

The Communist regime in Romania granted a higher importance to freight railway transportation than to that of passengers due to its ideological, political

---

[51]   This process started in 1957 with the withdrawal of Red Army troops from Romania and culminated with Gheorghe Gheorghiu Dej's 1964 Declaration of Independence – a political declaration that underlined the 'national path' of Romanian socialism, and with the speech by Nicolae Ceaușescu in 1968 that rejected the Soviet intervention in Czechoslovakia.

[52]   For an analysis of nostalgia, see Svetlana Boym, *The Future of Nostalgia* (New York 2001).

and economic goals of increasing production rather than consumption, and services.[53] This was both a strategy of political legitimisation and a path to fast modernisation, in imitation the Soviet model during the 1950s. By the middle of the 1960s, however, one finds the introduction of an autochthonous framework of development. For example, if one compares the content of newspapers from 1950s to that of 1960s, one notices a decrease in the number of articles that make references to the Soviet model.

The restrictions on passenger's facilities led to the finding of alternative, unofficial, but accepted solutions, such as the adding of passenger wagons to a freight train, or the frequent use of trains without paying a ticket. The railway management's incapacity to respond to shortages, the lack of resources, and poor management were among the factors that led to the lowering of travelling conditions in Romanian trains during the 1950s and 1960s.

At the same time, one observes a certain democratisation of train travel, as it became cheaper, and it was offered on a free basis to certain categories of people (such as high school pupils) during the 1950s and to even a larger extent towards the 1960s. The social and cultural impact of railways on passengers is significant in terms of the identity-building process, as train travel had a considerable influence in reducing distances and familiarising the passengers with parts of the country that were further away from their homes. However, it was not the existence of railways themselves that determined that, but the particular context of the 1950s and 1960s. This context meant increased access to schooling, and an inchoate process of industrialisation that required a larger number of workers, especially from the rural areas.

Finally, one should ask to what extent the passenger railway situation in Romania during the 1950s and 1960s was the result of a long backward tradition, as various scholars have argued, or of the presence of a newly installed Communist regime that was unwilling to invest in services.[54] In terms of railway development, Romania had one of the lowest rates of passenger travellers in Europe before World War Two, but the situation was relatively aggravated by the war; afterwards, the post-war reconstruction was slow due to the rather inefficient resource allocation system and poor management.[55]

---

[53]   Kornai, *The Socialist System: The Political Economy of Communism* (Princeton 1992).

[54]   See in this respect Andrew Janos, 'Modernization and Decay in Historical Perspective', in Kenneth Jowitt (ed.), *Social Change in Romania, 1860–1940: A Debate on Development in a European Nation* (Berkeley 1978), 72–116.

[55]   See Zaharia, *Traficul*, 8, and Tony Judt, *Postwar: A History of Europe since 1945* (New York 2005).

Bibliography

Bellu, Radu, *Mică monografie a căilor ferate din România*, vol. 1: *regionala Brașov* (Bucuresti 1995).

Boym, Svetlana, *The Future of Nostalgia* (New York 2001).

Câmpeanu, Pavel, *Ceaușescu. Anii numărătorii inverse* (Iași 2002).

Cratocvil, Silviu Dan, *Monografia Orașului Câmpina: Comitetul de Cultură a Județului* (Prahova 1990).

Crowther, William E., *The Political Economy of Romanian Socialism* (New York and others 1988).

Fitzpatrick, Shella, 'New perspectives on socialism', *Russian Review*, 45, 1986, 357–63.

Friedrich, Carl J. and Brzezinski, Zbigniew K., *Totalitarian Dictatorship and Autocracy* (Cambridge 1956).

Janos, Andrew, 'Modernization and Decay in Historical Perspective', in Kenneth Jowitt (ed.), *Social Change in Romania, 1860–1940: A Debate on Development in a European Nation* (Berkeley 1978), 72–116.

Judt, Tony, *Postwar: A History of Europe since 1945* (New York 2005).

Kornai, János, *The Socialist System: The Political Economy of Communism* (Princeton 1992).

Kotkin, Stephen, *Magnetic Mountain Stalinism as a Civilization* (Berkeley and Los Angeles 1995).

Murgescu, Bogdan, *România și Europa. Acumularea decalajelor economice 1500–2010* (Bucuresti 2010).

Neagoe, Stelian, *Istoria Guvernelor României de la începuturi 1859, până în zilele noastre, 1995* (Bucuresti 1995).

Payne, Mathew J., *Stalin's Railroad: Turksib and the Building of Socialism* (Pittsburgh 2001).

Pittaway, Mark, *Eastern Europe, 1939–2000: Brief Histories* (Oxford 2004).

Portelli, Alesandro, *The Death of Luigi Trastulli and Other Stories: Form and Meaning in Oral History* (New York 1991).

Portelli, Alesandro, *The Battle of Valle Giulia: Oral History and the Art of Dialogue* (Wisconsin 1997).

Rees, Arfon, *Stalinism and Soviet Rail Transport, 1928–1941* (New York 1995).

Tanase, Michel, 'Railways, Towns and Villages in Transylvania: Impact of the Railways on Urban and Rural Morphology', in Ralf Roth and Marie Noelle Polino (eds), *The City and the Railway in Europe* (Aldershot 2003), 45–59.

Teodorescu, P., 'Linia Bumbești-Livezeni', *Analele CFR*, issue 3, October 1948, 17–71.

Tismăneanu, Vladimir, *Stalinism for All Seasons. A Political History of Romanian Communism* (Berkeley, CA 2003).

Turnock, David, *An Economic Geography on Romania* (London 1974).

Verdery, Katerine, *National Ideology under Socialism: Identity and Cultural politics in Ceausescu's Romania* (Berkeley and Los Angeles 1991).

Zaharia, P., 'Traficul de călători' (The passenger railway traffic), *Analele CFR*, issue 3, October 1948, 3–17.

Chapter 14
Cold War Crisis on the Railway: Construction of the Berlin Wall

Tomáš Nigrin

One of the most important railway hubs in Europe, Berlin's railway network was deeply affected by tumultuous events in the twentieth century. Of these, the Second World War and the Cold War had the strongest impact. To this day, we can observe traces of the various phases of railway development in Berlin – its modest beginnings, its rapid modernisation, its wartime destruction, and the situation in which it found itself during the Cold War – in the form of overgrown, rusty tracks, abandoned embankments, unused bridges and derelict stations. Berlin's railway system suffered its most extensive decline as a result of the construction of the Berlin Wall in 1961. The objective of this study is primarily to describe and analyse the impact of the political confrontation that began in 1961 on railway transportation in Berlin. Adjustments in day-to-day operations and selected technical aspects of operation procedures for trains running close to the border are discussed as well.

The first railways on German territory opened in Bavaria in 1835, and the first railway connection in Prussia, linking Berlin with Potsdam, was inaugurated three years later. By 1846, five railways already went through Berlin. All the railway stations became interconnected in 1851. In 1871, the circular *Ringbahn* railway came into use. In 1882, a total of fourteen different railways entered Berlin, which was developing into one of the most important railway crossings in Prussia, the German empire and later also in the Weimar Republic. The advanced railway infrastructure and progressive concept of public transport in Berlin became symbols of modern railway operations in Europe. Before the start of the Second World War, Germany as a whole had approximately 54,000 kilometres of railway tracks.

Divided Berlin, United Railway

After the war, Berlin lay in ruins. Its renewal was slowed by complicated administrative divisions among the victorious Allied forces. During the first months of Allied control, the deep antagonisms between them had not yet surfaced, and in July 1945, a part of German territory occupied by US Army was exchanged for the Western part of Berlin, which had been conquered by the Soviets two months earlier. The three Western occupation sectors were created there shortly thereafter.

Representatives from the United States, the Soviet Union, Great Britain and France formed the Allied Command, the highest authority within the city. It would function until 1948, and was in many ways more effective than the Allied Control Commission, the highest governing body for the whole of Germany. On 1 September 1945, the Soviets put the responsibility for managing rail transportation in their occupied zone into German hands, namely to eight railway directorates (*Reichsbahndirektion*). One of those covered the whole territory of Berlin. Railway transport to Western sectors of Berlin, administered by the Deutsche Reichsbahn (DR), did not become a contentious issue until the first Berlin crisis in 1948 and 1949.[1]

That first Berlin crisis fully revealed how inappropriate the organisation and the structure of rail transportation in the city were. First, the de facto Soviet-controlled Deutsche Reichsbahn operated all transportation for the Western sectors as well. Second, tensions rose among DR employees, some of whom lived in the Western sectors and worked in the East and vice versa. Demands for wages paid in Western sector currency for all DR employees led to several mass strikes, the biggest and most destructive for the economy of the city following the first Berlin crisis.[2]

The Western Allies tried to limit the role of the DR in West Berlin after tensions had risen between the East and the West at the end of the 1940s. During the first Berlin crisis, the railway property was divided into inventory and real estate (*Vorratsvermögen*), and equipment necessary for operations (*Betriebsvermögen*). The former was transferred to the Deutsche Bundesbahn (DB), controlled by the West, in 1953, while the latter stayed under DR control and use. All personnel, cargo and military train service as well as the *S-Bahn* in West Berlin continued to be provided by DR trains. Thus, in West Berlin, the DR administered 145 kilometres of *S-Bahn* tracks, 78 railway stations (including *S-Bahn* stations), 1,000 kilometres of railway tracks and 1,038 hectares of land.[3]

In the 1950s, the Berlin Railway remained one of the last common elements in the city, but it was increasingly becoming divided between the two rival political blocs. After the bus and tramway transport systems were divided, only the railways ignored sectoral borders and functioned as an undivided company in the whole area. *S-Bahn* trains crossed the border on their usual routes, and railway-owned public facilities such as hospitals, cultural centres and sporting grounds served the

---

[1]   Burghard Ciesla, *Als der Osten durch den Westen fuhr. Die Geschichte der Deutschen Reichsbahn in Westberlin* (Köln 2006), 27.

[2]   The biggest strike of the Berlin railway workers led to a temporary cooperation between the Western Allies and the Soviet Union that was intended to stabilise the situation in the city. The coordination of activities with the Soviet Union was followed by huge consternation at the West Berlin population, because the Berlin Airlift, organised due to the Soviet blockade, was still in operation. See David E. Barclay, *'Schaut auf diese Stadt'. Der unbekannte Ernst Reuter* (Berlin 2000), 286–91.

[3]   Ciesla, *Als der Osten*, 29.

community in both parts of the city. The only difference was that DR employees living in West Berlin received part of their salaries in West German marks.[4]

The existence of interconnected railways started to present substantial difficulties for the German Democratic Republic (GDR). In the 1950s, Berlin became the place where it was easiest to get across the Iron Curtain, as borders within the city were still guarded only symbolically. Most escapees, including many from other states of the Eastern Bloc, left the GDR via the *S-Bahn*, simply staying on the West-bound train instead of getting out at the last station of the Eastern sector. The GDR's authorities and those of other Eastern bloc countries became uncomfortable with this situation.

Starting at the end of the 1950s, it became apparent both to GDR officials and to the Western powers that the situation of mass exodus through Berlin was politically and economically unsustainable for the GDR. The DR then started technical preparations for the possibility of running separate *S-Bahn* trains for the Eastern and the Western sectors. Construction of wide circular tracks around Berlin began, encircling West Berlin from the outside.[5]

Supported by the Soviets, the GDR's Walter Ulbricht decided to erect a wall within the city. What impact did the decision have on the railway system in Berlin? In the first phase, after 13 August 1961, all *S-Bahn* and *U-Bahn* service that crossed the sector border was discontinued. The only exceptions were the lines that only partially ran through the Eastern sector. These lines did not stop in stations in the Eastern bloc, which were guarded by People's Police and Border Guard units; they were the underground lines which are, today, U6 and U8, and the *S-Bahn* in the North–South Tunnel between the stations of Potsdammer Platz and Gesundbrunnen. In the Friedrichstrasse station, it was possible for West German commuters to change between *U-Bahn* (today U6) and *S-Bahn* lines heading to and from the Western sector and operating on the so-called *Stadtbahn*. It was, however, not possible for the West Berlin commuters to meet any passengers from East Berlin, nor to leave the station. The construction of the wall thus marked the beginning of the dismantling of the famous *Berliner Ringbahn*. The *S-Bahn* service between the sectors was shut down and numerous less important railway crossings at the border were closed. But various long-distance trains still operated from West Berlin, connecting it with West Germany. These passenger trains (called *Interzonenzug*), cargo trains and military trains only crossed through the territory of the GDR and did not make any stops there. After several successful unauthorised journeys by so-called 'freedom trains' to West Berlin, GDR authorities decided to dismantle seldom-used railway tracks connecting the sectors. Transit traffic was channelled to several well-guarded border-crossings, especially Wannsee and Spandau, where the border guard units took an active part in overseeing railway operations. The border guard command at each of the crossings had to authorise the departure of every train, and operated the derailer stop. Only after the permission

---

[4]   Barclay, *Schaut auf diese Stadt*, 190.
[5]   Bernd Kuhlmann, *Der Berliner Außenring* (Nordhorn 1997).

to depart was granted and the derailer stop deactivated could the regular railway personnel approve the transit passage.[6]

East–West Competition on the Berlin's Tracks

The immediate changes, such as limitations of the passenger railway service and modifications in the organisation of railway operations, were followed by more serious long-term transformations. The DR reacted to the political changes in Berlin by creating the Railway Office 4 (*Reichsbahnamt 4*) under the Berlin Railway directorate. Its organisational structure was the same as that of a regular railway directorate, which effectively meant that it became a specific and unique 'small directorate' for West Berlin.[7]

While the West tried to transform the whole of West Berlin into a showcase for capitalism, the DR attempted, starting in 1958, and then with increased intensity after 1961, to present the railway service in West Berlin as a showcase of socialism.[8] However, since the first period after the construction of the wall, the DR-operated *S-Bahn* service had faced a boycott by West Berlin citizens, called for in a speech by West Berlin mayor Willy Brandt on 16 August 1961. A common slogan at the time was, 'No marks for Ulbricht's barbed wire' (*Keine Mark für Ulbrichts Stacheldraht*), referring to the money paid as transit fees to the DR in West German marks for *S-Bahn* service in the Western sector.[9] The West Berlin public transport company *Berliner Verkehrsbetriebe* (BVG) immediately supported the boycott by organising bus lines that ran alongside the *S-Bahn*. Under these conditions, the DR wanted to improve the perception of the *S-Bahn* and the railway system as a whole, so it significantly increased the number of trains servicing West Berlin and shortened the intervals of all the lines. Even these measures did not help, and the *S-Bahn* became a target of West Berliners' revenge for the construction of the despised wall. Together with the boycott, physical attacks such as train derailings, vandalism and destruction of trains and other railway property became frequent.

The fact that the GDR Ministry for Transportation provided no railway police (*Transportpolizei*) contributed to the problem. Serving in these units had become highly dangerous after 13 August 1961, as the workers who often lived in West Berlin were often physically attacked, denounced or even 'pilloried', i.e. personal and publicly denounced, as servants of the detested GDR regime. As a result, the railway police was completely discontinued in West Berlin for several years. Furthermore, West German police patrolled neither on the DR trains nor on the adjacent DR property. This situation resulted in massive losses for the

---

6   Bernd Kuhlmann, *Züge durch Mauer und Stacheldraht* (Berlin 1998), 60.

7   Ciesla, *Als der Osten*, 11.

8   Ibid., 121.

9   Peter Merseburger, *Willy Brandt 1912–1992. Visionär und Realist* (Munich 2002), 400–401.

DR in the form of destroyed property. The unsuccessful efforts by the DR to create a showcase of socialism were repeated several times, no longer through strengthening of the transit service, but mainly through small beautification and modernisation campaigns, which had to be of limited extent and expense due to critical lack of West German marks.[10]

For the DR, the construction of the wall marked the beginning of a decline. It soon fell substantially behind the West German DB. Yet throughout the 1950s, the modernisation efforts still continued with similar speed in the DR and the DB. This included the implementation of new technologies and the replacement of old steam locomotives by diesel and electric trains. On both sides the planners used rough outlines of long-term plans that had been developed at the time when the country was still united. Meanwhile, starting in the early 1960s, the whole Bundesrepublik Deutschland (BRD) began to draw ahead of the GDR economically. The GDR's lack of resources became apparent in the DR, which cut its attempts at further modernisation.[11]

Operating the railway system in West Berlin including the *S-Bahn* turned out to create huge losses for the GDR. This loss only exacerbated the shortage of Western currency for the DR and the GDR as a whole. For the railway system in West Berlin, this meant that major investments to infrastructure were dramatically scaled down, and money was mainly granted only for basic maintenance. The DR management also tried to decrease the number of its West Berlin employees, whose salaries in West German marks were expensive for the DR to pay. To replace them with employees living in East Berlin was, however, impossible for political reasons. East Germans working in West Berlin represented more threatening instability for the GDR regime than the potential economy losses for DR caused by the lack of railway personal. Railway operations thus became drastically rationalised and reduced, but without concurrent implementation of modern technologies. Inefficiencies persisted. For example, for political and security reasons, to prevent communication between *S-Bahn* train operators in East Berlin and West Berlin, two frequencies were used, 81.8 MHz for the West and 84.75 MHz for the East.[12]

At the end of 1960s, the railways in West Berlin showed signs of severe lack of financing. Of the approximately one thousand kilometres of railway tracks, 15 per cent were closed down and 7 per cent were used very seldom or were foreseen to be closed down; 22 per cent of rail switches were also closed down and a further 10 per cent were also foreseen to be closed down in near future; 17 per cent of the railway buildings were in unusable conditions, and 1.26 kilometres of bridges and bridge constructions were closed down or would be soon. Because of the shortage of funds, the DR often discontinued service on long rail sidings, thus cutting off companies and factories from the railway network. This policy resulted in further losses due

---

[10] Ciesla, *Als der Osten*, 131–2.

[11] Ibid., 32.

[12] Kuhlmann, *Züge durch Mauer*, 73.

to decreased loading. Parallel with the efforts to save costs, there were increasing pressures to raise transit fees for each axle freight ton-kilometre in the interzonal passenger, cargo and military trains. For political reasons, the DR could not admit the true cause of the technical backwardness, the dilapidation of the infrastructure and the restrictive operating strategies. The prestige of the whole GDR was at stake.[13]

From a legal point of view, the period between 1961 and 1971 was not covered by any comprehensive transit agreement between the two countries.[14] In hindsight, it seems strange that this situation did not lead to more complications or confrontations. The legal vacuum ended in 1971, when a transit agreement was signed by the two German states.[15] It was only after 1990 that the railway system in West Berlin started to recover from the damage it incurred as a result of the construction of the wall. The process was very slow, requiring huge investments.

Starting in 1961, as the two blocs competed in raising the standard of living of their populations, availability of consumer goods, social welfare, social security, culture and architecture; they also confronted each other in the transportation sector. The DR-operated *S-Bahn* service competed with the BVG's new bus lines and new *U-Bahn* lines that were specifically designed to replace the *S-Bahn* (which has had quite unfortunate effects on the transit situation in unified Berlin today). An interesting footnote is that the division of Berlin appeared on the BVG's transit maps only in 1964. Until that time, the wall seemed not to exist and the *U-Bahn* lines still ran between the East and the West on the maps as if nothing had happened.

The contemporary situation of railway transport in Berlin, and particularly in its Western part, is an outcome of the Cold War period, where the only strategic concept in transportation management was political confrontation with the competing bloc and efforts to claim prestige. The Berlin Wall divided the city in two for almost 40 years. Today, nearly 60 years since its construction, not all of the dismantled and closed tracks and their related infrastructure have been reopened. The process is very costly, and with only a bit of hyperbole, we can say that the accounts for the Cold War and the Berlin Wall are not yet settled with respect to railway transportation, and may not be settled for some time to come.

Bibliography

Barclay, David E., *'Schaut auf diese Stadt'. Der unbekannte Ernst Reuter* (Berlin 2000).
Ciesla, Burghard, *Als der Osten durch den Westen fuhr. Die Geschichte der Deutschen Reichsbahn in Westberlin* (Köln 2006).

---

[13] Ciesla, *Als der Osten*, 32.

[14] See for example Forschungsinstituts der Deutschen Gesellschaft für Auswärtige Politik e.V (ed.), *Dokumente zur Berlin-Frage 1944–1966* (Munich 1987).

[15] Hermann Wentker, *Außenpolitik in engen Grenzen. Die DDR im internationalen System 1949–1989* (Munich 2007), 330–35.

Forschungsinstituts der Deutschen Gesellschaft für Auswärtige Politik e.V (ed.), *Dokumente zur Berlin-Frage 1944–1966* (Munich 1987).

Kuhlmann, Bernd, *Der Berliner Außenring* (Nordhorn 1997).

Kuhlmann, Bernd, *Züge durch Mauer und Stacheldraht* (Berlin 1998).

Merseburger, Peter, *Willy Brandt 1912–1992. Visionär und Realist* (Munich 2002).

Wentker, Hermann, *Außenpolitik in engen Grenzen. Die DDR im internationalen System 1949–1989* (Munich 2007).

PART III
After the Fall of the Iron Curtain: Changes – Problems – Modernisation

Chapter 15

Railway Integration in Europe: UIC – a Key Player of East–West Railway Integration

Paul Véron

Birth of a 'European' Railway System

The first railways were developed by private companies during the first half of the nineteenth century essentially on a national basis to serve the investors' business goals and were encouraged by governments which recognised early on the potential of this emerging mode of transport as a factor of economic growth and territorial unity. It was against this backdrop that railways were first developed in Great Britain, France, Belgium, Germany and Italy as well as on the North American and Asian continents. The first international railway service is generally considered to be the railway line linking Liege in Belgium to Cologne in Germany from 1843. Another pioneer for international railway operation in Europe was the industrialist Georges Nagelmaeckers who founded the Compagnie internationale des wagons–lits in 1876 and imagined from the beginning the operation of long-distance passenger trains across the European continent.

However, the specific idea of harmonising or unifying railway operations across Europe was mainly first pushed in Prussia and the constitutive states of the German Confederation in the mid nineteenth century. The German economist Friedrich List, who was behind the establishment of the *Zollverein*, the German customs union, advocated in the first half of the nineteenth century for the extension of the railway system to support territorial unity as well as trade and welfare development. Several milestones followed including the creation of a Prussian railway association in 1846 with a clear aim of harmonising railway operations, followed in 1847 by the foundation of a Union of German Railway Companies grouping 44 German networks, four networks from the Austro-Hungarian empire, including parts of the future Yugoslavia. The Union based in Hamburg was subsequently joined by railway companies of the Netherlands and Luxembourg and then Belgium, Russia, Poland and Romania, making a total of 105,450 kilometres of lines before the First World War. The working bodies and committees of this *Verein* (Union) were in charge of developing common standards on construction and use of infrastructure and rolling stock, loading gauges and the reciprocal and financial compensations between companies.[1]

---

[1]   See Verein Mitteleuropäischer Eisenbahnverwaltungen (ed.), *Vereins-Handbuch.* Herausgegeben anläßlich des 90jährigen Bestehens des Vereins im November 1936

Another pioneer of international railway harmonisation is Switzerland with its extensive railway network despite its small size. Located in the heart of Europe and a transit route for passenger and even more for freight trains, it has had to deal with a large variety of regulations in application in neighbouring countries. It is therefore not surprising that in 1875 the Federal Council – Switzerland's government – took the initiative to invite the governments and railway administrations (public and private) of the European States to an international conference in Bern in 1878. The first conference was followed by two others in 1881 and 1886 also held in Bern. The fourth conference in October 1890 ratified the Convention Relating to the International Carriage of Goods by Rail (*Convention internationale concernant le transport des marchandises par chemin de fer*, CIM), which imposed a genuine supranational law in the area of freight transport. Nine founding member states were signatories to the convention that entered into force in 1893. Additionally, a Central Office for International Carriage by Rail (*Office central des transports internationaux par chemins de fer*, OCTI) was also established in Bern, in charge of handling proposals to amend earlier conventions and convene revision conferences. The OCTI also acted as an arbitration court to solve disputes between railway companies and disseminated all information on decisions of the enforcement of these conventions. The OCTI was superseded in 1985 by the Intergovernmental Organisation for International Carriage by Rail originally named *L'Organisation intergouvernementale pour les transports internationaux ferroviaires* (OTIF) which remains to this day a key player in the development and adaptation of international rail transport law.

In parallel to these international agreements on legal aspects, several European conferences were signed with the objective of facilitating cross-border railway operations in commercial and operational terms. From 1872, the European Passenger Train Timetable Conference (*Conférence Européenne des horaires des trains de voyageurs*, CEH) defined the times of passenger trains as well as the composition of international trains and connections with domestic services. Railway experts met each year with a view to ensuring speedy, punctual, safe and comfortable passenger services. The CEH was followed by a European Conference on Direct Services which, by establishing seamless country-to-country links, enabled passengers to cross borders without having to change carriage. However, it was not before 1919 that a similar conference, the European Freight Timetable Conference (*Conférence Européenne des horaires des trains de marchandises*, CEM), addressed the freight train timetables and ensured an equivalent degree of international coordination.

A first important milestone in the unification of the European railway system in the technical and operational areas is the 'Technical Unity'. Again, an important initiative in the international railway field was taken by the Swiss Government. In August 1882, following the inauguration of the Saint–Gotthard Railway which perfectly illustrated the railway's international calling, the Swiss Federal Council

---

(without place of publication 1936).

invited the governments from neighbouring states to an international conference of experts on the Technical Unity of Railways. In October 1882, the state representatives signed a protocol ensuring that the rolling stock in compliance with the established standards could circulate on the networks of the member states. The first conference was followed by two others in 1886 and 1907 to address a range of technical issues as track gauge, loading gauges, methods for closing wagons, rolling stock standards such as buffers and couplings, facilitation of the access of customs officers to freight wagons, etc. The Technical Unity constitutes the basis for the standardisation of railways in Europe and its standards – for example track gauge, clearance, loading gauges for vehicles operated in international traffic – also apply today to a large number of railways across the world. These railway standards have been often complemented in more recent periods by *Union internationale des chemins de fer* (UIC) prescriptions or standards ('UIC Leaflets'). Only three European railway networks were set apart from the others due to their different 'broad' gauge tracks – those of Spain, Portugal and Russia.

Specific agreements also had to be signed at European level to address an important issue of cross-border railway operations: the exchange of freight wagons or coaches at the borders. In 1876, an international union for the exchange of rolling stock was established in Brussels. Members included railways from Germany, Austria-Hungary, Belgium, France, the Netherlands and Switzerland who were thus able to supply one another with valuable rolling stock. The Union was responsible mainly for the repatriation of empty freight cars, the carriage of vehicle parts to repair, the repair of damage, the payment of insurance claims, etc. The system, however, remained complicated and so under the impetus of Italian railways, the International Wagon Regulations (*Regolamento Internazionale Veicoli*, RIV) and International Coach Regulations (*Regolamento Internazionale delle Carrozze*, RIC) were agreed in Stresa in 1921, operating on a principle of mutual use, payment of utilisation fees, etc. One problem, however, due to the large number of freight wagons running empty, could not be solved until more recently. The RIV and RIC agreements were finally integrated into UIC. The RIV and RIC then had to be considered in the light of the new European legislation applicable to rail transport and the latest developments on this matter of cross-border wagon exchange was the creation in 2006 by UIC with European Rail Freight Association (ERFA) and Union internationale des wagons privés (UIP) of the General Contract for the Use of Wagons (GCU).

Thus, on the eve of the First World War, a wide range of conventions, agreements, regulations, unions, conferences, was in charge of harmonising or unifying various aspects of the European railway system, with focuses on rail transport law, operation rules, cross-border regulations and technical standards.

Figure 15.1   The current headquarters of the International Union of Railways
               (UIC) in Paris was inaugurated in 1963
Source: UIC.

Foundation of UIC, a Key Player for Railway Integration

The beginnings of the International Union of Railways (UIC) go back to the period immediately following the First World War. As the Paris Peace Conference took place in early 1919 to prepare the forthcoming Treaty of Versailles, the Allied powers entrusted a Commission of the International Regime of Ports, Waterways and Railways with the task of preparing a set of rules in the area of international transport. An inventory had to be taken of the rolling stock in Central Europe, notably in the now dismantled Austro-Hungarian empire, and this rolling stock redistributed. Article 366 of the Treaty of Versailles made provision for the Bern Convention to be revised, with the aim of facilitating the operation of German wagons on the railway lines of Allied powers, and conversely those of the Allied powers on German networks. Similar clauses were written in the treaties of Saint-Germain, Trianon and Neuilly, signed by Austria, Hungary and Bulgaria respectively.

The Council of the League of Nations (LON) officially formed in 1919 and established in Geneva in 1920, tasked a temporary committee for communication and transit 'to prepare project plans for general international conventions on transit, waterways and if possible railways'.[2] The documents prepared by this temporary committee of the LON, including the international regime of railways, were studied by the General Conference on Communications and Transit held in 1921 in Barcelona. Following discussions, it was agreed that it was better in the case of the railways to adopt general principles in the form of recommendations than to strictly bind member states to conventions.

In this context, the International Conference of Portorose in Italy (now Portorož in Slovenia) held in 1921 on the shores of the Adriatic sea, declared itself in favour of an 'association' of railways. The railways, which had been established under the Austro-Hungarian empire, fell under various national jurisdictions, but technical cooperation remained as vital as ever. Thus, delegates from the seven successor states of the Dual Monarchy (Austria, Hungary, Italy, Yugoslavia, Czechoslovakia, Serbia-Croatia-Slovenia and Romania, each of which inherited a portion of the former empire's territory and thereby its railways), as well as representatives from the United Kingdom and France, met in October–November 1921. Their task, pending a general European convention, was to establish rules to facilitate the international carriage of passengers, luggage and goods between the new networks.

The Romanian delegation played a particularly important role during the conference and it is worth mentioning engineer Alexandru Perieteanu, Director General of Romanian Railways (*Căile Ferate Române*, CFR), who supported the idea of forming an association of European railways and proposed that all the principles for standardising railway operations be ratified at a larger-scale conference planned shortly after in Genoa, so as to bind – pending a European convention – more than merely the administrations present in Portorose. The Romanian delegates also asked their French counterparts to prepare a substantial corpus of technical and legal documentation, and to make plans for a European railway conference in Paris.

The international conference in Genoa (April–May 1922) proposed that the standardisation of European railways be accelerated by conferring the continued management of this issue, previously given to diplomats, on the network operators. And it was France which found itself entrusted with the task of preparing an international conference, with the aim of founding a permanent railway institution endowed with broad competences. The Paris Conference was held in October 1922 with the participation of 27 States and 46 networks as well as two representatives from the League of Nations. With the exception of Finland, all European countries were represented bar USSR, whose pronouncement came in December 1922. Also present were the delegations of China and Japan, which boded well for the nascent organisation's potential influence. On opening the meeting, the German Secretary of State for Communications Karl von Stieler stressed the spirit of the conference in the following terms:

---

[2] Quoted from André Lewin and Paul Véron, *UIC: The Worldwide Association of Railways. Challlenges Past, Present Future* (Paris 2010), 24.

Our work is to renew the ties between European administrations that were severed by the war (...) our administration is resolved to create by any means necessary an association of all European railway administrations.[3]

The French proposals for the foundation of the International Union of Railways (UIC) with a permanent General Secretariat based in Paris were adopted. UIC did not work according to the principle of unanimity which governed the two railway treaties (the Bern Convention and the Technical Unity of Railways) but any decision had to be passed with a four-fifths majority and not give rise to subsequent opposition of 10 per cent or more of the total number of UIC votes. For the decisions obligatory in nature, members were required to obtain governmental approval. UIC was therefore politically and technically autonomous, whilst remaining bound to the laws and treaties. The statutes were adopted by 51 administrations from 29 countries in Europe and Asia. At the first formal meeting, one of the first decisions was the provisional admission of the Union of Soviet Socialist Republics (USSR). In autumn 1923 Chinese Railways requested to replace the word 'European' by 'international' in the UIC statutes.[4] The main mission in the UIC statutes is the:

l'unification et l'amélioration des conditions d'établissement et d'exploitation des Chemins de fer, en vue du traffic international (unification and improvement of conditions for establishment and operations of railways in view of international traffic).[5]

The technical harmonisation work within UIC was coordinated by five permanent committees: Passenger, Freight, Accounts and Exchange, Rolling Stock Exchange and Technical Issues. The work carried out in the five permanent committees resulted in the publication of UIC Leaflets, technical documents whose application was either obligatory or optional. These technical leaflets constituted the beginning of an international railway 'code', also known in practice as the UIC Code (103 leaflets in 1932, 197 in 1938). Today there are close to 700 leaflets covering all the main areas of railway activity (Statutes and Regulations, Passenger and Baggage Traffic, Freight Traffic, Finance-Accounts-Costs-Statistics, Operating, Rolling Stock, Traction, Way and Works, Technical Specifications, Information Technology). The UIC Leaflets constitute a universal technical benchmark. They were developed in close cooperation between technical experts from the member railways.

---

[3] Quoted from Lewin and Véron, *UIC*, 26.

[4] See ibid., 29.

[5] Union Internationale des Chemins de Fer (ed.), Statuts de l'Union Internationale des chemins de fer (UIC), *Bulletin de l'Union Internationale des chemins de fer*, 1, no. 1, November 1924, 35–39, here 35.

UIC: A Bridge for Railways in a Divided Europe

Following the World War Two disruptions, UIC resumed its activities towards the end of 1945. At the same time, 13 Allied countries (including the United States and USSR) set up ECITO (European Central Inland Transport Organisation) to address the urgent transport needs, since the war itself had severely damaged the railways. ECITO ceased its activities in 1948. For those countries which adhered, the United States' Marshall Plan proved generous in terms of loans and aid, particularly for the railways.

As an international association UIC was rapidly forced to confront the divisions within Europe and the world, starting with the political effects of the blocs and the Cold War. The first sign was the withdrawal of the Soviet Union Railways which is named in Russian Rossiiskie Zheleznye Dorogi (RŽD) from UIC in 1947 later rejoined the organisation in 2006 at the General Assembly in Montreal) and China took the same step the following year (note that today the China Railways (CR) of the People's Republic, as well as Taiwan High Speed Rail Corporation (THRSC) and Taiwan Railways Administration (TRA) of Taiwan, China, actively participate in UIC's work). Germany rejoined UIC in 1949.

In 1949, the United Nations Organisation (Economic and Social Council, Ecosoc) granted UIC consultative status to the UN to represent the railway sector worldwide. This administrative act was of symbolic value: it was the first mandate given to UIC by the international community to represent and promote this mode of transport in all regions of the world. This recognition of UIC's worldwide role as a spokesman for the railways which this status brought enabled it to serve as an international place of cooperation, oblivious to the rifts and divisions of post-war society. In particular it helped UIC build a strong bridge between railways and railway men and women hailing from countries which every other aspect of life contributed to keep apart.

In 1953, 16 Western European governments established the European Conference of Ministers of Transport (ECMT), in charge of addressing and harmonising the policies of these states with regard to transport, starting mainly with road transport (road quotas). The ECMT, which became the International Transport Forum, is hosted at the Organisation for Economic Co-operation and Development (OECD) headquarters in Paris, with which it shares several bodies. UIC has been regularly consulted by the ECMT since its creation on issues of international rail transport. Cooperation between International Transport Forum and UIC has recently strengthened over a set of issues, in particular those of sustainable development, security, and facilitation of cross-border operations (with a focus on former East–West borders).

In 1956, under the impetus of the Soviet Union, the socialist countries created the Organisation for Cooperation between Railways in Russian named Организация Сотрудничества Железных Дорог or ОСЖД (OSJD), based in Warsaw. Most of the OSJD member railways (bar the USSR, North Vietnam, North Korea and Cuba) were also members of UIC. This was notably the case

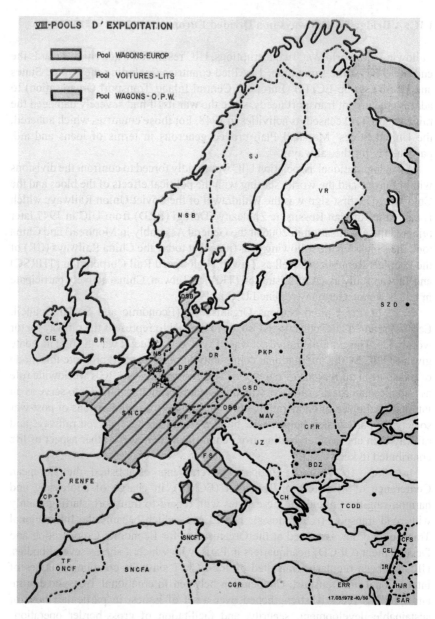

Figure 15.2   Map of wagon pools for the international management of the rolling stock fleet

Note: Several pools were constituted in Europe for the international management of the rolling stock fleet such as the Wagons-EUROP and sleeping car pools in Western Europe and the OPW-Wagons for central and Eastern Europe, including Soviet Railways.

Source: UIC.

of all OSJD's European members, which nearly all belong to the UIC founding members in 1922. During the period of the Iron Curtain, the national railways of central and Eastern European Countries (CEEC) – all OSJD members actively participated alongside the Western railways in the work of practically all the UIC Technical Committees and Sub–Committees (which had taken over from the 'Permanent Committees'). The OSJD operated – and still operates today – with two levels of cooperation: that of the transport ministers and of the presidents or directors general of national railway companies.

The desire to maintain ongoing professional dialogue and cooperation within the railway community was demonstrated by UIC Chairmen being appointed alternatively from the East and West, which was not a common rule at this time of division in Europe. UIC has thus been chaired successively by Donar Tarantowicz from Polskie Koleje Państwowe (PKP) (Polish State Railways) from 1965 to 1966, Karoly Rödönyi from Magyar Államvasutak (MÁV) (Hungarian State Railway) from 1971 to 1972, Volkmar Winkler (Deutsche Reichsbahn, DR), German Democratic Republic) from 1977 to 1978, Stanislav Houska from *Československé* státní dráhy (ČSD), (the Czechoslovak State Railways) in 1983, and Ladislav Blazek (ČSD) in 1984, Vesselin Pavlov (Balgarski darzhavni zheleznitsi (BDZ), Bulgarian State Railways) from 1989 to 1990 and finally Adam Wieldek (PKP, Poland) from 1998 to 1999.

An Un-Discontinued Cooperation between East and West

Railways of the East and West maintained and developed close cooperation in technical matters throughout the period of the 1960s to the end of the 1980s. Experts from Eastern European railway companies continuously participated in the UIC technical bodies (Committees for 'Research and Planning', 'Commercial–Passenger', 'Commercial-Freight', 'Finance', 'Movement-Operations', Traction and Rolling Stock", 'Personnel', 'Way and Works', 'Technical Specifications' and 'Information Technology').

Furthermore the technical work performed by UIC and OSJD focused on clearly identified cooperation issues and resulted in the edition of joint 'UIC-OSJD Leaflets', whose broad application extended over the vast territory of the entire Soviet Union. It is particularly worth mentioning the joint 'UIC-OSJD Technical Committees' and corresponding 'UIC-OSJD Joint Leaflets' on Automatic Couplings for Wagons, Standardised Digital Coding (standardisation of codes for IT-based railway communications), Documentation (exchange of scientific, statistical information) and more recently on Facilitation of Border-Crossings.

UIC's role in view of railway integration proved particularly useful when border-crossings between East and West opened. Being accustomed to working together and participating in the same system of technical cooperation and railway standards throughout the previous decades strongly facilitated the task of integrating the railways of the European Union and those of Central and Eastern

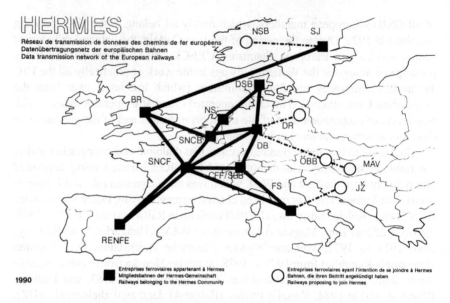

Figure 15.3   The HERMES data transmission network, 1990

Note: The HERMES data transmission network designed by UIC for the European railways in the 70s and 80s already planned extensions to the Deutsche Reichsbahn as well as Hungarian and Yugoslav Railways.

Source: UIC.

Europe (known at the time as CEEC) that began in the late 1980s and early 1990s. From the moment the borders began to open, UIC examined the impact of this new geopolitical and economic environment on the pan–European rail sector through a specially created body, the UIC East–West Task Force (it rapidly published a White Paper on the perspectives that the new political situation opened for the European rail sector). UIC immediately initiated closer cooperation with railways of all countries concerned (and with the Community of European Railways (CER), representing the railways of the European Union) in order to accelerate railway harmonisation at European level. The UIC East–West Task Force focused on the harmonisation of legislative, regulatory, technical and administrative measures between East and West.

UIC was notably associated with the CER in the pan–European conferences of Crete (1994) and Helsinki (1997) organised by the European Parliament and the Commission for the definition of pan–European transport corridors. The purpose of these conferences was to define transport routes in central and Eastern European countries that required major investments over the next 10 to 15 years to achieve a real integration of the continent. These 'Crete corridors' (ten rail transport corridors) were promoted by the European institutions and railway organisations, primarily UIC

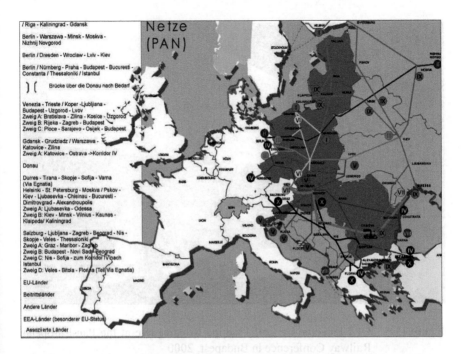

Figure 15.4   Map of the pan-European transport corridors, 1994

Note: Map of the Pan-European transport corridors defined at the 2nd Pan-European transport conference in Crete (1994) as routes in Central and Eastern Europe that required major investments over the next 10 to 15 years. Additions were made at the 3rd Pan-European conference in Helsinki in 1997. These 'Crete corridors' were actively promoted by the European institutions. Railway organisations – UIC together with CER – played an active role to promote and support these projects with professional expertise.

Source: UIC.

and CER. UIC published in this context a document entitled 'The Corridors Pan-European Rail Network – View point of the UIC East–West Task Force', in 1999.[6]

With the accession of practically all the central and Eastern European countries to the European Union, the railways of these parts of Europe gradually became fully integrated into the process of European transport and railway policy (within the CER framework) and UIC cooperation bodies. During the period 1990–2000 CEEC railways integrated the *Acquis Communautaire* relating to railway policy, meaning they began to adopt legislation and organisational structure as requested by the European directives (separation infrastructure/operations, separate accounts for infrastructure/operations, opening-up of networks to new entrants,

---

6   Union Internationale des Chemins de Fer (ed.), *The Corridors Pan-European Rail Network – View point of the UIC East-West Task Force* (Paris 1999).

Figure 15.5   UIC Director General Philippe Roumeguère at the Pan-European
Railway Conference in Budapest, 2000

Note: UIC Director General Philippe Roumeguère at the Pan-European Railway Conference
held in February 2000 in Budapest, at the invitation of Hungarian State Railways (MAV)
and with high-level representatives of the European institutions, European Commission
and Parliament.

Source: UIC.

liberalisation, etc.). Since the fifth wave of entries to the EU in January 2007,
all European (EU) railways have been fully integrated into the unification and
harmonisation process under the umbrella of the European institutions.

Today's European railway integration, carried out at four different levels, can
be summarised as follows:

- Political decision-making process: strong presence of CEEC countries
  in EU institutions as European Commission and Parliament, European
  Railway Agency (ERA).
- Professional representation towards political and economic institutions (in
  CER, European Rail Infrastructure Managers (EIM), etc.).
- Professional/technical cooperation mainly at UIC (with focuses on
  interoperability, development of a seamless, non-discriminatory, rail
  transport system.
- Business level, with a trend towards European alliances, joint ventures,
  private–public partnerships and new forms of joint business.

CIM vs SMGS

One of today's important challenges is the harmonisation of international transport law. In the area of international conventions governing the carriage of goods and passengers (CIM and CIV), UIC cooperated with OCTI, the international intergovernmental organisation established in 1893 in Bern, and superseded in 1985 by the International Organisation for International Carriage by Rail (OTIF). The latter managed the Convention on the International Carriage by Rail (COTIF), amended in 1999 by the Vilnius Protocol (with appendices applicable to the transport of hazardous goods and express parcels. One of OTIF's most important tasks today is reconciling CIM law on the carriage of goods (applicable in Western Europe and a substantial area of Central and Eastern Europe) and the so-called *Soglashenije o Meshdunarodnom Shelesnodoroshnom Grusowom Soobstschenii* (SMGS), a Russian acronym which stands for a legal system that was created under the impetus of the USSR to govern international freight transport in its sphere of influence – mainly OSJD railways – with *Soglashenije o Meshdunarodnom Passagierskom Soobstschenii* (SMPS) being the equivalent for the carriage of passengers.

An important outcome to note is that in September 2010 the Russian Ministry of Transport authorised the use of the CIM/SMGS joint consignment note over the Russian Federation's whole rail network (some 85,000 route kilometres and 5,000 stations). Shortly afterwards, Mongolian Railways took the same step, meaning that freight traffic by rail will now be able to move from the Atlantic to the Pacific under a single consignment note (transport document). Work has already started with the aim of facilitating freight movements between Europe and Asia.

Still with regard to legal integration, UIC is a member of the Executive Committee of *Comité international des transports ferroviaires* (CIT) (International Rail Transport Committee), an association of 200 railway undertakings from the West and from the CEEC, and shipping companies providing international freight transport and passenger services. CIT represents operators in international discussions on transport law, in particular work relating to international conventions.

Thus, after two decades devoted to abolishing political, administrative and technical borders inherited from the war period and the resulting East–West division, and following the full integration of CEEC countries into the policies of the European Union, the reunified European railway community is now facing a range of new challenges: increasing attractiveness and competitiveness to better cope with the competition of other modes, gaining a global dimension particularly in long-distance freight transport and logistics, making rail in Europe and around the world the most sustainable and preferred mode of transport.

Bibliography

Amsberg, A. v., 'Denkschrift an den Verein Deutscher Eisenbahnverwaltungen über Herbeischaffung von Material zum Entwurf eines Eisenbahnnetzes', *Eisenbahn Zeitung*, 1849, 201.

Ballet, Paul, Fontgalland, Bernard (de), 'Cinquante années de l'Union internationale des chemins de fer', *Revue Générale des Chemins de fer*, 91, issue 5 (May), 1972, 'Special issue: 1922 – U.I.C. – 1972', 335–40.

Göbertshahn, Rudolf, 'Eingliederung der Verbände RIC und RIV in die UIC', *Die Bundesbahn*, 57, 1981, S. 889–94.

Lewin, André and Véron, Paul, *UIC, the worldwide Association of Railways – Challenges Past, Present and Future* (Paris 2010).

Raczkiewicz, Marek and Boutté, Claude, 'La Mission Est/Ouest de l'UIC', 'The UIC East / West Task Force', 'Die Ost / West Task Force der UIC' (trilingual edition published for the UIC's 75th anniversary), *Revue Générale des Chemins de fer*, 116, nr. 9, September 1997, 39–43.

Ribeill, Georges, 'Vers une Europe ferroviaire sans frontières techniques. Histoire de l'interopérabilité des chemins de fer européens ou Les heurs et malheurs d'un enjeu majeur', *Chemins de fer*, 2011, 35–40.

Rödönyi, K., 'Le rôle de l'UIC dans la coopération internationale des chemins de fer', *Revue Générale des Chemins de fer*, 91, issue 5 (May), 1972, 'Special issue: 1922 – U.I.C. – 1972', 327–30.

Union Internationale des Chemins de Fer (ed.), *Assemblée Générale du 8 décembre 2009*. Communiqué de presse nr. 21, Paris 2009.

Union Internationale des Chemins de Fer (ed.), *The Corridors Pan-European Rail Network – View Point of the UIC East–West Task Force* (Paris 1999).

Union Internationale des Chemins de Fer (ed.), Statuts de l'Union Internationale des chemins de fer (U.I.C.), Bulletin de l'Union Internationale des chemins de fer, 1, no. 1, November 1924, 35–9.

Verein Mitteleuropäischer Eisenbahnverwaltungen (ed.), *Die Entwicklung der Lokomotive im Gebiet des Vereins Deutscher Eisenbahn Verwaltungen*, 2 vols and 2 vols including illustrations (Munich and Berlin 1930 and 1937).

Verein Mitteleuropäischer Eisenbahnverwaltungen (ed.), *Vereins-Handbuch. Herausgegeben anläßlich des 90jährigen Bestehens des Vereins im November 1936* (Munich and Berlin 1936).

Véron, Paul, 'De nouvelles responsabilités pour l'UIC en Europe et dans le monde / New responsibilities for the UIC in Europe and throughout the world / Die UIC stellt sich Europa- und weltweit neuen Verantwortungen', *La Revue Générale des Chemins de fer*, 116, issue 9, 1997, 7–20.

Chapter 16

Back to the Future? Russia's Railway Transport and the Collapse of the Soviet Union in Historical Perspective

Anthony Heywood[1]

When Mikhail Gorbachev became General Secretary of the Communist Party of the Soviet Union in 1985 the long-term future of the common-carrier Soviet railways (Sovetskie Zheleznye Dorogi – SZD) was seemingly secure.[2] The network was both vast and still growing: extending over nine time zones from the Baltic Sea in the west to the Pacific Ocean in the east and from the White Sea in the north to the Caspian Sea and central Asian deserts in the south, the route length totalled some 144,900 kilometres in 1985 – just over 10 per cent of the world's total length – and was planned to reach 147,200 kilometres in 1990 (Figure 16.1).[3]

Only the US system was longer at over 220,000 route kilometres, and no other system came close in size. Nor, despite Gorbachev's concern about 'stagnation' in the Soviet economy, was there any sign of the retrenchment that became common for railways in the West by the 1960s due to growing competition from other modes of transport. By the late 1980s the SZD was carrying just over half of the world's rail freight traffic.[4] Key features of the Soviet Union's transport geography favoured the railways, notably the country's enormous size (and relative lack of paved roads), the concentration of the population in western districts, and the concentration of the natural mineral resources in often remote areas of the north and east. Moreover, the Soviet government's long-standing transport strategy was

---

[1] For assistance with the preparation of this chapter I am very grateful to Robert Argenbright, Eileen Consey, Brandon Schneider and John Westwood. The maps are reproduced by courtesy of Russian Railways.

[2] The term common-carrier refers here to a railway system that is obliged by law to accept all the traffic that is offered for conveyance. In addition to its common-carrier system the Soviet Union had about 62,000 route kilometres of non-common-carrier feeder railways by 1991, usually operated by and for a specific industrial enterprise or group of enterprises.

[3] D.K. Zotov and S.S. Ushakov, *Problemy razvitiia transporta SSSR* (Moscow 1990), 13.

[4] P. Lydolph, *Geography of the USSR* (Elkhart Lake 1990), 373. I am grateful to Bob Argenbright for this point.

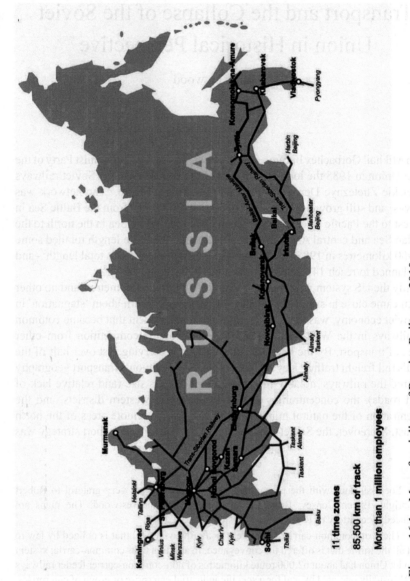

Figure 16.1   Map of mainlines of Russian Railways, 2010

Source: Russian Railways.

to maintain a unified and coordinated multi-modal system in state ownership.[5] Hence the volume of railway traffic had been growing almost continuously since the mid nineteenth century, and this pattern was projected to continue, with the railways expected to retain their dominant share of the Soviet non-pipeline freight and medium-distance passenger traffic. The key challenge for the railways was thus to find ever more capacity through raising technical and organisational efficiency, improving coordination with other forms of transport, and building more lines.

Table 16.1   Railways opened by year, 1838, 1845–1917 (route kilometres, excluding the Grand Duchy of Finland)

Year	Route opened	Cumulative total opened	Year	Route opened	Cumulative total opened
1838	26.50	26.50	1882	331.01	23,120.53
1845	116.39	142.89	1883	667.05	23,787.58
1846	133.12	276.01	1884	855.71	24,643.29
1847	87.75	363.76	1885	1,033.10	25,676.39
1848	13.66	377.42	1886	1,311.87	26,988.26
1849	0.00	377.42	1887	896.17	27,884.43
1850	117.99	495.41	1888	1,174.62	29,059.05
1851	497.89	993.30	1889	496.77	29,555.82
1852	0.00	993.30	1890	658.81	30,214.63
1853	44.34	1,037.64	1891	124.56	30,339.19
1854–56	0.00	1,037.64	1892	471.97	30,811.16
1857	120.01	1,157.65	1893	1,726.15	32,537.31
1858	0.00	1,157.65	1894	2,331.57	34,868.88
1859	165.12	1,322.77	1895	1,892.30	36,761.18
1860	254.40	1,577.17	1896	2,471.88	39,233.06
1861	599.39	2,176.56	1897	2,002.71	41,235.77

continued

---

[5]   For an introduction to this strategy as it was taught to students of transport economics in the mid 1980s see B.I. Shafirkin, *Edinaia transportnaia sistema SSSR i vzaimodeistvie razlichnykh vidov transporta*, 3rd edn (Moscow 1983).

Table 16.1   *concluded*

Year	Route opened	Cumulative total opened	Year	Route opened	Cumulative total opened
1862	1,271.12	3,447.68	1898	2,984.79	44,220.56
1863	0.00	3,447.68	1899	5,262.81	49,483.37
1864	94.08	3,541.76	1900	3,309.32	52,792.69
1865	224.91	3,766.67	1901	3,166.38	55,959.07
1866	712.42	4,479.09	1902	1,127.58	57,086.65
1867	463.26	4,942.35	1903	764.86	57,851.51
1868	1,743.97	6,686.32	1904	1,284.15	59,135.66
1869	1,379.40	8,065.72	1905	1,465.10	60,600.76
1870	2,504.72	10,570.44	1906	2,494.82	63,095.58
1871	2,838.27	13,408.71	1907	1,757.6	64,853.18
1872	680.77	14,089.48	1908	353.76	65,206.94
1873	1,839.60	15,929.08	1909	420.21	65,627.15
1874	1,970.15	17,899.23	1910	176.86	65,804.01
1875	802.80	18,702.03	1911	486.68	66,290.69
1876	598.00	19,300.03	1912	691.15	66,981.84
1877	1,504.39	20,804.42	1913	1,428.33	68,410.17
1878	1,252.28	22,056.70	1914	1,676.07	70,086.24
1879	305.87	22,362.57	1915	3,323.00	73,409.24
1880	197.32	22,559.89	1916	5,074.00	78,483.24
1881	229.63	22,789.52	1917	776.00	79,259.24

Note: Excludes (a) the railways of the Grand Duchy of Finland, opened 1862–1910, total 3,239.31 kilometres; (b) Chinese Eastern Railway in Manchuria. Versts are converted to kilometres at 1.06. The size of the active network at any given time may differ from cumulative total due to closures, war, etc.

Sources: Calculated and tabulated from G. M. Afonina (ed.), *Kratkie svedeniia o razvitii otechestvennykh zheleznykh dorog s 1838 po 1990 g.* (Moscow 1996), 7–93, and the revised edition *Kratkie svedeniia o razvitii otechestvennykh zheleznykh dorog s 1838 po 2000 g.* (Moscow 2002), 41–2.

Table 16.2   Railways opened by year, 1918–1991 (route kilometres, Soviet territory)

Year	Route opened	Cumulative total opened	Year	Route opened	Cumulative total opened
1918	894.0	894.0	1955	247.0	29,348.0
1919	102.0	996.0	1956	437.0	29,785.0
1920	354.0	1,350.0	1957	118.0	29,903.0
1921	197.0	1,547.0	1958	1,084.0	30,987.0
1922	113.0	1,660.0	1959	792.0	31,779.0
1923	174.0	1,834.0	1960	981.0	32,760.0
1924	1,463.0	3,297.0	1961	875.0	33,635.0
1925	459.0	3,756.0	1962	738.0	34,373.0
1926	1,190.0	4,946.0	1963	224.0	34,597.0
1927	1,026.0	5,972.0	1964	392.0	34,989.0
1928	403.0	6,375.0	1965	1,205.0	36,194.0
1929	316.0	6,691.0	1966	1,063.0	37,257.0
1930	942.0	7,633.0	1967	594.0	37,851.0
1931	2,542.0	10,175.0	1968	222.0	38,073.0
1932	853.0	11,028.0	1969	573.5	38,646.5
1933	486.0	11,514.0	1970	623.3	39,269.8
1934	597.0	12,111.0	1971	412.1	39,681.9
1935	299.0	12,410.0	1972	1,164.8	40,846.7
1936	799.0	13,209.0	1973	392.0	41,238.7
1937	76.0	13,285.0	1974	456.3	41,695.0
1938	0.0	13,285.0	1975	792.8	42,487.8
1939	1,288.0	14,573.0	1976	243.3	42,731.1
1940	2,524.0	17,097.0	1977	970.3	43,701.4
1941	1,758.0	18,855.0	1978	634.0	44,335.4
1942	2,726.0	21,581.0	1979	654.6	44,990.0

continued

Table 16.2   *concluded*

Year	Route opened	Cumulative total opened	Year	Route opened	Cumulative total opened
1943	1,170.0	22,751.0	1980	615.2	45,605.2
1944	1,765.0	24,516.0	1981	1,074.2	46,679.4
1945	263.0	24,779.0	1982	395.8	47,075.2
1946	137.0	24,916.0	1983	259.4	47,334.6
1947	793.0	25,709.0	1984	497.4	47,832.0
1948	0.0	25,709.0	1985	1,076.7	48,908.7
1949	122.0	25,831.0	1986	538.8	49,447.5
1950	538.0	26,369.0	1987	611.9	50,059.4
1951	633.0	27,002.0	1988	475.4	50,534.8
1952	604.0	27,606.0	1989	755.8	51,290.6
1953	1,386.0	28,992.0	1990	124.6	51,415.2
1954	109.0	29,101.0	1991	10.6	51,425.8

Note: It is unclear whether any railways were opened by anti-Bolshevik forces in the Civil War, but one presumes that this was very unlikely. There may be errors concerning the figures for sections of the Baikal-Amur railway in the 1980s. The size of the active network at any given time may differ from cumulative total due to war, territorial changes, closures, etc.

Sources: Calculated and tabulated from Afonina, *Kratkie svedeniia* (1996), 96–215, and Afonina, *Kratkie svedeniia* (2002), 215–17.

A mere six years later much of this picture was changing rapidly. Traffic on the SZD began to decline at the end of the 1980s as the Soviet economy lurched into crisis. Similarly, capital investment began to collapse, with, for instance, only 10.6 kilometres of new route being opened in 1991. Then came the implosion of the Soviet Union in December 1991, the replacement of its 15 constituent union republics by 15 separate sovereign states, and the corresponding partition of the SZD into 15 national railway systems, one for each of the former union republics. Inevitably the largest of these new states, the Russian Federation (Rossiiskaia Federatsiia – RF), founds itself in possession of the largest share of the Soviet railway network, which consisted of about 87,000 route kilometres or about 60 per cent of the old SZD. And this new national network, which became known as Russian Railways (Rossiiskie Zheleznye Dorogi – RZD), seemed to face some major uncertainties as of 1992. Under the leadership of President Boris Yeltsin the new Russian state was advocating radical economic reform that involved, in particular, the abandonment of the Soviet-era centrally planned economy in favour of a market-based mixed economy. In this difficult new environment would the concept of the unified transport system survive, or would inter-modal competition become the new norm? Would the volumes of railway freight and passenger traffic continue to decline, or would they resume growth? Would the railways retain their shares of freight and passenger traffic? Would the network continue to expand or would it shrink? Would the railways remain in state ownership or would they be privatised? And what would be the function of the railways ministry, the somewhat confusingly named Ministry of Ways of Communication (*Ministerstvo Putei Soobshcheniia* – MPS), which dated from 1865 and had functioned since Tsarist times as both network regulator and owner-operator of the common-carrier state railways.

An insightful book-length analysis of the impact of the transition on the RZD in the 1990s has been provided by John Westwood.[6] The rather different purpose of the present short chapter is to situate this upheaval in its long-term historical context. For want of more space this discussion concentrates on just three traditional core concerns: operating performance in terms of the volumes of freight and passenger traffic; network development and investment, primarily in terms of route length; and ownership. The analysis covers both the Tsarist imperial era to 1917 and the entire Soviet era from 1917 to 1991, and although it concentrates on highlighting long-term patterns it also briefly considers how far the post-Soviet transition can be compared with the two tremendous collapses in traffic turnover that afflicted the railways during the Russian Civil War from 1917 to 1922 and the Second World War from 1941 to 1945.[7] Where appropriate an effort is made to highlight incomplete data and discrepancies between the available sources (see Table 16.3 below).

Traffic

Traffic on the Imperial Russian and Soviet common-carrier railway networks grew virtually continuously from the Crimean War to 1989. The growth was perhaps most spectacular in the nineteenth century during the development of the core network. Freight was always more important than passenger traffic for revenue, so it is telling that the freight turnover quadrupled between 1865 and 1880, more

---

[6]   J.N. Westwood, *From Soviet Railways to Russian Railways* (Basingstoke 2002).

[7]   The main histories are: J.N. Westwood, *A History of Russian Railways* (London 1964); E.Ia. Kraskovskii and M.M. Uzdin (eds), *Istoriia zheleznodorozhnogo transporta Rossii, tom 1: 1836–1917* (St Petersburg 1994); V.E. Pavlov and M.M. Uzdin (eds), *Istoriia zheleznodorozhnogo transporta Rossii i Sovetskogo Soiuza, vol. 2: 1917–1945* (St Petersburg 1997). For detailed discussions of the two crises see R.T. Argenbright, 'The Russian Railroad system and the founding of the Communist state, 1917–1922', University of California at Berkeley PhD thesis, 1990, and G.A. Kumanev, *Voina i zheleznodorozhnyi transport SSSR, 1941–1945* (Moscow 1988).

Table 16.3   Railway traffic in the Russian empire, Soviet Union and Russian Soviet Federal Socialist Republic (RSFSR), 1900–1991

	Freight in billion tonne-kilometres	**Passenger in billion passenger-kilometres**
1900	37	12
1913	76	230
1917	63	22
1920	11	–
1924	36	16
1928	93	25
1932	169	84
1940	421	100
1945	314	66
1950	602	88
1960	1,504	176
1970	2,495	274
1980	3,440	342
1988	3,925	414
1990	3,717	417
1991 Soviet Union	3,365	383
1991 RSFSR	2,326	255

Note: – indicates data not available here and in tables below.

Source: G.M. Afonina et al., *Zheleznodorozhnyi transport: XX vek* (Moscow 2001), 9.

than doubled in the next decade, and then almost doubled again by 1900.[8] During the twentieth century the pattern of continual growth persisted despite the rise of motorised road transport and aviation, and in contrast to the decline that was caused in the West by competition from these rival technologies (see Table 16.3).

---

8   Westwood, *History of Russian Railways*, 78.

However, there were two exceptional periods of dramatic collapse in railway traffic: the main years of the Civil War (1917–20) and the first two or three years following the Nazi invasion of June 1941. The first of these crises began with the two 1917 revolutions and reached its nadir in 1920; the recovery that began in 1921 required about five years to attain the traffic levels of 1913, the last full peacetime year. The statistics for 1917–20 are highly unreliable due to the civil conflict and shifting international boundaries, with little if any information incorporated in the available figures for districts of the former empire that were not under Bolshevik control. Nonetheless it seems likely that, overall, the total freight traffic in the former empire in 1920 was at best roughly about one-quarter of the 1913 level, and formed an even smaller proportion of the Tsarist era peak in 1916 – a catastrophic collapse. As for the second crisis, the overall freight turnover fell during 1941–43 by about 50 per cent from the level in 1940, but at least this huge loss was proportionately not as bad as that in 1917–20, and the recovery to the pre-war level was achieved more quickly in just three years. Thereafter steady growth was the norm until 1989.[9]

Table 16.4   Railway traffic in the Russian Soviet Federal Socialist Republic and the Russian Federation, 1989–1993

	RSFSR 1989	RSFSR 1990	RSFSR 1991	RF 1992	RF 1993
Freight billion tonne-kilometres	2,626.7	2,539.1	2,325.9	1,961.9	1,850.4
percentage of 1989 level	100.0	96.7	88.5	74.7	70.4
Passenger billion passenger-kilometres	277.2	280.4	254.7	238.7	231.2
percentage of 1989 level	100.0	101.2	91.9	86.1	83.4

Source: V.I. Volkov et al. (eds), Doroga v rynok: Zheleznodorozhnyi transport v usloviiakh formirovaniia rynochnykh otnoshenii (Moscow 1994), 49.

---

[9]   For greater detail concerning 1913–1945 and careful caveats about the statistical data see J.N. Westwood et al., 'Transport', in R.W. Davies et al. (eds), *The Economic Transformation of the Soviet Union, 1913–1945* (Cambridge 1994), 161–8, and associated tables 304–306. For a comparison of traffic in the 1920s and 1990s see A.V. Poletaev and I.M. Savel'eva, 'Sravnitel'nyi analiz dvukh sistemnykh krizisov v rossiiskoi istorii (1920-e i 1990-e gg.)', *Ekonomicheskaia istoriia: ezhegodnik, 2000*, 121–5.

Table 16.5   Railway traffic in the Russian Soviet Federal Socialist Republic and the Russian Federation, 1990–2008

Year	Freight billion tonne-kilometres	% of 1990 level	Passenger billion pass.-kilometres	% of 1990 level
1990	2,523.0	100.0	274.4	100.0
1991	2,326.0	92.2	–	–
1992	1,967.0	78.0	–	–
1993	1,608.0	63.7	–	–
1994	1,196.0	47.4	–	–
1995	1,214.0	48.1	192.4	70.1
1996	1,125.0	44.6	181.2	66.0
1997	1,096.0	43.4	170.3	62.1
1998	1,006.0	39.9	152.5	55.6
1999	1,205.0	47.8	141.0	51.4
2000	1,373.0	54.4	167.1	60.9
2005	1,858.0	73.6	172.2	62.8
2006	1,951.0	77.3	177.6	64.4
2007	2,090.0	82.8	174.1	63.4
2008	2,116.0	83.9	175.9	64.1

Note: 1990 and 1991 figures are for the RSFSR. Galaburda et al. give figures that tally with the information from the Federal Statistical Service (Ul'ianov), and their freight figures for 1995–98 are higher than the figures given by Westwood, which were taken from RZD sources. The sources do not indicate whether the freight figures include empty-wagon workings, which may account for the discrepancies with the RZD annual reports. Overlaps between the sources show some slight variations.

Sources: freight 1990–2000: Westwood, *Soviet Railways*, 95 (taken from RZD sources); RSFSR freight and passenger 1990, passenger 1995–98: V.G. Galaburda et al. (eds), *Edinaia transportnaia sistema*, 2nd edn (Moscow 2001), 76; 2000–2008: I.S. Ul'ianov et al. (eds), *Transport v Rossii 2009: Statisticheskii sbornik* (Moscow 2009), 81 and 85; passenger 1999–2000: Afonina, *Zheleznodorozhnyi transport*, 9.

Table 16.6   Railway traffic in the Russian Federation, 2004–2009, as recorded in RZD Annual Reports

	2004	2005	2006	2007	2008	2009
Freight billion tonne-kilometres	1,797.3	1,852.9	1,944.9	2,312.6	2,423.8	2,271.4
% of 1990 level:	71.2	73.4	77.1	91.7	96.1	90.0
Suburban pass. in billion pass.-kilometres	36.3	52.0	52.8	–	46.7	38.2
Long-distance passenger in billion pass. kilometres	114.5	118.9	125.0	–	129.2	115.4
Total passenger in billion pass.-kilometres	150.8	170.9	177.8	174.1	175.9	153.6
% of 1990 level	55.0	62.3	64.8	63.4	64.1	56.0

Note: Freight figures include empty-wagon workings. Percentages calculated by the present author using 2,523 billion freight tonne-kilometres and 274.4 billion passenger-kilometres in 1990.

Sources: RZD annual reports 2005, 33; 2006, 42 and 48; 2007, 43; 2008, 34; 2009, 48, 85 and 95–6.

The economic crisis of the late 1980s and 1990s affected Russian railway traffic so badly that by 2010 neither the freight nor the passenger turnover had regained the levels of 1990. Tables 16.4, 16.5 and 16.6 collate traffic data from several different sources for the RF and its Soviet-era predecessor, the Russian Soviet Federal Socialist Republic (Rossiiskaia Sovetskaia Federativnaia Sotsialisticheskaia Respublika – RSFSR). They reveal a clear pattern despite some variations between the sources. A precipitous decline began in 1990–91 that lasted until about 1995, after which the decline continued more slowly to its trough in 1998, when the volumes of freight and passenger traffic were just 39.9 per cent (freight) and 55.6 per cent (passenger) of their 1990 levels. From that point the freight volume recovered steadily if gradually over the next 10 years, and was nearing its 1990 level by 2008 when that year's global financial crisis began to cause some slippage. Passenger traffic initially declined more slowly than freight, and did not fall nearly so far, but its recovery was weak and hesitant, and was shattered by the global financial crisis, the 2009 passenger turnover being only fractionally higher than the result for 1998. The crisis of the 1990s, then, involved a collapse of turnover that proportionately was worse than the Second World War experience but was not nearly as bad as the crisis during the Civil War. However, the subsequent recovery was far slower and much less steady than in the 1920s and 1940s, and it was clearly vulnerable to the vicissitudes of global economic and financial trends – a threat that did not apply to the relatively isolated Soviet economy in the times of Lenin and Stalin.

This turn of events might lead one to expect a significant number of line closures during the 1990s and beyond. In fact, the available information suggests that although some route losses have occurred, their scale has been relatively limited.[10] The RZD Annual Report for 2006 indicates that 2,500 route kilometres were closed between 1991 and 2005. Reports for the next three years suggest that only marginal changes occurred subsequently: the operating network is recorded as 85,216 route kilometres at 1 January 2007, then a fall to 85,155 kilometres is shown by 1 January 2008, followed by a rise to 85,194 kilometres at 1 January 2009 and 85,281 kilometres at 31 December 2009.[11] Furthermore, correlation of these figures with the statistical record of new routes opened suggests that some of the closed lines may have been reopened, having been merely mothballed. All things considered, the losses seem small in the circumstances, and are far short of the radical surgery experienced in countries like Great Britain several decades earlier. That said, one should also note that the non-common-carrier feeder lines have been much more troubled. Their freight turnover did rise from 26.9 billion tonne-kilometres in 1995 to 31.7 billion tonne-kilometres in 2006, but over the same period the extent of these lines fell by as much as one-third, from 64,000 kilometres in 1995 to 42,000 kilometres in 2006.[12]

---

[10]   For the details of the formal procedure for closing lines, as amended in August 2009, see Prikaz 137 at www.roszheldor.ru/regulatory_documents/akt_mintrans (last accessed 26 August 2010).

[11]   RZD Annual Reports 2006, 36; 2007, 49–50; 2008, 64; 2009, 105. These reports can be downloaded from the RZD website; they are filed in the Investor Relations section, subsection Financial Reports: http://eng.rzd.ru/isvp/public/rzdeng? STRUCTURE_ ID=21&layer_id=3290&id=381. Slightly different, cruder figures are given by Russia's Federal State Statistical Service: they show that the RZD operational network consisted of 87,000 route km in 1995 and that this figure dropped to 85,000 kilometres by 2005 before rising to 86,000 kilometres in 2008: I.S. Ul'ianov et al. (eds), *Transport v Rossii 2009: Statisticheskii sbornik* (Moscow 2009), 70 and 77. This publication and earlier editions can be downloaded from the Statistical Service's website at www.gks.ru/ wps/portal/OSI_P/ TRANS.

[12]   *Transport v Rossii 2009*, 88.

Table 16.7   Share of Soviet and Russian freight turnover by mode of transport, 1940–2010 (percentages of total tonne-kilometres)

	Railway	Sea	Inland waterway	Road	Oil pipeline	Gas pipeline	Air
Soviet Union							
1940	85.08	4.90	7.40	1.40	0.80	n/a	0.02
1960	79.27	6.90	5.30	5.20	2.70	0.60	0.03
1988	47.80	11.40	3.60	6.40	16.90	13.80	0.05
					Oil and Gas pipeline		
RSFSR							
1990	52.80	10.60	4.55	6.10	25.90		0.05
RF							
1995	49.80	11.60	3.70	8.16	26.70		0.04
	(32.90)	(8.80)	(2.50)	(4.20)	(51.50)		(0.04)
1998	49.40	7.90	3.30	6.00	33.30		0.10
2000	37.70	3.40	2.00	4.20	52.70		0.07
2005	39.70	1.30	1.90	4.10	52.90		0.06
2008	42.80	1.70	1.30	4.40	49.80		0.10

Note: The two sets of figures for 1995, from Galaburda and (in brackets) Ul'ianov respectively, indicate the nature of the discrepancies between these sources; n/a indicates not applicable.

Sources: 1940–88: N.N. Kazanskii et al. (eds), *Ekonomicheskaia geografiia transporta* (Moscow 1991), 54; 1990–98: Galaburda, *Edinaia transportnaia*, 54; (1995), 2000–2008: calculated from Ul'ianov, *Transport v Rossii 2009*, 72.

Part of the explanation for the relatively small amount of RZD line closures is the fact that the traffic downturn has affected most parts of the transport sector: a loss of traffic to other modes of transport is not the main issue. Tables 16.7 and 16.8 collate statistics from three sources showing the proportions of overall freight and passenger traffic handled by the various modes of transport, including pipelines. These figures do require considerable caution: there are evident discrepancies between them and the definitions of terms are often unclear. For example, given the pairs of figures for 1995, it would seem that earlier figures for railway passenger traffic include metro lines and that 'road' for 1940–90 groups buses, trolleybuses, taxis and probably trams – assumptions which I have incorporated into Table 16.8. Further work to develop a reliable sequence of figures would be useful, but meantime these tables can suffice for our present purpose of identifying broad trends. They show that the RZD has basically maintained its position with freight except in relation to pipeline traffic, which actually continues a trend that was being pressed by the Soviet regime, not least to help relieve railway congestion. The fact that pipeline traffic was least affected in the economic slump also helps to explain its greater prominence. Similarly, the main change with passenger traffic occurred with the post-war expansion of urban road transport, which reduced the railway share to 36.8 per cent by 1988. If that latter figure does include metro operations, then it seems likely that since 1990 rail has increased its share of the public transport passenger market – an understandable development in major cities like Moscow where the boom in private car ownership has led to horrendous road congestion that virtually paralyses bus and trolleybus services for much of the time.[13]

Table 16.8   Share of Soviet and Russian passenger turnover by mode of transport, 1940–2010 (percentages of total passenger-kilometres)

A. Soviet Union and RSFSR

	1940	1960	1988	1990
Railway and Metro	92.2	61.6	36.8	39.1
Road	3.2	31.9	43.5	37.4
Sea	0.8	0.5	0.1	0.1
Inland waterway	3.6	1.6	0.5	0.7
Air	0.2	4.4	19.1	22.7

continued

---

[13]   A useful case study of the private car and urban transport planning is R.T. Argenbright, 'Avtomobilshchina: Driven to the brink in Moscow', *Urban Geography*, 29, issue 7, 2008, 683–704.

Table 16.8   *concluded*

B. RF

	1995	1995	1998	2000	2005	2008
Railway	42.30	(34.80)	34.50	33.80	37.10	37.00
Metro		(8.40)		9.50	9.30	9.10
Buses	41.60	(34.10)	52.20	34.80	28.70	24.30
Taxi		(0.20)		0.04	0.02	0.02
Tram		(4.50)		5.10	2.90	1.70
Trolleybus		(4.80)		5.70	3.20	1.90
Sea	0.05	(0.05)	0.01	0.02	0.02	0.01
Inland waterway	0.25	(0.20)	0.18	0.20	0.20	0.20
Air	15.80	(13.00)	13.10	10.90	18.50	25.80

Note: The two sets of figures for 1995, from Galaburda and (in brackets) Ul'ianov respectively, are given to highlight the nature of the discrepancies between these sources. For 1940–90 I assume that 'road' means buses, trams, trolleybuses and registered taxis. Blank spaces indicate that the figure is subsumed in the nearest figure above.

Sources: 1940–88: Kazanskii, *Ekonomicheskaia geografiia*, 54; 1990–98: Galaburda, *Edinaia transportnaia*, 42; (1995), 2000–2008: calculated from Ul'ianov, *Transport v Rossii 2009*, 75.

Network Development, Investment and Ownership

How, then, has the collapse of Communism affected capital investment in the railways, particularly in terms of network development? In global terms the Tsarist and Soviet railways were rather unusual in that they opened new routes almost every year between the end of the Crimean War in 1856 and the collapse of the Soviet Union in 1991, so it is worth looking in some detail at the main trends. During the Imperial era there was a basic quick–slow pattern of network development (see Table 16.1). Briefly, the first public line was opened in 1838 between the capital, St Petersburg, and the nearby village of Tsarskoye Selo, where the Tsar's summer palace was located. A shortage of finance – this a recurrent theme – was a key reason why only three more noteworthy routes were opened in the empire during the next two decades. These were a line from Warsaw towards Vienna, a connecting line from St Petersburg to Warsaw, and the trunk line from St Petersburg to the former Russian capital Moscow. However, the Crimean defeat confirmed the strategic as well as the economic importance of railways for Russia, and thereafter the state promoted the construction of a national network as quickly as possible, with new routes being opened virtually every year to 1917. An investment boom began in the late 1850s but ended through financial scandals and a recession in the early 1870s, which was reflected after a couple of years in the lower levels of track opened in 1875 and 1876. The pace of development remained modest through the 1880s because of the way in which the Russo–Turkish War of 1877–78 disrupted the state's finances. By contrast, the 1890s brought a second construction boom as a key part of the state-led drive for rapid industrialisation that was masterminded by Sergei Witte, Minister of Finances during 1892–1903. Here more than ever the state used railway construction to drive the process of industrialisation through providing both a demand for industrial products and a transport service. Again, however, this virtuous circle was disrupted by recession from 1900 (reflected in the figures of 1902 and 1903 for routes opened in Table 16.1), and then by the financial stringency that followed another expensive war, this time the 1904–1905 conflict with Japan. Signs of a third construction boom began to appear from about 1910, and this continued through the Great War until the revolutionary turmoil began in 1917.[14]

The main debate concerning this legacy has been whether railway development under Tsarism was adequate for the country's needs. A chorus of criticism arose during World War One as the railways struggled to cope with the emergency, and this critique was naturally taken up in the Soviet period by managers, the Bolshevik political leadership and historians alike. The Tsarist regime, it was argued, had failed Russia by consistently refusing to provide enough investment to build the railways that the country desperately needed. For instance, in terms of route kilometres and density per head of population the network of the vast Russian empire was dwarfed by that of the United States and scarcely bore comparison with the dense systems of the major industrial powers of Western Europe. Hence the network could not cope with the enormous demands of the war, and unsurprisingly the resultant strain brought collapse.[15] This analysis, however, has been challenged by Westwood and others. They contend that the rate of development reflected a broadly sensible compromise given the impossibility of raising enough capital to produce an ideal railway network. International comparisons of distance and

---

[14]   For good overviews see Westwood, *History of Russian Railways*, 20–34, 38–50, 59–78, 107–17, 125–8, 140–5, and B.E. Hurt, 'Russian economic development, 1881–1914, with special reference to the railways and the role of the government', University of London PhD thesis, 1963.

[15]   For example, N.V. Ivanovskii, 'Kak osushchestvit' vozrozhdenie transporta', *Zheleznodorozhnaia tekhnika i ekonomika*, 1, issue 2, 1919: 21–6. This analysis echoed the more general argument that Tsarist economic development was too slow. Perhaps the most influential critique was by V.I. Grinevetskii, *Poslevoennye perspektivy russkoi promyshlennosti* (Moscow 1922). On the railways see especially ibid., 108–37. This approach is also found in Western literature, such as the statistical data about relative industrial progress of world powers 1860–1910 at A. Nove, *An Economic History of the USSR* (Harmondsworth 1980), 15.

density per head of population make no sense if, as was common, no allowance was made for the country's special circumstances, notably the vast areas that were uninhabitable or very sparsely populated. Not least, it is unreasonable to condemn the railway system for being unprepared for a very exceptional, prolonged wartime emergency that not even the military experts predicted.[16]

For all its criticism of the Tsarist state's approach to railway development, the Bolshevik regime did not expand the network as much as engineers initially hoped. To be sure, it retained the concept of using railway-building to stimulate economic development, and new routes continued to be opened in almost every year, yielding a network of over 147,000 route kilometres by 1991 (Table 16.2). The overall tally of routes opened during 1918–1891 (51,425.8 kilometres) contrasts starkly with the widespread closures that occurred in Western Europe and North America after the Second World War. Yet this total represented only about two-thirds of the amount built by the Tsarist regime, and the growth rate never matched the high average tempo of the empire's last 25 years. Nothing came of the protracted discussions during the Civil War about building a network of so-called 'supermainlines' (*sverkhmagistrali*) for high-speed long-distance freight traffic, not to mention such apparently impracticable ideas as a railway to the Bering Strait.[17] The reality was that the World War and Civil War had impoverished Russia, and moreover Lenin became captivated by the idea of using a more recent technology – electric power – to drive the next stage of Russian industrialisation. The railways thus had to make do with a relatively modest level of investment. Ironically but logically and unsurprisingly, many of the actual railway construction projects of the 1920s and 1930s were based on plans that had been formulated before the revolution, such as the famous Turksib line linking Turkestan with Siberia via Semipalatinsk.[18] True, a radical change of direction was mooted after the Second World War in the form of a grandiose plan to build a network of lines across the inhospitable northern half of the country, and a start was made using prison-camp labour. But despite considerable expenditure and thousands of prisoner fatalities this work was abandoned almost immediately after Stalin's death in 1953.[19]

---

[16]   See Westwood et al., 'Transport', 169–78.

[17]   On supermainlines see, for example, Grinevetskii, *Poslevoennye perspektivy*, 124–5; L.N. Bernatskii, 'O sverkhmagistraliakh', *Tekhnika i ekonomika putei soobshcheniia*, 19–20, 1922, 243–7. The proposed Siberia–Alaska Railway, complete with tunnel under the Bering Strait, was much discussed in the early twentieth century: S. Marks, *Road to Power: The Trans-Siberian Railroad and the Colonization of Asian Russia, 1850–1917* (London 1991), 206, and extensive records survive in the French national archives (I am grateful to Brandon Schneider for this information). More generally on the debate about railway modernisation during 1917–20 see A.J. Heywood, *Modernising Lenin's Russia: Economic Reconstruction, Foreign Trade and the Railways* (Cambridge 1999), 56–63.

[18]   The history of the Turksib is the subject of M.J. Payne, *Stalin's Railroad: Turksib and the Building of Socialism* (Pittsburgh 2001).

[19]   A.A. Berzin, 'Doroga v nikuda: Materialy o stroitel'stve zheleznoi dorogi Salekhard–Igarka, 1947–1953 gg.', *Voprosy istorii estestvoznaniia i tekhniki*, 1, 1990, 38–48.

Thereafter the biggest and best known Soviet project was the Baikal–Amur main line (Baikalo-Amurskaia *magistral* – BAM) in Siberia, which was built from Lena across the northern tip of Lake Baikal to Tynda, Urgal and Komsomol'sk-na-Amure in the 1970s and 1980s. Dubbed the 'railway of the century', and intended as ever to spur large-scale economic development, the 3,200 kilometre link was an enormously difficult and costly line to build in a very inhospitable environment, and it was still struggling to establish itself when the Soviet Union imploded.[20]

In this context the impact of the Soviet Union's demise on railway development appears dramatic to say the least. Table 16.9 collates data from three official Russian sources about new routes opened in the Russian Federation during 1992–2009. Even when allowance is made for the disappearance of the other 14 union republics, which accounted for about 60,000 route kilometres or roughly 40 per cent of the Soviet network at 1991, it is clear that there was an unprecedented complete collapse of construction work in the 1990s and only a very modest revival during 2000–2009. Official sources sometimes emphasised that priority was given to maintenance and repair in the 1990s, and the same point is implicit in RZD annual reports from 2005.[21] That may be so, and it would be logical in such an economic crisis, but it was not a matter of choice. There was simply a total collapse of investment in railway development from 1988 that lasted through the 1990s. During 1985–87 the annual figure for development investment varied between 2.56 and 2.67 billion roubles, but then came a precipitate slump to 870 million roubles in 1988, 440 million in 1991 and just 15 million in 1992.[22]

That said, investment in electrification was, like line closures, an area where the RZD tried to hard not to retreat. Electrification had begun in earnest on the erstwhile SZD at the end of the 1940s and continued for four decades at an impressive average of about 1,100 route kilometres per year (for 1947–1991 see Table 16.10). Significantly, electrification continued on the RZD throughout the 1990s at an annual average rate of about 340 kilometres for 1992–2000. Obviously this rate was much lower than in Soviet times but it was a very considerable achievement in the tough economic circumstances. For the following decade the picture is less clear: either the average dropped to around 200 kilometres per year, to judge by fragmentary evidence in RZD annual reports, or it stayed at much the

---

[20]   The BAM was started in the 1930s, with the sections to Lena and from Komsomol'sk-na-Amure being built then and during 1947–1953, when the project was abandoned. A good example of the regime's efforts to popularise the revived project is A. Druzenko et al., *Trassa* (Moscow 1985), written by journalists from the *Izvestiia* newspaper.

[21]   For example: N.S. Konarev et al. (eds), *Zheleznodorozhnyi transport: Entsiklopediia* (Moscow 1994), entry 'Zheleznodorozhnoe stroitel'stvo', 135, and RZD Annual Report 2009, 106.

[22]   Volkov, *Doroga v rynok*, 50–51. The source is not clear about whether these figures relate to the Soviet Union or the RSFSR and RF, but the basic point holds whichever is correct.

same level, according to the State Statistical Service's data, which, however, may include non-RZD industrial feeder lines.

Table 16.9 Railway route kilometres opened and route kilometres electrified, Russian Federation, 1992–2009

Year	Opened Afonina	Opened Kevesh and Ul'ianov	Opened RZD	Electrified Afonina	Electrified Kevesh and Ul'ianov	Electrified RZD
1992	45.1	–	–	210.7	–	–
1993	6.0	–	–	121.4	–	–
1994	0.0	–	–	347.0	–	–
1995	0.0	–	–	152.7	152.7	–
1996	0.0	–	–	302.4	–	–
1997	78.5	–	–	424.6	–	–
1998	–	–	–	326.2	–	–
1999	–	–	–	494.0	–	–
2000	–	1.7	–	690.6	588.3	1958.0
2001	–	197.2	–	–	683.4	
2002	–	175.3	–	–	641.1	
2003	–	36.8	–	–	356.0	
2004	–	26.7	–	–	34.2	
2005	–	127.8	–	–	507.4	
2006	–	208.2	–	–	46.4	
2007	–	40.7	–	–	0.0	0.0
2008	–	84.4	8.2	–	225.7	187.1
2009	–	–	47.7	–	–	–

Note: With electrification no distinction is made between single- and multi-track routes. Blank spaces indicate that the figure is subsumed in the nearest figure above.

Sources: Calculated and tabulated from Afonina, *Kratkie svedeniia* (2002), 218–26; M.N. Sidorov et al. (eds), *Transport v Rossii 2003: Statisticheskii sbornik* (Moscow 2003), 24; A.L. Kevesh et al. (eds), *Transport v Rossii 2005: Statisticheskii sbornik* (Moscow 2005), 24; A.L. Kevesh et al. (eds), *Transport v Rossii 2007: Statisticheskii sbornik* (Moscow 2007), 19; Ul'ianov, *Transport v Rossii 2009*, 28; RZD Annual Report 2006, 50; RZD Annual Report 2007, 49; RZD Annual Report 2008, 38 and 73; RZD Annual Report 2009, 48.

Table 16.10   Main-line electrification, 1924–1991

Year	Route-kilometres electrified	Year	Route-kilometres electrified	Year	Route-kilometres electrified
1924	11.2	1947	113.0	1970	1,411.3
1925	0.0	1948	361.1	1971	390.4
1926	20.0	1949	130.8	1972	1,103.8
1927	0.0	1950	275.1	1973	982.3
1928	0.0	1951	418.2	1974	781.4
1929	17.8	1952	182.6	1975	773.7
1930	34.6	1953	570.1	1976	816.4
1931	9.2	1954	574.4	1977	642.4
1932	67.4	1955	526.5	1978	492.5
1933	221.5	1956	1,019.0	1979	1,117.0
1934	27.2	1957	1,268.8	1980	898.1
1935	655.3	1958	1,748.4	1981	1,048.2
1936	181.9	1959	1,612.1	1982	926.1
1937	411.3	1960	2,255.1	1983	1,094.7
1938	58.5	1961	1,854.9	1984	1,092.3
1939	135.1	1962	2,290.0	1985	474.9
1940	0.0	1963	2,232.7	1986	2,601.4
1941	30.1	1964	2,136.4	1987	1,144.2
1942	9.5	1965	2,314.2	1988	1,192.0
1943	51.2	1966	2,077.9	1989	891.4
1944	90.4	1967	1,919.2	1990	417.2
1945	269.8	1968	1,293.2	1991	426.2
1946	57.5	1969	1,619.3	**Total**	**51,870.4**

Sources: Calculated and tabulated from Afonina, *Kratkie svedeniia* (1996), 102–215; and Afonina, *Kratkie svedeniia* (2002), 216–17.

As for future investment, the official view remains determinedly optimistic to judge by the long-term railway development strategy to 2030 that was approved by the Russian federal government in 2008 and that is aligned with the government's national transport strategy for the same period.[23] Assuming that the network will remain absolutely fundamental for the economy, economic growth and defence, and that traffic will grow substantially, the railway strategy calls not only for wholesale renovation work and the modernisation of much of the rolling stock, but also for large-scale railway construction 'to create conditions for new centres of economic growth', especially in Siberia and the Far East.[24] Costed at 13,812 billion roubles (US$450 billion), the plan specifies as much as 20,700 route kilometres to be built, mostly during 2016–30 – a tempo that we can see is much higher than the average for the Soviet era, close to the average for 1845–1917, but not as high as the rate for 1892–1917. Included are 1,500 kilometres of dedicated high-speed (350 kilometres per hour) passenger routes and a 1,866 kilometres line in the far northeast from Nizhnii Bestiakh through Moma to the Pacific Coast at Magadan, with the possibility after 2030 of reviving a spectacular old dream – a line from Moma to Uelen at the Bering Strait (Figure 16.2 and 16.3).[25]

Electrification is planned to continue at the rate of 3,918 kilometres by 2015 and then up to 3,580 kilometres during 2016–30 – figures that imply an average rate of about 325 kilometres per year for 2008–30.[26]

The RZD contends that by implementing this strategy 'it will be possible to develop a qualitatively new, 'intelligent' transport (system), realise transit potential and create the necessary conditions for the innovation-based development of key areas of the national economy'. In short:

---

[23]   For a short summary of the railway strategy in English see RZD Annual Report 2009, 40–43. Maps showing the proposed new routes occupy 41–2, though some of the marked routes are planned for after 2030. The full document is 'Strategiia razvitiia zheleznodorozhnogo transporta v Rossiiskoi Federatsii do 2030 goda', ratified by the government on 17 June 2008. It can be downloaded from the website of the Ministry of Transport of the Russian Federation: www.mintrans.ru subsection Transportnaia strategiia/ transportnaia strategiia (last accessed 26 August 2010). At the same location is the national transport strategy to 2030: 'Transportnaia strategiia Rossiiskoi Federatsii na period do 2030 goda', ratified on 22 November 2008, and a very detailed multi-modal map of proposed developments entitled 'Transportnaia infrastruktura Rossii 2010–2030 gg.'

[24]   For the detailed forecasts of traffic growth to 2030 for the whole transport sector see 'Transportnaia strategiia Rossiiskoi Federatsii', appendix 2.

[25]   The strategy has minimum and maximum versions, costed respectively at 11,447.8 billion roubles and 13,812.4 billion roubles (prices at 1 January 2007). The minimum plan envisages 16,017 kilometres of new routes, whereas the maximum version specifies 20,730 new route kilometres: 'Strategiia', 8–9, 36–7, 62–3, appendices 1, 7 and 9. The line to Magadan is specified in Appendix 9, 1, and the Moma–Uelen extension is marked and dated as post-2030 on the map 'Transportnaia infrastruktura Rossii 2010–2030 gg.'

[26]   'Strategiia', 32.

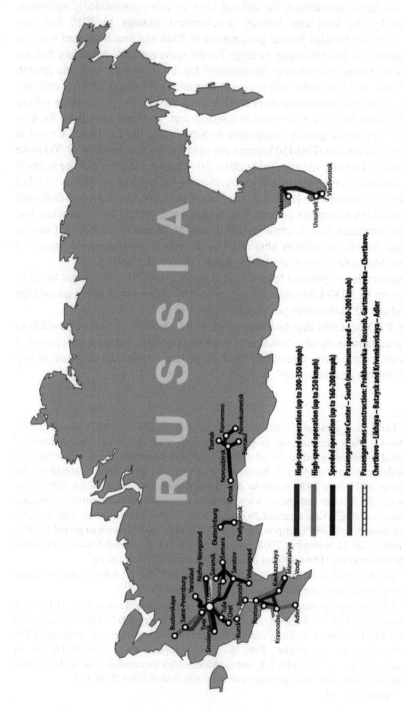

Figure 16.2   High-speed passenger transport system planned for completion by 2030
Source: Russian Railways.

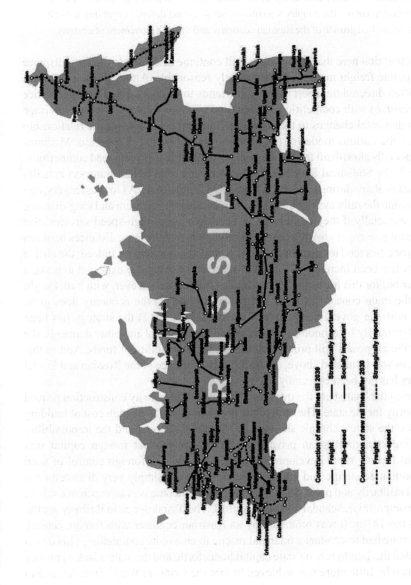

Figure 16.3 Russian Federation railway network development to 2030
Source: Russian Railways.

> The Strategy will (...) result in the fundamental modernization of infrastructure, the qualitative renovation of (rolling) stock, including full replacement of stock that has exceeded its useful life, large-scale expansion of the rail network and enhanced efficiency and safety in the industry. Infrastructure conditions will be created to ensure the country's territorial integrity and defence capability as well as intensified growth of the Russian economy and the free movement of citizens.[27]

The assumption here that the railways will continue to dominate the long-distance non-pipeline freight market seems perfectly reasonable. Although the concept of the unified directed transport system now tends to mean a unified transport space (*prostranstvo*) with competition, the national transport strategy does not envisage any fundamental changes to the country's transport geography or the relationship between the various modes of transport during the period in question. Medium- and especially short-haul freight may prove vulnerable to private road competition, though if the Statistical Service's data are correct, road freight transport actually lost market-share during the decade from 1998 (Table 16.4). As for passengers, one can imagine the railways retaining their current share of medium and long-distance traffic, especially if they do manage to develop a net of high-speed services. But significant passenger growth seems unlikely given that the large distances between the major cities tend to favour aviation in a market environment. Indeed, the airline industry has been increasing its market-share and can also be expected to make a stronger bid for this traffic (see Table 16.5). Ultimately, however, with bulk freight being the main concern as ever, and assuming that (1) the economy does grow in line with the government's optimistic forecasts, and (2) the strategy has been shaped primarily by economic criteria rather than political and other demands, the fate of the proposals will probably hinge on the availability of funds. And in this regard, as was intimated above, the historical experience of the Russian and Soviet railways has not been especially happy.

During the Tsarist era the question of how to fund railway construction proved very thorny for the state. The crux of the problem was that the high cost of building railways, the state's chronic shortage of investment capital and the impossibility of raising enough Russian private investment meant that foreign capital was essential for any rapid development of the network. Yet foreign control of such an important economic and military resource was not simply very distasteful but seemed militarily and politically dangerous. The outcome was an expensive tale of delay, compromise, scandal and state control. The Tsarskoye Selo Railway set the tone in the 1830s. It was promoted by an Austrian engineer with foreign capital, but the state had to conduct a financial rescue to ensure its completion. This fiasco persuaded the Tsar to rely on state capital henceforth, and the state's lack of money explains why little more was achieved before the Crimean War.[28] That defeat and

---

[27]   RZD Annual Report 2009, 40.

[28]   For detailed discussions see R.M. Haywood, *The Beginnings of Railway Development in Russia in the Reign of Nicholas I, 1835–1842* (Durham 1969); and R.M.

a change of Tsar produced a decision to rely on foreign private capital, but by the 1870s this tactic was discredited by financial scandals, such that state financing again became the norm for new routes and the state began to nationalise privately owned railways. The railway boom of the 1890s was largely funded by foreign capital, but now this money was channelled through the government instead of foreign private companies, and the nationalisation policy continued. After the 1900 recession and Russo-Japanese War, however, the 30-year consensus about state funding disintegrated. The MPS still wanted state funding exclusively and further nationalisation, whereas the Ministry of Finances saw private capital as the only realistic option. Usually the latter prevailed with the understanding that privately owned lines would eventually pass to state ownership.[29]

The Bolshevik revolution simplified the picture considerably, if not very helpfully. The fiercely anti-capitalist new regime imposed full state control, the remaining private companies being nationalised without compensation in February 1918. Accordingly, the state would now also provide all investment. The problem was that with Russia impoverished and politically isolated by 1920, there was no serious prospect of large-scale foreign loans to help rebuild and expand the economy. There was some talk in the West in the early 1920s about using the railways as collateral for loans, but the Soviet government had no intention of relinquishing state control over an asset that it regarded as vital for defence as well as the economy.[30] No further change would occur for the rest of the Soviet era, and with investment priority passing to nationwide electrification, heavy industry and elsewhere, the railways had to make do with much less money than they would have liked.

The collapse of Communism has brought – eventually – a sea-change in this arena. As Westwood has shown, the MPS spent the 1990s trying with some success to resist the pressure for radical reform and to mitigate the effects of the economic crisis on its workforce and business.[31] But the MPS was abolished in 2003: its policy-making and regulatory functions were passed to the Ministry of Transport and its operating responsibilities were transferred to the RZD as a wholly state-owned share company. Now Russia's largest employer with 1.2 million employees, the RZD is supporting the reformist agenda. Although it is likely to remain in state hands as owner of the network's fixed assets and traction, the RZD does now see private capital as an essential partner with continuing state support. For instance, by 2009 66.2 per cent of the freight-wagon stock was owned by RZD or its subsidiaries and associates, whereas other owners had as much as 33.8 per cent of the stock.[32] Crucially, private sources are earmarked to play a major role in funding the 2008 development strategy alongside central

Haywood, *Russia Enters the Railway Age, 1842–1855* (Boulder, CO 1998).

[29]   See especially Westwood, *History of Russian Railways*, 40–5, 48–50, 64–78, 133–8, and 142–5, and Hurt, *Russian Economic Development*.

[30]   See Heywood, *Modernising Lenin's Russia*, 187.

[31]   Westwood, *Soviet Railways to Russian Railway*.

[32]   RZD Annual Report 2009, 87.

government, regional governments and RZD sources (including, for example, bond issues).[33] Accordingly, a fundamental question for the federal government, transport ministry and RZD board will be the extent to which the private sector will prove willing to back their railway vision.

To some degree the answer to that question will hinge on factors well beyond the control of the RZD board, including politics, the pattern of national economic growth and the levels of confidence in the Russian economy as a whole. But it is worth noting in the RZD's favour that the principal geographical and social conditions that helped to drive the process of railway expansion during the nineteenth and twentieth centuries remain fundamentally unchanged. The Soviet Union may have disappeared, but the Russian Federation is still a huge country that stretches from the Baltic Sea to the Pacific, albeit with its population still concentrated in its European regions. Pipelines aside, the infrastructure for medium- and long-distance transport is much the same as it was in the 1980s, notwithstanding increased investment in road-building, and it is not expected to change radically during the next few decades. Not least, the lure of natural resources located in poorly accessible regions of the north and east may well spur the construction of new railways into those regions, as the plans suggest. So the RZD board does have good reason to be confident that railway transport will remain absolutely critical for the bulk of Russia's long-distance freight for the foreseeable future.

Conclusions

The collapse of the Soviet Union has clearly had a tremendous – and in key respects unprecedented – impact on the railways of Russia that continues to be felt. Yet a considerable degree of important continuity is also evident with each of the three main issues discussed above. In the crude terms of overall turnover, with no regard for such major issues as changes in the commodities transported, the collapse in the volume of traffic must be situated between the two great catastrophes of 1917–20 and 1941–43. In the same terms, the recovery since 1999 has been much slower and more complex than was the case in the 1920s and 1940s. So, seen from this basic perspective and taken as a whole comprising both collapse and recovery, the post-Soviet traffic crisis could arguably be ranked as the worst in the history of the Russian railways. As for the outcomes, the stable transport geography of Russia suggests that freight traffic will almost certainly regain and surpass its pre-crisis peak, but the medium- and long-distance railway passenger traffic may fail to recover fully if the airline industry can itself make more competitive and continue to build its market-share.

Also unprecedented for Russia was the hiatus in railway development during the 1990s, and it was only marginally mitigated by the RZD's determined effort

---

[33]   'Strategiia', 63.

to maintain electrification at a level of some 230–50 route kilometres per year during the first two post-Soviet decades. And yet, ironically, the RZD's strategy for future development is heavily influenced by the past. Understandably it has been shaped to a degree by the geographical issues noted above. But its grandiose scale also owes much to traditional thinking, including the core idea that railway-building in remote areas can be used to promote regional economic and social development. The optimism of this document in a difficult economic climate recalls the passionate but ultimately fanciful discussions about network expansion in the Soviet press at the height of the Civil War, but hopefully the 2008 plan will have a happier fate.

The organisational and financial changes seem no less dramatic with the abolition of the MPS after more than 135 years, the reform of the RZD as a share company and the reappearance for the first time since 1917 of major role for private capital in railway construction and operations. Back in Tsarist and Soviet times the MPS was widely regarded as a state within the state, complete with its own housing, health-care, education, food supply and communications systems, not to mention its own security services. The RZD has inherited this empire, but it does seem to be making an effort to develop a different, more responsive corporate culture with the possibility of far-reaching reorganisations. Yet here too there is a substantial measure of continuity. For instance, the RZD remains committed to fulfilling what it calls its 'social responsibilities', primarily towards its workforce. Above all, the company remains – and is highly likely to remain – in state ownership. Specifically, private enterprises will be able to own rolling stock and organise services, but the state via the RZD will retain ownership of the track infrastructure and probably most if not all of the locomotives.[34]

Since 1991, then, the Russian railways have experienced a profound upheaval that compares with – and arguably surpasses – the two worst crises in their history. Some of the key Soviet transport policies like centrally planned inter-modal coordination have disappeared, and some momentous reforms have been instigated. But there are also significant continuities in mindset and policy that are deeply rooted in the culture and traditions of the Russian railways. Faced with an uncertain future, the Russian railways have not simply rejected their past, but have sought to meld large parts of it with the new national priorities associated with running a mixed state-private economy.

---

[34]   A comparison can be made with Gazprom, which controls the gas pipeline network and sets the terms of access for other gas companies. I am grateful to Bob Argenbright for this point.

Bibliography

Afonina, G.M. (ed.), *Kratkie svedeniia o razvitii otechestvennykh zheleznykh dorog s 1838 po 1990 g.* (Moscow 1996).

Afonina, G.M. (ed.), *Kratkie svedeniia o razvitii otechestvennykh zheleznykh dorog s 1838 po 2000 g.* (Moscow 2002).

Afonina, G.M. et al., *Zheleznodorozhnyi transport: XX vek* (Moscow 2001).

Argenbright, R.T., 'Avtomobilshchina: Driven to the brink in Moscow', *Urban Geography*, 29, issue 7, 2008, 683–704.

Argenbright, R.T., 'The Russian railroad system and the founding of the Communist state, 1917–1922', University of California at Berkeley PhD thesis, 1990.

Bernatskii, L.N., 'O sverkhmagistraliakh', *Tekhnika i ekonomika putei soobshcheniia*, 19/20, 1922, 243–7.

Berzin, A.A., 'Doroga v nikuda: Materialy o stroitel'stve zheleznoi dorogi Salekhard–Igarka, 1947–1953 gg.', *Voprosy istorii estestvoznaniia i tekhniki*, 1, 1990, 38–48.

Druzenko, A. et al., *Trassa* (Moscow 1985).

Galaburda, V.G. et al. (eds), *Edinaia transportnaia sistema*, 2nd edn (Moscow 2001).

Grinevetskii, V.I., *Poslevoennye perspektivy russkoi promyshlennosti* (Moscow 1922).

Haywood, R.M., *Russia Enters the Railway Age, 1842–1855* (Boulder, CO 1998).

Haywood, R.M., *The Beginnings of Railway Development in Russia in the Reign of Nicholas I, 1835–1842* (Durham 1969).

Heywood, A.J., *Modernising Lenin's Russia: Economic Reconstruction, Foreign Trade and the Railways* (Cambridge 1999).

Hurt, B.E., 'Russian economic development, 1881–1914, with special reference to the railways and the role of the government', University of London PhD thesis, 1963.

Ivanovskii, N.V., 'Kak osushchestvit' vozrozhdenie transporta', *Zheleznodorozhnaia tekhnika i ekonomika*, 1, issue 2, 1919, 21–6.

Kazanskii, N.N. et al. (eds), *Ekonomicheskaia geografiia transporta* (Moscow 1991).

Kevesh, A.L. et al. (eds), *Transport v Rossii 2005: Statisticheskii sbornik* (Moscow 2005).

Kevesh, A.L. et al. (eds), *Transport v Rossii 2007: Statisticheskii sbornik* (Moscow 2007).

Konarev, N.S. et al. (eds), *Zheleznodorozhnyi transport: Entsiklopediia* (Moscow 1994).

Kraskovskii, E. Ia. and Uzdin, M.M. (eds), *Istoriia zheleznodorozhnogo transporta Rossii, tom 1: 1836–1917* (St Petersburg 1994).

Kumanev, G.A., *Voina i zheleznodorozhnyi transport SSSR, 1941–1945* (Moscow 1988).

Lydolph, P., *Geography of the USSR* (Elkhart Lake 1990).

Marks, S., *Road to Power: The Trans-Siberian Railroad and the Colonization of Asian Russia, 1850–1917* (London 1991).

Nove, A., *An Economic History of the USSR* (Harmondsworth 1980).

Pavlov, V.E. and Uzdin, M.M. (eds), *Istoriia zheleznodorozhnogo transporta Rossii i Sovetskogo Soiuza*, vol. 2: *1917–1945* (St Petersburg 1997).

Payne, M.J., *Stalin's Railroad: Turksib and the Building of Socialism* (Pittsburgh 2001).

Poletaev, A.V. and Savel'eva, I.M., 'Sravnitel'nyi analiz dvukh sistemnykh krizisov v rossiiskoi istorii (1920-e i 1990-e gg.)', *Ekonomicheskaia istoriia: ezhegodnik, 2000*, 98–136.

RZD Annual Reports 2006–2009 (can be downloaded from the RZD website at: http://eng.rzd.ru/isvp/public/rzdeng?STRUCTURE_ID=21&layer_id=3290&id=381).

Shafirkin, B.I., *Edinaia transportnaia sistema SSSR i vzaimodeistvie razlichnykh vidov transporta*, 3rd edn (Moscow 1983).

Sidorov, M.N. et al. (eds), *Transport v Rossii 2003: Statisticheskii sbornik* (Moscow 2003).

'Strategiia razvitiia zheleznodorozhnogo transporta v Rossiiskoi Federatsii do 2030 goda' (2008) (can be downloaded from the website of the Ministry of Transport of the Russian Federation: www.mintrans.ru sub-section Transportnaia strategiia/transportnaia strategiia).

'Transportnaia strategiia Rossiiskoi Federatsii na period do 2030 goda' (2008) (can be downloaded from the website of the Ministry of Transport of the Russian Federation: www.mintrans.ru sub-section Transportnaia strategiia/transportnaia strategiia).

'Transportnaia infrastruktura Rossii 2010–2030 gg.' (2008) (can be downloaded from the website of the Ministry of Transport of the Russian Federation: www.mintrans.ru sub-section Transportnaia strategiia/transportnaia strategiia).

Ul'ianov, I.S. et al. (eds), *Transport v Rossii 2009: Statisticheskii sbornik* (Moscow 2009).

Volkov, V.I. et al. (eds), *Doroga v rynok: Zheleznodorozhnyi transport v usloviiakh formirovaniia rynochnykh otnoshenii* (Moscow 1994).

Westwood, J.N., *A History of Russian Railways* (London 1964).

Westwood, J.N. et al., 'Transport', in R.W. Davies et al. (eds), *The Economic Transformation of the Soviet Union, 1913–1945* (Cambridge 1994), 161–8 and 304–6.

Westwood, J.N., *From Soviet Railways to Russian Railways* (Basingstoke 2002).

Zotov, D.K. and Ushakov, S.S., *Problemy razvitiia transporta SSSR* (Moscow 1990).

Chapter 17

The Unification of East and West German Railways into the Deutsche Bahn

Ralf Roth

State and Railway in a Divided Country

The capitulation of the Nazi regime on 8 May 1945 meant the occupation of Germany by four Allies which divided the country into four occupied zones (*Besatzungszonen*) and four separate railway administrations. Initiatives were taken to revive the former Reichsbahn and lay the ground for a central solution to the great traffic problems under which the destroyed country suffered; however, these initiatives failed. All that could be achieved was the establishment of a railway committee which was installed as a separate department of the Allied Control Council (*Kontrollrat*). The committee discussed the advice of the Control Council in so far as it was related to matters of railway transport, for example agreements on inter-zone traffic, and fixing general tariffs.[1]

Most railway men were convinced that the character of the Reichsbahn should be preserved. They saw their company not as an enterprise led by business values, but as a governmental institution or department which took on social responsibility from its national importance. The general director of the railway in the Bizone (the combined American and British zone) was of the opinion that the Reichsbahn must be the clamp that clips together the German people in times of need. Although the railway leaders failed to implement a mighty national railway in the destroyed and divided country, recovery started, at first in the American zone, at the level of the former states (*Länder*). The denazification campaign caused some delays, because, for example, in the Bizone alone, 55 per cent of the upper railway employees and 54 per cent of the middle level had to leave the Reichsbahn. This was even though the Allies were not very systematic, and Germans in the administration opposed and hindered the plans. The second struggle the still-mighty railway organisation fought was against decentralisation. The railway administration successfully opposed the ambition of the states to make the railway part of their governments.[2] It is well known that the four Allies became separated in two factions, and that

---

[1]   See Anthony James Nicholls, 'Zusammenbruch und Wiederaufbau: Die Reichsbahn während der Besatzungszeit', in Lothar Gall and Manfred Pohl (eds), *Die Eisenbahn in Deutschland. Von den Anfängen bis zur Gegenwart* (Munich 1999), 245–79, here 246.

[2]   Ibid., 249, 258–64 and 278.

similarly, in 1949, Germany was divided into West and East, into two republics called Bundesrepublik Deutschland (Federal Republic of Germany) and Deutsche Demokratische Republik (German Democratic Republic). At the same time, the Reichsbahn was divided into the Deutsche Bundesbahn for West Germany and the Deutsche Reichsbahn for East Germany. In each of the two Germanys, the railway became part of the state administration. In West Germany, the provisional constitution, the *Grundgesetz*, precisely prescribed the position of the railways in the new nation. The railway was to exist as an institution of the Federation with limited influence from the states. The railway was not to dominate the transport ministry. Nor was it to be an independent enterprise of the state, as the *Reichsbahngesellschaft* had been during the Weimar Republic. The Allies forced the railway in the Federal Republic to drop the name *Reich*. This was the reason for the name Deutsche Bundesbahn. But the change of name did not solve the problem of a problematic state tradition that still continued. The mentality or the spirit of state officials was probably stronger in the Bundesbahn than in the Reichsbahn of the German Democratic Republic.[3]

Although the railways in East and West remained state railways, their developments were nevertheless totally different. This was not only a function of the kinds of societies the transportation systems were confronted with, but also of the specific type of competition each railway company experienced with other transport systems.

In West Germany, the general framework for economic activities shifted toward integration with the West (*Westingegration*) and toward cooperation within the emerging European institutions. The law related to the Bundesbahn called for an administrative council (*Verwaltungsrat*) led by a president. The members of this council were elected by the government via proposals from the Federal Council, or *Bundesrat* (the second chamber of the Federal Republic, comprising representatives of the federal states), and via proposals by the most important organisations of the economy and trade unions. The council made its decisions independently of advice from the government. The board of the Bundesbahn had to follow the decisions of the council, although the board's employer was the Minister of Transport.

West Germany's railway was still a mighty force. It was one of the biggest customers for industry of the Federal Republic. In 1952, for example, the Bundesbahn ordered goods with a value of 2.3 billion marks and consumed 16 per cent of the coal taken that year from Germany's coal mines. But in contrast to the end of the nineteenth century the financial situation of West Germany's railway was not the best in the middle of the twentieth century. It suffered under a huge pile of old debts, and felt more and more the competition from motor vehicles. Also, it needed money for the rationalisation and modernisation of business, administration and technology to become more attractive to its own customers.[4]

---

[3]   Ibid., 278–9.

[4]   See Adolf Sarter and Theodor Kittel, *Die Deutsche Bundesbahn. Ihr Aufbau und Arbeitsgrundlage* (Frankfurt am Main 1952), 19–20. On the background see Günther

One of the main tasks for the Ministry of Transport in West Germany was to set up a new traffic and transport policy that took into consideration the new situation in the traffic market. The role of the railways had to be redefined. In the 1920s and 1930s, the competition between railways and trucks had been regulated by the state, which protected the railways so that they could bear the burden of reparations and fulfil social tasks. The railway could handle this from its own income alone by making profits in certain parts of its business, for example long-distance goods transport, and then using this profit to fill the holes in the budget caused by cheap regional passenger fares – a system of vertical subsidies. This system worked satisfactorily for the first half of the twentieth century. But it became imbalanced during the upsurge of motor vehicles in the 1950s. Some statistics illustrate this. From 1949 to 1989, the network of the Deutsche Bundesbahn shrank from 30,344 kilometres to 27,045, and the number of employees decreased from 539,000 to only 254,491. In 1949 the West German railway carried 1.3 billion passengers, and in 1989 only one billion – though over longer distances, on average. The goods traffic carried on rail increased from 216 million tons to 273 million. But the railway's portion of total goods traffic decreased from 56 to only 22 per cent, while the debts had skyrocketed to 44 billion marks by the end of the 1980s.[5]

In the 1950s, a bus service organised by the Bundesbahn itself replaced many short-distance rail lines of secondary importance.[6] The railway's monopoly in transport was lost as bus lines competed more and more for short-distance travellers. In goods transport, the railways were confronted with trucks; river and canal shipping, too, gained a growing part of the market. At the same time, the demand for shipped coal decreased. More and more, coal was converted to electricity by power plants in the direct neighbourhood of mines. And finally, in the 1950s, oil began to be transported in pipelines, replacing coal in some areas.[7] Thus it became necessary to define the role of railways in a time of the liberalisation of the transport market. The German national parliament, the *Bundestag*, debated these issues beginning at the end of the 1950s, and initiated several expert studies, such as the *Brand-Gutachten* of 1960 and the *Leber-Plan* of 1967–68. Broader European transport policies influenced Germany's own. The harmonisation

---

Schulz, 'Die Deutsche Bundesbahn 1949–1989', in Gall and Pohl, *Die Eisenbahn in Deutschland*, 317–76, here 318–19, 323, and Paul Roth, 'Die deutsche Bundesbahn als Auftraggeberin der deutschen Wirtschaft', in *Die deutsche Bundesbahn und ihre Industrie* (Frankfurt am Main 1953), 63–71.

[5]   Andreas Predöhl, *Verkehrspolitik*, 2nd edn (Göttingen 1964), 280, and Horst Weigelt and Ulrich Lamper, *40 Jahre Deutsche Bundesbahn 1949–1989* (Darmstadt 1989), 52 and 667.

[6]   Schulz, *Die Deutsche Bundesbahn*, 324, 331 and 335.

[7]   Marlene Müller, *Die Finanzkrise der Deutschen Bundesbahn, ihre Ursachen und Sanierungsmöglichkeiten* (Innsbruck 1958), 42–3.

of railways in Europe started in 1965 with the Harmonisation Decision of the European Economic Community 65/271.[8]

So far this chapter has considered the hard factor responsible for the decline of Germany's railway – that is, its financial situation. But the loss in all domains was not only a question of hard facts but also of soft ones. The automobile appeared on the scene as a metaphor for freedom, independence, privacy, self-responsibility and individuality, while public transport was more and more seen as a transport system for the masses, associated with the idea of an economy centrally planned by the state, and with inefficiency, ponderousness and bureaucracy.

As the railway's share of the transport market shrank, the financial problems increased, and rising personnel costs also contributed to the general problem. Beginning at 8.8 billion marks in the 1950s, the salary costs had increased to 20.7 billion marks in 1982, compounding a debt that reached 36 billion marks and continued to grow. These debts had to be balanced out by the state, creating a vicious circle. The growing deficit forced higher debts, the higher debts meant increased interest payments, and this diminished the scope for financial actions, leading to new debts.[9]

These financial problems worsened despite the fact that there had been a period of tough modernisation and rapid change in infrastructure and technical innovations. Indeed, one could not find many similarities between the Deutsche Bundesbahn of 1949 and that of 1989. The Bundesbahn of 1989 was based on electric and diesel locomotives that drove up to 200 kilometres per hour and sometimes more. Many stations featured modern architecture, and were attractive and highly functional. All were open for the public, and not closed up by gates and barriers, as had been the case earlier. And the civil servants began to accept their role as providers of customer service. But despite these great strengths in modernisation, and the reduction of staff and administration, and the electrification, and more comfort in better trains, and a shrinking network whose non-profitable lines had been closed – despite these advances, the formerly profitable system became a bottomless barrel for subsidies.[10]

This was the situation in the Federal Republic of Germany. The situation in the German Democratic Republic was totally different, not only because of the German Democratic Republic's incorporation into the Soviet bloc of states in Eastern Europe. At the time of the foundation of the German Democratic Republic, the Deutsche Reichsbahn stayed in poor condition. After the war, the Soviet Union had dismantled 4,000 kilometres of railway tracks for reparation reason, which led to a decrease in efficiency and safety, and an increase in wear and tear on the remaining infrastructure. The cut off of coal delivery from mines in West Germany

---

[8]   Schulz, *Die Deutsche Bundesbahn*, 341 and 347.

[9]   Lothar Dernbach, 'Die Strategie DB '90. Entwicklung und Stand der Realisierung', *Journal des Eisenbahnwesens*, 36, 1985, 12–19.

[10]   Lothar Dernbach, 'Bahnreform '94 setzt Schlußstrich unter Staatsbahn-Ära. Maßnahmen zur Lageverbesserung in der Nachkriegszeit', *Jahrbuch der Eisenbahn* 1994/95, 116–54, here 154.

caused additional problems. High quality West German coal was replaced by brown coal with a lower caloric value. Moreover, funding for investment in new railways was consumed by the project of building railway networks around West Berlin – a project that went on until 1963. Berlin had been a railway hub until the separation of the Germanys, and now part of it was off limits to the East.

The Reichsbahn of the Democratic Republic became again – as it had been in the Nazi period – part of the Ministry of Transport. But now the economic planners undertook the attempt to plan the total transport demand, and to distribute it across the capacities of trains, ships and trucks.[11] In West Germany's free market society, the principle of competition guided transport policy. In East Germany, in contrast, transport was planned centrally and distributed among the different transport systems, which were organised as socialised or people-owned enterprises, *Volkseigene Betriebe*. This did not mean all competition between trains and trucks was abolished. Because short-distance transport created relatively high strain on the railway, because it was labour-intensive and costly, the Ministry of Transport enacted a reform of goods traffic in 1958. But compared with the Federal Republic, the Democratic Republic undertook only relatively minor innovations and modernisations in tracks and facilities. Not only that, its investments in the rail sector decreased between 1960 and 1988 from 9.8 per cent of all investments in the country to only 6.5 per cent. Unlike the Federal Republic, the Democratic Republic did not invest more than necessary, although the demand for transport increased. After 1965, the situation became a bit better for the Deutsche Reichsbahn: the railway was able to catch up in investments and modernisation.[12] But industry received comparatively much more investment. While in West Germany, electrification made speedy progress in the 1960s, East Germany did not start its electrification programme until the 1980s. On 21 February 1980, the Minister of Transport, Otto Arndt, spoke about electrification as the most important measure for rationalisation of the Reichsbahn. Nevertheless, it took the state more than half a year to present an action plan for the far-reaching use of electricity in the five-year plan for 1981 to 1985.[13] Because the total level of investment stayed the same while electrification was taking place, the Reichsbahn had to stop other projects, such as a fundamental modernisation and rationalisation of the Reichsbahn as a whole; the reconstruction of lines for higher speed; and the modernisation of the car stock. Finally, there was a lack of money for automatic

---

[11]   See Christopher Kopper, 'Die Deutsche Reichsbahn 1949–1989', in Gall and Pohl, *Die Eisenbahn in Deutschland*, 281–316, here 281–4 and 299–300, and Paul Olbrich, 'Permanente Struktur-Revolution der *Deutschen Reichsbahn*', in *SBZ-Archiv*, 6, 1955, 198–202.

[12]   Karl Hofmann, Ökonomik, Organisation und Planung der Eisenbahn (Berlin 1968), 148–50, and Kopper, ibid., 302 and 309–10.

[13]   Kopper, ibid., 312.

Figure 17.1   Travellers of the GDR in the Bavarian city of Hof, 1989
Source: Fotosammlung Deutsche Bahn Museum, 1989_NN171224a.

Figure 17.2   People of the GDR standing in queue for the 'welcome grant'
                (*Begrüßungsgeld*) at the railway station in the Bavarian city of Hof,
                1989
Source: Fotosammlung Deutsche Bahn Museum, 1989_NN184731.

switching and signalling systems. Because of all this, the Reichsbahn could not make use of the full potential that the electrification of the main lines offered.[14]

On the bright side, in East Germany, the competition with motor vehicles was much less harsh than in West Germany because of the state control of truck traffic. By law, all persons wishing to ship goods more than 50 kilometres had to request the service of railways. The railway's portion of the transport market stayed stable longer and did not shrink as rapidly as it did in West Germany. There was no rapid loss of staff and no closure of lines. But the costs for this policy were tremendous and had to be borne by the whole society. Moreover, the delay in investments and the inefficiency of the transport sector were among the problems that undermined the society of the Democratic Republic, contributing to its collapse in the late 1980s.

State and Railway in the Decade of Reunification and Liberalisation of Railway Transport

After the collapse of East Germany, the Bundesbahn and the Reichsbahn remained separate for a couple of years. Most politicians were very sceptical about the future of both companies and about railways in general. The staggering railway debts in West Germany and the tremendous delay in technical and organisational modernisation in East Germany provided good reasons for that view. No one would have imagined that a commission called together in 1989 would deliver a reform concept that would lead to a fundamentally new organisation of Germany's railway in January 1994. No one would have foreseen a successful transformation of the two sick dinosaurs into a single shareholder company led by a management convinced of the advantages of a free market transport economy and convinced that the money should not come primarily from the state but had to be earned on the market.[15]

The reform of the two railway companies and the problems of German reunification were closely linked. The Eastern railway was an explosive topic of discussions around the time of the 1990 reunification treaty. Many billions of marks were foreseen for far-reaching and costly investments in the railway network in the East. Necessary projects included through-going lines and large investments into the railway hub of the formerly divided capital of Berlin. After reunification, it was necessary to decrease the staff of the Reichsbahn from 500,000 to 250,000 employees within four years, and to develop a concept of how the railways should be organised in the future. For all these problems, the commission had to find solutions. Some figures shed light on the dimensions of the situation. The network of the Deutsche Reichsbahn was denser than that of the Bundesbahn – it was made

---

[14]   See Brian Rampp, *Verkehrswirtschaft Ostdeutschlands* (München 1993), 234–7.

[15]   See Hans-Peter Schwarz, 'Wiedervereinigung und Bahnreform 1989–1994', in Gall and Pohl, *Die Eisenbahn in Deutschland*, 377–418, here 378, and Gerd Aberle and Andrea Bermer, *Bahnstrukturreform in Deutschland. Ziele und Umsetzungsprobleme* (Cologne 1996).

up of no less than 14,000 kilometres of track, more than half as much as the Federal Republic's 27,000 kilometres. But this network was antiquated. Only 30 per cent had been electrified. Not more than 30 per cent had been expanded to a two track or multiple track system, while in West Germany, nearly 50 per cent was electrified and multiple tracked. On this old-fashioned network, twice as many people were transported per year as in the Federal Republic. One can imagine what this meant for the state of the tracks and facilities, and what renovation would cost.

A closer look at the deficit shows how dramatic the situation was. The Bundesbahn of the Federal Republic piled up a deficit of 9.4 billion marks each year, and the Reichsbahn of the former Democratic Republic contributed to this with an additional deficit of 6.1 billion per year. One could ask why it had taken so long for a fundamental reform, and why the situation needed to escalate that way, although the problems were very well known. There were many examples of other countries, such as the USA, Japan, Sweden and the United Kingdom, treating this problem by taking drastic measures like deregulation, and instating legislative conditions that allowed their railways to conform to the free market. One reason why this did not happen in Germany was probably the good economic development in the 1980s, which covered the railway debts in the state budget for a while. But at the end of the 1980s, speedily increasing debt directed attention to the problematic trend again. In September 1987, the Minister of Transport received a report by the US-based McKinsey & Company management consulting firm that caused a sensation. It was clear from the report that the market position of the Bundesbahn had permanently dropped, and had become worse since the 1960s. In the 1980s, it had reached only half of its former position in a growing transport market in passenger and goods traffic. The shrinking market position, according to the McKinsey report, resulted in principle in debt. Although the amount of debt was sometimes stable for a while, the railway budget had developed into a permanent burden of the state, and the problem could get worse. The media characterised this part of the report as revealing one of the worst dangers to the state budget. Under normal conditions, the railway would have had to declare bankruptcy at this time. And in the following years, the state was confronted with additional burdens of the Reichsbahn, not to mention the costs of reunification itself. Some extrapolations of the report's data to the next decade led to horrifying figures up to a deficit of 180 billion marks in 2001, and that moved the debate forward. A deficit of 180 billion marks would have required a total of 400 billion marks for the debt itself, for the management of the debt, for additional subsidies from the state budget and for new lines of credit.[16]

The prospect of joining the two railways caused further unsolvable problems. The stuff of the Reichsbahn was more numerous than the staff of the Bundesbahn,

---

[16]   McKinsey & Co., *Deutsche Bundesbahn. Neuordnung des DB-Konzerns. September 1987*. Historische Sammlung of the Deutsche Bahn AG, 01-01-0098. See also Gerd Aberle, *Zukunftsperspektiven der Deutschen Bundesbahn* (Heidelberg 1988). On the background see Schwarz, *Wiedervereinigung und Bahnreform*, 379–91.

although their network was only half as big. In total, both companies would have 500,000 employees. When officials of the government and members of the parliament calculated the costs for the salaries of all railway employees for the next decade, a second shock wave ran through the whole political body of Germany.

Besides politicians of the ministry and the parliament, two other groups fostered the debate: the Railway Commission called together by the government in 1990, and the boards of both the Bundesbahn and the Reichsbahn, which became unified in 1991 under the leadership of the charismatic entrepreneur Heinz Dürr. Dürr was later described as the father of the railway reform of 1993–94. Other leading figures in the railway reform included the four ministers of transport in the years between 1987 and 1993, Werner Dollinger, Friedrich Zimmermann, Günther Krause and Matthias Wissmann. The installation of the Railway Commission in February 1989 was one of the first consequences of the McKinsey report and a second internal report on the situation of railways. In the following years, the Commission and the united boards of both railways worked closely together. Initial analyses showed the situation was worse than expected. The income of the Bundesbahn sank dramatically. The need for more money skyrocketed to an additional 25 billion marks and was extrapolated to 40 billion in 1995. This was why the Commission presented the concept of a metamorphosis of the two German railways into one shareholder company at a very early point in time. The Commission argued that only under that condition would entrepreneurial leadership be possible.[17] The more the Commission and board analysed the situation, the more it became clear that fundamental reform was necessary so that the whole system would not break down. Two decades of reform debate without consequences now resolved into practical activities in the years between 1991 and 1993. Within only three years, the German railways were made ready for privatisation, a process that ended a tradition of state railways that had begun in 1879 (or 1920, the beginning of the national railway). An independent company was formed, named Deutsche Bahn AG. It was to be run like a private company, although the state owned it fully. But after a period of time and an 80 billion mark modernisation programme, the company prepared to gather its investment capital from its own profit, and to attract capital for investment on the stock exchange.

To go public, a lot had to be done in advance. Everyone could see the problems of the *Bundesbahn* and its railway stations, which were in serious need of modernisation, in contrast to the country's modern, comfortable airports. So the goals for a 'Renaissance of the Railway Station' were presented in an attractive catalogue combined with an exhibition that moved from city to city, expressing the vision of what twenty-first century railway stations should be, including comfort and shops like in airports. The advantage would be to offer both in the middle of cities. The renewal of railway stations was seen as one of the most important investments both for attracting new customers and for presenting a new image of the railways.

---

[17]   Ibid., 392–401.

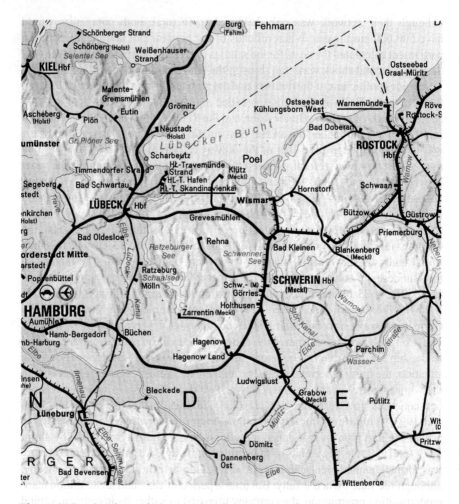

Figure 17.3   Section of the north of Germany of the official railway map
              (*Reisekarte*) of DB and DR, 1993

Note: The section shows dead ended railway lines alongside the former border between
FDR and GDR and the first restored through-going lines.

Source: DB Mobility Logistik, MG-18–13–1993.

For that reason it was decided to organise the real estate function of both railways –
their stations and land – as a special company, later named DB Immobile.[18]

---

[18]   See Bund Deutscher Architekten, Deutsche Bahn AG, Förderverein Deutsches
Architekturzentrum in cooperation with Meinhard von Gerkan (eds), *Renaissance der
Bahnhöfe. Die Stadt im 21. Jahrhundert* (no date and place of publication), and Schwarz,
Wiedervereinigung und Bahnreform, 407–408.

The state railways officially ended on 31 December 1993 and started their new career as a single company on 1 January 1994. The Deutsche Bahn AG is still owned by the state but is now managed independent of the state administration, like a private company. The process of privatisation has not yet been completed. But the success of the reform cannot be overlooked. The reform brought a solution for the speedy increase of deficits and debts. In 1997, the Deutsche Bahn AG made a profit for the first time, a profit of 245 million marks. This was not very much compared with the turnover of 30 billion and with a labour force of 230,000 employees, but the profits have steadily increased ever since. In its first three years, Deutsche Bahn AG invested 41 billion marks, and a further 81 billion were planned for the following years. Today the annual profit is around one billion Euros. But more important than the profit is probably how the railway looks today. The Deutsche Bahn has become visibly more modern. Many stations have been reconstructed and some new ones have been built. They are modern and attractive locations. The image is no longer that of a bankrupt state company.[19]

In 15 years, the Deutsche Bahn AG invested in new, modern technology, and it modernised tracks and railway stations, trains and locomotives. The number of employees declined from nearly 500,000 to 230,000; they run service on a shrinking network. But at the same time, new strategic lines have been constructed for high-speed travel. The Deutsche Bahn has transported an increasing number of passengers and an increasing amount of goods. And important international activities have led to a diversification of the staff, with 1 per cent located outside Germany.

Bibliography

Aberle, Gerd and Bermer, Andrea, *Bahnstrukturreform in Deutschland. Ziele und Umsetzungsprobleme* (Cologne 1996).

Aberle, Gerd, *Zukunftsperspektiven der Deutschen Bundesbahn* (Heidelberg 1988).

Bund Deutscher Architekten, Deutsche Bahn AG, Förderverein Deutsches Architekturzentrum in co-operation with Meinhard von Gerkan (eds.) Renaissance der Bahnhöfe. Die Stadt im 21. Jahrhundert (no date and place of publication).

Dernbach, Lothar, 'Bahnreform '94 setzt Schlußstrich unter Staatsbahn-Ära. Maßnahmen zur Lagerverbesserung in der Nachkriegszeit', *Jahrbuch der Eisenbahn* 1994/95, 116–54.

Dernbach, Lothar, 'Die Strategie DB '90. Entwicklung und Stand der Realisierung', *Journal des Eisenbahnwesens* 36, 1985, 12–19.

Hofmann, Karl, Ökonomik, Organisation und Planung der Eisenbahn (Berlin 1968).

---

[19]   Ibid., 416–17.

Kopper, Christopher, 'Die Deutsche Reichsbahn 1949–1989', in Lothar Gall and Manfred Pohl (eds), *Die Eisenbahn in Deutschland. Von den Anfängen bis zur Gegenwart* (Munich 1999), 281–316.

McKinsey & Co., *Deutsche Bundesbahn. Neuordnung des DB-Konzerns. September 1987.* Historische Sammlung of the Deutsche Bahn AG, 01-01-0098.

Müller, Marlene, *Die Finanzkrise der Deutschen Bundesbahn, ihre Ursachen und Sanierungsmöglichkeiten* (Innsbruck 1958).

Nicholls, Anthony James, 'Zusammenbruch und Wiederaufbau: Die Reichsbahn während der Besatzungszeit', in Lothar Gall and Manfred Pohl (eds), *Die Eisenbahn in Deutschland. Von den Anfängen bis zur Gegenwart* (Munich 1999) 245–79.

Olbrich, Paul, 'Permanente Struktur-Revolution der *Deutschen Reichsbahn*', *SBZ-Archiv* 6, 1955, 198–202.

Predöhl, Andreas, *Verkehrspolitik*, 2nd edn (Göttingen 1964).

Rampp, Brian, *Verkehrswirtschaft Ostdeutschlands* (München 1993).

Roth, Paul, 'Die deutsche Bundesbahn als Auftraggeberin der deutschen Wirtschaft', in *Die deutsche Bundesbahn und ihre Industrie* (Frankfurt am Main 1953), 63–71.

Sarter, Adolf and Kittel, Theodor, *Die Deutsche Bundesbahn. Ihr Aufbau und Arbeitsgrundlage* (Frankfurt am Main 1952).

Schulz, Günther, 'Die Deutsche Bundesbahn 1949–1989', in Lothar Gall and Manfred Pohl (eds), *Die Eisenbahn in Deutschland. Von den Anfängen bis zur Gegenwart* (München 1999), 317–76.

Schwarz, Hans-Peter, 'Wiedervereinigung und Bahnreform 1989–1994', in Lothar Gall and Manfred Pohl (eds), *Die Eisenbahn in Deutschland. Von den Anfängen bis zur Gegenwart* (München 1999), 377–418.

Weigelt, Horst and Lamper, Ulrich, *40 Jahre Deutsche Bundesbahn 1949–1989* (Darmstadt 1989).

Chapter 18

Seen from the Driving Cab: The Consequences of German Railway's Privatisation since the Reunion of Deutsche Bundesbahn and Reichsbahn from the Engine Drivers' Perspective

Peter F.N. Hörz and Marcus Richter[1]

Looking over the Driver's Shoulder

In former times, notes the man in the blue waistcoat, assuming a casual attitude as he drives the *Regionalexpress* from Stuttgart to Würzburg, the bushes at the right and left hand side of the track used to be cut down regularly.[2] Today, however, the green stuff sometimes grows into the clearance gauge, and it is the job of an engine driver to report any greenery growing too close to the overhead lines.[3] Because of this uncontrolled growth along the track it had become more difficult to concentrate on the track, and driving not less safe, but more challenging for the engine driver.

---

[1]   A similar chapter had been published under the title '"Die Bahn macht mobil": Zum Berufsbild des Lokomotivführers im Kontext des liberalisierten Schienenverkehrsmarktes', in I. Götz, B. Lemberger, K. Lehnert and S. Schondelmayer (eds), *Mobilität und Mobilisierung: Arbeit im sozioökonomischen und kulturellen Wandel* (Frankfurt and New York 2010), 259–78.

[2]   Since driving cabs in most of new Deutsche Bahn railcar trains are separated only by glass doors from passenger compartments, engine drivers' workflow can be observed directly by interested passengers. In doing so, it becomes obvious, as in the scene outlined, that modern trains can be driven safely even in apparently relaxed postures: legs crossed or resting on briefcases or spatial structures of the cab, coffee in a paper cup stored next to the auxiliary equipment – all this indicates that train driving is possible under circumstances where any motorcar would end up in the ditch.

[3]   Clearance gauge is the space between moving railway vehicles and fixed structures along the track (e.g. buildings or vegetation). By making the growing stress a subject of complaints, engine drivers imply that rail operations could become less safe, because they cannot concentrate solely on their essential task – driving the train safely.

Figure 18.1   Driving cab of a German narrow-gauge steam locomotive, late 1930s

Note: The locomotive 99 6001 belonged to Harzer Schmalspurbahnen of the former Deutsche Reichsbahn of the GDR. Technical competences guaranteed by long and intensive training periods enable drivers and stokers to keep control over a technical system, which was mostly based on mechanics.

Source: Photo taken by the author Peter F. Hörz in May 2010.

The growth on both sides of the track may, even from the drivers' perspective, be of only marginal importance. At the same time, the complaints about neglect or delay of regular clearing indicate a subjective feeling of harder working conditions, since increasing difficulties on the track are only some of a multitude of engine drivers' experiences which reflect the development the Deutsche Bahn (DB) has been through during the last 15 years. In engine drivers' narratives as well as in those of railway managers, these developments always evolve between the space between 'former times' and 'today'. The turning point between these two poles is marked by 1 January 1994, the date when railway reforms came into force and Eastern Reichsbahn and Western Bundesbahn were reunited as the stock corporation Deutsche Bahn AG (DB AG). 'Former times' means the golden age of governmentally structured railways in East and West Germany.[4] In concrete terms, that golden age provided more social benefits, higher real income, longer recovery, layover and relay times, less pressure in general and, including on the technical side, better working conditions. 'In former times' there were up to 15 years' development time for new trains, more passing capacities, more vehicles on standby, more personnel on standby duty, more interchange stations and more points, better infrastructure in general, and, consequently, rail operations which were less stressful for the staff. However, from the perspective of a DB AG deputy manager who remembers an average railway cruising speed of less than 50 kilometres per hour and long coffee breaks due to irregular demand-oriented time tables, 'in former times' primarily means inefficiency, laziness and waste.[5]

The conflict sketched out so far has been deepening over the years, and has been occurring in many companies in the course of the transition to a 'Culture of a New Capitalism' as described by Richard Sennett.[6] However, the changes are all the more drastic from the point of view of the employees of the DB, because with the railways we are not only witnessing a change from old into new entrepreneurial structures but a transformation from state-run to entrepreneurial structures. Moreover, this transformation from an entity run by cameralistic administration

---

[4] Primarily caused by proprietary considerations, state-run GDR railway retained the company name Deutsche Reichsbahn which has been established during Weimar Republic and has been used in the days of Third Reich, too. Since railway workers played an important role in the development of German labour movement, and because of political patronisation of railway as a means of public and industrial transportation according to energy political reasons, the railway and its employees enjoyed particular reputation in GDR – much more higher than in the FRG where a strongly increasing automobilisation facilitated a change-over of transportation of goods and people from track to road.

[5] Conversation with a deputy of Deutsche Bahn middle management held by Peter Hörz in February 2007.

[6] R. Sennett, *The Corrosion of Character: The Personal Consequences of Work in the New Capitalism* (New York 1998), and R. Sennett, *The Culture of the New Capitalism* (New Haven and London 2006).

Figure 18.2   Looking over the driver's shoulder in a Deutsche Bahn class 612 diesel railcar

Note: Since the electronic systems of the vehicle must not be influenced by the driver his ability to take over control in case of technical problems is very limited.

Source: Photo taken by the author Peter F. Hörz in April 2009.

into a global player in the fields of mobility, networks and logistics preparing to go public on the stock market has taken place only in the last 15 years.[7]

So far, sociological and economic investigations have illuminated the process of liberalisation of the German railway market only on a macro level.[8] If they

---

[7]   Since the second step of German Railway Reform has come into force in 1999, the company Deutsche Bahn is operating as a multi-level holding which appears, according to the business divisions engaged in, as 'DB – Mobility. Networks. Logistics'.

[8]   See H. Hüning and U. Stodt, 'Regulierte Desintegration: Aspekte des internen Arbeitsmarktes der Deutschen Bahn', in H.M. Nickel, S. Völker and H. Hüning (eds), *Transformation – Unternehmensreorganisation – Geschlechterforschung* (Opladen 1999), 175–203; M. Frey, H. Hüning and H.M. Nickel, 'Unternehmen Zukunft – Börsenbahn? Beschleunigte Vermarktlichung, regulierte Desintegration und betriebliche Geschlechterpolitik', in T. Edeling, W. Jann, D. Wagner, and C. Reichard (eds), *Öffentliche Unternehmen: Entstaatlichung und Privatisierung?* (Opladen 2001), 125–55; T. Edeling, W. Jann, D. Wagner and C. Reichard, *Subjektivierung, Verunsicherung, Eigensinn: Auf der Suche nach Gestaltungspotentialen für eine neue Arbeits- und Geschlechtspolitik* (Berlin 2008); T. Engartner, 'Bahnwesen im Niedergang: Die (kapital)marktorientierte Neuvermessung des Schienenverkehrs in Deutschland und Großbritannien', in C.

inquire about it at all, researchers curious about the micro-effects of this process have only taken into consideration those employees that are directly involved with the new DB leitmotiv of customer orientation, the ones working in the service trenches.[9] But the engine drivers have been cut out of these investigations, though they see themselves and are seen by others as being on the front lines of rail transport service, and though they are considered by DB to be working in a most important 'job family'.[10] And this has happened despite the fact that their field of responsibility, their training, their workflow and their workplace have all changed dramatically in the 15 years since the reunion of the two German railways. There is, on the other hand, an astonishingly large number of popular memoirs and reminiscences from what is only now seen as the golden age of steam engines.[11] At the same time the engine drivers' profession has been made a subject of numerous books explaining their workflow and workplace in a more or less profound way to young and old railway enthusiasts.[12]

With our contribution we cannot balance out the paucity of social science investigations into the engine drivers' profession and the transformations it has recently been through. We can, however, shed a small light on the profession and on the consequences of the market orientation that was introduced by the railway reform following the reunion of the East German Reichsbahn and the West German Bundesbahn. At the centre of our investigation is the person of the engine driver in his socioeconomic and political contexts, in his cultural practices and his self-perceptions. The starting point of our thoughts has been the changing structures both of the DB AG and of the professional practice of engine drivers. We critically

---

Butterwegge, B. Lösch and R. Ptak (eds), *Neoliberalismus: Analysen und Alternativen* (Wiesbaden 2008), 277–97; T. Engartner, *Die Privatisierung der Deutschen Bahn:* Über *die Implementierung marktorientierter Verkehrspolitik* (Wiesbaden 2008).

[9] See the contributions in W. Dunkel and G.G. Voß (eds), *Dienstleistung als Interaktion: Beiträge aus einem Forschungsprojekt: Altenpflege, Deutsche Bahn, Call Center* (Munich and Mering 2004).

[10] Deutsche Bahn AG (ed.), *Personal- und Sozialbericht 2001* (Berlin 2002), 26. The account is published on the website of *Deutsche Bahn*: http://www.deutschebahn.com/site/shared/de/dateianhaenge/berichte/personalbericht_2001.pdf (last accessed 15 May 2010). A job family is a cluster of jobs which are characterised by similar types of work, types of training, skills, knowledge and expertise.

[11] See e.g. H. Arnold, *Von der Dampfromantik zum 'Swiss-Express': Als SBB-Lokomotivführer erlebt* (Chur 1986); J. Kretschmann, *Feuer, Wasser, Kohle – Ein Lokführer erinnert sich* (Berlin 1988); A. Katzenbeisser, *Zwischen Dampf und Diesel: Meine Ausbildung zum Lokführer 1956–1965* (Vienna, Cologne and Graz 1988); A.-W. Aufderheide, *Bremszettelmemoiren: Erinnerungen und Bilder aus dem Lokführeralltag* (Lübbecke 1995), and A. Richter and K. Richter, *Großvater und sein Dampfroß: Aus dem Leben eines königlich-sächsischen Dampflokführers* (Stuttgart 1999).

[12] See e.g. M. Weltner (ed.), *Beruf Lokführer: Hintergründe und Fakten – Ein Traumberuf in Geschichte und Gegenwart* (Munich 2005), and K. Haderer, *Der Lokomotivführer* (Munich 2009).

evaluated German-language resources describing the profession of the engine driver and gained insight into the everyday work routines and self-perceptions of engine drivers by carrying out five two-hour-long narrative interviews.

Profession and Professionals

According to the German sociologist Max Weber, a profession or occupation should be understood as 'the mode of specialisation, specification, and combination of the functions of an individual in so far as it constitutes for him the basis of continuous opportunity for income or earnings.'[13] Nevertheless, as Weber argued elsewhere, a profession is not only for breadwinning but is also a calling that takes over one's whole life and acts as an important fulfilment of duties.[14] Profession as a vocation? This formula, moulded by the Protestant work ethic, is applied to the engine driver in the DB's documents as well as by the public and by the engine drivers themselves.

'But what is it about the profession of the engine driver that holds such a great attraction?'[15] The question appears in a 1964 Schweizer Bundesbahnen (SBB) brochure. What shapes the specific professional profile of an engine driver? What ennobles the engine driver as the 'King of the Track', as he is seen in popular literature?[16] The SBB answers:

> The man in the cabin can only rely on himself. This means, of course, a great deal of responsibility, as he has been entrusted with the lives of numerous people. Undoubtedly, there are negative aspects of the profession such as the irregular working hours. But a profession like that offers great satisfaction to those who love it with heart and soul.[17]

This exposition brings up two central characteristics of the profession. The man at the front of the train has to fend for himself for long periods of his professional day-to-day performance, and at the same time bears responsibility for passengers and machine by dealing with technical systems.[18]

---

[13]   M. Weber, *Economy and Society: An Outline of Interpretive Sociology* (Berkeley 1978), 140.

[14]   See M. Weber, *The Protestant Ethic and the Spirit of Capitalism* (London and New York 1992), 39–50.

[15]   Schweizerische Bundesbahnen (ed.), *Wie werde ich Lokomotivführer?* (1964).

[16]   Weltner, *Beruf Lokführer*, 113.

[17]   Schweizerische Bundesbahnen, *Lokomotivführer?* (1964).

[18]   Because of the great responsibility they carry, engine drivers – like pilots and doctors – are rated by German insurance companies as an occupational group with an extraordinary liability risk.

In a more sober way, but similar in its core statements, the profession is presented by the DB in its 'Competence Profile for Track Engine Drivers' for the year 2000. Along with the specific tasks, there is a demand for the 'ability to cope with emotional pressure', 'a sense of responsibility', 'conscientiousness', 'reliability' and 'identification with the profession'.[19] In these occupational profiles, responsibility, irregular working hours and extraordinary pressure are burdens which are described as only manageable with the help of a moral and professional commitment. The strains must be coped with as a unique aspect of the profession, and they are contrasted with those of other professions. From the 29-year-old engine driver Christoph F., we learn that this profession requires 'enthusiasm' and that the work in the cabin offers 'satisfaction'. But not only that: Though he could be earning more money doing something else, F. would again choose the profession that he has chosen:

> I think all railroaders, even if they deny it (...) without a hankering, you can't do this job. It's a good business for enthusiasts who do their job with conviction and passion, and, last but not least, as a vocation. On the balance, someone working on the Daimler assembly line earns the same, but has more leisure time and less responsibility. Whether this job satisfies him in the same way, is something completely different. And, of course, each person must sort this out for himself. Nevertheless, I would decide for the job over and over again. It's just great. There are little things: Driving into the rising sun, or into the setting sun, yeah, just things like that (...).

Asked what prerequisites he thinks are necessary to be an engine driver, F. says, 'You have to be born for it.'

On a superficial level, this and a number of similar expressions show the drivers' close relationship to the profession, their technical expertise, their experience of working at irregular times in shifts, at weekends and on public holidays. At the same time they reflect identification, a need for distinction and self-legitimisation, especially in combination with criticism of the situation at the Deutsche Bahn. There should be no doubt about the fact that the engine drivers consider themselves the true productive workforce of the *Bahn*, as Christoph F. explains:

> The system only works because people are still more involved than they have to be. If this involvement went down one day the system would collapse. Because the railway still depends on its people. Actually, if all railroaders would work according to their regular requirements as written in their labour agreement we wouldn't have to go on strike anymore because the system would collapse on its own.

---

[19]   Deutsche Bahn AG (ed.), *Personal- und Sozialbericht 2001* (Berlin 2002), 26.

Such seemingly self-confident statements of indispensable professionals contrast with others in which the development of the company *Bahn* and the profession of the engine drivers are portrayed as being in decline. Rudolf P., who has passed through all stages of the profession since he has started his career as a fireman on a steam locomotive of GDR Reichsbahn in the 1960s, complains that today, faced with the modern engine types, the 'railway-specific' characteristics of the *Bahn* are being lost:

> This has nothing whatsoever to do with railway. The whole issue isn't so railway specific-anymore, I'd say. Just because, in former times (...) A locomotive is a locomotive: You had passenger cars behind you. You didn't have contact with passengers, you were on your own, or with a fellow. And today, you are sitting in the driving cab with all the people directly behind you. In some ways it's like driving a bus. Of course, it's not a bus, it's a railroad train, but everywhere there is electronics, and sometimes it doesn't work, and all you can do is be annoyed.

As we have seen, P. compares the new engine types with busses and reports from the times when they were introduced in the second half of the 1990s:

> There was one colleague who resigned because he couldn't cope. He said, 'This has got nothing to do with railway anymore. I'm not a bus driver!'[20]

There is more to those superficially humorous remarks than meets the eye. With the introduction of a new generation of engines came a devaluation of the vast technical knowledge older engine drivers naturally still have at their disposal, but which plays no role in the age of electronics. Against this background, even the dirty steam engine, responsible for numerous profession-related illnesses, is remembered in a positive light. Werner D., who was trained in his profession on a steam locomotive, states:

> With a steam locomotive you knew what was wrong. There was no defect you couldn't see. But if something goes wrong nowadays the engine driver can't do anything. Nobody can control modern electronics (...).

As a consequence both of the lower technical competences engine drivers are trained for and of the increasing computerisation, the engine drivers' ability to take over control in case of technical failure and to fix the problem has been reduced. Rudolf P. clarifies:

---

[20] Modern railcar trains operating in German regional traffic are not only not taken seriously as 'trains', and sometimes critically, sometimes ironically considered as 'motorbuses' by engine drivers, but are indeed partly constructed out of components which normally are used by the lorry construction industry (e.g. railcars of DB series 628, 641, and 650).

In former times, you knew exactly what kind of technology was inside the engine. If anything didn't work, normally you could help yourself. That's how we've been raised, how we've been trained. And today you are just trained in basic knowledge, no more, no less. And if anything doesn't work, there's nothing you can do, because of all the electronics. In former times, we were punished when we broke down on the track. Today that's not happening anymore, just because, mostly, it's not your fault. It's all electronics that doesn't work, and then you get stuck.

Instead of being able to help themselves in case of a defect as they used to, engine drivers today can only alert the dispatcher and call for the breakdown service. D.'s plain analysis:

> If anything goes wrong with the railcar there is not much we can do ourselves. There is a checklist for looking for defects which you have to follow and either it works again or not. And if not, you have to call for a reserve locomotive to tow you away.[21]

This reflects a policy put into action a few years ago: the DB devalued the profession of the track engine driver by making the old technical qualifications unnecessary, reducing responsibilities, and focusing the drivers' concentration on the engine and its functions. Up until the middle of the 1990s, the precondition for becoming an engine driver was a professional training as a machine fitter. Today, anyone who has a secondary school qualification and who has passed an aptitude test can start to train as an engine driver. The engine drivers consider these changes not only a devaluation of their profession but also a downward shift of the *Bahn* system as a whole. Trade unionists call it an attack targeting the qualifications of engine drivers.[22]

---

[21]   In any situation in which technical failure occurs in modern railcar trains, especially in the execution of a checklist such as mentioned by Werner D., a particular problem crops up in regard to the *interaction of man and machine*. *This problem* has been discussed by Lisanne Bainbridge in respect to the increasing automation of technical systems in general. Engine drivers of modern railcars primarily operate and monitor the railcar system, which usually operates correctly and mostly operates autonomously. However, they do not control the machine actively. Their limited training and the system's complexity prevent any profound insight into the computerised system. Thus, in the event that something goes wrong, engine drivers are able neither to take control immediately nor to find and fix the defect quickly – if ever. Instead, they have to execute a checklist step by step to gain insight into how the system is running and to get an idea of what might be wrong. So when the system breaks down, knowledge and skills are becoming necessary that are not required in normal operations, and, at the same time, knowledge and skills, which require costly special training and therefore have been aspired to, pare down by automation. See L. Bainbridge, 'Ironies of automation', *Automatica*, 19, 1983, 775–79.

[22]   Accounting for the gradual reduction of occupational qualifications since railway reform has come into force, the German railway worker union (*Gewerkschaft Deutscher*

As engine drivers readily concede, as the new engine types have been brought into service, their job has become undoubtedly cleaner, quieter and altogether physically less stressful than it was in the days of steam traction or older types of diesel locomotives. However, driving a train evokes a new type of stress, unconnected to driving the vehicle or to solving technical problems, but resulting from greater proximity to the passengers. Formerly, the engine driver concentrated only on controlling and driving the train. He was not disturbed by the fireman working next to him in the steam locomotive cab, nor by the shaking of the vehicle or its massive noise level. Today's engine drivers, though, are directly faced with the passengers and their requests. The driving cab in most of new Deutsche Bahn railcar trains is separated only by a glass door from passenger compartments, and regional trains, more and more frequently, are operated without any conductors. Thus, in case of delay, malfunctions or problems with the ticket machine, the engine driver is the only contact person travellers can ask for information or help:

> Driving a railcar train is much less difficult than driving a steam locomotive. But in a way, it's more stressful, because drivers have become closer to the passengers, and because they often drive alone, which was never the case in the past, when there was always at least one attendant on each train. So now, when the train is delayed the travellers want information: 'Will we reach our connection?' If there is no train attendant, where do they go? To the engine driver! That's normal, that's understandable. They want to know whether I'm going to reach all the connecting trains. So that's a bit nerve-racking (...) You have to drive the train, pay attention to your driving and to the track, which is, of course, still your primary responsibility. Anyway, passengers want to be informed. All you can say in such a situation is, 'Just a moment, while I'm driving, I can't take care of anything else. I can do only one thing at a time!' Maybe I can call the dispatcher and tell him: 'I have travellers who want to reach their next train.' And maybe you receive information via text message, eventually: 'Connection granted!' or 'Not granted!' There's nothing else I can do.[23]

Lokomotivführer, GDL) persistently criticizes a 'narrow gauge apprenticeship' which is only orientated to necessities and which restricts the engine drivers' skills more and more. From trade unionists' perspective, a return to high qualification standards is absolutely necessary. See the GDL's statement at http://www.gdl.de (last accessed 15 May 2010).

[23]   Since the *Technikbasierte Abfertigungsverfahren* (TAV), a system of computer-aided train dispatch has set the technical conditions. Not only relatively easily observable small railcar trains can be operated *only* by the engine driver, but regional trains consisting of a locomotive and up to five (double-decker) coaches carrying hundreds of passengers can, too. So train conductors, of whom formerly at least one had to be on board each train monitoring the platform, closing the doors or signalling the engine driver before departure that all doors have been cleared, are not needed urgently anymore. Where required by public contractors ordering regional traffic, the TAV, furthermore, has made it possible to employ less-qualified and therefore lower-paid conductors to attend trains without having any operational tasks.

As indicated in these descriptions by Werner D., aside from transformations in the profession of the engine driver enforced on the level of man and machine, engine drivers are witnessing changes in interpersonal interactions, too. These changes are not only a function of the engine drivers' greater proximity to travellers caused by the design of new railcar trains and the abolition of train attendants. They are also about the relationships between the engine drivers and the railway administration. Despite the fact that the range of engine drivers' duties has increased, they do not seem to be treated as competent partners by the higher levels of the DB management. Instead, claims Rudolf P., they are treated as an economic liability:

> If you have a personal contact person, you can speak face to face, you feel much better than dealing with someone by phone, over long distances, without knowing the guy at the other end of the line. There was a time when you really didn't know the man you were talking to on the phone. Today it's getting better (...) Today you know him, you know with whom you are speaking. Nowadays things have changed. But when he's directly on site, it's totally different. If he is around you, you can say: 'You are a fool, stop doing things like that, do it this way!' Of course, you can't talk like that to your boss. Anyway, it's different – the personal contact. For instance, think about personnel matters, the personnel office: Today they're all located in Leipzig. And, actually, they don't have any overview. For them, you're merely a number, nothing else. You have your personnel number, that's all (...) There is no more face-to-face communication (...) It's a big company where all this doesn't count anymore.

Although the Deutsche Bahn and trade unions unanimously emphasise the key role of the engine driver in the railway system, there is little opportunity for drivers to get involved in decision-making by telling their officials about their practical experiences. In addition to that, the engine drivers' autonomy has been sharply restricted. Engine drivers obey orders from distant dispatchers and are supervised through a combination of signalling, punctual automatic train running and radio messages.[24] And that is still not all: On all high-speed tracks, engine drivers are in charge only of supervision, rather than driving per se. There is no doubt that trains without drivers are no longer a question of feasibility, but are prevented only by the lack of acceptance from train passengers.

At their workplace, engine drivers experience their profession as a kind of double act combining the roles of remotely controlled puppets and single-combat fighters. They see themselves as puppets because the larger number of responsibilities does not cover the tasks of a 'driver', and because their expertise

---

[24]   Punctual automatic train running is a technical system controlling trains by magnetic induction, which is why it is also called inductive train control. For instance, if an engine driver does not slow the train according to a displayed speed limit or did not acknowledge a signal by pushing a kind of biased off-switch, the train is braked to a halt automatically.

as machinists is no longer needed. They see themselves as fighters in single combat because they meet fewer and fewer colleagues working in and around the train. In trains without conductors, engine drivers have to take over their tasks, as well as more and more of the duties formerly carried out by the technical staff concerning the preparation and final inspection of the train. The start and end of work as well as the handing over of the railcar trains has increasingly been individualised. Werner D. complains:

> It's often said: 'The company remains one unit – one *Bahn*!' In former times it was one *Bahn*! You knew your dispatcher, just because you had to deal with him face to face before and after every shift. Nowadays you're alone with the railcar. Almost nobody is at the stations anymore. You look out of your window and start driving. You're on your own. You have to do the work that used to be carried out by others, by colleagues who did the groundwork. Today this is all your business. You're your own pump attendant. Before you take over the train, you have to check the brakes, which was done by a coach inspector in the past. At the platform there was a colleague for monitoring and signalling departure. Today that's all your business. Furthermore, there is no train attendant, that's your business, too. There are lots of things like this. Tasks and responsibilities which had been loaded onto several shoulders in former times are yours alone today (...) Without being paid more, you're doing other people's work.

Whereas in former times engine drivers had interacted with colleagues being responsible for locomotive control, station surveillance and train attending, nowadays it is only the engine driver who has to carry out most of these tasks. Rudolf P. says:

> When you're on a normal shift, you get a slip of paper containing everything you have to do. Your train number; whether you are being relieved; if you have to put away the engine, or if you have to refuel (...) And if all this works according to plan, there's no reason to talk with anyone all day.

But not only in day-to-day work engine drivers are experiencing a level of individualisation they did not have to consider before: one further example is the planning and organisation of their career within the company. In the times of state railways every engine driver could hope to climb the ladder, driving passenger or high-speed trains, after he had passed his exam and done 10,000 kilometres of freight train duty without any forced braking. Today, in consequence of the breaking up of the Deutsche Bahn into different divisions, each engine driver is forced to take career planning into his own hands, as we learn from Christoph F.'s insight:

> You have to apply in the corporate division, if you want to move, as I moved, for example, from regional traffic to long-distance traffic. You have to make

an application. You will have an interview. You have to pass through a kind of assessment centre where you're asked about your knowledge. What kind of qualifications do you have? What do you offer? What further qualifications do you think you might need for the job you are applying for? The employer wants to know whether he has to invest in you. Of course, it also depends on how you sell yourself in an interview, as is common on the free market. How do I promote myself? Indeed, you have to commit yourself. If you really want to go further, you have to tell yourself: 'Okay, I'm going to apply, I'm going to take care of myself!'

Because punctuality and reliability at the beginning of each shift as well as driving without forced braking are now basic conditions for the profession of the engine driver, there is little room for distinction. Drivers are also unable to increase turnover, productivity or customer satisfaction. Their only opportunity to deliver superior performance is to drive in an energy-efficient way. Due to the fact that there is no hope of automatic career advancement as a result of good performance, each engine driver has to ask himself in which DB division or in which non-state railway company he wants to work if he wants to try to climb the career ladder. This leads to demands for mobility, flexibility and self-promotion, none of which was necessary in the age of the state railway.[25]

Conclusion

Seen from the driving cab, the market-oriented reform of the Deutsche Bahn carried out since the reunion of the two German railways in 1994 means more than a loss of income and habitual social benefits. For engine drivers, it means a sudden farewell to high technical qualification standards, long training periods and vast decision-making competence and authority. Today, they feel they have become mere operational assistants, carrying out instructions which they can barely influence. This development feels like a decline and is mainly subliminally lamented. At the same time it forces engine drivers to sing the song of songs of the reliable, trustworthy engine driver burdened with responsibility, when it comes to defending their income, justifying their choice of profession, and defending

---

[25] In other passages of the interview conducted with F., we learned that he sometimes has to finish his paperwork at home, because – today – at his workplace there's sometimes not enough time for it. Such developments, combined with the need for active career planning, can be interpreted as indicating that engine drivers, like many other workers, are increasingly affected by a development 'Towards a "self-entrepreneurial" work force', and are becoming so-called 'entreployees', to use the term of H.J. Pongratz and G.G. Voß, 'From employee to "entreployee": Towards a "self-entrepreneurial" work force?', *Concepts and Transformation*, 8, issue 3, 2003, 239–54.

the way they see themselves as professionals.[26] But the gap between the actual situation in the driving cab and the professional self-concept of the engine driver is widening, as it puts a strain on those qualities and qualifications that marked the profession of the engine driver as extraordinary during the first 160 years of German railway history. These qualities and qualifications are tending to become, if not completely obsolete, then at least less and less meaningful as the railways carry out their reforms.

For comprehensible business management reasons, the DB must rationalise the profession of the engine driver. However, the DB administration has so far found it impossible to contradict the image of these qualities and qualifications, mainly because the company also profits from this image of the engine driver as a highly qualified, competent and responsible specialist. For the engine drivers and their trade union representatives, but also for their employer, it is of vital importance that they are perceived not in their actual professional practice but in their former 'believed' reality built upon the way things used to be. This is important as long as the idea of an engine without a driver is not widely accepted. Because it is in the common interest of engine drivers and their employer not to destroy this legacy image of the engine driver, it is important that concurring employees' and employers' interests are ultimately dealt with without too much polarisation. At the same time, following Zygmunt Bauman, the engine drivers' work ethic (created by discourses from the Deutsche Bahn management, the engine drivers and the trade unions about the importance of the engine drivers' profession for the railway system, as well as about the burdens engine drivers carry day by day) can be read as an indication of the conflicts between the company DB AG and its employees, especially the engine drivers, which are caused by the transformation German railway recently went through:

> Whenever you hear people talking about ethics, you should be pretty sure that someone somewhere is dissatisfied with the way some other people behave and would rather have them behaving differently. Hardly ever has this advice made more sense than in the case of work ethic. Since it erupted into the European consciousness in the early stages of industrialisation, and in its many avatars throughout the twisted itinerary of modernity and 'modernisation', the work ethic served politicians, philosophers and preachers alike as a clarion call to, or

---

[26] A development similar to the one we have discussed concerning the engine drivers' profession, especially focusing on the changes in interactions between man and machine, as well as the gap between actual professional practice on the one hand and exterior public representation on the other hand, has been outlined by Ingo Matuschek and Frank Kleemann for the profession of pilots: see I. Matuschek and F. Kleemann, 'Simulator und Autopilot: Zur Virtualisierung der Pilotentätigkeit', in G. Herlyn, J. Müske, K. Schönberger and O. Sutter (eds), *Arbeit und Nicht-Arbeit: Entgrenzung und Begrenzung von Lebensbereichen und Praxen* (Munich and Mering 2009), 161–80.

an excuse for, attempts to uproot, by hook or by crook, the popular habit which they saw as the prime obstacle to the new brave world they intended to build.[27]

Regarding the engine drivers' position, this means that in the end, the ambiguity of their professional self-perception, fed by the narratives of reliability and responsibility on the one hand, and the decline of the *Bahn* and the profession on the other, highlights the qualifications of those who – under more difficult circumstances – still carry out this profession in a responsible and reliable way. This recalls the observation at the beginning about the wild growth along the track and its increasingly rare removal: despite the growth of the difficulties of their working conditions, the engine drivers who hold high the virtues of their profession still ensure the safe transportation of passengers and goods.

Bibliography

Arnold, H., *Von der Dampfromantik zum 'Swiss-Express': Als SBB-Lokomotivführer erlebt* (Chur 1986).

Aufderheide, A.-W., *Bremszettelmemoiren: Erinnerungen und Bilder aus dem Lokführeralltag* (Lübbecke 1995).

Bainbridge, L., 'Ironies of automation', *Automatica*, 19, 1983, 775–9.

Bauman, Z., *Work, Consumerism and the New Poor* (New York 2005).

Deutsche Bahn AG (ed.), *Personal- und Sozialbericht 2001* (Berlin 2002).

Dunkel, W. and Voß, G.G. (eds), *Dienstleistung als Interaktion: Beiträge aus einem Forschungsprojekt: Altenpflege, Deutsche Bahn, Call Center* (Munich and Mering 2004).

Edeling, T., Jann, W., Wagner, D. and Reichard, C., *Subjektivierung, Verunsicherung, Eigensinn: Auf der Suche nach Gestaltungspotentialen für eine neue Arbeits- und Geschlechtspolitik* (Berlin 2008).

Engartner, T., 'Bahnwesen im Niedergang: Die (kapital)marktorientierte Neuvermessung des Schienenverkehrs in Deutschland und Großbritannien', in C. Butterwegge, B. Lösch and R. Ptak (eds), *Neoliberalismus: Analysen und Alternativen* (Wiesbaden 2008), 277–97.

Engartner, T., *Die Privatisierung der Deutschen Bahn: Über die Implementierung marktorientierter Verkehrspolitik* (Wiesbaden 2008).

Frey, M., Hüning, H. and Nickel, H.M., 'Unternehmen Zukunft – Börsenbahn? Beschleunigte Vermarktlichung, regulierte Desintegration und betriebliche Geschlechterpolitik', in T. Edeling, W. Jann, D. Wagner and C. Reichard (eds), *Öffentliche Unternehmen: Entstaatlichung und Privatisierung?* (Opladen 2001), 125–55.

Haderer, K., *Der Lokomotivführer* (Munich 2009).

---

[27]   Z. Bauman, *Work, Consumerism and the New Poor* (New York 2005), 6.

Hörz, Peter F.N. and Richter, Marcus, '"Die Bahn macht mobil": Zum Berufsbild des Lokomotivführers im Kontext des liberalisierten Schienenverkehrsmarktes', in I. Götz, B. Lemberger, K. Lehnert and S. Schondelmayer (eds), *Mobilität und Mobilisierung: Arbeit im sozioökonomischen und kulturellen Wandel* (Frankfurt and New York 2010), 259–78.

Hüning, H. and Stodt, U., 'Regulierte Desintegration: Aspekte des internen Arbeitsmarktes der Deutschen Bahn', in H.M. Nickel, S. Völker and H. Hüning (eds), *Transformation–Unternehmensreorganisation–Geschlechterforschung* (Opladen 1999), 175–203.

Katzenbeisser, A., *Zwischen Dampf und Diesel: Meine Ausbildung zum Lokführer 1956–1965* (Vienna, Cologne and Graz 1988).

Kretschmann, J., *Feuer, Wasser, Kohle – Ein Lokführer erinnert sich* (Berlin 1988).

Matuschek, I. and Kleemann, F., 'Simulator und Autopilot: Zur Virtualisierung der Pilotentätigkeit', in G. Herlyn, J. Müske, K. Schönberger and O. Sutter (eds), *Arbeit und Nicht-Arbeit: Entgrenzung und Begrenzung von Lebensbereichen und Praxen* (Munich and Mering 2009), 161–80.

Pongratz, H.J. and Voß, G.G., 'From employee to "entreployee": Towards a "self-entrepreneurial" work force?', *Concepts and Transformation*, 8, issue 3, 2003, 239–54.

Richter, A. and Richter, K., *Großvater und sein Dampfroß: Aus dem Leben eines königlich-sächsischen Dampflokführers* (Stuttgart 1999).

Schweizerische Bundesbahnen (ed.), *Wie werde ich Lokomotivführer?* (1964).

Sennett, R., *The Corrosion of Character: The Personal Consequences of Work in the New Capitalism* (New York 1998).

Sennett, R., *The Culture of the New Capitalism* (New Haven and London 2006).

Weber, M., *Economy and Society: An Outline of Interpretive Sociology* (Berkeley 1978).

Weber, M., *The Protestant Ethic and the Spirit of Capitalism* (London and New York 1992).

Weltner, M. (ed.), *Beruf Lokführer: Hintergründe und Fakten – Ein Traumberuf in Geschichte und Gegenwart* (Munich 2005).

Chapter 19

The Reopening of Murska Sobota–Zalalövő Railway: A Paradox of the European Reunification in Central Europe?

Kevin Sutton

Reopening a railway axis is not only a technical choice. It can be seen as a spatial event, due to its important political signification. Transport axes do not present structuring effects by their own being. Their appropriations by political sphere offer more than a technical event, particularly when it takes place in a border changing context. From a historical point of view, the railway carries a political speech. A present illustration of it is the reopening of the Murska Sobota–Hodos–Zalalövő-Railway axis between Slovenia and Hungary.

The reopening of this railway in 2001 takes sense in a regional geopolitical context characterised by the European integration of the two countries. The original railway line had been opened in 1907, during the imperial era, to provide maritime access for the central part of the Habsburg empire. This fact has to be put in its railway context: the first years of the twentieth century saw the openings of several routes in what is now Slovenian territory, for example, the Karawanken axis. All these routes defined a kind of railway convergence to this space, identifying it as a territorial articulation in the empire peripheries. The post-Second World War era changed the position of the railway net into a kind of an unstructured in-between, in association with the reorganisation of maritime transport.

Since 1968, after a while without traffic following the Second World War, the former line was closed. Then, the single railway axis from Slovenia to Hungary and Central Europe passed through Croatia and Murakeresztur. Thus activities to re-establish the Hodos line were started in the 1980s. Nevertheless, in 1991, the young Slovenian state and its own strategic maritime gate of Koper did not get a logistical way in parallel with its political independence.

Geopolitical changes of the 1990s offered a new background to this question. Both the Slovenian and Hungarian states began to study ways to reconstruct the axis. But the decisive event was the announced European integration and the associated financial and technical help.

The European programmatic choice to go along with the bi-national project seems to interrogate the cohesion of the new European Union space (Figure 19.1). It directly deals with the question of the border dynamic, as a management of the inherited border from the era when the EU had only 15 members, as well as

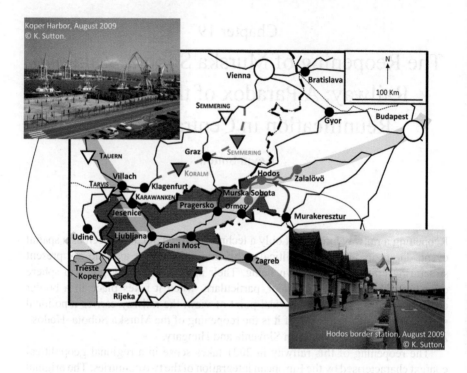

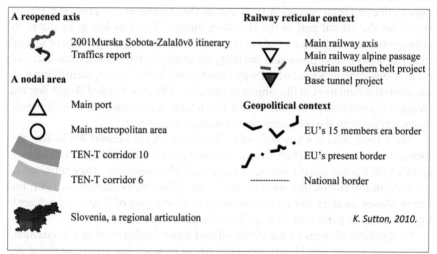

A reopened axis

〰 2001Murska Sobota-Zalalövö itinerary
   Traffics report

A nodal area

△ Main port

◯ Main metropolitan area

▨ TEN-T corridor 10

▨ TEN-T corridor 6

⬛ Slovenia, a regional articulation

Railway reticular context

—— Main railway axis
▽ Main railway alpine passage
   Austrian southern belt project
▼ Base tunnel project

Geopolitical context

〜 EU's 15 members era border

⌐ EU's present border

------ National border

K. Sutton, 2010.

Figure 19.1   The reopening of Murska Sobota–Zalalövő Railway through its reticular and territorial-associated recomposition

Source: Illustration created by author.

the adaptation to the new needs of the inner territorial coherence. The reopened axis is, indeed, parallel to the present border with Croatia. So that, in a way, the reopening of this railway appears as a mirror of the regional competitive context. But does it not appear more as an introduction to the paradoxical railway context?

The Railway Reopening as a Mirror of a Regional Competitive Context

One of the main issues associated with the Slovenian railway's background is the distribution of maritime traffic to and from Koper harbour. The different modernisation projects, still in progress in the southern part of the national network, show it. The maritime traffic has really exploded in this port, although the site is quite reduced (Figure 19.1), so the strategic stake for this growing dynamic is the free flow of the outgoing continental itineraries.[1] This issue is thrown out until the cross-border facilities question. But the previous obligation to transport goods through Croatia in order to access Central European markets was not the surest way to assure this free flow of traffic or the continuity, of the relations.

The first analyses of the traffic structure passing through the 'reinvented' railway axis shows the political dimension of the project. The reopening did not lead to more traffic. The quantity of cargo transported by rail between Slovenia and Hungary has decreased since 2001. A traffic report from the Croatian line to the Slovenian passage happened. This report has been encouraged, since 2001, by special price reductions offered to transport firms for using the new line.[2] Slovenia made a frame agreement with the Slovakian railway to attract traffic to Italy over the Tarvisio Pass. Mutual agreements for transporting services from Ukraine and Romania have been signed too.[3] The idea is really, on the one hand, to assert the new axis as the Central European way to an Adriatic harbour, and, at the same time, to attract new traffic to Koper.

Two competitors are facing Koper: Rijeka and Trieste. The new logistical situation reveals the marginalisation of the Croatian competitor, enforced by Slovenian integration in the EU on 1 May 2004. The 'European reunification' is

---

[1]   Different articles present the evolution of the traffic in the harbour of Trieste. The most recent one we can indicate is A. Beyer and J.C. Savin, 'Les ports-frontières de Trieste, Koper et Rijeka, futurs débouchés pour les conteneurs d'Europe centrale', *Méditerranée*, 111, 2008, 39–49.

[2]   Different official audits have been made to follow the evolution of the costs and benefits of the renewing works. See for example L. Podonyi and J. Vrabic (eds), *Audit Report on Railway Construction Zalövö-Bajansenye-Hodos-Murska Sobota* (Budapest 2003), 61. An analysis of the traffic reports directly after the reopening of the line is made in République de Slovénie, Ministère des Transports and Direction des chemins de fer (eds), *Le Transport intermodal dans la République de Slovénie. Situation actuelle, possibilités et défis* (September 2004).

[3]   See Podonyi and Vrabic, *Audit Report*, 58.

a kind of paradox in the region: more than a real reunification, the new context appears as a new composition of the border situation. Rijeka cannot appear, like Koper does, as a direct gate to the communitarian space. This reduces the competitiveness of the Croatian harbour in this northern Adriatic port region.

The other regional competitor, Trieste, remains the most important harbour of the region. It benefits from its historical setting in the logistical networks, which connect it with the inner European markets. Several logistic programmes, like the Alpine Freight Railway, enforce Trieste's position by supporting logistics through the Tarvisio Pass. The particularity of this alpine passage is that it is quite specialised for cargo traffic. Only a few regional trains on the Italian side and some international passenger night trains use it. Advantages offered by this passage are the free flow of traffic (the route allows to bypass the main nodal points like Udine or Villach) and a high level of connectivity. Villach is an important inner Alpine railway crossroad where the Tauern (to Salzburg–Munich–Czech Republic) and the Semmering (Vienna–Budapest–Slovakia) axes are connected to the Tarvisio and the Karawanken (Slovenia) ones.

Despite the traffic realities, the new line between Murska Sobota and Zalalövő is identified as part of the Trans-European Transportation Network (TEN-T) corridor programme six, on the fifth Pan-European corridor.[4] This institutionalisation is a kind of technical paradox, because of the gap of traffic between it and its competitors, like the Tarvisio and Semmering axes, which are not placed at the same level in the programme. In fact, during the summer of 2009, only 60 trains per day went through Hodos, while at the same time between 150 and 200 trains per day went through the Semmering tunnel.[5] So, if the reopened line won the competition with the Croatian access to Hungary, Semmering definitely stays number one of the Central European market access.

The three itineraries mentioned (Tarvisio–Semmering, Slovenia–Semmering, and Hodos–Zalalövő) present, to a regional scale, the same horizon: connecting Central Europe to the Adriatic. This is the historical meaning of the constitution of the regional railway network and of its present renewal. The articulation of this network identifies a single territory in the European railway geography: Slovenia. During the first construction of the network, during the imperial era, the space of the present Slovenian territory was defined as a kind of extended gateway to the sea. After the Second World War, it became a northern Yugoslavian reticular dead-end. Nowadays, it is a southeastern belt located along a territorial end of the European Union's space.

---

[4]   The programmatic plan is accessible on the website of the European Commission. http://ec.europa.eu/transport/infrastructure/maps/maps_en.htm (last accessed 2 November 2010). See also Union Européenne des Chambres de Commerce et d'Industrie (UECC) (eds), *Pour la politique des transports, Maillons manquants et goulets d'étranglement dans le réseau européen des transports* (Basel 2007).

[5]   Datas given by the traffic regulators of Hodos and of Semmering in August 2009.

The Hodos railway's spatial trajectory is a mirror of these evolutions of the political context. Its opening stood for the vision of a maritime opening for the Austro-Hungarian territories; its closing is associated with the identification of Rijeka as the main regional port in the Yugoslavian system, which undervalued Koper. The present reopening expresses the new regional era, so that this reopening can appear as a kind of événement *spatial* (spatial event). This is a manifesto of the will to ensure connections within the EU, parallel to the new border, and to give visibility to the European Union in these territories. A trip from Ljubljana to Hodos is, indeed, punctuated by EU's investment communication boards.

The Invention of a Competitive Belt around Vienna?

Identifying the route between Slovenia and Hungary into the TEN-T can constitute a surprise. Another set of modernisation projects is indeed thought along the main regional axis, the Semmering. The Semmering axis should not be considered only in its Austrian aspect. Projected to the European scale, it appears as a southern extension of the Baltic rail axis.[6] The continental scale sense of the new thinking of the Semmering axis is to realise an isthmus between Baltic and Adriatic.[7] Then this set of projects take meaning to different scales. On a national scale, the main objective is to integrate Graz into a national southern belt using two basis-tunnel projects: Semmering and Koralm. These two tunnel projects are associated to a regional scale too. Their association with Vienna's new main station in Austrian territorial marketing shows the will to reinvent the European position of Vienna in association with the new geopolitical context.[8] The regional scale issue is also a

---

[6] H. Eicher, 'Kärnten und die Baltisch-Adriatische-Verkehrsachse', in *Kärntner Landesregierung* (ed.), *Schriftenreihe der Verkehrsplanung in Kärnten*, vol. 4 (Klagenfurt 2006), 1–58.

[7] For a reflexion upon the sense of the Semmering axis and the evolution of its position in front of the evolution of Austrian urban network, see H. Eicher, 'Der Ostsee-Adria-Korridor und die Steiermark', in Institut für Geographie Karl-Franzens-Universität (ed.), *Beiträge zur Geographie der Steiermark. Festschrift für W. Leitner* (Graz 1997), 79–118.

[8] For a history of the Viennese central station project, see W. Kos and G. Dinhobl (eds), *Großer Bahnhof. Wien und die weite Welt* (Vienna 2006), 427–41. This association is manifested by the territorial marketing promoting the central station project City of Vienna (ed.), *More than Just a Railway Station* (Vienna 2009), 4. The document is published at http://www.hauptbahnhof-wien.at/de/Presse/Publikationen/Folder/VIENNA_CENTRAL_STATION_Imagefolder_engl.pdf (last accessed 2 November 2010). See also on Semmering Basis Tunnel One ÖBB Infrastruktur Bau (ed.), *Semmering Base Tunnel Project* (Vienna 2008), 2. The document is published at http://www.oebb.at/bau/en/Servicebox/Brochures_and_Folders/2008_08__FSBT_en.pdf (last accessed: 2 November 2010), and the summary in Austrian Railway Planification (ed.), *Document GVP-Ö. Generalverkehrsplan Kurzfassung* (Vienna 2002). From a historical point of view, the association between the city's station and the tunnel is developed in R. Kassal-Mikula and P. Haiko, 'Vom

metropolitan. The sense of Semmering axis is, in a historical dimension, to be the Viennese maritime gate. And the dream of the Semmering basis-tunnel belongs finally to the ambition to set Vienna at the heart of a corridor between two maritime fronts, as an articulation 'in' and 'of' Europe. So, the whole Austrian project is a serious competitor for the Murska Sobota–Zalalövő axis. Services offered by the first one cannot be equalled by the second one (Figure 19.2).

The stake for Vienna is thus maritime, but also continental: the question of the logistical metropolitan competitive context with Budapest. The Hungarian capital profits from a connectivity improvement thanks to the reopening of the Murska Sobota–Zalalövő axis. Then we can consider the constitution of a kind of competitive belt set around the Austrian southern metropolitan one (Figure 19.2).

The market objectives of the Austrian set of projects are very similar to those of the eastern competitive belt.[9] Since the dissolution of the Austro-Hungarian empire, Vienna has been mostly integrated into a west–east axis, allowing the city to figure as a remote head of the Austrian urban network. This dimension is still predominant, and this means Vienna West Station is still the first station of the city. But, with the European Union's opening to the east, the Vienna's western terminus logic turned into a Central European articulation issue. Therefore, Vienna needs to recover a strong southern gate towards dynamic centres on the Adriatic, opening Balkan and Italian roads to the new EU members. Reaffirming this role of pivot renews Vienna's historical purpose in urban and transport networks. The location chosen for the new central station – the former location of the East and South Stations – is deeply symbolic: it underlines the link between the Semmering basis-tunnel project and the central station. The tunnel project is presented as fulfilling the new central station, and, in return, the station offers to it a financial and an infrastructural pertinence. But, if the tunnel is not identified as a European priority project, the new station is.

A Railway Reopening for Questioning the Regional Sense of Europe

The registration of Murska Sobota–Zalalövő Railway to support the TEN-T in the region calls into question the whole regional territorial dynamics, from the enlargement of the EU to its consequences in terms of metropolitan competition. And these two aspects cannot be dissociated: the urban issue is mostly a European reunification one. The choice of the Adriatic exit itinerary presented to European decision-makers is the choice of the continental regional hub of reference (Figure

---

"Arsenalstil" zur "Wiener Renaissance"', in W. Kos and G. Dinhobl (eds), *Großer Bahnhof* (Vienna), 86–101. and W. Kos 'Tanne und Palme. Das imaginative Potenzial der Südbahn', in W. Kos and G. Dinhobl (eds), *Großer Bahnhof* (Vienna), 130–3.

   [9] This common objective is clear when we compare the Vienna main station and Semmering basis-tunnel project communication with the audit on the efficiency of the reopening of the Slovenian-Hungarian axis.

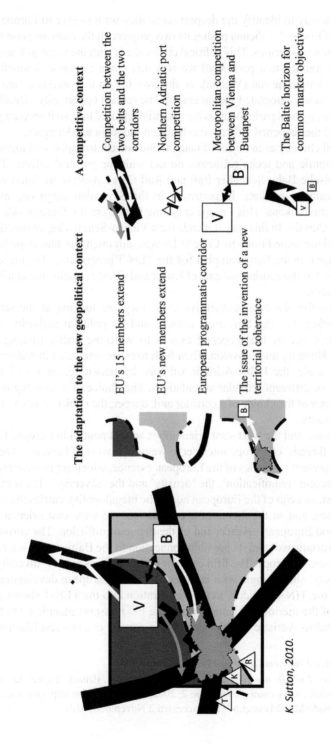

Figure 19.2 The railway reopening, a mirror of the European reunification paradox

Source: Illustration created by the author.

19.2). It is also a way to identify the deepest sense they want to give to Europe in this 'fragment of Europe'.[10] Vienna pushes its two projects all the more because the regional competition is serious. This political choice deals with the sense of Europe to spread to its southeastern part: shall we arm this urban region to a junction symbolising the long-time run (Vienna), or shall we bet on the 'interlude' era to homogenise the newly integrated spatial entity? The second opportunity identifies Budapest, former regional parliament, as the potential regional hub, so it encourages the promotion of the reopened railway axis between Slovenia and Hungary.

This political choice has to be coordinated to the current transport and logistic dynamics. Economic and technical actors do not wait for political effects. The forwarders Deutsche Bahn Schenker Rail and Rail Cargo Austria are interested in the Balkan railway markets, in particular in the Slovenian cargo one as a 'bridgehead' to the Balkans. This Europe is getting built from the Western side of the former Iron Curtain. In this way it pleads for a Vienna–Semmering connection to organise Adriatic expeditions to Central Europe, although the tunnel project still does not appear in the European plan for the TEN-T programme. The present corridor identified as the continental gate of Koper and Trieste remains the number five (Lisbon–Kiev).

One thing unifies the two competitive axes: they are looking at the same commercial market. For the Slovenian railway and its political authority, the economical pertinence of the reopened axis is to welcome traffic running to Poland through Hungary and Slovakia. Then both axes are interested in realising, on a European scale, the Baltic-Adriatic isthmus, by transiting, on a regional scale, through two different reticular articulations. The choice of a main regional junction is a matter of the choice of a corridor and, deeper, the choice of what kind of Europe one wants.

The north–south and the west–east orientations are not neutral in Europe. Two dynamics, two 'threads' of Europe intersect to weave the west of Europe.[11] These two elements represent two poles of the European essence, which are two concrete issues for the present 'reunification', the 'density' and the 'diversity'. The north–south orientation, an echo of the European heart (the megalopolis), carries the first European essence, and so the theme of accumulation; the west–east orientation carries the second European essence, and so the theme of diffusion. The corridor choice for the Adriatic exit and its possible connection to the Baltic space is a real speech whose topic is Europe. The fifth corridor carries this essence of 'diversity', which the 'density' shall mingle with in order to build a European development. The passage of the TINA corridors to their integration into the TEN-T shows the reinforcement of the meridian orientation into the EU transport planning. On the one hand, the Baltic–Adriatic corridor carries this density essence and illustrates

[10]   M. Foucher, *Fragments d'Europe* (Paris 1998).

[11]   See J. Lévy, *Europe: une géographie* (Paris 1997), and R. Brunet, 'Lignes de force de l'espace européen', *Mappemonde*, 66, issue 2, 2002, 14–19. See also http://www.mgm. fr/PUB/Mappemonde/M202/Brunet.pdf (last accessed 2 November 2010).

this last point. On the other hand, the choice of the fifth corridor carries a speech upon a dynamic of diffusion. We are really facing a political choice: what is the European sense of this political reunification?

The reopening of the Murska Sobota–Zalalövő Railway leads us to present questions which the European construction is nowadays confronted with. The sentence of François Mitterrand, '*L'Europe se construit par les transports*', is not denied. The course is at the depths of the Europe idea, of *europeanity* and of European citizenship. For many new European citizens, the accession to this title meant, first of all, new horizons for their individual routes, which reinforced the issues around Hodos–Zalalövő Railway from a passenger traffic point of view.

The choice of the sense to give to this European axis is, therefore, function of the political project for this area. The border is the key theme. The question of the management of the inner border inherited from the era when the EU had only 15 members is latent behind the corridor choice. This border, marked by its north-south orientation, is only crossed by the Salzburg–Vienna–Budapest and Salzburg–Graz–Maribor axis. The risk that the European choice of the meridian corridor (supported by the Semmering) could bring is the reinforcement of this effect by strengthening the western pivots. The fifth corridor would be a way to lessen this heritage and the impact of another border problem, created this time by the 2004 enlargement of Europe.

The question raised by this maritime exit is the consistency of the European funds orientations. The issue is the invention of a kind of conciliation between all of the elements constituting the European mood. These elements meet in a single geographic area, and, above all, in a single country in this region: Slovenia. From Slovenia to Austria, the course also reveals the stake of Vienna's sense in Central Europe, as well as its capacity to recover its urban network.

Conclusion

The reopening of the Murska Sobota–Hodos-Zalalövő Railway axis proposes a reading of several paradoxes in the context of the enlargement of the EU to Central Europe. The main one is, certainly, the gap between the programmatic logic and the reality of the traffic. It allows us to interrogate the political sense of this revival in the context of the regional border situation. If the strategic financial support is a speech about the territorial coherence value of this axis, it could be at the same time a negative sign proposed to Croatia: this new itinerary does not make new traffic being produced but keeps the present ones that previously went through Murakeresztur. This choice cannot be disconnected from the strategy built to encourage the development of Koper harbour, whose traffic has been increasing for a decade.

The continuing importance of the Semmering route and the confrontation of both ambitions to realise a kind of isthmus, by connecting Polish and Slovakian markets to the Adriatic, reveals the real regional competitive dimension of the 'reunification'. It belongs to the metropolitan hierarchical organisation:

metropolitan issues thus meet maritime and border ones in a multi-scalar confrontation.

Bibliography

Beyer, A. and Savin, J.C., 'Les ports-frontières de Trieste, Koper et Rijeka, futurs débouchés pour les conteneurs d'Europe centrale', *Méditerranée*, 111, 2008, 39–49.

Brunet, R., 'Lignes de force de l'espace européen', *Mappemonde*, 66, 2002, 14–19 (online version under: http://www.mgm.fr/PUB/Mappemonde/M202/Brunet. pdf).

City of Vienna (ed.), *More than Just a Railway Station* (Vienna 2009) (online version under: http://www.hauptbahnhof-wien.at/de/Presse/Publikationen/ Folder/VIENNA_CENTRAL_STATION_Imagefolder_engl.pdf).

Eicher, H., 'Der Ostsee-Adria-Korridor und die Steiermark', in Institut für Geographie Karl-Franzens-Universität (ed.), *Beiträge zur Geographie der Steiermark. Festschrift für W. Leitner* (Graz 1997), 79–118.

Eicher, H., 'Kärnten und die Baltisch-Adriatische-Verkehrsachse', in Kärntner Landesregierung (ed.), *Schriftenreihe der Verkehrsplanung in Kärnten*, vol. 4 (Klagenfurt 2006), 1–58.

Foucher, M., *Fragments d'Europe* (Paris 1993).

GVP-Ö, *Generalverkehrsplan. Kurzfassung from* January 2002 (Vienna 2002).

Kassal-Mikula, R. and Haiko, P., 'Vom "Arsenalstil" zur "Wiener Renaissance"', in W. Kos and G. Dinhobl (eds), *Großer Bahnhof. Wien und die weite Welt* (Vienna 2006), 86–101.

Kos, W. and Dinhobl, G. (eds), *Großer Bahnhof. Wien und die weite Welt* (Vienna 2006).

Kos, W., 'Tanne und Palme. Das imaginative Potenzial der Südbahn', in W. Kos and G. Dinhobl (eds), *Großer Bahnhof. Wien und die weite Welt* (Vienna 2006), 130–3.

Lévy, J., *Europe: une géographie* (Paris 1997).

ÖBB Infrastruktur Bau, *Semmering Base Tunnel Project* (Vienna 2008) (online version under: http://www.oebb.at/bau/en/Servicebox/Brochures_and_Folders/ 2008_08__FSBT_en.pdf).

Offner, J.M., 'Les "effets structurants" du transport: mythe politique, mystification scientifique', *L'espace géographique*, 3, 1993, 233–42.

Pap, R., *UNESCO Weltkulturerbe Semmeringbahn* (Semmering 2003).

Podonyi, L. and Vrabic, J. (eds), *Audit Report On Railway Construction Zalövö-Bajansenye-Hodos-Murska Sobota* (Budapest 2003).

République de Slovénie, Ministère des Transports, Direction des chemins de fer (eds), *Le Transport intermodal dans la République de Slovénie. Situation actuelle, possibilités et défis* (Ljubljana 2004).

Union Européenne des Chambres de Commerce et d'Industrie (UECC) Pour la politique des transports, *Maillons manquants et goulets d'*étranglement *dans le réseau européen des transports* (Basel 2007).

Chapter 20

'More is Less': Regular Interval Timetable in Central Eastern Europe

Viktor Borza, Vít Janoš and István Neumann

The Problem and Approaches to Overcoming It

Public transport in the central Eastern region of Europe currently faces a situation quite similar to Western European experience in the decades that followed 1960. The current curse could be turned into a blessing, as we are now in a position to select, as a point of departure towards progress, the most suitable and most tried and tested method from amongst a number of approaches.

By the early 1980s, virtually all railways in Western Europe had been experiencing a prolonged crisis, mainly due to the dramatic surge of road and air transport. Given the environmental impacts of that development, a gradual shift towards a transport policy more in harmony with the requirements of environmental protection and towards an increasingly human-centric, client-friendly approach to meeting transport needs took place in a number of Western European countries. This included efforts to modernise transport systems and rail infrastructure and led to a revival of rail transport there, most markedly from the 1990s onwards. In many cases, however, efforts to modernise the railways did not necessarily result in the elimination of basic structural problems, nor in a comprehensive rise in the quality of public transport. Decision-makers frequently favoured prestigious investment schemes and costly high-speed projects without due attendance to the 'software-type' problems of organisational and service structures next to the systematic timetable-driven development of national rail networks. Thus, rail transport again became the most attractive transport mode, but typically in a number of modernised relations favoured by the makers of transport policy. Such a limited approach did not compensate for the decline of national rail networks and public transport in general.

The passenger railways of the central Eastern European region continue to face problems that the West confronted years before. Typical of the situation is that rail becomes less competitive due to the general availability and flexibility of individual road transport as well as cheap air transport, ageing infrastructure and rolling stock, more or less constant decline in passenger numbers, and corporate losses on the rise partly caused by restrictions due to excessive deficits of national budgets.

In the face of the increasing decline in the modal split share of rail transport, one country stands out against the general central Eastern European trend. In the

Czech Republic, both an integrated regular timetable scheme and regional transport systems have been implemented, resulting in a marked rise of the public transport system's modal split share. Passenger numbers increased by 20 to 120 per cent over a four-year period on railway lines subject to reorganisation and enhanced services with more train kilometres and connections.[1] Hungary is another central Eastern European country where a regular interval timetable was partially adopted on a national scale. Success has been much more subdued in Hungary, where regional transport schemes are lacking, ticket prices are up sharply and almost four dozen railway lines have been closed. During the first two decades following the 1989 change of political system there has been no consistent transport policy implementing efforts to integrate transport services. As a result the share of both public transport and railways has continued to decrease, except for some railway lines with enhanced service based on a regular interval timetable. Following the partial introduction of the new timetable scheme on the Hungarian network, annual losses in passenger numbers amounted to 10 to 12 per cent on network elements not served on a regular timetable basis. Thanks to the success of the regular interval timetable, these losses were partially counterbalanced and overall annual passenger losses of Hungarian railways were reduced to 3 to 4 per cent in the two years following the scheme's introduction in Eastern Hungary.[2]

Regular Timetable and Integration in Western Europe: The Swiss and French Experiences

Historically, two major approaches dominated in response to a similar situation within the more highly developed regions of Europe. The best results were achieved by the Swiss model based on a set of organising principles known as *Integraler Taktfahrplan* (ITF).

The Swiss ITF timetable model was inspired by an earlier Dutch timetable scheme, made to suit a topographically diverse landscape and the necessities of the integration of bus and rail, city, regional and long-distance transport. But what we would (historically) call the 'French model' also brought about some distinctive economic and territorial progress, even though on the bottom line it resulted in growing losses and an increasing importance of state subsidies.[3]

---

[1]   V. Janoš, K. Baudyš and J. Pospíšil, 'Railway timetable in the Czech Republic', Vilnius Gediminas University PhD thesis, 2009, 7–11.

[2]   V. Borza, Gy. István, L. Kormányos and B. Gy. Vincze, 'Integrált ütemes menetrend', part 3. Published online in 2008 at http://itf.hu/index.php, paragraph 6 (last accessed 15 June 2010).

[3]   As early as 1927 Netherlands Railways (NS) introduced a regular service with electric trains every hour following the electrification of their most important line, Amsterdam–Haarlem–The Hague–Rotterdam. Soon this was augmented to every 30 minutes, but only for the expresses. The stopping trains, although also mostly electric, ran to

The main characteristics of the French model are that they (1) only operate 'full trains' concentrating on peak times, (2) focus on state-of-the-art rolling stock and infrastructure and (3) pursue a preferential approach accepting market segmentation, e.g. privileged high-speed networks, such as the *Train à grande vitesse* (TGV), next to ultra-modern suburban trains and networks like the *Réseau express régional* (RER).

Basic business economics inspire this model. The aim is to improve financial efficiency, so service is only provided in the event that the demand matches the capacity. This is called the Demand Steered Service Model. The real problem with this approach is that, due to its obvious commitment to cutting expenses, it does not sufficiently take into consideration the dominance of general expenses in rail transport and the basic asymmetries of demand typical of the entire public transport sector.

Besides ostensibly improving financial efficiency, the French model, even at its best, resulted in overall passenger losses because it excluded or impeded passengers of the services that were cancelled because of less than optimal demand. On a network level, this meant that quite a few passengers stopped using the railways who would have used one of the more cost-efficient 'full trains' on their way back or on their onward trip.

This phenomenon was observed in Hungary when due to a misguided political decision the national railways Magyar Államvasutak (MÁV), along with limited innovation and modernisation efforts, was ordered to radically reduce its services in the 2004–2005 timetable with the aim of cutting costs. This resulted in 5.7 per cent fewer train/kilometres and in 6.4 per cent fewer passengers on a network level, a greater loss than expected.

As for the cost structure of MÁV passenger railways, more than a third is spent on rail infrastructure and another two-fifths on rolling stock. In 2005, MÁV-Start Zrt paid 3 per cent less in track access fees, 4 per cent less in traction fees, and 2.4 per cent more in overhead costs. This was mainly due to greater idle times of personnel

---

somewhat erratic schedules in between the expresses. Gradually this new form of timetable was extended to other lines, but the big change came in 1934 with the introduction of new diesel-electric trains on the lines radiating from Utrecht. These trains ran every hour on a regular schedule, always on the same minute of the hour. Connecting trains at the end of these new diesel services were adjusted too in the same way, even in the outlying districts of the country. By 1939 a majority of NS trains ran to a regular interval timetable – every hour, every 30 minutes or even every 20 minutes, and always on the same minute of the hour, all day long. Only on some less frequented regional lines the interval between trains could be as much as two hours, but again always on the same minute of the hour. Goods traffic, in the Netherlands always less important than the passenger side of the business, was largely run in the night. This simplified timetable facilitated travelling by rail enormously. After World War Two the regular interval timetable was finally introduced on all lines, with trains running every hour, every 30 minutes or even less on some much frequented lines. Remark is based on Guus Veenendaal, *Spoorwegen in Nederland van 1834 tot nu*, 2nd edn (Amsterdam 2008), 357–58.

and rolling stock, as well as to specific cost increase due to system standstill.[4] Not only did they fail to meet the projected cost decrease, but the losses were transferred to the infrastructure, traction and maintenance branches of business.

A similar development has been experienced in Slovakia for years, resulting in operators facing repeated rises of track access fees. In contrast, in the Czech Republic, a regular interval timetable was adopted, resulting in a better performance level with more train kilometres. Regional transport schemes and territorial ownership of regional rail transport have also been introduced.

In the current central Eastern European setting, even carefully prepared and executed downscaling of train services will likely result in a loss of passengers, which is detrimental to European Union (EU) transport policy, to energy efficiency and sustainability targets. In the French model, in order to gain passengers, the appeal of the remaining services must be significantly increased by extremely costly development of infrastructure and rolling stock. All in all, this is likely to result in (1) rising passenger numbers in the preferred segments, partly to the detriment of traditional segments (cannibalisation), (2) a further decrease of the share of rail transport and (3) ever more costly railway systems, necessitating excessive state budget commitments.

Meanwhile, the model termed 'French' is no longer consistently applied in France and, naturally, decisions based on demand-driven service models are also taken elsewhere, even in countries with ITF-type transport schemes, The German national timetable scheme called *Deutschlandtakt*, for instance, was delayed and diluted on several occasions. Meanwhile the Société nationale des chemins de fer Français (SNCF), the French national railway, has in fact adopted a regular interval timetable structure in significant parts of its network, and has decided to operate an ITF-type timetable on the entire *Réseau ferré de France* from 2012 onwards.[5] In the Swiss model introduced in 1982, a regular timetable scaled to match peak period demand is maintained all day and all week long. When ITF was introduced, the Swiss had some of the oldest rolling stock in Western Europe, though it was well maintained. Speed was relatively low even on main lines, 80 to 140 kilometres per hour. Between 1982 and 1992, infrastructure development was limited to a few low-cost interventions intended to maintain or create service levels in harmony with the timetable requirements. The Swiss national transport scheme is characterised by broad inter-modal cooperation based on timetable integration that is also extended to bus and city transports.

---

[4] V. Borza, 'Integrált Ütemes Menetrend, avagy Lehet nyereséges a vasúti közszolgáltatás', Corvinus University PhD thesis, 2007, 9.

[5] Meanwhile in Germany the political decision to introduce *Deutschlandtakt* is still pending, and the conservative–liberal coalition pledged since 2009 to 'investigate the possibility' of its introduction. See *Verkehrspolitische Ziele der Initiative Deutschland-Takt* (Berlin 2009), http://www.deutschland-takt.de/deutschlandtakt/ (last accessed 21 December 2010).

Unlike the French model, where demand-driven interventions are typical, the supply-driven service model applied in Switzerland takes into account the high overhead costs in public transport, rail in particular. 'Nothing is more expensive than an idle train!' as experienced railway professionals say. Supply-driven performance results in the maximum amount of services that can be performed by a given personnel and rolling stock. Because such performance does not cause a significant rise in cost, in Switzerland the available public transport capacity runs at peak performance most of the day, resulting in a more flexible, attractive system serving as a true alternative to individual road transport. In a full-fledged ITF-type system, passengers are able to travel at least hourly between any two points in the network. Even without high-speed tracks, a symmetric timetable structure geared to quick changes of a few minutes creates a passenger-friendly, highly available and efficient system. Such an increase in performance and quality of service resulted in Swiss railways having a modal split share four times the European average. Indeed, the entire public transport sector experienced dynamic passenger growth, and an economic basis was created to facilitate significant infrastructure and rolling stock development serving the increasing passenger flows. All this resulted in sustainable, even profitable (!) rail passenger transport.

Essential cost factors of rail passenger service include (1) track access fees and other fees related to infrastructure, (2) traction fees and other fees related to rolling stock, (3) depreciation and maintenance costs of rolling stock itself, (4) personnel costs related to passenger services, (5) real estate, accounting, corporate and administrative overhead and (6) marketing costs.

The share of variable costs in Hungarian passenger rail transport was only about 2.5 per cent, one-fortieth of the entire cost. All the rest was by and large independent of the level of performance.

The expenses of railway track infrastructure remains quite stable over the years and they can be recovered by access fees and state subsidies. Expenses must match income, because infrastructure railway companies are supposed to operate similar to not-for-profit businesses in the current setting. Thus the aggregated value of income from track access fees ought to remain pretty stable, independent of the performances of operators.

A given global performance level is determined by the minimum public service level. Public transport systems deal with similar peak-time demand in France, Switzerland and central Eastern European countries. If operators intend to cut costs by running 10 per cent fewer trains, they are likely to face a similar increase in track access fees, due to the fact that the number of trains ordered for the next year is a crucial factor when calculating next year's fees.

Traction fees behave in a similar manner, and even energy consumption does not strictly follow the level of actual performance. In fact, overhead costs dominate in all major cost elements. In the long run, costs can be cut only by down scaling the capacity. It is reasonable to scale capacity to peak demand on all parts of the network and then run the rolling stock at peak performance, attaining the level when extra income still matches marginal costs – essentially the larger energy intake of a running train compared to an idle train.[6]

Regular Timetable and Integration in Central Eastern Europe: Experiences and Potential

The Czech Experience

A demand-driven timetable structure was long typical for the Czech Republic (and former Czechoslovakia). Trains were operated at times of supposed demand. The 1983–84 timetable featured a first attempt at regularity: regional passenger trains (abbreviated 'Os' in Czech) of the Prague–Kolín line ran at a 60/30 minute interval with minor deviations, due to the circumstance that trains pulled by an engine are slower than electric multiple units. For years this timetable was continued there without modification or extension.

The 1993–94 timetable for the first time saw a degree of regularity for international trains. The traditional Vindobona and Hungaria express trains of the Eurotakt line linking Hamburg and Berlin with Vienna and Budapest via Prague ran on a regular timetable by then. Thanks to these trains, symmetry by the '00 minute' first appeared in the Czech timetable in 1994–95.[7]

Beginning in 1995–96, the regular interval timetable was extended to Prague suburban lines, first to Os trains of the Prague–Kralupy and Prague–Benešov lines. A year later, Os trains of the Prague–Beroun line were included, and from the 1997–98 timetable, with Prague–Nymburk–Kolín, the last double track line of the Prague suburban system was included. These local lines were island operations. They did not form a consistent network with through-links via Prague combining two lines. Their interval length varied during the daytime and each line used a different symmetry axis.

The timetable of 2000–2001 brought two major changes. Eurotakt trains were diverted to the Prague–Česká Třebová–Brno corridor line, which had been almost completely reconstructed and was 20 minutes faster, and the EgroNet project was launched, reorganising regional cross-border traffic including the Zwickau–Plauen–Cheb–Marktredwitz and Zwickau–Kraslice–Sokolov railway lines. EgroNet is operated partly by state railways and partly by the private company

---

[6]   This is called the optimum performance level, a critical success factor in public transport often ignored in the central Eastern European region.

[7]   '00 minute' refers to the fact that every regular timetable has a symmetry axis. Trains run symmetrically in both ways around that axis and in case of an XX:00 axis they meet in hubs around the full hour. Obviously in that year no ITF-type timetable existed in the country, but the first trains appeared that at least abroad followed this principle: starting in 2002–2003, Eurotakt trains ran symmetrically through the Czech Republic as well.

Viamont (train operator on the Kraslice–Sokolov line).[8] EgroNet traffic is part of a full-fledged regular interval traffic with '00-symmetry' and good connections in Bavaria and Saxony.

The EgroNet network provided a good pattern and a stimulus for the reshaping of national regional transport. Two pilot projects incorporating 00- symmetry were initiated to that end in the 2002–2003 timetable, the first in the northeastern Bohemian region featuring the Roudnice–Ústí nad Labem–Děčín and Ústí nad Labem–Chomutov–Karlovy Vary–Cheb lines, the other one in the Ostrava area with the Ostrava–Opava, Přerov–Ostrava–Český Těšín–Mosty u Jablunkova, Ostrava–Havířov–Český Těšín and Ostrava–Frenštát pod Radhoštěm lines. Besides these regional projects, in that year, regular intervals became dominant in national long-distance travel.

The 2002–2003 timetable brought about a distinctive break. This year was the last when decisions about timetable structures were the sole responsibility of České Dráhy (ČD), the Czech state railways. The Ministry of Transport started to order long-distance traffic (Ex and R-type fast trains), from the 2003–2004 timetable year. Also a regional structure of ownership by the 14 Bohemian and Moravian regions was created who are now in charge of Sp and Os-type regional trains. Thus the 2004–2005 timetable brought a huge amount of change, primarily in that national long-distance lines now operated in a standardised manner. The network was gradually brought in line with a unified national scheme based on ITF-type '00-symmetry', and ITF hubs were created. This first giant leap for the system was quite fiercely opposed within the railway organisation, the most prominent argument being that trains should continue to operate when most people need them rather than according to an 'unknown system', leading to many 'useless' connections and a lack of capacity for freight transport. It took about five years for the entire organisation to embrace the idea of a comprehensive national ITF-type timetable.

The regular interval concept not only created many new links and train services, it also terminated traditional direct links that did not fit the new scheme, such as the Prague–Jeseník or Most–České Budějovice direct express train services. Sections that lost their long-distance trains were branched into the national long-distance network. Such changes partly explain the opposition within the railway organisation. A decision was made to advance gradually. The new concept was progressively introduced within a five-year period as follows:

- 2003–2004 – drafting the new concept, first adaptations.
- 2004–2005 – first big system change, including a 7 per cent rise in total train kilometres.
- 2005–2006 – further system adaptation without additional train kilometres.

---

[8]   EgroNet is a regional rail transport scheme connecting towns in the Czech Republic, Bavaria and Saxony dating back to the year 2000. The Czech town of Cheb (Eger in German) is at the centre of that cross-border network, which is why the project was named EgroNet. See http://www.egronet.de/ (last accessed 21 December 2010).

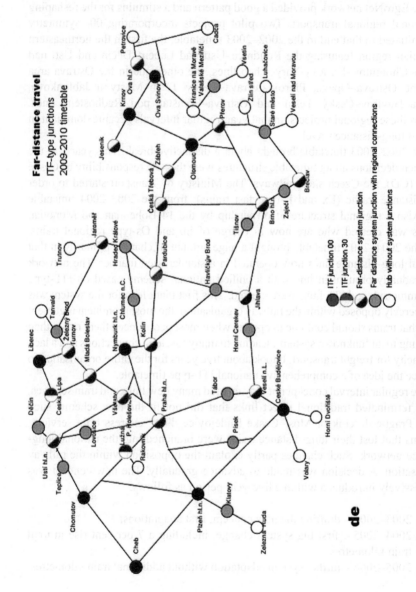

Figure 20.1   ITF-type junctions of the Czech long-distance rail network

Source: Map created by Vit Janoš.

- 2006–2007 – further adaptation including a 5 per cent rise in train kilometres.
- 2007–2008 – further adaptation including a 15 per cent rise in train kilometres. The Ministry of Transport orders the timetable of EuroCity and InterCity-type trains from now on. EC supplements are abolished, EC and IC trains form the upper service level within the national timetable, and thus a unique tariff scheme for the entire system is established.
- 2008–2009 – intervals are made shorter on main lines. A 12 per cent rise in train kilometres.
- From 2009–10 onwards – stabilising and realigning the scheme.[9]

For publicly ordered long-distance traffic, the success of the new concept became apparent after two years: the increase in passenger numbers ranged from 10 to 40 per cent for the railway lines realigned according to the ITF scheme. After four years it amounted to 20 to 120 per cent as compared with the base year. The most striking results were reported from the Prague–Ústí nad Labem line, where a two-segment order of services (a choice of several train types) with a consistent regular interval was established. The number of trains on this corridor line was almost doubled; instead of the initial two long-distance lines three lines serving a different set of stops carry almost six times as many passengers as four years ago – thousands of passengers daily who did not travel by rail before.

The role of the Ministry of Transport is limited to ordering long-distance public transport. Without such an order (that is without compensation payments), the state railways only operate their Super City (SC)-type Pendolino tilting trains between Prague and Ostrava. As regional transport now belongs to the regions, negotiations are necessary between the Ministry and the various regions. There is no such a thing in Czech Republic as an 'obligation of linkage' between regional and national systems: every owner is free to set their priorities. This explains why within the Czech system we can find many instances of excellent connections between regional and long-distance lines, but other linkups do not work well or do not exist at all.

Regional owners in favour of ITF-type timetables who have implemented a good set of linkups with long-distance lines are the Prague, Brno, Plzeň, Ústí nad Labem and Hradec Králové regions. The situation is acceptable but less than ideal in the Ostrava, Olomouc, Zlín and Liberec areas. To date, no national transport planning scheme for regional transport has set the pace for the development of the entire system. Each owner is responsible for planning, including coordination with neighbouring regions and with the Ministry. Most regions have installed a transport and conceptual work coordinator. The Ministry for its part has established close relationships with the Institute for Regional and Long-distance Transport Planning (*Institut für Regional- und Fernverkehrsplanung*, IRFP) in Dresden and the České

---

[9]   V. Janoš and K. Baudyš, 'Railway timetable in the Czech Republic', in Wydawnictwo Politechniki Ślaskiej (ed.), *The development of transportation systems* (Gliwice 2010), 181–6.

Vysoké Učení Technické (ČVUT), the technical university of Prague.[10] Beside the problem of the reluctance of the entire railway organisation to adopt an 'ITF mindset', another set of problems is related to quality issues. The railway company uses old rolling stock for most long-distance services, the daily circulation of which has been optimised through ITF. The comfort offered by current stock does not match twenty-first century expectations, and the intensive use of old stock puts additional strain upon it which can be detrimental to reliability and punctuality. Construction due to the developments of corridor lines also affects punctuality.

The regular interval timetable scheme has brought many new passengers to railways. If we want them to remain, we cannot allow the pace of change to slow down. Following the first two essential steps of introducing regular timetables and integrating public transport modes, the biggest potential now is to develop the rolling stock. Also, more time and effort must be dedicated to annual timetable planning, including the simulation of bottlenecks and the creation of intervention scenarios for cases of disturbances and unforeseen events.

The present Czech regular interval timetable scheme cannot yet be regarded as final. Much remains to be achieved, such as diminishing intervals on busy relations resulting in more trains on lines with sufficient demand, introducing accelerated services on modernised lines and creating new hubs through infrastructure investments. The aim is to create an efficient system demonstrating to passengers that railways can be the backbone of an attractive, flexible alternative to private transport.

The Hungarian Experience

The Hungarian ITF pilot project was organised in 2004 in the Danube bend region north of Budapest, which was already served by a semi-regular timetable. A new system of regional 'slow trains' and faster so-called 'zonal trains' with fewer stops was scheduled according to the principles of ITF. It provided better services for the vast majority of passengers, making possible a much better use of existing rolling stock. A 30 per cent performance increase was realised for a cost increase of only 0.4 per cent.[11]

In 2006–2007, an ITF-type regular interval timetable was introduced to the eastern Hungarian long-distance network. As for regional lines, a degree of regularity – e.g. a train every other hour during part of the day – was introduced for some, while others were left with an irregular timetable. This timetable scheme was subsequently extended to parts of the western half of Hungary in a half-hearted manner, and was diluted in the east in order to meet political requirements restricting performance. Other factors dimming the positive effects of the initial stage of national ITF, both external and internal to railways, included the general lack of long-term transport policy, including the lack of targets to be

---

10   See their websites www.irfp.de and www.cvut.cz (last accessed 15 October 2010).

11   Borza, 'Integrált Ütemes Menetrend', 20.

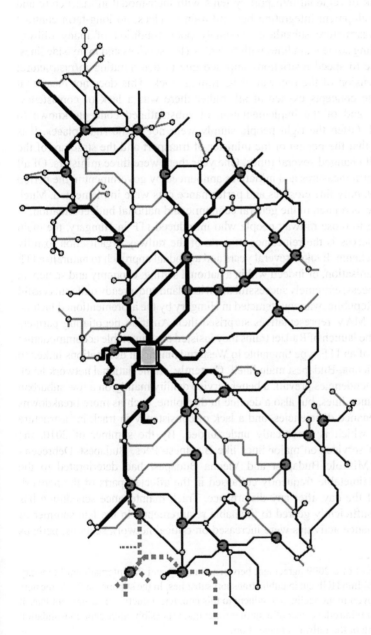

Figure 20.2 ITF-type hubs created in the Hungarian network, 2006–2008

Legend: Thick lines were served hourly or more frequently, thin black lines every other hour or less frequently in a regular or somewhat regular timetable, grey lines did not have a regular timetable.

Source: Map created by Viktor Borza.

met by MÁV and other operators; substantial ticket price increases in and after 2007; the lack of regional transport systems with inter-modal infrastructure and timetable development integrating bus and train services; no long-term contract for state infrastructure subsidies; extremely poor condition of many railway tracks, including some main lines with InterCity (IC) services and many side lines; slow response to speed restrictions imposed due to deteriorating infrastructure; and the suspension of the renewal of IC rolling stock. This does not mean that no appropriate concepts existed at all; rather there was a lack of consistency, of leadership and of the implementation of substantiated concepts known to be successful. Often the right people simply were not in the right places. It is symptomatic that the person of the minister of transport and the structure of the Ministry itself changed several times. One year there were three ministers. Of all structural reform measures and initiatives announced by government in the period of 2006–2009, only line closures and performance cuts were implemented. Much of the above was related to the general economic and national budget situation.[12]

According to those railway people who introduced ITF in Hungary, the main obstacle to success is the reluctance of parts of the railway organisation to fully embrace the scheme. It takes several years and a gradual approach to naturalise ITF within an organisation, or indeed within a national setting, economy and society at large. This process, extremely successful in Switzerland and already quite successful in the Czech Republic, was counteracted in Hungary by the aforementioned factors. Nevertheless, MÁV representatives surprised their Austrian negotiating partners when before the launch of RailJet trains they insisted on a timetable accommodating the extension of an ITF-type timetable to Western Hungarian destinations linked to hubs on the Vienna–Budapest main line.[13] Currently, on the national network level, contradictory tendencies prevail: a better service quality mainly on a few suburban and long-distance lines, but also a decline in discipline, such as more breakdowns due to maintenance deficiencies, and a lack of consistency in track infrastructure maintenance, which is chronically underfunded. By the summer of 2010, the punctuality of services on major lines like Budapest–Pécs, Budapest–Debrecen–Nyíregyháza–Miskolc–Budapest and Vienna–Budapest had deteriorated to the point that the timetable frequently collapsed in the affected parts of the network for the rest of the day after any disturbance. Track maintenance scheduling has not yet been sufficiently geared to timetable requirements. In the late summer of 2010, maintenance activities were increased on critical network sections, perhaps

---

[12]   Also, part of a 2009 agreement between Hungary and the International Monetary Fund was a 40 billion HUF cut in public transport subsidies. In the summer of 2010, the new conservative government declined to adhere to this counterproductive measure, but later it was intended to reintroduce cuts of a similar magnitude (possibly after debt consolidation and restructuring of the railway organisation).

[13]   New international speed train service of the Österreichische *Bundesbahn* (ÖBB) in cooperation with German *Deutsche Bahn AG* (DB AG) and Hungarian MÁV. See Borza, István, Kormányos and Vincze, 'Integrált ütemes menetrend', part 3.

also due to government's new transport policy incorporating a pro-rail stance to be introduced to Parliament in 2011.[14]

A timetable with regular intervals remains in effect for a significant section of the network, including main lines with IC trains and other long-distance services, but the scheme has not been extended to the entire network, nor even to all Budapest suburban railways.[15] Regionalisation of public transport has not been implemented to date. On lines served hourly or every other hour, some pairs of trains – commonly in late morning – have been suspended because of performance constraints imposed by one minister of transport.[16] Meanwhile, even the available poor statistics clearly show the adverse results of performance cutbacks. As long as overhead system expenses are not decreased, when train operators pay less track fees, but infrastructure costs remain the same, the amount that has been saved must sooner or later be returned to the infrastructure companies.

Summing up the aggregated performance function of costs and revenues in a manner true to measure will establish the business result of passenger transport activities. Passenger railway companies operate with losses throughout Europe, except for very few operators with full-fledged ITF timetables. Therefore the question is, at which performance level can losses be minimised by increasing passenger numbers and optimising revenues? As long as Hungarian (and other central Eastern European) state railways operate far below their optimal performance level, performance cuts will generally not result in savings. On the contrary, the level must be raised to the point where individual lines and the entire network are able to attract more passengers by offering better service with more trains and connections. 'More is less' – in central Eastern Europe more train kilometres would result in less losses within a matter of months, as long as changes are managed professionally, part of a long-term transport policy aiming

---

[14]   In July 2010, Minister Tamás Fellegi refuted news that public transport subsidiaries would be reduced by 40 billion HUF based on an agreement between the International Monetary Fund and the preceding Hungarian government. Fellegi stated that withholding these funds would probably result in the collapse of public transport, and would certainly cause the further deterioration of service levels and modal split share. See http://www.magyarkozlekedes.hu/ index.php/kozlekedespolitika/7607-fellegi-megalapozatlan-az-imf-nek-tett-vallalas (last accessed 30 July 2010). In October 2010, a one-time payment and a credit guarantee to the infrastructure railway were effectuated. Starting in 2011, a five-year contract will determine state contributions to rail infrastructure, and in July 2011 a decision was taken to consolidate railway debts.

[15]   Lines 142, 75, 78 and 77 could become part of the suburban system but have no ITF-type regular interval timetable. Line 77 and part of line 142 were discontinued in December 2009, one of which was put back to service in July 2010, with only two pairs of trains a day.

[16]   According to insiders, the poor initial timetable of the five Hungarian lines on which passenger service was resumed on 3 July 2010 is the responsibility of a senior ministry officer, who insisted that a performance limit decreed by Minister Pál Szabó must still be adhered to.

at the integration of transport modes. The art of optimising performance levels is a balancing act, as interdependences within the system must be adequately considered and weighed. Besides inappropriate performance cuts, another classic misjudgement is overrating the savings potential of downsizing the network. From the times of the 'Beeching Axe' in the 1960s to the recent Hungarian closures, it became apparent that such measures fall short of realising the expected savings even if services are only 'suspended', temporarily avoiding the costly rehabilitation of discontinued railway tracks.[17] Due to the requirements of climate protection and energy efficiency, the large-scale closure of railway lines goes against common sense and the interests of each national economy. Considering the political situation, the move to close down lines was even more likely to produce a loss for the state budget.[18] Given MÁV's current level of service, a further performance reduction would represent a threat to the sustainability of MÁV's core activities. The goal of a railway company operating in a rational manner is to reach the point of minimal losses by establishing an optimal service level. ITF, when it is systematically applied like a 'software program', allows operators to attain the level where the value of marginal revenues is still in excess of marginal costs in order to maximise efficiency and minimise losses.

With regard to the potential of ITF in the central Eastern European region, companies and owners must take care to operate their regular interval timetable system in a reasonable and sensitive way, taking into account the local infrastructure situation and the local mentality, traditions and organisational structures. While it is not always possible or appropriate to change these factors, the question remains: what corporate and transport policy measures – including legal and institutional background, integral tariff system, investment scheduling, etc. – are necessary to realise all the benefits of ITF, including optimal proportions of cost and size?

Conclusion

The current crisis of rail transport in central Eastern European countries is very similar to one that Western Europe faced 30 years ago, even though circumstances and the intensity of problems differed. From amongst the possible approaches to overcome the crisis, the Swiss model appears to be the most effective and appropriate blueprint for improvement and progress in central Eastern European

---

[17] The 'Beeching Axe' is an informal name for the British government's attempt in the 1960s to reduce the cost of running British Railways, mainly by drastically downsizing the network and by discontinuing many stops which generated little traffic.

[18] Politicians of the new 2010 government had announced long before their foreseeable landslide election victory a stance in favour of rail development, and had promised that they would put discontinued lines back to service. In 2010, 10 lines were reactivated, and further lines were short-listed for reactivation later on in the process of elaborating and implementing a sustainable transport policy.

railways. In the past, ITF-based operations proved to be the only way for some (mainly Swiss) passenger railway companies to operate without losses.

Given the macroeconomic performance of central Eastern European states, an important aspect of the Swiss model is that an almost immediate rise in the level and efficiency of services can be attained without the need for very costly investments. Based on the Swiss experience, within one to seven years and with a 4 per cent cost increase, a 10 to 40 per cent rise in revenues can be attained. The Czech and – to a lesser extent – Hungarian experience matches these results. Thus an ITF-type timetable is able to improve the situation of companies afflicted by losses amounting to billions of Euros to be compensated from the state budget. A transport system organised alongside a full-fledged ITF scheme not only improves the modal split but also helps to decrease the costs borne by society.

Improving efficiency includes the planning processes. An ITF-based system favours an expedient concept of infrastructure development priorities as it points out which possible developments are not a priority. It favours efficient management of human resources, which still makes up for 45 per cent of MÁV's cost structure. Due to ITF's transparent, periodic nature, planning efforts can be reduced to a fraction of previous levels, the remaining tasks not necessarily requiring in-depth railway related knowledge. If by increasing the service level, the share of public transport increases, the need to downsize staff will be much lower or not necessary at all. Achieving the structural adjustments necessary for such progress to take place is certainly not an easy task. If they are undertaken successfully, however, the workplace retaining effects of a stronger public transport system – including infrastructure and rolling stock developments, as well as overall economic and social benefits – would appear to make it easier for politicians, owners and corporate leaders to take the necessary decisions.

As the process of railway liberalisation advances in line with EU transport policy, track access for all operators without discrimination is a critical expectation. This requires an objective set of rules based on clear standards. A regular interval timetable is a viable setting for that.

If an ITF-type system can be extended to the whole region, to entire national networks, and to all branches of public transport, it seems likely, based on what we know, that within a decade rail passenger transport could be turned into a profitable business in central Eastern Europe, too. Why should we, instead of adopting an ITF-type regular interval timetable, maintain any more expensive and less efficient system of railway transport?

Bibliography

Borza, V., 'Integrált Ütemes Menetrend, avagy Lehet nyereséges a vasúti közszolgáltatás', Corvinus University PhD thesis, 2007.

Borza, V., István, Gy., Kormányos, L. and Vincze, B. Gy., 'Integrált ütemes menetrend', parts 1–3. Articles published online in 2007-9 at http://itf.hu/index.php (last accessed 15 June 2010).

Janoš, V. and Baudyš, K., 'Railway Timetable in the Czech Republic', in Wydawnictwo Politechniki Ślaskiej (ed.), *The Development of Transportation Systems* (Gliwice 2010), 181–6.

Janoš, V., Baudyš, K. and Pospíšil, J., 'Railway timetable in the Czech Republic', Vilnius Gediminas University PhD thesis, 2009.

Veenendaal, Guus, *Spoorwegen in Nederland van 1834 tot nu*, 2nd edn (Amsterdam 2008).

Chapter 21

Railway Heritage Protection Policy in Hungary

Zsuzsa Frisnyák

The Hungarian history of railway heritage protection is made up of three distinct periods. During the first phase, which lasted from the end of the nineteenth century until the 1960s, the safekeeping, collection and presentation of railway objects were performed by a single institution, the Hungarian Royal Museum of Transport.[1] The collection of the museum, which opened on 1 May 1899, consisted of objects displayed at the millennium exhibition in 1896, which had been organised to celebrate the one thousandth anniversary of the Hungarian conquest. Ninety per cent of the exhibits were railway-related and 10 per cent were nautical.[2] In the transportation hall of the millennium exhibition, art collections were displayed to represent the 50 year history of domestic railways.

A series of models showcasing the development of Hungarian railway vehicles were prepared in 1:5 scale and in a special quality, without regard to expenses. Between 1896 and 1942, a total of 119 pieces were manufactured from the 1:5 scale models, which are lifelike to the last bolt. The designers aimed for a perfect structural copy, and the models are, therefore, theoretically operable.[3] In addition to the models, the Museum's exhibitions also featured interlocking equipment, substructure models, track types, communications tools, photos, maps and more. Between 1899 and 1966 the Museum was maintained by the Hungarian State Railways, the Magyar Államvasutak (MÁV), whose directors and their co-workers were railway experts. Due to a lack of space, the museum did not collect out-of-service vehicles. Railway engineers believed that the development of the vehicles was perfectly demonstrated by the impressive models.

---

[1]   Starting in 1945, the official name of the Museum was the Museum of Transport, and since 2008 it has been the Museum of Science, Technology and Transport.

[2]   Five months later a very similar museum opened in Nuremberg, Germany, the Royal Bavarian Railway Museum. The two museums were the first ones of their kind in the world. See the contribution of Rainer Mertens in this volume.

[3]   József Soltész, 'A Közlekedési Múzeum 1:5 méretarányú vasúti járműmodell gyűjteménye' (Collection of 1:5 scale railway vehicle models of the Museum of Transport), in András Katona (ed.), *Közlekedési Múzeum Évkönyve, vol. 11: 1996–1998* (Budapest 1999), 81–126, here 93–7, 105–107, 111, 113–16.

Figure 21.1   Models of a Hungarian Locomotive, 1:5 scale, 1920s
Source: Museum of Science, Technology and Transport, Budapest.

In 1944, the museum building was twice hit by bomb attacks. In addition, the museum suffered not only from the requisitions of the Red Army but also from looting by locals as well. By 1948, the 3,200-piece railway collection had melted away to a mere 560.[4] In the museum, vegetating in a decrepit building closed to the public, the collecting of new railway objects and the replacement of destroyed ones were both out of the question. During the times of the dictatorship in the 1950s, the Museum of Transport offered a relative shelter to a few railway engineers considered to be enemies of the Communist regime. Despite the general poverty and repressive atmosphere, the engineers, who as museum staff were hidden from the watchful eyes of the commissars, performed valuable work that influenced the heritage protection activities of later decades. In the course of the 1950s and 1960s, data-rich handwritten databases were prepared on the vehicles of Hungarian railways, on their development and on other railway equipment. These databases, and the professional knowledge they contained, served as a foundation for the revival and modernisation of the Hungarian railway heritage protection policy.

---

[4]   Ákos Vaszkó, 'A vasúti gyűjtemény' (The Railway Collection), in Béla Czére (ed.), *Közlekedési Múzeum* Évkönyve, *vol. 1: 1896–1971* (Budapest 1971), 55–92, here 63.

Figure 21.2   Destruction of the Railway Collection, 1944
Source: Museum of Science, Technology and Transport, Budapest.

The Modernisation of Railway Heritage Protection

The second period of railway heritage protection, which began in the 1960s and lasted until 1985, was characterised by theoretical and practical modernisation. The revival of the heritage protection activity cannot be tied to a certain person or institution; nor has it yet been summarised in a single document. The process of modernisation took place in a series of smaller or greater steps and it resulted from everyday practice and the debates taking shape throughout the years. All of this luckily coincided with the state modernisation programme of the Hungarian railways in 1968. Railway heritage preservationists had to find answers to the events accompanying the modernisation of railways: the mass scrapping of steam locomotives, the closure of tracks with low traffic volumes, dieselisation and electrification, etc. Consequently, in this era the museum started to engage in active collection, and gave up its former policy of not acquiring original vehicles.

The Museum of Transport was reopened to the public in 1966. The museum was taken out of the supervision of MÁV and became an independent but state-run institution of national importance, Visitors were faced with a cultural institution which – despite not having recovered from the destruction of Second World War – offered a more youthful tone. The rich pre-war installations in Secession style were not rebuilt, so the spectacle definitely became poorer in a way. However,

Figure 21.3   The reopening of the museum, 1966
Source: Museum of Science, Technology and Transport, Budapest.

the informative quality of the new, permanent exhibition was of a higher standard because the organisers abandoned the pre-war concept that an exhibition was nothing but a group of objects lined up next to one another. The new exhibition presented the technical development of railways chronologically and in historical context. This was definitely a significant step forward, both in terms of approach and methodology. The idea that railways are not purely technological developments but also economic, social and cultural products did not occur to the earlier curators, who had been trained as railway engineers.

The fate of the scrapped railway vehicles was decided as part of an agreement between the Museum of Transport and MÁV in 1970. The experts of the museum and the railway company jointly decided which of the vehicles taken out of service needed to be preserved.[5] However, the museum did not have a large enough warehouse to store the railway vehicles taken into its stock, so the trains remained in MÁV territory and were stored in the open air. Everybody was aware that this was an emergency measure. In the 1970s and 1980s the museum acquired more and more vehicles, and at the turn of the millennium the museum had a total of

---

[5]   Mariann Koltai, 'A hazai nagyvasúti gőzmozdonyok megőrzése' (Preservation of inland steam locomotives), in Béla Czére (ed.), *Közlekedési Múzeum Évkönyve, vol. 4: 1976–1978* (Budapest 1979), 49–74, here 53.

96 of them. The display of old steam locomotives at traffic-heavy railway stations became fashionable. Most often, the local communities of railway employees took care of the maintenance of steam locomotives set up as memorials.

During this period of railway heritage protection, there were no institutions other than the Museum of Transport which would have focused on this task in an organised way. However, several influential experts among the leading officials of MÁV embraced the idea of railway heritage protection. In 1985, railway experts who were strongly committed to the cause formed a work committee within the MÁV, the MÁV History Commission. The heritage protection activity of the next decades was shaped by the work of this commission.

Railway Heritage Policy with Multiple Players

The third period of Hungarian railway heritage protection, which leads us to the present times, is characterised by professionalisation, the activity of multiple players, and an ever-increasing social base. Established in 1985, the MÁV History Commission joined in the cause of railway heritage protection. Its influence, and its ability to enforce its interests, were incomparably greater than those of the Museum of Transport. All this occurred in a way that the Commission did not have any decision-making authority or independent funding, but it functioned as the consulting and advisory board of MÁV, while its members worked as volunteers. The members of the Commission started lobbying to have MÁV restore an occasional vehicle by using its own budget. In the decades to come, the Commission's influence and the results it achieved kept on increasing. The Commission developed a vehicle reconstruction programme. Vehicles were selected for restoration in such a way that they could constitute a complete train. For engines that were restored to operational condition, passenger cars were sought so that their age matched, and in 1987, MÁV's vintage 1870 old-timer train – pulled by a steam locomotive hauling a tender – was featured on the 150th anniversary celebrations of the Austrian Federal Railways (Österreichische Bundesbahn, ÖBB). Participants considered it a great success that the Bogie-type fast railcar 'Árpád' constructed in 1935 and a dining car of the Compagnie internationale des wagons-lits (CIWL) built in 1912 – both restored in less than six months and in operable condition – were also among the vehicles presented at the Wien Nord railway station.

The political transition of 1990 did not have a direct impact on railway heritage protection. In the new economic environment, MÁV founded Nosztalgia Ltd., an independent company, to operate old-timer trains. The economic crisis, the mass layoffs and loss of jobs following the regime change threw into disarray the local workplaces and small communities whose members ensured the conservation of engines displayed at railway stations from time to time. Consequently, the 1990s brought a drastic and spectacular decline in the condition of old-timer railway vehicles stored in the open air.

Figure 21.4   One of the old-timer trains

Note: This train is operated by Nosztalgia Ltd. Its engine was manufactured in 1870.

Source: Hungarian Railway Heritage Park, Budapest.

At the same time, however, the MÁV History Commission placed an increasing premium on vehicle restoration and on assuring the operability of restored vintage vehicles. To this end, János Csárádi, the Chief Executive Officer of MÁV, issued decrees to regulate the traffic and technical conditions of the operation of old-timer vehicles. The Museum of Transport and the MÁV History Commission identified and registered each vehicle and building of historic value and every machine that belonged to the railway infrastructure. Some of the vehicles and equipment were taken under state protection by the Museum of Transport. The museum supported the vehicle restoration programme so that the usage rights of the vehicles – which had became the property of the museum several decades earlier and were stored in the open air – were given to Nosztalgia by the museum free of charge. In exchange, Nosztalgia had to cover the expenses of restoration, operation and maintenance. The ownership of the old-timer railway vehicles did not change, they remained property of the Museum of Transport. The Commission had the vehicles restored as close to their original state as possible.

In 1987 MÁV created a regulation on the protection of historic buildings. It classified protected buildings in three categories. Today MÁV owns a total of 117

Figure 21.5   The permanent exhibition in the Museum of Transport, 1996
Source: Museum of Science, Technology and Transport, Budapest.

protected railway buildings; 25 of them have won the national historic building status, which entitles them to the highest category of protection available.[6]

The events of railway heritage protection did not leave the Museum of Transport unaffected either. The museum's energies had been freed up from the burden of vehicle reconstruction and maintenance, and the museum launched a new, permanent exhibition. In the 1990s, historians accepted that the history of railways must be interpreted and researched from the point of view of economy and social history, and that old-timer vehicles are more than the mere representation of the phases of technical development. So the research staff of the museum examined in detail the exhibitions of the National Railway Museum in York, the Museum of Science and Industry in Manchester and the Science Museum in London, and compared them to the exhibition practice in Austria and Germany, mainly to the Deutsches Museum in Munich and the Technisches Museum in Vienna.

In 1996 the new, permanent railway exhibition was opened with a floor space of some 2,400 square metres. As a result of the shift in the approach, the exhibition presented railway history from the point of view of passengers. What was the life

---

[6]   György Heller et al., *Oldtimer Railway Vehicles in Hungary* (Budapest 1990), 55, and István Kummér, 'Műemlékvédelem a magyar vasúton' (The Protection of Monuments in the Hungarian Railway), in Antal Fejes (ed.), *25 éves a MÁV História Bizottsága 10 éves a Magyar Vasúttörténeti Park Alapítvány* (Budapest 2009), 33–44, here 36.

Figure 21.6   Contest of locomotives in Hungarian Railway Heritage Park, 2008
Source: Hungarian Railway Heritage Park, Budapest.

of a small town railway station like, what were the travelling circumstances like for a middle-class woman in the 1880s, how did the railway organise the travelling of the royal family? Moreover, following the English examples, it also reflected visual humour. The exhibition featured a small town railway station; visitors could take a peek into the traffic room or into the ticket office, and were even able to enter the waiting hall. The objective of the exhibition was to present as many relics in their own historical environment as possible. Exhibitors were only able to fit five old-timer railway vehicles into the exhibition space. One of them, a vehicle manufactured in 1861, is the oldest remaining steam locomotive that ran in Hungary. One of the three old-timer passenger cars is open for visitors to step in and look around.

A dream of several decades came true for railway fans when the Hungarian Railway Heritage Park opened in 2000 in honour of the thousandth anniversary of the foundation of the Hungarian state. The establishment of this open air railway museum was financed by state funds. But the heritage park was created by the voluntary public work of Hungarian railway employees. The open air museum was set up in Budapest, in the Northern Engine House built between 1909 and 1911. The soil was exchanged on the entire 12-hectare territory of the open air museum. Then came landscaping, afforestation, outdoor lighting, the renewal of public utilities, etc.[7]

---

[7]   Ferenc Holcsik and György Villányi, *Hungarian Railway Heritage Park* (Budapest 2002), 203.

Figure 21.7   The Railway Heritage Park viewed from above
Source: Hungarian Railway Heritage Park, Budapest.

The Hungarian Railway Heritage Park works as a foundation. Operation of the park was mandated by the foundation to the MÁV Nosztalgia Ltd. The foundation takes care of the maintenance and restoration of the exhibited vehicles, organises exhibitions. The foundation, the MÁV and the MÁV Nosztalgia Ltd. arranged their relationship with an agreement of cooperation. The Museum of Transportation signed an agreement with the foundation about issues concerning vehicles owned by the museum but located at the Railway Heritage Park.

In the railway history park in 2000, visitors were able to view 53 restored vehicles. In 2001 the number increased to 66. As a result of the effort to preserve vehicles, the park is able to offer a considerable collection to its visitors.

These days, the following numbers and types of vehicles are in operable condition: 9 steam locomotives, 11 diesel locomotives, 2 electric locomotives, 13 diesel railcars, and 47 passenger cars. The list of vehicles waiting to be restored still contained 180 items in 2010. According to general opinion, due to the technical underdevelopment of Hungarian railways and less discipline, in scrapping many vehicles survived that would have been destroyed a long time before in Western European countries that were developing in a more balanced way. Nowadays old-timer railway trips are organised with various destinations every weekend. However, the operation of old-timer vehicles raises such questions to which the answers are yet to materialise in Hungary: how long are these vehicles supposed to be used? At present, the interests related to the operation of old-timers are still stronger than those related to the general protection of works of art.

Table 21.1   Collection of vehicles in the Hungarian Railway Heritage Park

	Number	Year
Steam locomotives	31	1870–1956
Diesel locomotives	11	1954–75
Diesel railcars and trailers	12	1927–62
Electric locomotives	7	1914–75
2-wheel passenger cars	18	1854–1931
Bogie-type passenger cars	20	1895–1974
Freight wagons	14	1884–1954
Snow remover machines	6	1929–43
Track construction machines	4	1960–72
Railway cranes	2	1942–43
Rail auto cars and motor draisines	8	1949–73
Draisines	5	?

Source: Holcsik and Villányi, *Hungarian Railway Heritage Park*, 206–19.

The Museum of Science, Technology and Transport and the Hungarian Railway Heritage Park can expand their railway collection only if they can obtain funding for it. The short-term future of the railway heritage protection policy is mostly determined by sponsorship from private capital and the available tendering funds. What will the heritage protection policy look like in the long run? Hungary will probably follow the European railway heritage protection trend, especially that of Germany and Austria because of the traditionally stronger relationship with these two countries and the closer relationship with their museums.

Consequently, the 2000s brought along a significant increase in the efforts to protect our railway heritage. Its mass base has also expanded, and the popularity of the Railway History Park has continued. Nowadays the club of railway fans is organised, strengthened and focused by the Internet. Some fans collect the sounds of railway engines, others take pictures of station buildings and prepare descriptions of railway lines. There are timetable aficionados and, naturally, almost every locomotive type has its own devotees. The highest quality Internet portal presents the railway stations and train stops of Hungary in a historical context.[8] At the same time, in parallel with the successes of railway heritage protection, the conditions for scientific research have also improved significantly. Hungary's only archive, which is nearly fully digitalised, is in the possession of MÁV.[9] Close to 5,000 railway-related postcards – mostly dated prior to 1944 – can be researched online.[10] The Museum of Transport has taken over MÁV's old technical drawing collection. As a result of the efforts of several decades, the collection comprising some 100,000 drawings is now available for research. It has become extremely useful for vehicle restoration. And today, the museum collections of railway-related objects include more than 7,500 works of art.

Conclusion

The history of the Hungarian railway heritage protection is not an unbroken chain of successes. Today's institutional structure with its multiple players is relatively stable, but there is still a lack of methodical and predictable development in the area of vehicle restoration. That era of the Hungarian railway heritage protection has not yet arrived. Because the state's contributions are unpredictable, and the railway companies are encumbered with debts, planning is impossible even for the short term.

Bibliography

Heller, György et al., *Oldtimer Railway Vehicles in Hungary* (Budapest 1990).

Holcsik, Ferenc and Villányi, György, *Hungarian Railway Heritage Park* (Budapest 2002).

Koltai, Mariann, 'A hazai nagyvasúti gőzmozdonyok megőrzése' (Preservation of inland steam locomotives), in Béla Czére (ed.), *Közlekedési Múzeum Évkönyve, vol. 4: 1976–1978* (Budapest 1979), 49–74.

Kummér, István, 'Műemlékvédelem a magyar vasúton' (The Protection of Monuments in Hungarian Railway), in Antal Fejes (ed.), *25 éves a MÁV História Bizottsága 10 éves a Magyar Vasúttörténeti Park Alapítvány* (Budapest 2009), 33–44.

Soltész, József, 'A Közlekedési Múzeum 1:5 méretarányú vasúti járműmodell gyűjteménye' (Collection of 1:5 scale railway vehicle models of the Museum

---

8   See http://www.vasutallomasok.hu (last accessed 30 October 2010).

9   MÁV Central Archives. www.mavintezet.hu/jkp/leveltar_en (last accessed 30 October 2010. In digital format 2.5 million documents are available for research.

10   Magyar Múzeumi Képeslap Katalógus. http://muzeum.arcanum.hu/kepeslapok/opt/a100525.htm?v=pdf&a=start ((last accessed 30 October 2010.

of Transport), in András Katona (ed.), *Közlekedési Múzeum* Évkönyve, *vol. 11: 1996–1998* (Budapest 1999), 81–126.
Vaszkó, Ákos, 'A vasúti gyűjtemény' (The Railway Collection), in Béla Czére (ed.), *Közlekedési Múzeum Évkönyve, vol 1: 1896–1971* (Budapest 1971), 55–92.

Chapter 22

The Heritage of the Deutsche Reichsbahn and its Presentation in the Deutsche Bahn Museum in Nuremberg

Rainer Mertens

Some Basic Facts about the DB Museum

German railways were born on 7 December 1835 when the first steam train departed from Nuremberg on a six-kilometre journey to the neighbouring town of Fürth. This marked the start of developments that would catapult Germany into the industrial age within a few decades. The 'Royal Bavarian Railway Museum' – the first public museum in the world dealing with the railways, their technology and history – opened its doors just 65 years later, on 1 October 1899. Including its postal section, which opened in 1902, the Museum of Transportation, as it became known, has been one of the most famous museums in Germany since its inception.

In 1996, the railway section, which occupies some 80 per cent of the museum area, was renamed the DB Museum, becoming the official museum of the recently formed Deutsche Bahn AG (DB AG) railway company, which had been created 3 years earlier by the unification of the Deutsche Bundesbahn (DB) and the Deutsche Reichsbahn (DR), the railway services of the former West and East Germany, respectively.

When DB AG took over management, the long-established railway museum underwent extensive renovation. The museum was visualised as playing an important role in presenting DB AG's corporate image to the public.[1] During the following years, the exhibits were fully updated both in terms of form and content, the collections were rearranged and catalogued in a computer database, and services were expanded and modernised. Out-of-date sections were removed and new areas of activity were launched. Furthermore, new locations were established nationwide to house the large collection of more than 120 pieces of rolling stock, giving the museum a presence throughout Germany.

---

[1]   The basics of the renovation are described in: Rainer Mertens, 'DB Museum in Nuremberg, The Home of German Railway History', *Japan Railway and Transport Review*, 43/44, March 2006, 17–23.

Figure 22.1   Entrance of the Deutsche Bahn Museum, 2010
Source: Deutsche Bahn Museum, Nuremberg.

Figure 22.2   Poster of the DR for the festivities of the *Tag des Deutschen Eisenbahners* (Day of Railwaymen), 1972. The poster heralded the friendship between GDR and USSR.

Source: Deutsche Bahn Museum, Nuremberg.

New Directions

Following the renovation of several parts of the main Nuremberg building, general renovation started in 1999. A new permanent exhibition covering an area of 3,700 square metres and dealing with the history of the railways in Germany was then installed. This project showed the new direction the museum was taking. At first, the museum had been seen as dealing with the history of technology, so its main task was to demonstrate the technological development of the railways as a transportation system. As a consequence, original rolling stock was exhibited, along with signals and signal boxes, communication devices, and other technology related to railway construction. However, there was no social, economic and cultural context showing the significance of the railways beyond the purely industrial one.

The 'Eras of Railway History' exhibition, which opened in the anniversary year of 1985, was the first to examine the economic and political conditions in the nineteenth and twentieth centuries that brought about the development of the railways, although priority was still given to railway technologies.

With the new permanent exhibition, the technological development of Germany's railway system is integrated into a holistic consideration of the railway's history and its reciprocal interactions with politics, economics, culture and society. Visitors move chronologically through 200 years of railway history, from its beginnings in England around 1800 until German reunification in 1989. The presentations are designed not to overwhelm visitors with information. The construction of artificial historical settings was actively avoided. The inclusion of an educational expert on the team made it possible to account for the interests of first-time visitors when designing the exhibition, selecting the exhibits and writing explanatory text. The spaces of the old building prevented the exhibition designers from achieving some of their aims.

The exhibitions were planned by a team of four historians and one educational expert under my leadership. We received support and advice from a museum advisory committee set up by the DB AG Board containing historians, railway experts and politicians, including the historian Lothar Gall; Hermann Schäfer, director of the Bonn Museum of History; Dietrich Conrad, former director of the Transport Museum in Dresden; and Günther Gottmann, former director of the German Technology Museum in Berlin.

Sources, Relics and Database

When we started to schedule the new exhibition we became aware of the fact that there was not much that we could build upon concerning the history of the East

German railway. That had not been part of the 1985 exhibition, and there was not much literature about it.[2]

On the other hand, we had many relics from the Reichsbahn. When the Reichsbahn and Bundesbahn were integrated into the new Deutsche Bahn AG, many technical and administrative units were dissolved; among them were the document archives and *Bildstellen* (photo archives) of the former *Reichsbahndirektionen* (directorates), the collections of construction plans of the repair workshops, and many other things which were no longer used for railway operations. While the document archives became part of the state archives, most of the *Bildstellen* and many plans and objects came to the Deutsche Bahn. Some of the most interesting were:

- The working locomotives and vehicles from the historical collection of the Reichsbahn, among them the 03 001 locomotive (one of the first *Einheitslokomotiven* (standard locomotives), built in 1924), and a replica built in 1985 of the Saxonia, the first really operational German locomotive, originally built in 1838.[3]
- The photo archives of a number of pre-World War Two *Reichsbahndirektionen*, including those of Berlin, Dresden and Halle, which became part of East Germany. These photographs, of which there are more than 50,000, are kept in the DB Archive in Berlin, while the photographs from the *Reichsbahndirektionen* that became part of West Germany are kept in the DB Museum. Both inventories are accessible through the *Informationssystem Bahn- und Konzerngeschichte* (IBK) (information system railways and corporate history) IT database.
- Copies of Reichsbahn films (about 1,000), which were mainly made for training, but also for political propaganda.
- A collection of 227 propaganda posters dating from 1950 to the 1980s.

To put all those things in order and give them a structure, we not only studied reports and journals of the Reichsbahn, we also relied on the support of East German railway employees. During this work in 2000, we came into contact with many employees of the former Reichsbahn and received many pointers as to where we could find other interesting documents and objects. It was not always easy to deal with the workers because many of their departments were destined to be closed down soon. Accordingly, we sometimes felt like looters. But in most

---

[2]   At the same time, in September 1999, a publication about German railway history appeared, edited by the Deutsche Bahn. It contained a chapter about the Reichsbahn in the GDR written by Christopher Kopper. See Christopher Kopper, 'Die Deutsche Reichsbahn 1949–1989', in Lothar Gall and Manfred Pohl (eds), *Die Eisenbahn in Deutschland. Von den Anfängen bis in die Gegenwart* (Munich 1999), 281–319.

[3]   In accordance with the railway reform of 1989 and following years, the historical collection of the Reichsbahn was divided into working vehicles which were given to the DB Museum, and non-working vehicles which went to the Verkehrsmuseum Dresden.

cases, people were very helpful and were often happy that the testimonies of a long working life were to be kept for posterity.

Moreover, we put out a call for help with our research in the corporate publication *Bahnzeit* (now *DB Welt*), which brought us many other contacts to former Reichsbahn railway employees who provided us with stories, documents and objects. In the end, we were able to save many remarkable objects, such as the complete *Traditionskabinett*[4] of the repair workshop in Potsdam, a large collection of almost every type of passenger coach built in the GDR from the Dessau repair shop, and a considerable stock of Reichsbahn uniforms and service clothing.

'On Separate Tracks': Integration of the Reichsbahn History into the Permanent Exhibition

Within a few months, the exhibition team had a broad collection for the scheduled exhibition: objects, photographs, models (on loan from East German locomotive factories and the Dresden Verkehrsmuseum), films and even the original driver's cab of the GDR E 10 electric locomotive. The challenge now was to integrate all these objects into the permanent exhibition, illustrating the history of the Reichsbahn in its multiple contexts of politics, economics, technology and social development.

The first room of the exhibition, 'Collapse and reconstruction', shows the situation between 1945 and 1949, especially the separation of Germany and the Reichsbahn into four zones, the merger of the three Western zones, the influence of the Cold War and the radical dismantling of railway facilities and rolling stock in the Soviet Zone. At the exit of this room, an original border post and two uniforms of the newly founded Deutsche Bundesbahn and the transformed Deutsche Reichsbahn mark the beginning of the 'separate tracks'.

The idea behind this exhibition unit was to show the Reichsbahn's history in parallel with that of its western sister, the Bundesbahn. The main exhibition area – almost 700 square metres – was divided lengthwise. On one side is the history of the DB, on the other that of the DR.

The topics for each railway – 24 for the East, 22 for the West – are loosely arranged in a chronological order. Many of the topics are represented both in East and West. Both railways suffered starting problems, implemented an extensive electrification programme and employed a growing percentage of women. The parallel set-up enables visitors to directly compare the situation in East and West.

---

4   'Almost every factory (in the GDR; RM) had a so-called "tradition chamber" (Traditionskabinett), a small museum consisting of objects, photographs, and other materials showing the history and the overall development of the place. They were visited regularly by staff members, as well as by official guests and delegations.' Andreas Ludwig, 'Discursive Logics in the Material Presentation of East German History. Exhibitions and History "Ten Years After"': Paper given to the conference 'Ten Years After – German Unification', University of Michigan, Ann Arbor, 1999.

Figure 22.3　Internal Reichsbahn poster for raising the quality of work

Note: The poster should remind dispatchers (Fahrdienstleiter) to pay attention to the hierarchic order of trains. It was seen as a question of honour doing this. The symbolic 'Q' stood for quality (Qualität).

Source: Deutsche Bahn Museum, Nuremberg.

Figure 22.4   Boundary Post of the Iron Curtain: Installation of the permanent
exhibition of the museum

Source: Deutsche Bahn Museum, Nuremberg.

Thus, they learn that electrification at the Reichsbahn (official slogan: 'Campaign for electrification') took place 10 years after it did at the Bundesbahn (official slogan: 'Our locomotives are giving up smoking') and that the percentage of female employees and the variety of professions was much higher in the East than in the West. Other topics are specifically connected with the Reichsbahn: the general lack of everything which was necessary for a smoothly operating railway, from high-quality coal to durable concrete; the dark chapter of uranium transport to the Soviet Union; and the 'Pioneer railways', small-scale railway installations where young people could simulate railway operations under realistic conditions.

Walking a Fine Line

Dealing with the history of the German Democratic Republic always means walking a fine line. On the one hand, you have to avoid the arrogant '*Wessi*' (Western) attitude. On the other, you must not succumb to the temptation of trafficking in '*Ossi*' (Eastern) nostalgia. Working with authentic objects and media can lead to nostalgia; creating the possibility to compare developments in East and West can lead to arrogance. It was our challenge to avoid both. To achieve

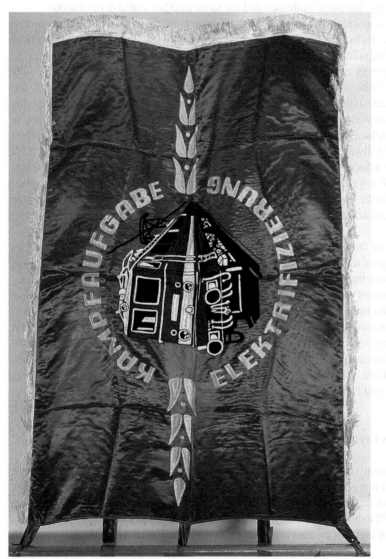

Figure 22.5   Banner of the 'Campaign for electrification'
Source: Deutsche Bahn Museum, Nuremberg.

maximum objectivity view without avoiding any statement on social and political circumstances, we used the following principles:

- The presentation of the two railways is basically equal. We used the same space, the same materials and the same number and size of objects.
- The critical points and dark chapters in history are clearly shown: the railways' loss of importance in the West, the impact of political manipulation in the East, and, of course, the negative consequences of German separation.
- In spite of the unfavourable circumstances, the railway service of the Reichsbahn ran amazingly well – a result of the widespread talent for improvisation among the East German railway employees. This fact is emphasised in our exhibition, as is the Reichsbahn's relative high standard of railway technology. For example, the electric locomotive class 234, introduced in 1984, is still being used by several German S-Bahn urban railways. And the typical double-deck carriages of *VEB Waggonbau Görlitz* became the prototypes of the contemporary standard vehicle for German short-distance traffic.

By virtue of its vast number of objects and documents, its variety of media and its wide range of topics, 'On separate tracks' is one of the most important exhibitions dealing with the history of the GDR. It was created by a process in which many interest groups were involved: the exhibition team, the advisory committee, former Reichsbahn railway employees, contemporary witnesses and railway enthusiasts. In the museum's opinion, the result is a vivid and authentic picture of the East German railway and its place in the great stream of history.[5] The public's response has been almost unanimously positive; there have been only a few critical voices. Visitors from the East of Germany, especially, praise the exhibition as being objective and close to reality.

Activities beyond the Permanent Exhibition

The museum's activities in respect of the heritage of the Reichsbahn are not limited to our permanent exhibition. The history of the railway in the GDR has become an integral part of our temporary exhibitions as well. In the case of our 2007–2008 exhibition 'Go easy – Go Bahn' about the history of railway advertising, the exhibition team created a unit about Reichsbahn advertising that was based on

---

[5] The catalogue is published as DB Museum (ed.), *Auf getrennten Gleisen. Reichsbahn und Bundesbahn 1945–1989. Katalog zur neuen Dauerausstellung des DB Museums*, vol. 3 (Nuremberg 2001).

completely new research.[6] The current exhibition, '*Transportwunder*' (transport miracles), about the past and present of freight transport and logistics, also contains a section on rail freight transport in the GDR.

Figure 22.6   Locomotives in the Halle branch museum
Source: Deutsche Bahn Museum, Nuremberg.

Outside Nuremberg, the DB Museum has also undertaken some activities to preserve the heritage of the Deutsche Reichsbahn. The main activity is the Museum's branch in Halle an der Saale. The Halle branch is located in a historical engine roundhouse that previously belonged to the Fahrzeug Versuchsanstalt (Research Institute for Locomotives), which made a considerable contribution to the high technological level attained by railways in the GDR. A particular attraction of the Halle location is its collection of high-speed Reichsbahn steam locomotives.

The Halle facility – like the Museum's 'Western' branch in Koblenz – is partially supported by volunteers who focus on the preservation and restoration of historical stock – work that is very labour-intensive. This cooperation has great benefits for both sides. The railway enthusiasts can pursue their hobby, while the Museum has an inexpensive means of caring for its historical railway fleets.

---

[6]   Steffen Koch, '"Laß andere lenken" – Reichsbahn-Werbung 1949–1989', in DB Museum (ed.), *Go easy, Go Bahn. 200 Jahre Bahn und Werbung* (Nuremberg 2008), 122–49.

In addition to the stock collection, the Halle branch hosts a small permanent exhibition about the history of the site. The doors are open, depending on the season, two or four days a month. The yearly number of visitors is about 7,000.

DB Museum – Home for the History of German Railways in East and West

Since its renovation, the Nuremberg Railway Museum has changed from a technology-oriented museum of the West German Bundesbahn and pre-war railways to a culture-oriented museum of the pan-German Deutsche Bahn and its predecessors. The history of the Deutsche Reichsbahn in East Germany is one of the central topics of the new DB Museum. The exhibition 'On separate tracks' in the main museum in Nuremberg contains one of the largest and most important presentations of GDR history in Germany. The Museum's branch in Halle an der Saale is an authentic home for a considerable number of Reichsbahn locomotives. Many other locomotives and rolling stock are lent to railway clubs in East Germany. In this way, the Museum stays in close contact with many former railway employees and benefits from their voluntary work concerning maintenance and restoration of the historical railway vehicles.

Thus, the DB Museum has become a home for the history of German railways in both East and West Germany.

Figure 22.7   *Bestarbeiter* RAW H. Mattern

Note: 'RAW' stood for *Reichsbahnausbesserungswerk* and meant a repair shop of the Deutsche Reichsbahn. '*Bestarbeiter*' was a worker who managed to deliver the best working results. The shield should animate workers to compete with each other for more efficient work.

Source: Deutsche Bahn Museum, Nuremberg.

Bibliography

DB Museum (ed.), *Auf getrennten Gleisen. Reichsbahn und Bundesbahn 1945–1989. Katalog zur neuen Dauerausstellung des DB Museums*, vol. 3 (Nuremberg 2001).

Koch, Steffen, '"Laß andere lenken" – Reichsbahn-Werbung 1949–1989', in DB Museum (ed.), *Go easy, Go Bahn. 200 Jahre Bahn und Werbung* (Nuremberg 2008), 122–49.

Kopper, Christopher, 'Die Deutsche Reichsbahn 1949–1989', in Lothar Gall and Manfred Pohl (eds), *Die Eisenbahn in Deutschland. Von den Anfängen bis in die Gegenwart* (Munich 1999), 281–319.

Ludwig, Andreas, 'Discursive Logics in the Material Presentation of East German History. Exhibitions and History "Ten Years After"': Paper given to the conference 'Ten Years After – German Unification', University of Michigan, Ann Arbor, 1999.

Mertens, Rainer, 'DB Museum in Nuremberg, the home of German Railway History', *Japan Railway and Transport Review*, 43/44, March 2006, 17–23.

Index

Modern Economic and Social History Series

General Editor
Derek H. Aldcroft, University Fellow, Department of Economic and
Social History, University of Leicester, UK

Derek H. Aldcroft
Studies in the Interwar European Economy
1 85928 360 8 (1997)

Michael J. Oliver
Whatever Happened to Monetarism?
Economic Policy Making and Social Learning in the United Kingdom
Since 1979
1 85928 433 7 (1997)

R. Guerriero Wilson
Disillusionment or New Opportunities?
The Changing Nature of Work in Offices,Glasgow 1880–1914
1 84014 276 6 (1998)

Roger Lloyd-Jones and M.J. Lewis with the assistance of M. Eason
Raleigh and the British Bicycle Industry
An Economic and Business History, 1870–1960
1 85928 457 4 (2000)

Barry Stapleton and James H. Thomas
Gales
A Study in Brewing, Business and Family History
0 7546 0146 3 (2000)

Derek H. Aldcroft and Michael J. Oliver
Trade Unions and the Economy: 1870–2000
1 85928 370 5 (2000)

Ted Wilson
Battles for the Standard
Bimetallism and the Spread of the Gold Standard in the Nineteenth Century
1 85928 436 1 (2000)

Patrick Duffy
The Skilled Compositor, 1850–1914
An Aristocrat Among Working Men
0 7546 0255 9 (2000)

Robert Conlon and John Perkins
Wheels and Deals
The Automotive Industry in Twentieth-Century Australia
0 7546 0405 5 (2001)

Sam Mustafa
Merchants and Migrations
Germans and Americans in Connection, 1776–1835
0 7546 0590 6 (2001)

Bernard Cronin
Technology, Industrial Conflict and the Development of Technical
Education in 19th-Century England
0 7546 0313 X (2001)

Andrew Popp
Business Structure, Business Culture and the Industrial District
The Potteries, c. 1850–1914
0 7546 0176 5 (2001)

Scott Kelly
The Myth of Mr Butskell
The Politics of British Economic Policy, 1950–55
0 7546 0604 X (2002)

Michael Ferguson
The Rise of Management Consulting in Britain
0 7546 0561 2 (2002)

Alan Fowler
Lancashire Cotton Operatives and Work, 1900–1950
A Social History of Lancashire Cotton Operatives in the Twentieth Century
0 7546 0116 1 (2003)

John F. Wilson and Andrew Popp (eds)
Industrial Clusters and Regional Business Networks in England, 1750–1970
0 7546 0761 5 (2003)

John Hassan
The Seaside, Health and the Environment in England and Wales since 1800
1 84014 265 0 (2003)

Marshall J. Bastable
Arms and the State
Sir William Armstrong and the Remaking of British Naval Power, 1854–1914
0 7546 3404 3 (2004)

Robin Pearson
Insuring the Industrial Revolution
Fire Insurance in Great Britain, 1700–1850
0 7546 3363 2 (2004)

Andrew Dawson
Lives of the Philadelphia Engineers
Capital, Class and Revolution, 1830–1890
0 7546 3396 9 (2004)

Lawrence Black and Hugh Pemberton (eds)
An Affluent Society?
Britain's Post-War 'Golden Age' Revisited
0 7546 3528 7 (2004)

Joseph Harrison and David Corkill
Spain
A Modern European Economy
0 7546 0145 5 (2004)

Ross E. Catterall and Derek H. Aldcroft (eds)
Exchange Rates and Economic Policy in the 20th Century
1 84014 264 2 (2004)

Armin Grünbacher
Reconstruction and Cold War in Germany
The Kreditanstalt für Wiederaufbau (1948–1961)
0 7546 3806 5 (2004)

Till Geiger
Britain and the Economic Problem of the Cold War
The Political Economy and the Economic Impact of the
British Defence Effort, 1945–1955
0 7546 0287 7 (2004)

Anne Clendinning
Demons of Domesticity
Women and the English Gas Industry, 1889–1939
0 7546 0692 9 (2004)

Timothy Cuff
The Hidden Cost of Economic Development
The Biological Standard of Living in Antebellum Pennsylvania
0 7546 4119 8 (2005)

Julian Greaves
Industrial Reorganization and Government Policy in Interwar Britain
0 7546 0355 5 (2005)

Derek H. Aldcroft
Europe's Third World
The European Periphery in the Interwar Years
0 7546 0599 X (2006)

James P. Huzel
The Popularization of Malthus in Early Nineteenth-Century England
Martineau, Cobbett and the Pauper Press
0 7546 5427 3 (2006)

Richard Perren
Taste, Trade and Technology
The Development of the International Meat Industry since 1840
978 0 7546 3648 9 (2006)

Roger Lloyd-Jones and M.J. Lewis
Alfred Herbert Ltd and the British Machine Tool Industry,
1887–1983
978 0 7546 0523 2 (2006)

Anthony Howe and Simon Morgan (eds)
Rethinking Nineteenth-Century Liberalism
Richard Cobden Bicentenary Essays
978 0 7546 5572 5 (2006)

Espen Moe
Governance, Growth and Global Leadership
The Role of the State in Technological Progress, 1750–2000
978 0 7546 5743 9 (2007)

Peter Scott
Triumph of the South
A Regional Economic History of Early Twentieth Century Britain
978 1 84014 613 4 (2007)

David Turnock
Aspects of Independent Romania's Economic History with
Particular Reference to Transition for EU Accession
978 0 7546 5892 4 (2007)

David Oldroyd
Estates, Enterprise and Investment at the Dawn of the Industrial Revolution
Estate Management and Accounting in the North-East of England, c.1700–1780
978 0 7546 3455 3 (2007)

Ralf Roth and Günter Dinhobl (eds)
Across the Borders
Financing the World's Railways in the Nineteenth and Twentieth Centuries
978 0 7546 6029 3 (2008)

Vincent Barnett and Joachim Zweynert (eds)
Economics in Russia
Studies in Intellectual History
978 0 7546 6149 8 (2008)

Raymond E. Dumett (ed.)
Mining Tycoons in the Age of Empire, 1870–1945
Entrepreneurship, High Finance, Politics and Territorial Expansion
978 0 7546 6303 4 (2009)

Peter Dorey
British Conservatism and Trade Unionism, 1945–1964
978 0 7546 6659 2 (2009)

Shigeru Akita and Nicholas J. White (eds)
The International Order of Asia in the 1930s and 1950s
978 0 7546 5341 7 (2010)

Myrddin John Lewis, Roger Lloyd-Jones, Josephine Maltby
and Mark David Matthews
Personal Capitalism and Corporate Governance
British Manufacturing in the First Half of the Twentieth Century
978 0 7546 5587 9 (2010)

John Murphy
A Decent Provision
Australian Welfare Policy, 1870 to 1949
978 1 4094 0759 1 (2011)

Robert Lee (ed.)
Commerce and Culture
Nineteenth-Century Business Elites
978 0 7546 6398 0 (2011)

Martin Cohen
The Eclipse of 'Elegant Economy'
The Impact of the Second World War on Attitudes to Personal
Finance in Britain
978 1 4094 3972 1 (2012)

Gordon M. Winder
The American Reaper
Harvesting Networks and Technology, 1830–1910
978 1 4094 2461 1 (2012)

Julie Marfany
Land, Proto-Industry and Population in Catalonia, c. 1680–1829
An Alternative Transition to Capitalism?
978 1 4094 4465 7 (2012)

Lucia Coppolaro
The Making of a World Trading Power
The European Economic Community (EEC) in the GATT Kennedy Round
Negotiations (1963–67)
978 1 4094 3375 0 (2013)

For Product Safety Concerns and Information please contact our
EU representative GPSR@taylorandfrancis.com Taylor & Francis
Verlag GmbH, Kaufingerstraße 24, 80331 München, Germany